L
7.4.04

James Joyce's
A Portrait of the Artist as a Young Man

A CASEBOOK

CASEBOOKS IN CRITICISM

General Editor, William L. Andrews

JAMES JOYCE'S

A Portrait of the Artist as a Young Man

◆ ◆ ◆

A CASEBOOK

Edited by

Mark A. Wollaeger

OXFORD
UNIVERSITY PRESS

2003

OXFORD

UNIVERSITY PRESS

Oxford   New York

Auckland   Bangkok   Buenos Aires   Cape Town   Chennai
Dar es Salaam   Delhi   Hong Kong   Istanbul   Karachi   Kolkata
Kuala Lumpur   Madrid   Melbourne   Mexico City   Mumbai   Nairobi
São Paulo   Shanghai   Taipei   Tokyo   Toronto

Copyright © 2003 by Oxford University Press, Inc.

Published by Oxford University Press, Inc.
198 Madison Avenue, New York, New York 10016

www.oup.com

Library of Congress Cataloging-in-Publication Data
ᵇ James Joyce's A portrait of the artist as a young man : a casebook /
edited by Mark A. Wollaeger.
p. cm. — (Casebooks in criticism)
Includes bibliographical references.
ISBN 0-19-515075-9; 0-19-515076-7 (pbk.)
1. Joyce, James, 1882–1941. Portrait of the artist as a young man.   2.
Dublin (Ireland)—In literature.   3. Young men in literature.   I.
Wollaeger, Mark A., 1957–   II. Series.
PR6019.O9 P6453 2003
823'.912—dc21   2002008818

1 3 5 7 9 8 6 4 2

Printed in the United States of America
on acid-free paper

For Corey and Mia

Acknowledgments

Essay collections throw into relief the collaborative dimension of all books; many friends and colleagues helped out with this project. First, I want to thank Maud Ellmann and Joseph Valente for providing me with revised and expanded versions of previously published material. Marjorie Howes, Vicki Mahaffey, Emer Nolan, and Patrick Parrinder were good enough to offer timely interventions in the permissions process. I am also indebted to Gayle Rogers for his careful research, proofreading, and multiform assistance, and to Daniel C. Turner for running down some information late in the process. Jay Clayton, Kevin Dettmar, Roy Gottfried, Brandon Kershner, William Kupinse, Douglas Mao, Jennifer Shelton, Karin Westman, and Lon Wilhelms all responded generously and constructively to drafts of my introduction and my essay contribution, "Between Stephen and Jim: Portraits of Joyce as a Young Man." I lay claim, of course, to all remaining errors. I am also grateful to Victor Luftig for alerting me to Austin Clarke's memoirs, Dori Mikus for her expert secretarial labors, Jeremy Lewis and Stacey Hamilton at Oxford University Press for answering endless procedural questions and expediting the production process, William Andrews for inviting me to do this casebook, and the anonymous press readers of my proposal for their useful suggestions.

Credits

Wayne Booth, "The Problem of Distance in *A Portrait of the Artist*," in Booth, *The Rhetoric of Fiction*, 2d ed. (Chicago: University of Chicago Press, 1983), 323–36. Reprinted with permission of the University of Chicago Press.

Hélène Cixous, "The Style of the Troubled Conscience," in *The Exile of James Joyce*, trans. Sally A. J. Purcell (New York: Lewis, 1972), 323–31. Reprinted with permission of the author.

Marian Eide, "The Woman of the Ballyhoura Hills: James Joyce and the Politics of Creativity," *Twentieth Century Literature* 44, no. 4 (Winter 1998): 377–91. Reprinted with permission.

Maud Ellmann, "The Name and the Scar: Identity in *The Odyssey* and *A Portrait of the Artist as a Young Man*." Based on Maud Ellmann, "Polytropic Man: Paternity, Identity, and Naming in *The Odyssey* and *A Portrait of the Artist as a Young Man*," in *James Joyce: New Perspectives*, ed. Colin MacCabe (Bloomington: Indiana University Press, 1982), 73–104. The essay is reprinted here, newly revised and expanded for this volume, with permission of the author.

Marjorie Howes, " 'Goodbye Ireland I'm Going to Gort': Geography, Scale, and Narrating the Nation," in *Semicolonial Joyce*, ed. Derek Attridge and Marjorie Howes (Cambridge: Cambridge University Press, 2000), 58–77. Reprinted with the permission of Cambridge University Press.

Hugh Kenner, "The *Portrait* in Perspective," in Kenner, *Dublin's Joyce* (1956; reprint, New York: Columbia University Press, 1987), 109–33. Copyright Indiana University Press. Reprinted with permission.

Michael Levenson, "Stephen's Diary in Joyce's *Portrait*—The Shape of Life," *English Literary History* 52, no. 4 (1985): 1017–35. Copyright the Johns Hopkins University Press. Reprinted by permission of the Johns Hopkins University Press.

Vicki Mahaffey, "Framing, Being Framed, and the Janus Faces of Authority" in *Critical Essays on James Joyce's "A Portrait of the Artist as a Young Man,"* ed. Philip Brady and James E. Carens (New York: Hall, 1998), 290–315, an abridged and redacted version of *"A Portrait of the Artist as a Young Man,"* in Mahaffey, *Reauthorizing Joyce* (Cambridge: Cambridge University Press, 1988; reprint, University Press of Florida, 1995). Copyright Cambridge University Press. Reprinted with the permission of Cambridge University Press.

Emer Nolan, "Portrait of an Aesthete," in Nolan, *James Joyce and Nationalism* (New York and London: Routledge, 1995), 36–47. Reprinted with permission.

Patrick Parrinder, *"A Portrait of the Artist* and *Exiles,"* in Parrinder, *James Joyce* (Cambridge: Cambridge University Press, 1984), 71–105. Reprinted with the permission of Cambridge University Press.

Fritz Senn, "The Challenge: *ignotas animum* (An Old-fashioned Close Guessing at a Borrowed Structure)," *James Joyce Quarterly* 16, nos. 1–2 (Fall 1978–Spring 1979): 123–34. Reprinted by permission.

Joseph Valente, "Thrilled by His Touch: Homosexual Panic and the Will to Artistry in *A Portrait of the Artist as a Young Man,"* *James Joyce Quarterly* 31, no. 3 (Spring 1994): 167–88. Reprinted by permission in newly revised and expanded form.

Contents

James Joyce's
A Portrait of the Artist as a Young Man

A CASEBOOK

Introduction

MARK A. WOLLAEGER

❖   ❖   ❖

SINCE ITS PUBLICATION in 1916, *A Portrait of the Artist as a Young Man* has probably drawn more attention than affection from literary critics. *Dubliners* (1916) virtually invented the modern short story; *Ulysses* (1922) pushed the novel form to its limit; *Finnegans Wake* (1939) turned English into a foreign language. Critics have also made the case for *Portrait*'s place in the canon of modern literature: Joyce's first novel is generally considered the epitome of the modernist *Bildungsroman*, or novel of education, and Hugh Kenner has called its first page the most radically innovative page of prose fiction in the twentieth century. But *Portrait* has also inspired critiques with titles such as "A Portrait of the Artist as a Young Misogynist" (Henke), and Wayne Booth considers the book something of a failure.[1] My first Joyce teacher in college edited a collection of essays on Joyce and yet confessed privately to not caring much for *Portrait*. It may be that for every literary critic who loves *Portrait*, there's another who dislikes it. Perhaps I exaggerate, but while most readers enjoy the vulnerable young Stephen Dedalus of the first two chapters, the experience of seeing the world through the increasingly complex mediation of Stephen's developing mind seems to make strongly divergent responses inevitable.

There are many reasons to enjoy or recoil from peering at the world through Stephen-colored glasses. Or, perhaps, smell the world through his nose would be more accurate. For many early reviews express their repugnance at Joyce's olfactory emphasis in *Portrait*, their disgust with what they considered the excessive realism of the book registering most forcefully in their nostrils, which they tilted into the air in a vain attempt to remain uncontaminated. Probably what they were really objecting to was Joyce's frankness about sex and bodily functions. H. G. Wells's much-quoted comment that in *Portrait* Joyce reveals "a cloacal obsession" (an opinion Joyce himself eventually came to share) is representative of the negative reaction to Joyce's naturalism, his willingness to admit taboo bodily sensations into fiction with an intensity that Victorian canons of taste had forbidden. (These canons still obtained for the reviewers themselves, who therefore did not openly complain about Stephen's whoring and masturbation.) But Wells also admired the novel and asserted that "one believes in Stephen Dedalus as one believes in few characters in fiction" (Deming 86, 87). Similarly, a reviewer in the *New Republic* praised Joyce's candor in *Portrait* as "a nobility" even as a more fastidious reviewer for the *Irish Book Lover* admitted *Portrait*'s "brilliant descriptive style" while averring that "no clean-minded person could possibly allow it to remain in reach of his wife, his sons or daughters" (Deming 97, 102). In her contribution to this volume, Maud Ellmann suggests that critical response has duplicated what reviewer Clutton-Brock called Stephen's own "conflict of beauty and disgust" (Deming 90), "with the disgusted lining up on one side, and those enraptured with the novel's beauty on the other." But the disgust, I believe, has less to do with Joyce's putative obsession with the smell of "horse piss and rotted straw" (*Portrait* 86) than with his ability to make readers intermittently identify with the character who enjoys inhaling it. What Clutton-Brock aptly called "the unwilled intensity of dreams," even when interrupted by a sudden sense of ironic distance, is not always a happy experience, and if readers are drawn to the little boy who breaks his glasses on the cinder track, fewer feel comfortable with the young man in chapter 5 who coldly rejects the friendship tendered by Cranly and snubs E. C., once the girl of his dreams.

It makes sense, then, that *Portrait* criticism was dominated for many years by the problem of how to take Stephen, a self-absorbed aesthete who prefers "the contemplation of an inner world of individual emotions mirrored perfectly in a lucid supple periodic prose" to language that reflects "the glowing sensible world" (*Portrait* 166–67). The contrasting responses of professional and nonprofessional readers are instructive in this regard. Often taught in advanced placement courses in U.S. high schools, *Portrait* typically goes down well with smart teens on the brink of leaving home to forge new experiences in the smithy of the soul. However much recent criticism has aimed to entangle Joyce in the nets of religion, nationality, and language that Stephen tries to elude (*Portrait* 203), the appeal of *Portrait* to young readers is grounded precisely in Stephen's hunger for autonomy. College students trying on intellectual identities for the first time tend to like *Portrait* for the same reason. Religion also enters the equation: anyone who grew up rebellious and Roman Catholic (as I did) will instantly recognize Stephen's struggles with sin, guilt, sex, and damnation. Or maybe any young man will, for gender no doubt divides reader response to some extent. Women in *Portrait* appear largely as symbolic projections of Stephen's imagination, and Stephen's textbook virgin-whore complex has put off some readers over the years. Feminist criticism has done much to reveal how some critical responses unconsciously reproduce Stephen's misogyny, but feminist responses to *Portrait* have themselves been divided, with critics such as Sandra Gilbert and Susan Gubar arguing that Joyce's women are confined to their bodies and a purely material existence, and others, such as Maud Ellmann and Karen Lawrence, discussing how Joyce's texts expose the operations of male desire in response to women.[2] Nonetheless, Stephen's struggles with authority and self-understanding, however implicated in his less-appealing qualities, have made it possible for diverse readers to find versions of themselves in Joyce's fictional self-portrait.

For writers, the appeal of *Portrait* has always been over-whelming. As a *Künstlerroman*, or story of an artist's growth into vocation (a subset of the *Bildungsroman*), *Portrait* speaks to the difficulty, anguish, and exhilaration of trying to gain command over language. For writers early in the twentieth century, moreover, Stephen's commitment to flying by the nets thrown over his soul perfectly expresses the desire for artistic freedom that motivated modern artists aspiring, in Ezra Pound's famous slogan, to "make it new." Irish writers in particular have been drawn to the novel, and not simply because Ireland is a predominately Catholic nation. *Portrait*'s historical dimension, greatly underplayed for most of its critical history, has long been as important to Irish writers as its elaborate symbolism was to American New Critics.

Testimony to the fullness of Joyce's sense of Irish identity in *Portrait* is not hard to come by. The Irish poet Austin Clarke offers a particularly vivid account of Joyce's place in the imagination of Irish authors in his recollection of sitting with Joyce in a cafe in Paris as a young man in his twenties. While Joyce, "a tall melancholy bearded figure in a black overcoat," sat in silence, Clarke began to feel increasingly like a small boy afraid to raise his hand in class:

> I was scarcely aware of him, for in the intolerable circumstance of silence, a dismal force constrained my mind back to the past. "The Portrait of the Artist" [*sic*] had long since become confused with my own memories or had completed them and, set up by his recollecting presence, I heard, as in correspondence, the murmur of classes and chalk squealing on the blackboard until teeth cringed, saw the faces of boys that I had hated and Jesuits in black soutanes, the brass candlesticks turned upon some common lathe that had seemed to him like "the battered mail of angels," and, with heart in shoes, I waited, having had, as I fancied, those thoughts that are forbidden by the Sixth Commandment, for the fatal sound of the sliding

panel of the confession box, until suddenly the tenuous voice of Dedalus broke the silence like falling glass—and Jesuits, boys, candlesticks and sins against the Blessed Virgin and all the abracadabra of childhood vanished down the trapdoors of the mind to lie in wait for the next dream or perilous temperature. (26–27)

Joyce's representation of Irishness has a hallucinatory power that usurps Clarke's own memories. Indeed, so powerful a presence is *Portrait* in Clarke's mind that he sees Joyce as Stephen and later chooses not to describe his own school days at Clongowes Wood because Joyce, who attended the same school a generation earlier, had already done it so well.[3] It is of course ironic that the role of confessor in Clarke's *Portrait*-inflected imagination is played by Joyce, who like Stephen turned his back on the priesthood at an early age. Given Joyce's obsession with cuckoldry, in contrast, Clarke's association of the author of *Ulysses* and *Exiles* (Joyce's 1918 play) with the Sixth Commandment's injunction against adultery could not be more appropriate.

For the Nobel Laureate Seamus Heaney, Joyce is just as powerful, but the influence works to very different ends. In Heaney's "Station Island," a dream vision modeled on Dante's *Purgatorio*, Joyce returns as a ghost to reprove Heaney for his excessive earnestness about Irish politics. If Joyce has a centripetal effect on Clarke, driving him inward toward his Irish past, the effect for Heaney is centrifugal. "Keep at a tangent," Joyce advises the poet:

> When they make the circle wide, it's time to swim
> out on your own and fill the element
> with signatures on your own frequency. (93–94)

Enjoining the poet to shake off his felt obligation to write about the history of Irish oppression, Joyce tells him that he has "listened long enough. Now strike your note" (93). When Heaney only half-jokingly refers to Stephen's diary entry of April 13 (Heaney's own birthday) as "the Feast of the Holy Tundish," Joyce rebukes him, saying that Stephen's concerns about writing in English as an Irishman are no longer worth worrying over: "The English language/belongs to us" (93).[4] It makes sense that Heaney, desiring a reprieve from history, would summon a writer who was deeply engaged with history. Who better to give permission to widen one's scope than a writer who never ceased writing about his native Dublin?

So, given the broad appeal of *Portrait*, what gets under the skin of literary critics? In the wake of Joyce epigone Thomas Pynchon, who sends a character down through the toilet in an excremental vision far more graphic than anything in *Portrait*, the time for holding one's nose is long past. The answer may lie in the contradictory effect of the novel on Clarke and Heaney, in its power to absorb readers into Stephen or send them off at tangents into the world beyond. The charged dialectic between self-absorption and engagement characteristic of Stephen's relation with his surroundings (and ours with Stephen) raises questions about literary intellectuals, who, ever attentive to the developing processes of their own minds, follow in his footsteps. As Stephen lords it over his intellectual inferiors and condescends to his "dull-witted" Irish nationalist friend Davin, it is hard not to ask the question: Are our own intellectual pretensions being mocked? In his "conversation" with Lynch—more a lecture, really—Stephen's desire to remain cloistered "in a mental world" by fending off Lynch's fond recollections of eating cowdung as a child is mocked by a "dray laden with old iron," which suddenly silences Stephen's "hypothesis" with "the harsh roar of jangled and rattling material," like a student punctuating "the true scholastic stink" of his discourse with a loud fart (*Portrait* 206, 209, 214). Are articles produced pretty much just for their own sake, as Stephen's aesthetic theory may be, or do they make contact with the world Stephen occasionally glimpses beyond the veil of his imagination? Are they seminal, like the epiphanies Stephen imagines placing in libraries all over the world in *Ulysses*, or is such a notion, as Kenner was the first to say of Stephen's villanelle, merely a wet dream? Perhaps to pose the question in this way is already to fall into the trap of self-absorption. But, as I indicated earlier, the problem of assessing Joyce's ironic treatment of Stephen has been a major concern of

Portrait criticism, and if the issue has typically been couched as a purely formalist one, having to do with authorial "distance" from the protagonist, it need not be.

The complexity of Joyce's attitude toward Stephen can be traced in the genesis of the novel. Several months after the death of his mother, Joyce drafted an essay in January 1904 entitled "A Portrait of the Artist" for submission to *Dana*, a new magazine edited by Fred Ryan and William Magee (who wrote as John Eglinton). Ryan and Magee (who probably did not know that George Russell had written to Yeats that Joyce was "certainly more promising than Magee" [Mikhail 15]) rejected the essay on the grounds that it was largely incomprehensible and what could be understood had too much to do with sex. It may be, however, that the essay was also too new, for to call "A Portrait of the Artist" an essay does not do justice to its unusual mixture of essay, narrative, philosophical disquisition, and lyric poem. Complicating matters further, this early attempt at self-portraiture already displays traces of the variant of free indirect discourse that Joyce would refine in *Portrait* and later deploy in more radical forms in *Ulysses*. Richard Ellmann has described the technique as the "magnetization of style and vocabulary by the context of person, place, and time" (Ellmann 146). That is, just as *Portrait* advances more through stylistic contrast than plot, each contrast marking a stage in the growth of Stephen's mind, the style of the essay changes along with its content and imbues each moment with a particular kind of subjective bias, whether mocking, appreciative, or awestruck. Kenner's coinage for the technique has stuck: the Uncle Charles Principle (Kenner 15–38).

Given that many of the debates about how to assess Joyce's attitude toward Stephen can be traced back to the novel's distinctive narrative voice, it is worth pausing over the Uncle Charles Principle in order to distinguish it from closely related narratological terms, such as *style indirect libre* (the French term from which the English "free indirect discourse" derives), *erlebte Rede* (the German term, which means "experienced discourse"), or Dorrit Cohn's suggested alternative, "narrated monologue." These largely synonymous terms describe the technique of representing a character's thoughts in her own idiom while remaining in the third person and the same tense as the surrounding narration. First used extensively in English by Jane Austen at the turn of the nineteenth century and later more systematically in French by Gustave Flaubert in *Madame Bovary* (1856), narrated monologue (to adopt Cohn's lucid term) is Joyce's preferred method for representing consciousness in *Portrait*, and the ambiguity between narrative and characterological voices that is fundamental to narrated monologue accounts in part for readers' difficulty in disentangling sympathetic and ironic attitudes toward Stephen. Cohn suggests that the test of narrated monologue is that it can be translated into interior monologue with a simple shift in person and tense, and she takes her example from Stephen's confession at the end of chapter three (Cohn 100–3): "God could see that he was sorry" (*Portrait* 143) translates to "God can see that I am sorry."

Although Kenner's definition of the Uncle Charles Principle sounds much like a definition of narrated monologue—*"the narrative idiom need not be the narrator's"* (Kenner 18)—what he is describing in *Portrait* is a more subtle, intermittent effect in which only a few words or a distinctive syntactical turn lend the sentence a subjective cast without coalescing into a representation of consciousness. The language functions as narration, describing a narrative event, even as it implies the character's *likely perspective* on the event, not the flow of the character's thoughts. What's more, the narrative idiom shifts not only in response to the subjectivity of the character, as in narrated monologue, but also, as Richard Ellmann notes, in response to place and time.[5] Kenner coined the term in response to Joyce's contemporary Wyndham Lewis, who had cited a single word from *Portrait* as evidence of Joyce's failure to purge his lexicon of dated verbiage: Uncle Charles "repairs" to the outhouse, Kenner explains, because that is the word the fastidious older man would use to describe the action (Kenner 17). By not citing precedents for the Uncle Charles Principle, Kenner may be guilty of the common tendency in Joyce criticism of implying that before Joyce, consciousness was not subtly rendered in fiction; but Joyce's evanescent suggestions of subjective coloring in "A Portrait of the Artist" undoubtedly herald the emergence

of fictional techniques that would overshadow those of his predecessors.[6]

In addition to adumbrating Joyce's developed method in *Portrait*,
"A Portrait of the Artist" explains the need for such a method in
its opening paragraph: Literary portraiture should trace "the
curve of an emotion" because the past is a "fluid succession of
presents" ("A Portrait of the Artist" 257–58). No one has offered
a better account of the cinematic character—the paradoxical flu-
idity of discontinuous images—of *Portrait*'s narrative sequence. But
theory is one thing, practice another, and it took ten years for
Joyce to transform "A Portrait of the Artist" into *Portrait*. In the
meantime, the story began to take shape as a long narrative with
the satirical title *Stephen Hero*. In what remains of this version,
Joyce's attitude toward Stephen is at least as sympathetic as it is
satiric, but *Stephen Hero*'s meandering, loosely focused narrative
lacks the symbolic compression, stylistic virtuosity, or provocative
disjointedness of *Portrait*. Joyce abandoned *Stephen Hero* in 1905 in
order to complete *Dubliners* and did not begin to rewrite it as
Portrait until 1907. The writing did not come easily, and in 1911,
infuriated and bitter over his difficulties publishing *Dubliners*, Joyce
angrily threw the manuscript of *Portrait* into the fire. Only his
sister Eileen's quick action saved the pages from the flames. *Portrait*
required saving one more time before it could find a readership,
this time by Ezra Pound. Pound, who heard of Joyce through
Yeats, solicited material from Joyce in late 1913 and instantly saw
the value of what he received in return: the first chapter of *Portrait*
and the full manuscript of *Dubliners*. Thanks to Pound, the progressive review the *Egoist* began serializing the novel, fifteen pages
per issue, on February 2, 1914, Joyce's thirty-second birthday. This
breakthrough had the salutary effect of encouraging Joyce to finish the novel he had begun as an essay ten years before in Dublin.
(Hans Walter Gabler offers evidence that Joyce may have begun
Stephen Hero before "A Portrait of the Artist," but I choose to honor
Joyce's own postscript to *Portrait*: "Dublin 1904 / Trieste 1914.")
Serialized through September 1915, *Portrait* would not be published
as a book until 1916, by B. W. Huebsch in New York, after no
fewer than five other publishers passed on it.

Reviewing the book, Pound recognized that *Portrait* emerged more from European fiction than from a narrowly English or Irish tradition and asserted, "James Joyce produces the nearest thing to Flaubertian prose that we now have in English" (Pound 89). French fiction was often a touchstone in early discussions of modernism in England. Henry James lamented what he considered the lack of rigorous form and style in the English novel compared with the French, and many modern novelists looked to the master craftmanship of Flaubert and Maupassant as a model for their efforts to bring the art of the novel into the twentieth century—or, to register more distinctly the characteristically modernist disdain for Victorian fiction, to bring the novel into the twentieth century *as* art. Thus Ford Madox Ford was greatly pleased that his modernist landmark *The Good Soldier* (1915) was once called (or so Ford claimed) the best French novel ever written in English. Ford's description of "the intricate tangle of references and cross-references" (3) he worked into *The Good Soldier* also captures the verbal complexity of *Portrait*. For if many of Joyce's contemporaries, as we have seen, were struck by the graphic physicality of Joyce's naturalism, today's readers, schooled by modernism to read novels as if they were poems, are more likely to attend to *Portrait*'s complicated patterns of symbolic imagery, from the birds linking back to the Icarus myth and the red and green hairbrushes evoking Irish politics, to the recurring images of water, flower petals, and bats. In many ways *Portrait* epitomizes modernism understood as the confluence of the symbolist and naturalist movements of the late nineteenth century: Joyce opens his fiction to the everyday effluvia of lower-middle-class Dublin while also investing naturalistic details with polyvalent symbolic significance.[7]

Pound's comparison of Joyce with Flaubert, who is widely considered the father of modern fiction's attempt to synthesize the realms of fact and symbol, evokes this literary historical context. But Pound also wanted to invoke a more political context by highlighting Joyce's status as a European Irishman whose book was written in Trieste and published in New York because "the Irish . . . are slow in recognizing their own men of genius" (Pound

89). For Joyce, the truth of this claim was writ large in the martyrdom of Charles Stewart Parnell, the champion of Irish political autonomy in the House of Commons whose adultery cost him the support of the Church, leading to his disgrace, loss of political power, and early death. Joyce's first literary work was a memorial poem, "Et Tu, Healy" (written when he was a child and now lost), denouncing Timothy Healy, one of the many politicians and churchmen who, in Joyce's view, betrayed Ireland's best hope for independence. The theme of betrayal is woven throughout Joyce's work, and in *Portrait* Parnell's death makes a deep impression on Stephen at Clongowes Wood. Stephen's subsequent suspension between a native Irish identity that fascinates him in the person of a pregnant peasant woman and the allure of the more cosmopolitan identity he associates with Europe derives in part from his angry fear that Ireland is "the old sow that eats her farrow" (*Portrait* 203)—a mother who consumes her own children. The importance of Parnell's sad story to Joyce's imagination can be gauged by his decision to have Stephen attend Clongowes Wood from 1891 to 1892 instead of a few years earlier, as Joyce himself had, so that Parnell's death in 1891 could coincide with Stephen's battle against injustice when he is unfairly pandied in class for having broken his glasses.

The year 1891 was a particularly bad one for Joyce. The eldest of ten children, Joyce was always given the best education his father's station in life would permit. But when Parnell died, Joyce was no longer at Clongowes, considered the best school in Ireland, because in June of that year the family's declining finances forced his father, John Joyce, to withdraw him. Joyce would briefly attend a Christian Brothers school for the poor, a fact he never acknowledged in later years. He was fortunate, however, to be able to move without fees from the Christian Brothers to Belvedere College in 1893 because of his father's chance meeting with Belvedere's new rector, who remembered Joyce from Clongowes. In 1898, he entered University College, Dublin, and left with his B.A. in 1902. Later that year, he made his first trip to the Continent, the momentous journey Stephen anticipates at the end of *Portrait*. As Michael Levenson's contribution to this volume shows, Stephen's final diary entry poises him on the verge of leaving while also drawing him back into the past through the figure of the "old father" that ends the book. Though relations between Stephen and Simon Dedalus in *Portrait* might suggest otherwise, Joyce always remained close to his father, certainly much closer than his brother Stanislaus ever did, even though his father often made life very difficult for the entire family.

John Joyce had inherited properties in Cork and held an undemanding yet well-paying job when James was born, but he was a spendthrift who squandered the family fortune and was pensioned off his job. Joyce was born in the comfortable Dublin suburb of Rathgar, but the family's subsequent itinerary traces their momentary rise in standing followed by the steady decline that weighs on the Dedalus family in *Portrait*. From Rathgar, the Joyces moved closer to the more fashionable suburb of Bray in 1887, then closer to Dublin in Blackrock in early 1892, and finally, with income declining and some of the Cork properties sold to pay off debts, the Joyce family arrived in Dublin later that year. Briefly staying in a lodging house, they soon moved into a comfortable large house off Mountjoy Square before falling into a downward spiral of one bad address after another, all in Dublin. Such were the circumstances Joyce left behind when he entered into voluntary exile from Ireland in 1904 with his future wife, Nora Barnacle, and traveled to Pola and Trieste, where he finally finished *Portrait*.

The relationship between *Portrait* and Joyce's life has always been a concern in Joyce studies, in part because Joyce relied so heavily on memory, in part because some readers are tempted to use biography to unriddle what otherwise might seem opaque. Knowledge of Joyce's life can only enrich one's experience of *Portrait*, and students of Joyce are blessed with many good studies, none of which is more important that Richard Ellmann's biography. But readers should remain wary of using contextual information to dispense with ambiguities or contradictions that the novel itself refuses to resolve. For instance, the oddness of Stephen's gazing at the word "Lotts" while recovering from his humiliation at the school play should not be overshadowed by the fact that a Dublin lane a short way from the northern quays of the Liffey still bears that name. The charged materiality of language that cannot be assimilated into the densely woven symbolic patterns of the novel is part of the meaning of the moment, as is the fact that Joyce, who liked to believe that Dublin could be rebuilt from the pages of his fiction, always clung tenaciously to the actual urban topography of the city his fiction so carefully mapped. Text and context, in other words, are mutually illuminating but do not fully disclose each other's secrets. Thus it is entirely appropriate that the most interesting problem to emerge from a biographical perspective—how to construe the relationship between Joyce and Stephen—is mirrored within the text in the problematic relationship between narrator and protagonist. Several of the essays included here address that relationship; my own contribution, "Between Stephen and Jim: Portraits of Joyce as a Young Man," takes up the biographical issue.

CHOOSING ESSAYS FOR A CASEBOOK on *Portrait*, one cannot help feeling haunted by the possibilities each selection ousts. My choices have been guided by the desire to speak to many audiences, from the first-time reader hoping for guidance to the professional critic looking for new insights. I have consequently included several essays that seem to me indispensable to general understanding and invaluable to teachers of *Portrait* as well as essays intended for a more restricted audience. The essays by Hugh Kenner and Patrick Parrinder speak to everyone and include a great deal of useful information for first-time readers about literary and historical allusions as well as commentary on symbolism. For more detailed glosses on the text, student readers may also want to consult Don Gifford's *Joyce Annotated* (1982) or the annotated editions of the novel listed in the suggested reading section. Though a few essays, such as those by Joseph Valente and Maud Ellmann, may best be appreciated by readers well versed in literary theory and criticism, by contemporary standards all the contributions in this volume are quite readable. A full account of the evolution of Joyce criticism is beyond the scope of this introduction, but the historical arrangement of the selections is intended to suggest not only the breadth of Joyce criticism but the way the field has changed over time. The essays therefore begin with a mixture of formalism, biography, and intellectual history before entering into literary historical, rhetorical/narratological, and poststructuralist approaches, and ending with samples of the more recent turn to sex and gender, history and politics. Some of these essays will be familiar to seasoned Joyceans; a few have been revised specifically for this volume and appear here in this form for the first time; others may be less well known to all but highly specialized scholars.

The first essay in this collection, Hugh Kenner's "The *Portrait* in Perspective," a version of which was first published in 1948, is a touchstone for subsequent criticism and still provides the single best introduction to the novel. Comprehensive in its treatment, the chapter demonstrates why Kenner is often considered Joyce's best close reader. Kenner discusses everything from the genesis of the story and its dominant themes and structure to its recurring images, distinctive idiom, and ironic mode. His discovery that "the first two pages, terminating in a row of asterisks, enact the entire action in microcosm" has been seminal. Equally influential, Kenner's judgment that "the priest of the eternal imagination" (Joyce's words, Stephen's notion) turns out to be laughably and "indigestibly Byronic" set the terms for subsequent debate about the degree to which Joyce treats Stephen with sustained irony. Finally, in addition to its intrinsic value, the book from which the version reprinted here is taken, *Dublin's Joyce* (1956), carries the additional historical interest of having first been drafted as a 1950 Yale dissertation under the direction of Cleanth Brooks, who in the 1940s taught at Yale the first university course in the United States ever to include Joyce's work.

Wayne Booth's "The Problem of Distance in *A Portrait of the Artist*," excerpted from his magisterial *Rhetoric of Fiction* (first published in 1961), was the first to formulate the issue of irony in the novel as a structural problem, even a defect. It does not do a disservice to Booth's subtle and far-reaching argument to observe that the fundamental question is, in his words, "Is Stephen a pompous ass or not?" Booth locates the issue in a literary historical perspective by observing that the clear distinction between authorial and characterological norms, taken for granted in earlier fiction, begins to erode in modern fiction and becomes thoroughly problematic in *Portrait* as Joyce effaces all explicit authorial commentary. The problem becomes particularly acute when trying to gauge how seriously to take Stephen's aesthetic theory and his villanelle. The uneven quality of Joyce's own poems in his collections *Chamber Music* (1907) and *Pomes Penyeach* (1927) only exacerbates the difficulty of evaluating Stephen's youthful effort, and the notebooks in which Joyce commented on the aesthetic theories of Aquinas and Aristotle do not enable a definitive assessment of Stephen's discourse in *Portrait*. Booth points out that no one thought to read Stephen ironically before the publication of *Ulysses* in 1922, in which Stephen is explicitly presented as more fallen Icarus than soaring Daedalus, and that "ironic readings did not become popular, in fact, until after the fragment of *Stephen Hero* was published in 1944." Once you see the irony, you can't *not* see it, and yet no amount of immanent reading or invocations of external evidence will permit the reader to ascertain precisely how Joyce intended Stephen to be read. Criticism today is unlikely to care as much about authorial intentions in quite this way, and Booth seems unaware of the complications produced by free indirect discourse, but among the many virtues of his argument is that he not only pinpoints a distinctive feature of *Portrait*'s reception but presents it as a teachable problem that corresponds to the way most readers first experience the story.

Hélène Cixous's short excerpt, like Kenner's, began as a dissertation project. The big book that evolved from her Sorbonne thesis, *The Exile of James Joyce* (1972), includes this brief yet illuminating commentary on the episode in chapter 3 that most criticism passes over in silence: the retreat in which Stephen hears fire-and-brimstone sermons that, for a time, restore his faith. Students often complain about the length of the sermons, and criticism typically does little more than point out that they reproduce mimetically in the reader what Stephen himself is undergoing. Cixous's more subtle reading is not only of interest as an early instance of her continuing engagement with Joyce, whose fiction influenced her theoretical writings much as it did the psychoanalytic theory of her compatriot Jacques Lacan; it is valuable in its own right for her argument about the double significance of *Portrait*'s third chapter. In Cixous's account, the retreat shows external reality, through the agency of the priest's voice, taking revenge on Stephen's mind for having distorted it; it also anticipates Joyce's later technique in *Ulysses* of rendering objective reality subjective and inward without sacrificing its autonomy. Stephen himself, she suggests, ultimately discovers from the sermons that "sin and fear are better spiritual stimulants for the poet's imagination than virtue and piety are."

Patrick Parrinder is one of the few critics apart from Cixous who discusses the retreat in any detail, and his treatment of the entire novel rivals Kenner's as a comprehensive introduction. Parrinder's wide-ranging discussion, which comments on fundamental issues of structure, style, and theme, also sets *Portrait* in literary historical perspective by surveying, among other things, generic influences on the novel and Joyce's debts to romanticism, decadence, and aestheticism and to writers such as Henrik Ibsen (the idol of young Joyce), Walter Pater, and Oscar Wilde; he also finds illuminating points of comparison in figures as diverse as Keats and Conrad, Dostoevsky and D. H. Lawrence. Parrinder shares Booth's no-nonsense unwillingness to see Joyce as the infallible God of Modernism and meticulously demonstrates why it is "naive to pretend that Joyce's artistic control, as he revised the manuscript, was total or that the end-product is altogether seamless." Parrinder is particularly good on the narrative ellipses and disjunctions that are obscured by too narrow a focus on the lyrical continuity of *Portrait*'s recurring images.

Fritz Senn is one of Joyce's best close readers. Certainly no one matches his philological virtuosity, on display in "The Challenge: *ignotas animum*" (1978) in what Senn wryly calls a "minute epigraphic hieroglyphing" of the quotation from Ovid's *Metamorphoses* that Joyce selected as the epigraph for *Portrait*, the only one in his oeuvre. The essay carefully unpacks Ovid's Latin (*"Et ignotas animum dimittit in artes"*) in order to model the problems of reading that

Joyce poses not only in *Portrait* but throughout his work. Slowing down and patiently mapping the reader's movements of mind in the act of reading, Senn shows how *Portrait* aims to circumvent limitations imposed by syntax so as to approximate the kind of verbal juxtapositions that came easier to poets such as Ovid, who enjoyed the relative freedom of a fully inflected language. The forward and backward shuttling solicited by Joyce's style evokes, Senn shows, "the gropings of a developing mind at crucial stages." Elegant and masterful, the essay persuasively finds the Joycean world in the grain of his language.

As Senn's wit and ingenuity pay homage to Joyce's, so do Maud Ellmann's in "The Name and the Scar: Identity in *The Odyssey* and *A Portrait of the Artist as a Young Man*," which revises and expands her earlier essay "Polytropic Man: Paternity, Identity, and Naming in *The Odyssey* and *A Portrait of the Artist as a Young Man*" (1982). At once concentrated and capacious, this poststructuralist reading is as finely attuned to linguistic nuance as Senn's and also takes up Pound's *Cantos*, Homer, Wordsworth, and all of Joyce's writings in order to tease out connections between scars, identity, paternity, and language that culminate in a reading of the enigmatic moment in which Stephen reads the word *Fœtus* carved into a student's desk while looking for his father's initials. Poststructuralism has often targeted modernism's investment in origins, but far from a mechanical debunking of what Jacques Derrida has called the illusion of metaphysical presence—that is, the typically unarticulated assumption that something like a speaking voice guarantees the stability of written language (Derrida 280–81)—Ellmann's essay persuasively demonstrates that Stephen's charged response to *Fœtus*, which encodes multiple threats to paternity and a correlative anxiety about the maternal, should be considered the omphalos, or navel, not just of *Portrait* but of Joyce's oeuvre. It is also instructive to note the way Ellmann and Parrinder converge on similar features of *Portrait*—loose ends, disjointedness, opacities—but respond differently owing to their divergent critical assumptions: Parrinder reads them as signs of the text's troubled genesis and its highlighting of memory, Ellmann as manifestations of a peculiarly Joycean textual logic that resonates with similar moments in other authors and throws into relief the nature of literary language.

Michael Levenson's "Stephen's Diary in Joyce's *Portrait*—The Shape of Life" modestly claims to be filling a gap in Joyce studies by paying close attention to the diary as a genre but ends up doing much more. Levenson's insight into the ways in which the seriality intrinsic to the diary form subverts the narrative of development proper to the *Bildungsroman* offers a new perspective on the long-standing issue of irony by complicating our sense of how characterization operates in *Portrait*. Undaunted by Booth's vigorous rejection of the "absurd hypothesis" that Joyce had come "to look upon all of Stephen's actions as equally wise or equally foolish, equally sensitive or equally meaningless," Levenson argues that, by the end of the novel, its competing generic impulses present us with "at least four forms of the individual life: a pattern of *Bildung* . . . a pattern of repetition . . . a pattern of reversal . . . and a pattern of regression." To Booth, he responds, "What judgment is more appropriate for youth than to connect its ambition to all its possible issues?" Levenson clinches his argument with exquisitely detailed readings of the ways in which Stephen's closing diary, ostensibly "committed to the sentiments of the present as they prepare for the future, is haunted with echoes of early life which recur with a mocking persistence." Levenson thus offers a cubist understanding of character in which multiple perspectives are rendered simultaneously, and his view of irony (though he does not say so explicitly) is consonant with the model proposed long ago by Kenneth Burke, who understood irony as a dialogic structure in which multiple possibilities are suspended nonhierarchically. Stephen is a maturing artist, failure, and fœtus all at once.

Vicki Mahaffey's *Reauthorizing Joyce* (1988), from which the essay included in this volume, "Framing, Being Framed, and the Janus Faces of Authority," has been redacted, argues that in *Portrait* Stephen fails to understand that the authority he desires is split between the mental and the sensual, and this failure prevents him from grasping his necessary implication in the various "nets" he would elude. Stephen accepts the received notion of authority as transcendent—the authority of the Church provides a good model here—and yet his sensitivity to forms of "unauthorized knowledge" (knowledge grounded in sensory perception and the waywardness of figurative language) continually delegitimizes the forms of transcendence he seeks through religion and art. Mahaffey probes deeply into what Parrinder and Levenson refer to in passing as a kind of textual or linguistic unconscious in *Portrait* in order to show how Stephen remains bound by an either-or logic that is belied by the complexity of the linguistic matrix in which his character is embedded. In addition to illuminating readings of how subconscious verbal echoes operate independently of Stephen's intentions and how Stephen's misogyny derives from "his identification with a Janus-faced authority whose faces are both male," the larger yield of Mahaffey's approach is her demonstration that language in *Portrait* "acts as a complex frame of reference for the perceptions of author, character, and reader without compelling any recognition [in contrast to the verbal pyrotechnics of *Ulysses*] that it *is* the dominant system of reference." Like Levenson, Mahaffey thus gains critical purchase on the long-standing debate about aesthetic distance by challenging its terms. Critics worrying over the problem of sympathy versus judgment in effect reenact Stephen's own false dilemma by limiting themselves to mutually exclusive options.

Newly revised and expanded for this volume, Joseph Valente's "Thrilled by His Touch: The Aestheticizing of Homosexual Panic in *A Portrait of the Artist as a Young Man*" offers a significantly new reading of *Portrait* by focusing on the shaping influence of the text's homoerotic energies. Drawing on the work of Eve Sedgwick, D. A. Miller, and Judith Butler, queer theory and gender studies have found fertile ground in Joyce. In this groundbreaking essay Valente revises Miller's idea of the "open secret" in order to propose a new theoretical concept, the "open closet," which instead of establishing essential truths while pretending to disguise them, as in an open secret, *obscures* truths in the act of pretending to divulge them. Intrinsically valuable as a contribution to queer theory, the open closet also reconfigures the irony crux in *Portrait* by generating a potent claim about the vexed relation between Stephen and Joyce: "Dedalus's sexual ambivalences veil Joyce's while putting them on display and display them while putting them under a veil of doubt." Valente also offers fresh perspectives on Stephen's green rose, his corporal punishment at Clongowes, his epiphanic vision of the bird girl, and his refusal of the priesthood, all the while conducting detailed close readings in support of the bold claim that Stephen's phobic denial of homosexual energies constitutes "a *fundamental determinant* of the novel's basic structure and hence of Stephen's destiny."

Emer Nolan's "Portrait of an Aesthete," excerpted from her *James Joyce and Nationalism* (1995), offers an outstanding example of the historicizing turn in recent criticism, in particular the effort to restore the Irishness of Joyce's work. Nolan critically assesses and advances discussions of Joyce's relation to Irish cultural nationalism by arguing that Stephen's apparently aestheticist effort of self-creation is structurally homologous with the nationalist project it ostensibly opposes. Too often, she argues, the political message of *Portrait* is taken to be that Art can provide a haven beyond politics and ideology. But such aestheticist readings miss two crucial points: first, that Joyce writes *about* an aesthete, not *as* one; and second, that Joyce's specifically *European* brand of nationalism is "an ideology devoted to self-creation and self-expression, education and art—a lonely project, in advance of the creation of the ideal national community." Nolan's approach revises the critical tendency to see Yeats and Joyce as antithetical in their responses to nationalism by taking seriously Stephen's stated ambition to "forge the uncreated conscience" of his race.

Marian Eide's "The Woman of the Ballyhoura Hills: James Joyce and the Politics of Creativity" (1998) extends the kind of thinking Nolan undertakes by showing how sexuality is entwined with aesthetics and national politics in *Portrait*. If earlier criticism, as Booth suggested, often turned to *Stephen Hero* for evidence of the irony operating in *Portrait*, Eide and Nolan mine it for Stephen's more explicit engagement with politics and cultural nationalism. For Eide, Stephen's complex attitude toward Irish cultural politics in *Stephen Hero* provides an important context for the peasant

woman that Stephen's nationalist friend Davin recalls having encountered in *Portrait*. By turning away from the woman's sexual
invitation, Davin spurned an opportunity that Stephen, who sees
the woman as a symbol of authentic Irishness, longs to seize. In
this figure, Eide argues, Joyce refashions the popular mythology
of the Irish woman as betrayer of the nation and suggests that
"the coming into consciousness of a nation" depends in part on
"the coming into consciousness of desire" that was denied in
dominant models of Irish nationalism.

In " 'Goodbye Ireland I'm Going to Gort': Geography, Scale,
and Narrating the Nation" (2000), Marjorie Howes also discusses
Stephen's attraction to Davin's peasant woman, but Howes locates
this moment as an instance of *Portrait*'s interest in "teasing out the
complex relations between metaphorical and material space" that
underlie the construction of national identity. Howes argues that
Joyce explores competing narratives of nation in "The Dead"
(1914) and *Portrait* by interrogating the interrelation of the various
geographical scales—local, regional, and international—invoked
in any effort to imagine a coherent national identity. The metaphorizing of material spaces is fundamental to this project, as are
the disjunctions between the material and the symbolic that such
metaphorization entails. Thus, "Stephen's actual travel through
the space of rural Ireland has helped him produce an imaginary
and specifically national geography, in which a national male subject performs the integration of the local into the national by his
movement through space and his symbolic appropriation of the
peasant women as national types." And yet, the old Irish-speaking
man who haunts Stephen's diary reasserts the incommensurability of different scales in his dismissal of Mulrennan's comments
about the universe and stars: "Ah, there must be terrible queer
creatures at the latter end of the world" (*Portrait* 251). Howes's
contribution exemplifies the best of what the recent confluence
of Joyce studies and postcolonial theory has to offer. Rather than
"apply" theory, Howes takes up theoretical concepts proposed by
Homi Bhabha and subjects them to the test of history and her
own skeptical intelligence, redeploying Bhabha's influential concept of "narrating the nation" only after restoring its submerged

spatial coordinates and rethinking it within the specific context of Ireland's uneven rural development. The essay's synthesis of historical and theoretical approaches achieves the kind of authority and balance to which this casebook aspires.

The volume closes with my essay, written for this volume and published here for the first time, "Between Stephen and Jim: Portraits of Joyce as a Young Man." As the contributions by Booth, Valente, and Mahaffey make clear, the space between Stephen and Joyce can be construed in many ways, and a good deal is at stake in how critics choose to do so. The problem does not permit a definitive answer, but it is my hope that my chapter, which is intended to give some sense of the biographical figure "within or behind or beyond or above" the pages of Joyce's autobiographical novel (*Portrait* 215), and this collection as a whole will help readers, critics, and teachers of *Portrait* make sense of this challenging novel in their own ways.

Notes

1. See also Moretti, who finds chapter 5 "strikingly blank and pointless" (55)—but fortunate insofar as *Portrait*'s consequent failure spurred Joyce on to *Ulysses.* Levenson's essay in this volume, though published before Moretti's, can be read as a refutation of this argument.

2. The intersection of Joyce and feminist studies, though often controversial, has proved to be a remarkably productive site. In addition to Lawrence, see Scott.

3. For the tendency in criticism to efface distinctions between Joyce and Stephen, see my essay in this volume, "Between Stephen and Jim: Portraits of Joyce as a Young Man."

4. Although Heaney may have had second thoughts on this score: He omits this portion of the poem in a recent reprinting. See Heaney, *Opened Ground.*

5. This dimension of the technique becomes most pronounced in *Ulysses.* When Leopold Bloom eats lunch in a restaurant the narrative discourse becomes infected by tropes of food and digestion, producing a particularly funny version of what might be called Joycean food poisoning: "Ham and his descendants musterred and bred there" (*Ulysses* 8: 742).

6. For other instances of subtle variants of narrated monologue, see

Cohn (132–34). I am indebted to the skepticism of Kevin Dettmar for provoking this definitional excursus.

7. Wilson was the first to situate Joyce in this confluence, though he sees *Ulysses*, not *Portrait*, as combining the resources of symbolism and naturalism (204–8). Levin, developing Wilson's insight, also sees *Portrait* as largely naturalistic and *Ulysses* as an attempted dialectical synthesis (3–20).

Works Cited

Burke, Kenneth. "The Four Master Tropes." In Burke, *A Grammar of Motives*. 1945. Reprint, Berkeley: University of California Press, 1969.

Clarke, Austin. *Twice Round the Black Church*. London: Routledge & Kegan Paul, 1962.

Cohn, Dorrit. *Transparent Minds: Narrative Modes for Presenting Consciousness in Fiction*. Princeton, N.J.: Princeton University Press, 1978.

Deming, Robert H. *James Joyce: The Critical Heritage*. Vol. 1. London: Routledge & Kegan Paul, 1970.

Derrida, Jacques. *Writing and Difference*, translated by Alan Bass. London: Routledge, 1978.

Ellmann, Richard. *James Joyce*. New York: Oxford University Press, 1982.

Ford, Ford Madox. *The Good Soldier*. 1915; reprint, New York: Oxford University Press, 1990.

Gabler, Hans Walter. "The Genesis of *A Portrait of the Artist as a Young Man*." In *Critical Essays on James Joyce's "A Portrait of the Artist as a Young Man,"* edited by Philip Brady and James F. Carens, 83–112. New York: Hall, 1998.

Gilbert, Sandra M., and Susan Gubar. "Sexual Linguistics: Gender, Language, Sexuality." *New Literary History* 16 (1985): 515–43.

Gifford, Don. *Joyce Annotated: Notes for "Dubliners" and "A Portrait of the Artist as a Young Man."* 2d ed. Berkeley: University of California Press, 1982.

Heaney, Seamus. *Opened Ground: Poems, 1966–96*. London: Faber and Faber, 1998.

———. *Station Island*. New York: Farrar, Straus, Giroux, 1985.

Henke, Suzette. "Stephen Dedalus and Women: A Portrait of the Artist as a Young Misogynist." In *Women in Joyce*, edited by Suzette Henke and Elaine Unkeless, 82–107. Urbana: University of Illinois Press, 1982.

Joyce, James. *Chamber Music*, edited by William York Tindall. New York: Columbia University Press, 1954.

———. *Exiles*. New York: Huebsch, 1924.

———. *Pomes Penyeach*. Paris: Shakespeare, 1927.

———. "A Portrait of the Artist." In *A Portrait of the Artist as a Young Man*, edited by Chester G. Anderson, 257–72. New York: Penguin, 1977.

———. *A Portrait of the Artist as a Young Man*, edited by Chester G. Anderson. New York: Penguin, 1977.

———. *Ulysses: The Gabler Edition*. New York: Random House, 1986.

Kenner, Hugh. *Joyce's Voices*. Berkeley: University of California Press, 1978.

Lawrence, Karen. "Joyce and Feminism." In *The Cambridge Companion to James Joyce*, edited by Derek Attridge, 237–58. Cambridge: Cambridge University Press, 1990.

Levin, Harry. *James Joyce*. 1941. Revised and augmented. New York: New Directions, 1960.

Mikhail, E. H. *James Joyce: Interviews and Recollections*. New York: St. Martin's, 1990.

Moretti, Franco. "'A useless longing for myself': The Crisis of the European Bildungsroman," in *Studies in Historical Change*, edited by Ralph Cohen, 43–59. Charlottesville: University of Virginia Press, 1992.

Pound, Ezra. *Pound/Joyce: The Letters of Ezra Pound to James Joyce with Pound's Essays on Joyce*, edited by Forrest Read. London: Faber and Faber, 1967.

Scott, Bonne Kime. *Joyce and Feminism*. Bloomington: Indiana University Press, 1984.

Wilson, Edmund. *Axel's Castle*. 1931. Reprint, New York: Norton, 1984.

The *Portrait* in Perspective

HUGH KENNER

◆　◆　◆

From wrong to wrong the exasperated spirit
Proceeds, unless restored by that refining fire
Where you must move in measure, like a dancer.
　　　　　　　　　　　　　　　—T. S. Eliot

Faites votre destin, âmes désordonnées,
Et fuyez l'infini que vous portez en vous!
　　　　　　　　　　　　　　　—Baudelaire

And yet he felt that, however he might revile and
mock her image, his anger was also a form of
homage.
—Joyce, *A Portrait of the Artist as a Young Man*

A *Portrait of the Artist as a Young Man* was some ten years in the writing. A thousand-page first draft was written around 1904–1906, about the same time as the bulk of *Dubliners*. This was scrapped and a more compressed version undertaken in 1908; the third and final text was being composed in 1911, and was finished early in 1914.[1] About one third of the first draft (the *Stephen Hero* fragment) survives to show us what was going on during the gestation of this book, the only one which it cost Joyce far more trouble to focus than to execute.

Joyce first conceived the story of Stephen Dedalus in a picaresque mode. The original title was meant to incorporate the ballad of Turpin Hero, a reference to which still survives in the final text (P252/244).[2] Turpin spends most of the ballad achieving gestes at the expense of a gallery of middle-class dummies, beginning with a lawyer:

> As they rode down by the powder mill,
> Turpin commands him to stand still;
> Said he, your cape I must cut off,
> For my mare she wants her saddle cloth.
>> O rare Turpin Hero,
>> O rare Turpin O.
> This caus'd the lawyer much to fret,
> To think he was so fairly bit;
> And Turpin robb'd him of his store,
> Because he knew he'd lie for more.
>> O rare Turpin Hero,
>> O rare Turpin O.

The lawyer's mistake was to admit the plausible stranger to his intimacy. Stephen in the same way achieves a series of dialectical triumphs over priests, parents, and schoolfellows. The typical dialogue commences amid courtesies:

> Stephen raised his cap and said "Good evening, sir." The President answered with the smile which a pretty girl gives when she receives some compliment which puzzles her—a "winning" smile:
> —What can I do for you? he asked in a rich deep calculated voice.

But cut-and-thrust soon follows:

> —May I ask if you have read much of [Ibsen's] writing? asked Stephen.
> —Well, no . . . I must say . . .
> —May I ask if you have read even a single line?
> —Well, no . . . I must admit . . .

Stephen always relieves the interlocutor of his complacence:

—I should not care for anyone to identify the ideas in your essay with the teaching in our college. We receive this college in trust . . .

—If I were to publish tomorrow a very revolutionary pamphlet on the means of avoiding potato-blight would you consider yourself responsible for my theory?

—No, no, of course not . . . but then this is not a school of agriculture.

—Neither is it a school of dramaturgy, answered Stephen. (895/8)

The ballad ends with Turpin in jail condemned to the gallows; *Stephen Hero* was presumably to end, as the *Portrait* does, with Stephen Protomartyr on the brink of continental exile, acknowledged enemy of the Dublin people. This Stephen is an engaging fellow with an explosive laugh (S59/49), an image of the young Joyce whom Yeats compared to William Morris "for the joyous vitality one felt in him," or of the student Joyce who emerges from his brother's *Memoir*:

Uncompromising in all that concerned his artistic integrity, Joyce was, for the rest, of a sociable and amiable disposition. Around his tall, agile figure there hovered a certain air of youthful grace and, despite the squalors of his home, a sense of happiness, as of one who feels within himself a joyous courage, a resolute confidence in life and in his own powers. . . . Joyce's laugh was characteristic . . . of that pure hilarity which does not contort the mouth.[3]

When Stephen's uncompromising side occasionally becomes absurd, Joyce the recorder is always at hand to supply a distancing phrase: "the fiery-hearted revolutionary"; "this heaven-ascending essayist" (S80/67); "he was foolish enough to regret having yielded to the impulse for sympathy from a friend" (S83/70). Toward the end of the existing fragment we find more and more of these excusing clauses: "No young man can contemplate the fact of death with extreme satisfaction and no young man, specialised by fate or her stepsister chance for an organ of sensitiveness and intellectiveness, can contemplate the network of falsities and trivialities which make up the funeral of a dead burgher without extreme disgust" (S168/150). This clumsy sentence, its tone slithering between detachment, irony, and anger, is typical of the bad writing which recurs in the *Stephen Hero* fragment to signal Joyce's periodic uncertainty of Stephen's convincingness.

The book ran down unfinished in 1906, stalled partly by its own inner contradictions, partly by the far maturer achievement of *Dubliners.* It had never, Joyce saw, had a theme; it was neither a novel, nor an autobiography, nor a spiritual or social meditation. It contained three sorts of materials that would not fuse: documentation from the past, transcribed from the Dublin notebooks; Joyce's memories of his earlier self, transmuted by a mythopoeic process only partly controlled; and his present complex attitude to what he thought that self to have been.

Fortunately, the catalytic theme was not long in coming. In the late fall of 1906, he wrote from Rome to his brother about a new story for *Dubliners,* "Ulysses." On February 6, 1907, he admitted that it "never got any forrarder than the title." It coalesced, instead, with the autobiographical theme, and both subjects were returned to the smithy. A novel, *Ulysses,* as Joyce told a Zurich student ten years later, began to be planned as sequel to a rewritten *Portrait.* In 1908 *Stephen Hero* was discarded for good, and the job of lining up the two works began. And once the final balance of motifs for the *Portrait* had been at last struck and the writing of the definitive text completed, the last exorcism, *Exiles,* took only three spring months. *Ulysses* and *Finnegans Wake* took seven and seventeen years, but their recalcitrance was technical merely. The *Portrait* includes their scenario: first "the earth that had borne him" and "the vast indifferent dome" (Penelope, Ithaca), then sleep and a plunge into "some new world, fantastic, dim, uncertain as under sea, traversed by cloudy shapes and beings" (P200/196). These are lyric anticipations of the dense epic and dramatic works to come; the actual writing of those works went forward during the next quarter century with scarcely a false step.

Linking Themes

In the reconceived *Portrait* Joyce abandoned the original intention of writing the account of his own escape from Dublin. One cannot escape one's Dublin. He recast Stephen Dedalus as a figure who could not even detach himself from Dublin because he had formed himself on a denial of Dublin's values. He is the egocentric rebel become an ultimate. There is no question whatever of his regeneration. "Stephen no longer interests me to the same extent [as Bloom]," said Joyce to Frank Budgen one day. "He has a shape that can't be changed."[4] His shape is that of aesthete. The Stephen of the first chapter of *Ulysses* who "walks wearily," constantly "leans" on everything in sight, invariably sits down before he has gone three paces, speaks "gloomily," "quietly," "with bitterness," and "coldly," and "suffers" his handkerchief to be pulled from his pocket by the exuberant Mulligan, is precisely the priggish, humorless Stephen of the last chapter of the *Portrait* who cannot remember what day of the week it is (P206/201), sentimentalizes like Charles Lamb over the "human pages" of a secondhand Latin book, (P209/204), conducts the inhumanly pedantic dialogue with Cranly on mother love, (P281/271), writes Frenchified verses in bed in an erotic swoon, and is epiphanized at full length, like Shem the Penman beneath the bedclothes (F176), shrinking from the "common noises" of daylight:

> Shrinking from that life he turned towards the wall, making a cowl [!] of the blanket and staring at the great overblown scarlet flowers of the tattered wall-paper. He tried to warm his perishing joy in their scarlet glow, imaging a roseway from where he lay upwards to heaven all strewn with scarlet flowers. Weary! Weary! He too was weary of ardent ways. (P260/252)

This new primrose path is a private Jacob's ladder let down to his bed now that he is too weary to do anything but go to heaven.

To make epic and drama emerge naturally from the intrinsic stresses and distortions of the lyric material meant completely new lyric techniques for a constation exact beyond irony. The *Portrait* concentrates on stating themes, arranging apparently transparent words into configurations of the utmost symbolic density. Here is the director proposing that Stephen enter the priesthood:

> The director stood in the embrasure of the window, his back to the light, leaning an elbow on the brown crossblind, and, as he spoke and smiled, slowly dangling and looping the cord of the other blind, Stephen stood before him, following for a moment with his eyes the waning of the long summer daylight above the roofs or the slow deft movements of the priestly fingers. The priest's face was in total shadow, but the waning daylight from behind him touched the deeply grooved temples and the curves of the skull. (P178/175)

The looped cord, the shadow, the skull, none of these is accidental. The "waning daylight," twice emphasized, conveys that denial of nature which the priest's office represented for Stephen; "his back to the light" cooperates toward a similar effect. So "crossblind": "blind to the cross,"[5] "blinded by the cross." "The curves of the skull" introduces another death image; the "deathbone" from Lévy-Bruhl's Australia, pointed by Shaun in *Finnegans Wake* (F193), is the dramatic version of an identical symbol. But the central image, the epiphany of the interview, is contained in the movement of the priest's fingers: "slowly dangling and looping the cord of the other blind." That is to say, coolly proffering a noose. This is the lyric mode of *Ulysses*'s epical hangman, "The lord of things as they are whom the most Roman of Catholics call *dio boia*, hangman god" (U210/201).

The Contrapuntal Opening

According to the practice inaugurated by Joyce when he rewrote "The Sisters" in 1906, the *Portrait*, like the two books to follow,

opens amid elaborate counterpoint. The first two pages, terminating in a row of asterisks, enact the entire action in microcosm.
An Aristotelian catalog of senses, faculties, and mental activities
is played against the unfolding of the infant conscience.

> Once upon a time and a very good time it was there was
> a moocow coming down along the road and this moocow that
> was down along the road met a nicens little boy named baby
> tuckoo. . . .
>
> His father told him that story: his father looked at him
> through a glass: he had a hairy face.
>
> He was baby tuckoo. The moocow came down along the
> road where Betty Byrne lived: she sold lemon platt.
>
> > *O, the wild rose blossoms*
> > *On the little green place.*
>
> He sang that song. That was his song.
>
> > *O, the green wothe botheth.*
>
> When you wet the bed, first it is warm then it gets cold.
> His mother put on the oilsheet. That had the queer smell.

This evocation of holes in oblivion is conducted in the mode of
each of the five senses in turn; hearing (the story of the moocow),
sight (his father's face); taste (lemon platt), touch (warm and
cold), smell (the oil sheet). The audible soothes the visible disturbs. Throughout Joyce's work, the senses are symbolically dis-
posed. Smell is the means of discriminating empirical realities
("His mother had a nicer smell than his father" is the next sentence), sight corresponds to the phantasms of oppression, hearing
to the imaginative life. Touch and taste together are the modes
of sex. Hearing, here, comes first, via a piece of imaginative literature. But as we can see from the vantage point of *Finnegans
Wake*, the whole book is about the encounter of baby tuckoo with
the moocow: the Gripes with the mookse.[6] The father with the
hairy face is the first Mookse avatar, the Freudian infantile analogue of God the Father.

In the *Wake*

>Dersherr, live wire, fired Benjermine Funkling outa
th'Empyre, sin right hand son. (F289)

Der Erzhefrr (archlord), here a Teutonic Junker, is the God who
visited his wrath on Lucifer; the hairy attribute comes through
via the music-hall refrain, "There's hair, like wire, coming out of
the Empire."

Dawning consciousness of his own identity ("He was baby tuckoo") leads to artistic performance ("He sang that song. That was
his song"). This is hugely expanded in chapter IV:

>Now, as never before, his strange name seemed to him a
prophecy . . . of the end he had been born to serve and had
been following through the mists of childhood and boyhood,
a symbol of the artist forging anew in his workshop out of the
sluggish matter of the earth a new soaring impalpable imperishable being. (P196/192)

By changing the red rose to a green and dislocating the spelling,
he makes the song his own ("But you could not have a green
rose. But perhaps somewhere in the world you could" [P8/13]).

>His mother had a nicer smell than his father. She played
on the piano the sailor's hornpipe for him to dance. He danced:
>
>*Tralala lala,*
>*Tralala tralaladdy,*
>*Tralala lala,*
>*Tralala lala.*

Between this innocence and its Rimbaudian recapture through
the purgation of the *Wake* there is to intervene the hallucination
in Circe's sty:

THE MOTHER

(*With the subtle smile of death's madness.*) I was once the beautiful May Goulding. I am dead. . . .

STEPHEN

(*Eagerly.*) Tell me the word, mother, if you know it now. The word known to all men. . . .

THE MOTHER

(*With smouldering eyes.*) Repent! O, the fire of hell! (U565/547)

This is foreshadowed as the overture to the *Portrait* closes:

He hid under the table. His mother said:

—O, Stephen will apologise,

Dante said:

—O, if not, the eagles will come and pull out his eyes.—

Pull out his eyes,
Apologise,
Apologise,
Pull out his eyes.

Apologise,
Pull out his eyes,
Pull out his eyes,
Apologise.

The eagles, eagles of Rome, are emissaries of the God with the hairy face: the punisher. They evoke Prometheus and gnawing guilt: again-bite. So the overture ends with Stephen hiding under the table awaiting the eagles. He is hiding under something most of the time: bedclothes, "the enigma of a manner," an indurated rhetoric, or some other carapace of his private world.

Theme Words

It is through their names that things have power over Stephen:

> —The language in which we are speaking is his before it is
> mine. How different are the words *home, Christ, ale, master,* on
> his lips and on mine! I cannot speak or write these words
> without unrest of spirit. His language, so familiar and so for-
> eign, will always be for me an acquired speech. I have not
> made or accepted its words. My voice holds them at bay. My
> soul frets in the shadow of his language. (P221/215)

Not only is the Dean's English a conqueror's tongue; since the
loss of Adam's words, which perfectly mirrored things, all language has conquered the mind and imposed its own order, askew
from the order of creation. Words, like the physical world, are
imposed on Stephen from without, and it is in their canted mirrors that he glimpses a physical and moral world already dyed
the color of his own mind since absorbed, with language, into
his personality.

> Words which he did not understand he said over and over
> to himself till he had learnt them by heart; and through them
> he had glimpses of the real world about him. (P68/70)

⌈Language is a Trojan horse by which the universe gets into the
mind.⌋The first sentence in the book isn't something Stephen sees
but a story he is told, and the overture climaxes in an insistent
brainless rhyme, its jingle corrosively fascinating to the will. It
has power to terrify a child who knows nothing of eagles, or of
Prometheus, or of how his own grown-up failure to apologize
will blend with gathering blindness.

It typifies the peculiar achievement of the *Portrait* that Joyce
can cause patterns of words to make up the very moral texture
of Stephen's mind:

Suck was a queer word. The fellow called Simon Moonan that name because Simon Moonan used to tie the prefect's false sleeves behind his back and the prefect used to let on to be angry. But the sound was ugly. Once he had washed his hands in the lavatory of the Wicklow hotel and his father pulled the stopper up by the chain after and the dirty water went down through the hole in the basin. And when it had all gone down slowly the hole in the basin had made a sound like that: suck. Only louder.

To remember that and the white look of the lavatory made him feel cold and then hot. There were two cocks that you turned and the water came out: cold and hot. He felt cold and then a little hot: and he could see the names printed on the cocks. That was a very queer thing. (P6/12)

"Suck" joins two contexts in Stephen's mind: a playful sinner toying with his indulgent superior, and the disappearance of dirty water. The force of the conjunction is felt only after Stephen has lost his sense of the reality of the forgiveness of sins in the confessional. The habitually orthodox penitent tangles with a God who pretends to be angry; after a reconciliation the process is repeated. And the mark of that kind of play is disgraceful servility. Each time the sin disappears, the sinner is mocked by an impersonal voice out of nature: "Suck!"

This attitude to unreal good and evil furnishes a context for the next conjunction: whiteness and coldness. Stephen finds himself, like Simon Moonan,[7] engaged in the rhythm of obedience to irrational authority, bending his mind to a meaningless act, the arithmetic contest. He is being obediently "good." And the appropriate color is adduced: "He thought his face must be white because it felt so cool."

The pallor of lunar obedient goodness is next associated with damp repulsiveness: the limpness of a wet blanket and of a servant's apron:

He sat looking at the two prints of butter on his plate but could not eat the damp bread. The table-cloth was damp and limp. But he drank off the hot weak tea which the clumsy scullion, girt with a white apron, poured into his cup. He wondered whether the scullion's apron was damp too or whether all white things were cold and damp. (P8/13)

Throughout the first chapter an intrinsic linkage, white-cold-damp-obedient, insinuates itself repeatedly. Stephen after saying his prayers, "his shoulders shaking," "so that he might not go to hell when he died," "curled himself together under the cold white sheets, shaking and trembling. But he would not go to hell when he died, and the shaking would stop" (P16/20). The sea, mysterious as the terrible power of God, "was cold day and night, but it was colder at night" (P14/19). We are reminded of Anna Livia's gesture of submission: "my cold father, my cold mad father, my cold mad feary father" (F628). "There was a cold night smell in the chapel. But it was a holy smell" (P14/19). Stephen is puzzled by the phrase in the Litany of the Blessed Virgin: Tower of Ivory. "How could a woman be a tower of ivory or a house of gold?" He ponders until the revelation comes:

> Eileen had long white hands. One evening when playing tig she had put her hands over his eyes: long and white and thin and cold and soft. That was ivory: a cold white thing. That was the meaning of *Tower of Ivory*. (P36/40)

This instant of insight depends on a sudden reshuffling of associations, a sudden conviction that the Mother of God, and the symbols appropriate to her, belong with the cold, the white, and the unpleasant in a blindfold morality of obedience. Contemplation focused on language is repaid:

> *Tower of Ivory. House of Gold.* By thinking of things you could understand them. (P45/48)

The white-damp-obedient association reappears when Stephen is about to make his confession after the celebrated retreat; its patterns provide the language in which he thinks. Sin has been associated with fire, while the prayers of the penitents are epi-phanized as "soft whispering cloudlets, soft whispering vapour, whispering and vanishing" (P164/163). And having been absolved:

> White pudding and eggs and sausages and cups of tea. How simple and beautiful was life after all! And life lay all before him. . . .
>
> The boys were all there, kneeling in their places. He knelt among them, happy and shy. The altar was heaped with fragrant masses of white flowers: and in the morning light the pale flames of the candles among the white flowers were clear and silent as his own soul. (P168/166)

We cannot read *Finnegans Wake* until we have realized the significance of the way the mind of Stephen Dedalus is bound in by language. He is not only an artist; he is a Dubliner.

The *Portrait* as Lyric

The "instant of emotion" (P251/244), of which this 300-page lyric is the "simplest verbal vesture," is the exalted instant, emerging at the end of the book, of freedom, of vocation, of Stephen's destiny, winging his way above the waters at the side of the hawk-like man: the instant of promise on which the crushing ironies of *Ulysses* are to fall. The epic of the sea of matter is preceded by the lyric image of a growing dream; a dream that like Richard Rowan's in *Exiles* disregards the fall of man; a dream nourished by a sensitive youth of flying above the sea into an uncreated heaven:

> The spell of arms and voices: the white arms of roads, their promise of close embraces and the black arms of tall ships that stand against the moon, their tale of distant nations. They are held out to say: We are alone—come. And the voices say with them: We are your kinsmen. And the air is thick with their company as they call to me, their kinsman, making ready to

go, shaking the wings of their exultant and terrible youth.
(P298/288)

The emotional quality of this is continuous with that of the *Count
of Monte Cristo*, that fantasy of the exile returned for vengeance
(the plot of the *Odyssey*) which kindled so many of Stephen's
boyhood dreams:

> The figure of that dark avenger stood forth in his mind for
> whatever he had heard or divined in childhood of the strange
> and terrible. At night he built up on the parlour table an image
> of the wonderful island cave out of transfers and paper flowers
> and strips of the silver and golden paper in which chocolate
> is wrapped. When he had broken up this scenery, weary of its
> tinsel, there would come to his mind the bright picture of
> Marseilles, of sunny trellises and of Mercedes. (P68/70)

The prose surrounding Stephen's flight is empurpled with transfers and paper flowers too. It is not immature prose, as we might
suppose by comparison with *Ulysses*. The prose of "The Dead" is
mature prose, and "The Dead" was written in 1908. Rather, it is
a meticulous pastiche of immaturity. Joyce has his eye constantly
on the epic sequel:

> He wanted to meet in the real world the unsubstantial im-
> age which his soul so constantly beheld. He did not know
> where to seek it or how, but a premonition which led him on
> told him that this image would, without any overt act of his,
> encounter him. They would meet quietly as if they had known
> each other and had made their tryst, perhaps at one of the
> gates or in some more secret place. They would be alone,
> surrounded by darkness and silence: and in that moment of
> supreme tenderness he would be transfigured. (P71/73)

As the vaginal imagery of gates, secret places, and darkness implies, this is the dream that reaches temporary fulfillment in the
plunge into profane love (P113/114). But the ultimate "secret

place" is to be Mabbot Street, outside Bella Cohen's brothel; the unsubstantial image of his quest, that of Leopold Bloom, advertisement canvasser; Monte Cristo, returned avenger, Ulysses; and the transfiguration, into the phantasmal dead son of a sentimental Jew:

> *Against the dark wall a figure appears slowly, a fairy boy of eleven, a changeling, kidnapped, dressed in an Eton suit with glass shoes and a little bronze helmet, holding a book in his hand. He reads from right to left inaudibly, smiling, kissing the page.* (U593/574)

That Dedalus the artificer did violence to nature is the point of the epigraph from Ovid, *Et ignotas animum dimittit in artes*; the Icarian fall is inevitable.

> In tedious exile now too long detain'd
> Dedalus languish'd for his native land.
> The sea foreclos'd his flight: yet thus he said,
> Though earth and water in subjection laid,
> O cruel Minos, thy dominion be,
> We'll go through air; for sure the air is free.
> *Then to new arts his cunning thought applies,*
> *And to improve the work of nature tries.*

Stephen does not, as the careless reader may suppose, become an artist by rejecting church and country. Stephen does not become an artist at all. Country, church, and mission are an inextricable unity, and in rejecting the two that seem to hamper him, he rejects also the one on which he has set his heart. Improving the work of nature is his obvious ambition ("But you could not have a green rose. But perhaps somewhere in the world you could"), and it logically follows from the aesthetic he expounds to Lynch. It is a neoplatonic aesthetic; the crucial principle of epiphanization has been withdrawn. He imagines that "the loveliness that has not yet come into the world" (P297/286) is to be found in his own soul. The earth is gross, and what it brings forth is cowdung; sound and shape and color are "the prison gates of our soul";

and beauty is something mysteriously gestated within. The genuine artist reads signatures, the fake artist forges them, a process
adumbrated in the obsession of Shem the Penman (from *Jim the
Penman*, a forgotten drama about a forger) with "Macfearsome's
Ossean," the most famous of literary forgeries, studying "how
cutely to copy all their various styles of signature so as one day
to utter an epical forged cheque on the public for his own private
profit" (F181).

One can sense all this in the first four chapters of the *Portrait*,
and *Ulysses* is unequivocal:

> Fabulous artificer, the hawklike man. You flew. Whereto?
> Newhaven-Dieppe, steerage passenger. Paris and back. (U208/
> 199)

The Stephen of the end of the fourth chapter, however, is still
unstable; he had to be brought into a final balance, and shown
at some length as a being whose development was virtually ended.
Unfortunately, the last chapter makes the book a peculiarly difficult one for the reader to focus, because Joyce had to close it
on a suspended chord. As a lyric, it is finished in its own terms;
but the themes of the last forty pages, though they give the
illusion of focusing, don't really focus until we have read well
into *Ulysses*. The final chapter, which in respect to the juggernaut
of *Ulysses* must be a vulnerable flank, in respect to what has gone
before must be a conclusion. This problem Joyce didn't wholly
solve; there remains a moral ambiguity (how seriously are we
to take Stephen?) which makes the last forty pages painful reading.

Not that Stephen would stand indefinitely if *Ulysses* didn't top-
ple him over; his equilibrium in chapter V, though good enough
to give him a sense of unusual integrity in University College, is
precarious unless he can manage, in the manner of so many
permanent undergraduates, to prolong the college context for the
rest of his life. Each of the preceding chapters, in fact, works
toward an equilibrium which is dashed when in the next chapter
Stephen's world becomes larger and the frame of reference more

complex. The terms of equilibrium are always stated with disquieting accuracy; at the end of chapter I we find:

> He was alone. He was happy and free: but he would not be anyway proud with Father Dolan. He would be very quiet and obedient: and he wished that he could do something kind for him to show him that he was not proud. (P64/66)

And at the end of chapter III:

> He sat by the fire in the kitchen, not daring to speak for happiness. Till that moment he had not known how beautiful and peaceful life could be. The green square of paper pinned round the lamp cast down a tender shade. On the dresser was a plate of sausages and white pudding and on the shelf there were eggs. They would be for the breakfast in the morning after the communion in the college chapel. White pudding and eggs and sausages and cups of tea. How simple and beautiful was life after all! And life lay all before him. (P168/166)

Not "irony" but simply the truth: the good life conceived in terms of white pudding and sausages is unstable enough to need no underlining.

The even-numbered chapters make a sequence of a different sort. The ending of IV, Stephen's panting submission to an artistic vocation—

> Evening had fallen when he woke and the sand and arid grasses of his bed glowed no longer. He rose slowly and, recalling the rapture of his sleep, sighed at its joy. (P201/197)

—hasn't quite the finality often read into it when the explicit parallel with the ending of II is perceived:

> He closed his eyes, surrendering himself to her, body and mind, conscious of nothing in the world but the dark pressure of her softly parting lips. They pressed upon his brain as upon

his lips as though they were the vehicle of a vague speech; and between them he felt an unknown and timid pressure, darker than the swoon of sin, softer than sound or odour. (P114/115)

When we link these passages with the fact that the one piece of literary composition Stephen actually achieves in the book comes out of a wet dream ("Towards dawn he awoke. O what sweet music! His soul was all dewy wet" [P254], we are in a position to see that the concluding "Welcome, O life!" has an air of finality and balance only because the diary form of the last seven pages disarms us with an illusion of auctorial impartiality.

Controlling Images:
Clongowes and Belvedere

Ego versus authority is the theme of the three odd-numbered chapters. Dublin versus the dream that of the two even-numbered ones. The generic Joyce plot, the encounter with the alter ego, is consummated when Stephen at the end of the book identifies himself with the sanctified Stephen who was stoned by the Jews after reporting a vision (Acts 7:56) and claims sonship with the classical Daedalus who evaded the ruler of land and sea by turning his soul to obscure arts. The episodes are built about adumbrations of this encounter: with Father Conmee, with Monte Cristo, with the whores, with the broad-shouldered moustached student who cut the word *Fœtus* in a desk, with the weary mild confessor, with the bird girl. Through this repeated plot intertwine controlling emotions and controlling images that mount in complexity as the book proceeds.

In chapter I the controlling emotion is fear, and the dominant image Father Dolan and his pandybat; this, associated with the hangman god and the priestly denial of the senses, was to become one of Joyce's standard images for Irish clericalism—hence the jack-in-the-box appearance of Father Dolan in Circe's nightmare imbroglio, his pandybat cracking twice like thunder (U547/531). Stephen's comment, in the mode of Blake's repudiation of the God who slaughtered Jesus, emphasizes the inclusiveness of the image: "I never could read His handwriting except His criminal thumbprint on the haddock."

Chapter II opens with a triple image of Dublin's prepossessions: music, sport, religion. The first is exhibited via Uncle Charles singing sentimental ballads in the outhouse; the second via Stephen's ritual run around the park under the eye of a superannuated trainer, which his uncle enjoins on him as the whole duty of a Dubliner; the third via the clumsy piety of Uncle Charles, kneeling on a red handkerchief and reading above his breath "from a thumb-blackened prayerbook, wherein catchwords were printed at the foot of every page" (P67/69). This trinity of themes is unwound and entwined throughout the chapter, like a net woven round Stephen; it underlies the central incident, the Whitsuntide play in the Belvedere chapel (religion), which opens with a display by the dumbbell team (sport) preluded by sentimental waltzes from the soldier's band (music).

While he is waiting to play his part, Stephen is taunted by fellow students, who rally him on a fancied love affair and, smiting his calf with a cane, bid him recite the *Confiteor*. His mind goes back to an analogous incident, when a similar punishment had been visited on his refusal to "admit that Byron was no good." The further analogy with Father Dolan is obvious; love, art, and personal independence are thus united in an ideogram of the prepossessions Stephen is determined to cultivate in the teeth of persecution.

The dreamworld Stephen nourishes within himself is played against manifestations of music, sport, and religion throughout the chapter. The constant ironic clash of Dublin versus the Dream animates chapter II, as the clash of the ego versus authority did chapter I. All these themes come to focus during Stephen's visit with his father to Cork. The dream of rebellion he has silently cultivated is externalized by the discovery of the word *Fœtus* carved in a desk by a forgotten medical student:

It shocked him to find in the outer world a trace of what he had deemed till then a brutish and individual malady of his own mind. His monstrous reveries came thronging into his memory. They too had sprung up before him, suddenly and furiously, out of mere words. (P101/102)

The possibility of shame gaining the upper hand is dashed, however, by the sudden banal intrusion of his father's conversation ("When you kick out for yourself, Stephen, as I daresay you will one of these days, remember, whatever you do, to mix with gentlemen"). Against the standards of Dublin his monstrous reveries acquire a Satanic glamour, and the trauma is slowly diverted into a resolution to rebel. After his father has expressed a resolve to "leave him to his Maker" (religion) and offered to "sing a tenor song against him" (music) or "vault a fivebarred gate against him" (sport), Stephen muses, watching his father and two cronies drinking to the memory of their past:

An abyss of fortune or of temperament sundered him from them. His mind seemed older than theirs: it shone coldly on their strifes and happiness and regrets like a moon upon a younger earth. No life or youth stirred in him as it had stirred in them. He had known neither the pleasure of companionship with others nor the vigour of rude male health nor filial piety. Nothing stirred within his soul but a cold and cruel and loveless lust. (P107/108)

After one final effort to compromise with Dublin on Dublin's terms has collapsed into futility ("The pot of pink enamel paint gave out and the wainscot of his bedroom remained with its unfinished and illplastered coat" [P110/111]), he fiercely cultivates his rebellious thoughts, and moving by day and night "among distorted images of the outer world" (P111/112) plunges at last into the arms of whores. "The holy encounter he had then imagined at which weakness and timidity and inexperience were to fall from him" (P112/113) finally arrives in inversion of Father Dolan's and Uncle Charles's religion; his descent into night-town is accompanied by lurid evocations of a Black Mass (cf. Ulysses 583/565):

> The yellow gasflames arose before his troubled vision against the vapoury sky, burning as if before an altar. Before the doors and in the lighted halls groups were gathered arrayed as for some rite. He was in another world: he had awakened from a slumber of centuries. (P113/114)

Controlling Images: Sin and Repentance

Each chapter in the *Portrait* gathers up the thematic material of the preceding ones and entwines them with a dominant theme of its own. In chapter III the fear-pandybat motif is present in Father Arnall's crudely materialistic hell, of which even the thickness of the walls is specified; and the Dublin-versus-dream motif has ironic inflections in Stephen's terror-stricken broodings, when the dream has been twisted into a dream of holiness and even Dublin appears transfigured:

> How beautiful must be a soul in the state of grace when God looked upon it with love.
>
> Frowsy girls sat along the curbstones before their baskets. Their dank hair trailed over their brows. They were not beautiful to see as they crouched in the mire. But their souls were seen by God; and if their souls were in a state of grace they were radiant to see; and God loved them, seeing them. (P162/160)

A *rapprochement* in these terms between the outer world and Stephen's desires is too inadequate to need commentary, and it makes vivid as nothing else could the hopeless inversion of his attempted self-sufficiency. It underlines, in yet another way, his persistent sin, and the dominant theme of chapter III is sin. A fugue-like opening plays upon the Seven Deadly Sins in turn; gluttony is in the first paragraph ("Stuff it into you, his belly counselled him"), followed by <u>lust</u>, then <u>sloth</u> ("A cold lucid indifference reigned in his soul"), <u>pride</u> ("His pride in his own sin, his loveless awe of God, told him that his offence was too grievous to be atoned for") <u>anger</u> ("The blundering answer stirred the embers of his contempt for his fellows"), finally, a recapitulation fixes each term of the mortal catalog in a phrase, enumerating how "from the evil seed of lust all the other deadly sins had sprung forth" (P120/120).

Priest and punisher inhabit Stephen himself as well as Dublin: when he is deepest in sin he is most thoroughly a theologian. A paragraph of gloomy introspection is juxtaposed with a list of theological questions that puzzle Stephen's mind as he awaits the preacher:

> Is baptism with mineral water valid? How comes it that while the first beatitude promises the kingdom of heaven to the poor of heart, the second beatitude promises also to the meek that they shall possess the land? . . . If the wine change into vinegar and the host crumble into corruption after they have been consecrated, is Jesus Christ still present under their species as God and as man?
>
> Here he is! Here he is!
>
> A boy from his post at the window had seen the rector come from the house. All the catechisms were opened and all heads bent upon them silently. (P120/120)

Wine changed into vinegar and the host crumbled into corruption fits exactly the Irish clergy of "a church which was the scullery-maid of Christendom." The excited "Here he is! Here he is!" following hard on the mention of Jesus Christ and signaling nothing more portentous than the rector makes the point as dramatically as anything in the book, and the clinching sentence, with the students suddenly bending over their catechisms, places the rector as the vehicle of pandybat morality.

The last of the theological questions is the telling question. Stephen never expresses doubt of the existence of God nor of the essential validity of the priestly office—his *non serviam* is not a *non credo*, and he talks of a "malevolent reality" behind these appearances (P287/277)—but the wine and bread that were offered for his veneration were changed into vinegar and crumbled into corruption. And it was the knowledge of that underlying validity clashing with his refusal to do homage to vinegar and rot that evoked his ambivalent poise of egocentric despair. The hell of Father Arnall's sermon, so emotionally overwhelming, so picayune beside the horrors that Stephen's imagination can generate, had no more ontological content for Stephen than had "an eternity of bliss in the company of the dean of studies" (P282/273).

The conflict this central chapter is again between the phantasmal and the real. What is real—psychologically real, because realized—is Stephen's anguish and remorse and its context in the life of the flesh. What is phantasmal is the "heaven" of the Church and the "good life" of the priest. It is only fear that makes him clutch after the latter at all; his reaching out after orthodox salvation is, as we have come to expect, presented in terms that judge it:

> The wind blew over him and passed on to the myriads and myriads of other souls, on whom God's favour shone now more and now less, stars now brighter and now dimmer, sustained and failing. And the glimmering souls passed away, sustained and failing, merged in a moving breath. One soul was lost; a tiny soul; his. It flickered once and went out, forgotten, lost. The end: black cold void waste.
>
> Consciousness of place came ebbing back to him slowly over a vast tract of time unlit, unfelt, unlived. The squalid scene composed itself around him; the common accents, the burning gasjets in the shops, odours of fish and spirits and wet sawdust, moving men and women. An old woman was about to cross the street, an oilcan in her hand. He bent down and asked her was there a chapel near. (P162/160)

That wan waste world of flickering stars is the best Stephen has been able to do toward an imaginative grasp of the communion of saints sustained by God; "unlit, unfelt, unlived" explains succinctly why it had so little hold on him, once fear had relaxed. Equally pertinent is the vision of human temporal occupations the sermon evokes:

> What did it profit a man to gain the whole world if he lost his soul? At last he had understood: and human life lay around him, a plain of peace whereon antlike men laboured in brotherhood, their dead sleeping under quiet mounds. (P144/143)

To maintain the life of grace in the midst of nature, sustained by so cramped a vision of the life of nature, would mean maintaining an intolerable tension. Stephen's unrelenting philosophic bias, his determination to understand what he is about, precludes his adopting the double standard of the Dubliners; to live both the life of nature and the life of grace he must enjoy an imaginative grasp of their relationship which stunts neither. "No one doth well against he will," writes Saint Augustine, "even though what he doth, be well"; and Stephen's will is firmly harnessed to his understanding. And there is no one in Dublin to help him achieve understanding. Father Arnall's sermon precludes rather than secures a desirable outcome, for it follows the modes of pandybat morality and Dublin materiality. Its only possible effect on Stephen is to lash his dormant conscience into a frenzy. The description of Hell as "a strait and dark and foul smelling prison, an abode of demons and lost souls, filled with fire and smoke," with walls four thousand miles thick, its damned packed in so tightly that "they are not even able to remove from the eye the worm that gnaws it," is childishly grotesque beneath its sweeping eloquence; and the hair-splitting catalog of pains—pain of loss, pain of conscience (divided into three heads), pain of extension, pain of intensity, pain of eternity—is cast in a brainlessly analytic mode that effectively prevents any corresponding heaven from possessing any reality at all.

Stephen's unstable pact with the Church, and its dissolution, follows the pattern of composition and dissipation established by his other dreams: the dream for example of the tryst with Mercedes, which found ironic reality among harlots. It parallels ex-

actly his earlier attempt to "build a breakwater of order and elegance against the sordid tide of life without him" (P110/111),
whose failure, with the exhaustion of his money, was epiphanized
in the running dry of a pot of pink enamel paint. His regimen
at that time—

> He bought presents for everyone, overhauled his rooms, wrote
> out resolutions, marshalled his books up and down their
> shelves, pored over all kinds of price lists.

—is mirrored by his searching after spiritual improvement:

> His daily life was laid out in devotional areas. By means of
> ejaculations and prayers he stored up ungrudgingly for the
> souls in purgatory centuries of days and quarantines and years.
> ... He offered up each of his three daily chaplets that his soul
> might grow strong in each of the three theological virtues....
> On each of the seven days of the week he further prayed that
> one of the seven gifts of the Holy Ghost might descend upon
> his soul. (P170/167)

The "loan bank" he had opened for the family, out of which he
had pressed loans on willing borrowers "that he might have the
pleasure of making out receipts and reckoning the interests on
sums lent," finds its counterpart in the benefits he stored up for
souls in purgatory that he might enjoy the spiritual triumph of
"achieving with ease so many fabulous ages of canonical pen-
ances." Both projects are parodies on the doctrine of economy of
grace; both are attempts, corrupted by motivating self-interest, to
make peace with Dublin on Dublin's own terms; and both are
short-lived.

As this precise analogical structure suggests, the action of each
of the five chapters is really the same action. Each chapter closes
with a synthesis or triumph which the next destroys. The triumph of the appeal to Father Conmee from lower authority, of
the appeal to the harlots from Dublin, of the appeal to the
Church from sin, of the appeal to art from the priesthood (the

bird girl instead of the Virgin) is always the same triumph raised to a more comprehensive level. It is an attempt to find new parents: new fathers in the odd chapters, new objects of love in the even. The last version of Father Conmee is the "priest of the eternal imagination"; the last version of Mercedes is the "lure of the fallen seraphim." But the last version of the mother who said, "O, Stephen will apologise" is the mother who prays on the last page "that I may learn in my own life and away from home and friends what the heart is and what it feels." The mother remains.

The Double Female

As in *Dubliners* and *Exiles*, the female role in the *Portrait* is less to arouse than to elucidate masculine desires. Hence the complex function in the book of physical love: the physical is the analogue of the spiritual, as St. Augustine insisted in his *Confessions* (which, with Ibsen's *Brand*, is the chief archetype of Joyce's book). The poles between which this affection moves are those of St. Augustine and St. John: the Whore of Babylon and the Bride of Christ. The relation between the two is far from simple, and Stephen moves in a constant tension between them.

His desire, figured in the visions of Monte Cristo's Mercedes, "to meet in the real world the unsubstantial image which his soul so constantly beheld" draws him toward the prostitute ("In her arms he felt that he had suddenly become strong and fearless and sure of himself" [P114/114]) and simultaneously toward the vaguely spiritual satisfaction represented with equal vagueness by the wraithlike E——C——, to whom he twice writes verses. The Emma Clery of *Stephen Hero*, with her loud forced manners and her body compact of pleasure (S66/56), was refined into a wraith with a pair of initials to parallel an intangible Church. She is continually assimilated to the image of the Blessed Virgin and of the heavenly Bride. The torture she costs him is the torture his apostasy costs him. His flirtation with her is his flirtation with Christ. His profane villanelle draws its imagery from religion— the incense, the eucharistic hymn, the chalice—and her heart, following Dante's image, is a rose, and in her praise "the earth was like a swinging swaying censer, a ball of incense" (P256/248).

The woman is the Church. His vision of greeting Mercedes with "a sadly proud gesture of refusal"—

—Madam, I never eat muscatel grapes. (P68/71)

—is fulfilled when he refuses his Easter communion. Emma's eyes, in their one explicit encounter, speak to him from beneath a cowl (P76/78). "The glories of Mary held his soul captive" (P118/118), and a temporary reconciliation of his lust and his spiritual thirst is achieved as he reads the lesson out of the Song of Solomon. In the midst of his repentance she functions as imagined mediator: "The image of Emma appeared before him," and, repenting, "he imagined that he stood near Emma in a wide land, and, humbly and in tears, bent and kissed the elbow of her sleeve" (P132/131). Like Dante's Beatrice, she manifests in his earthly experience the Church Triumphant of his spiritual dream. And when he rejects her because she seems to be flirting with Father Moran, his anger is couched in the anticlerical terms of his apostasy: "He had done well to leave her to flirt with her priest, to toy with a church which was the scullery-maid of Christendom" (P258/250).

That Kathleen ni Houlihan can flirt with priests is the unforgivable sin underlying Stephen's rejection of Ireland. But he makes a clear distinction between the stupid clericalism which makes intellectual and communal life impossible, and his long-nourished vision of an artist's Church Triumphant upon earth. He rejects the actual for daring to fall short of his vision.

The Final Balance

The climax of the book is of course Stephen's ecstatic discovery of his vocation at the end of chapter IV. The prose rises in nervous excitement to beat again and again the tambours of a fin-de-siècle ecstasy:

His heart trembled; his breath came faster and a wild spirit passed over his limbs as though he were soaring sunward. His heart trembled in an ecstasy of fear and his soul was in flight. His soul was soaring in an air beyond the world and the body he knew was purified in a breath and delivered of incertitude and made radiant and commingled with the element of the spirit. An ecstasy of flight made radiant his eyes and wild his breath and tremulous and wild and radiant his windswept limbs.

—One! Two! . . . Look out!—

—O, Cripes, I'm drownded!— (P196/192)

The interjecting voices of course are those of bathers, but their ironic appropriateness to Stephen's Icarian "soaring sunward" is not meant to escape us: divers have their own "ecstasy of flight," and Icarus was "drownded." The imagery of Stephen's ecstasy is fetched from many sources; we recognize Shelly's skylark, Icarus, the glorified body of the Resurrection (cf. "His soul had arisen from the grave of boyhood, spurning her graveclothes" [P197/193]) and a tremulousness from which it is difficult to dissociate adolescent sexual dreams (which the Freudians tell us are frequently dreams of flying). The entire eight-page passage is cunningly organized with great variety of rhetoric and incident, but we cannot help noticing the limits set on vocabulary and figures of thought. The empurpled triteness of such a cadence as "radiant his eyes and wild his breath and tremulous and wild and radiant his windswept limbs" is enforced by recurrence: "But her long fair hair was girlish: and girlish, and touched with the wonder of mortal beauty, her face" (P199/195). "Ecstasy" is the keyword, indeed. This riot of feelings corresponds to no vocation definable in mature terms; the paragraphs come to rest on images of irresponsible motion:

He turned away from her suddenly and set off across the strand. His cheeks were aflame; his body was aglow; his limbs were trembling. On and on and on and on he strode, far out over the sands, singing wildly to the sea, crying to greet the advent of the life that had cried to him. (P200/196)

What "life" connotes it skills not to ask; the word recurs and recurs. So does the motion onward and onward and onward:

A wild angel had appeared to him, the angel of mortal youth and beauty, an envoy from the fair courts of life, to throw open before him in an instant of ecstasy the gates of all the ways of error and glory. On and on and on and on! (P200/196)

It may be well to recall Joyce's account of the romantic temper:

. . . an insecure, unsatisfied, impatient temper which sees no fit abode here for its ideals and chooses therefore to behold them under insensible figures. As a result of this choice it comes to disregard certain limitations. Its figures are blown to wild adventures, lacking the gravity of solid bodies. (S78/66)

Joyce also called *Prometheus Unbound* "the Schwärmerei of a young jew."

And it is quite plain from the final chapter of the *Portrait* that we are not to accept the mode of Stephen's "freedom" as the "message" of the book. The "priest of the eternal imagination" turns out to be indigestibly Byronic. Nothing is more obvious than his total lack of humor. The dark intensity of the first four chapters is moving enough, but our impulse on being confronted with the final edition of Stephen Dedalus is to laugh; and laugh at this moment we dare not; he is after all a victim being prepared for a sacrifice. His shape, as Joyce said, can no longer change. The art he has elected is not "the slow elaborative patience of the art of satisfaction." "On and on and on and on" will be its inescapable mode. He does not *see* the girl who symbolizes the full revelation; "she seemed like one whom magic had changed into the likeness of a strange and beautiful seabird" (P199/195), and he confusedly apprehends a sequence of downy and feathery incantations. What, in the last chapter, he does see he sees only to reject, in favor of an incantatory "loveliness which has not yet come into the world" (P197/286).

The only creative attitude to language exemplified in the book is that of Stephen's father:

—Is it Christy? he said. There's more cunning in one of those warts on his bald head than in a pack of jack foxes.

His vitality is established before the book is thirty pages under way. Stephen, however, isn't enchanted at any time by the proximity of such talk. He isn't as a matter of fact, even interested in it. Without a backward glance, he exchanges this father for a myth.

Notes

1. Herbert Gorman, *James Joyce* (New York: Farrar and Rinehart, 1939), V.iii, VII.i, VII.iii, VII.vi. See also Theodore Spencer's introduction to *Stephen Hero*, edited by Spencer (New York: New Directions, 1944).

2. A letter followed by two numbers is a page reference to standard American and English editions of one of Joyce's books. Thus P252/244 means that the quotation appears on page 252 of the Modern Library edition and on page 244 of the Jonathan Cape edition of *Portrait*. References to *Finnegans Wake* carry only one number since the pagination of both editions of that book is identical. D = *Dubliners* (Modern Library/Jonathan Cape); E = *Exiles* (New Directions/Jonathan Cape); F = *Finnegans Wake* (Viking Press/Faber and Faber); P = *A Portrait of the Artist as a Young Man* (Modern Library/Jonathan Cape); S = *Stephen Hero* (New Directions/Jonathan Cape); U = *Ulysses* (Modern Library/John Lane; Bodley Head).

3. Stanislaus Joyce, "James Joyce: A Memoir," *Hudson Review* 2, no. 4 (1950): 496.

4. Frank Budgen, *James Joyce and the Making of Ulysses* (London: Grayson and Grayson, 1934), 107.

5. "—You want me, said Stephen, to toe the line with those hypocrites and sycophants in the college. I will never do so.

—No. I mentioned Jesus.

—Don't mention him. I have made it a common noun. They don't believe in him; they don't observe his precepts" (S141/124).

6. Compare the opening sentence: "Eins within a space, and a weary-wide space it wast, ere wohned a Mookse" (F152). Mookse is moocow plus fox plus mock turtle. The German *Eins* evokes Einstein, who presides over the interchanging of space and time; space is the Mookse's "spatialty."

7. Joyce's names should always be scrutinized. Simon Moonan: moon: the heatless (white) satellite reflecting virtue borrowed from Simon Peter. Simony, too, is an activity naturally derived from this casually businesslike attitude to priestly authority.

The Problem of Distance in
A Portrait of the Artist

WAYNE BOOTH

◆   ◆   ◆

L ACK OF ADEQUATE WARNING that irony is at work; extreme complexity, subtlety, or privacy of the norms to be inferred; vivid psychological realism: Everyone recognizes that each of these three sources of difficulty is present in some modern fiction, frequently in forms more deceptive than anything encountered in earlier work. Any one of them alone can give trouble. And in some modern fiction all three are present. There is no warning, either explicitly or in the form of gross disparity of word and deed; the relationship of the ironic narrator to the author's norms is an extremely complex one, and the norms are themselves subtle and private; and the narrator's own mental vitality dominates the scene and wins our sympathy.

It is in the last of these three that modern fiction has gone far beyond anything experienced before Flaubert. Jane Austen's implicit apology for Emma said, in effect, "Emma's vision is your vision; therefore forgive her." But modern authors have learned how to provide this apology in much more insistent form. The deep plunges of modern inside views, the various streams-of-consciousness that attempt to give the reader an effect of living thought and sensation, are capable of blinding us to the possibility of our making judgments not shared by the narrator or reflector himself.

If a master puzzle maker had set out to give us the greatest possible difficulty, he could not have done more than has been done in some modern works in which this effect of deep involvement is combined with the implicit demand that we maintain our capacity for ironic judgment. The trouble with *Moll Flanders*, such a genius of confusion might be imagined as saying to himself, is that the obvious differences between the female heroine and the author provide too many clues. Let us then write a book that will look like the author's autobiography, using many details from his own life and opinions. But we cannot be satisfied with moral problems, which are after all much less subject to dispute than intellectual and aesthetic matters. Let us then call for the reader's precise judgment on a very elaborate set of opinions and actions in which the hero is sometimes right, sometimes slightly wrong, and sometimes absurdly astray. Just to make sure that things are not too obvious, let us finally bind the reader so tightly to the consciousness of the ambiguously misguided protagonist that nothing will interfere with his delight in inferring the precise though varying degrees of distance that operate from point to point throughout the book. We can be sure that some readers will take the book as strictly autobiographical; others will go sadly astray in overlooking ironies that are intended and in discovering ironies that are not there. But for the rare reader who can make his way through this jungle, the delight will be great indeed.

The giant whom we all must wrestle with in this regard is clearly Joyce. Except for occasional outbursts of bravado nobody has ever really claimed that Joyce is clear. In all the skeleton keys and classroom guides there is an open assumption that his later works, *Ulysses* and Finnegans Wake, cannot be read; they can only be studied. Joyce himself was always explicating his works, and it is clear that he saw nothing wrong with the fact that they could not be thought of as standing entirely on their own feet. The reader's problems are handled, if they are to be handled at all, by rhetoric provided outside the work.

But the difficulties with distance that are pertinent here cannot be removed by simple study. Obscure allusions can be looked up, patterns of imagery and theme can be traced; gradually over the years a good deal of lore has accumulated, and about some of it by now there is even a certain amount of agreement. But about the more fundamental matters the skeleton keys and guides are of little help, because unfortunately they do not agree, they do not agree at all. It is fine to know that in *Ulysses* Stephen stands in some way for Telemachus and Bloom for his wandering father, Ulysses. But it would also be useful to know whether the work is comic or pathetic or tragic, or, if it is a combination, where the elements fall. Can two readers be said to have read the same book if one thinks it ends affirmatively and the other sees the ending as pessimistic? It is really no explanation to say that Joyce has succeeded in imitating life so well that like life itself his books seem totally ambiguous, totally open to whatever interpretation the reader wants to place on them. Even William Empson, that perceptive and somewhat overly ingenious prophet of ambiguity, finds himself unable to be completely permissive toward conflicting interpretations. In a long, curious essay arguing that the basic movement of *Ulysses* is toward a favorable ending, with the Blooms and Stephen united, he admits that there are difficulties, and that they spring from the kind of book it is: it "not only refuses to tell you the end of the story, it also refuses to tell you what the author thinks would have been a good end to the story." And yet almost in the same breath he can write as if he thought previous critics somehow at fault for not having come to his inferences about the book. "By the way, I have no patience with critics who say it is impossible ever to tell whether Joyce means a literary effect to be ironical or not; if they don't know this part isn't funny, they ought to."[1] Well, but why should they be able to? Who is to mediate between Empson and those he attacks, or between Lawrance Thompson, in his interpretation of the book as comedy, and those critics with whom he is "decidedly at odds," Stuart Gilbert, Edmund Wilson, Harry Levin, David Daiches, and T. S. Eliot, each of whom assumes, he says, that "Joyce's artistic mode is essentially a non-comic mode, or that comedy in *Ulysses* is an effect rather than a cause"?[2]

Can it possibly make no difference whether we laugh or do not laugh? Can we defend the book even as a realistic mixture, like life itself, unless we can state with some precision what the ingredients are that have been mixed together?

Rather than pursue such general questions about Joyce's admittedly difficult later works, it will be more useful to look closely at that earlier work for which no skeleton key has been thought necessary, *A Portrait of the Artist as a Young Man* (1916). Everyone seems by now agreed that it is a masterpiece in the modern mode. Perhaps we can accept it as that—indeed accept it as an unquestionably great work from any viewpoint—and still feel free to ask a few irreverent questions.

The structure of this "authorless" work is based on the growth of a sensitive boy to young manhood. The steps in his growth are obviously constructed with great care. Each of the first four sections ends a period of Stephen's life with what Joyce, in an earlier draft, calls an epiphany: a peculiar revelation of the inner reality of an experience, accompanied with great elation, as in a mystical religious experience. Each is followed by the opening of a new chapter on a very prosaic, even depressed level. Now here is clearly a careful structural preparation—for what? For a transformation, or for a merely cyclical return? Is the final exaltation a release from the depressing features of Irish life which have tainted the earlier experiences? Or is it the fifth turn in an endless cycle? And in either case, is Stephen always to be viewed with the same deadly seriousness with which he views himself? Is it to artistic maturity that he grows? As the young man goes into exile from Ireland, goes "to encounter for the millionth time the reality of experience and to forge in the smithy" of his soul "the uncreated conscience" of his race, are we to take this, with Harry Levin, as a fully serious portrait of the artist Dedalus, praying to his namesake Daedalus, to stand him "now and ever in good stead"?[3] Or is the inflated style, as Mark Schorer tells us, Joyce's clue that the young Icarus is flying too close to the sun, with the "excessive lyric relaxation" of Stephen's final style punctuating "the illusory nature of the whole ambition"?[4] The young man takes himself and his flight with deadly solemnity. Should we?

To see the difficulties clearly, let us consider three crucial episodes, all from the final section: his rejection of the priesthood, his exposition of what he takes to be Thomistic aesthetics, and his composition of a poem.

Is his rejection of the priesthood a triumph, a tragedy, or merely a comedy of errors? Most readers, even those who follow the new trend of reading Stephen ironically, seem to have read it as a triumph: the artist has rid himself of one of the chains that bound him. To Caroline Gordon, this is a serious misreading. "I suspect that Joyce's *Portrait* has been misread by a whole generation." She sees the rejection as "the picture of a soul that is being damned for time and eternity caught in the act of foreseeing and foreknowing its damnation," and she cites in evidence the fall of Icarus and Stephen's own statement to Cranly that he is not afraid to make a mistake, "even a great mistake, a lifelong mistake and perhaps for eternity, too."[5] Well, which Portrait do we choose, that of the artistic soul battling through successfully to his necessary freedom, or that of the child of God, choosing, like Lucifer, his own damnation? No two books could be further from each other than the two we envision here. There may be a sufficient core of what is simply interesting to salvage the book as a great work of the sensibility, but unless we are willing to retreat into babbling and incommunicable relativism, we cannot believe that it is *both* a portrait of the prisoner freed and a portrait of the soul placing itself in chains.

Critics have had even more difficulty with Stephen's aesthetic theory, ostensibly developed from Aquinas. Is the book itself, as Grant Redford tells us,[6] an "objectification of an artistic proposition and a method announced by the central character," achieving for Joyce the "wholeness, harmony, and radiance" that Stephen celebrates in his theory?[7] Or is it, as Father Noon says, an ironic portrait of Stephen's immature aesthetics? Joyce wanted to qualify Stephen's utterances, Noon tells us, "by inviting attention to his own more sophisticated literary concerns," and he stands apart from the Thomist aesthetics, watching Stephen miss the clue in his drive for an impersonal, dramatic narration. "The comparison of the artist with the God of the creation," taken "straight" by many critics, is for Father Noon "the climax of Joyce's ironic development of the Dedalus aesthetic."[8]

Finally, what of the precious villanelle? Does Joyce intend it to be taken as a serious sign of Stephen's artistry, as a sign of his genuine but amusingly pretentious precocity, or as something else entirely?

> Are you not weary of ardent ways,
> Lure of the fallen seraphim?
> Tell no more of enchanted days.
>
> Your eyes have set man's heart ablaze
> And you have had your will of him.
> Are you not weary of ardent ways? (*P* 223)

Hardly anyone has committed himself in public about the quality of this poem. Are we to smile at Stephen or pity him in his tortured longing? Are we to marvel at his artistry, or scoff at his conceit? Or are we merely to say, "How remarkable an insight into the kind of poem that would be written by an adolescent in love, if he were artistically inclined?" The poem, we are told, "enfolded him like a shining cloud, enfolded him like water with a liquid life: and like a cloud of vapour or like waters circumfluent in space the liquid letters of speech, symbols of the element of mystery, flowed forth over his brain" (*P* 223). As we recall Jean Paul's formula for "romantic irony," "hot baths of sentiment followed by cold showers of irony," we can only ask here which tap has been turned on. Are we to swoon—or laugh?

Some critics will no doubt answer that all these questions are irrelevant. The villanelle is not to be judged but simply experienced; the aesthetic theory is, within the art work, neither true nor false but simply "true" to the art work—that is, true to

Stephen's character at this point. To read modern literature properly we must refuse to ask irrelevant questions about it; we must accept the "portrait" and no more ask whether the character portrayed is good or bad, right or wrong than we ask whether a woman painted by Picasso is moral or immoral. "All facts of any kind," as Gilbert puts it, "mental or material, sublime or ludicrous, have an equivalence of value for the artist."[9]

This answer, which can be liberating at one stage of our development in appreciating not only modern but all art, becomes less and less satisfactory the longer we look at it. It certainly does not seem to have been Joyce's basic attitude, though he was often misleading about it.[10] The creation and the enjoyment of art can never be a completely neutral activity. Though different works of art require different kinds of judgment for their enjoyment, the position taken in chapters 3–5 must stand: no work, not even the shortest lyric, can be written in complete moral, intellectual and aesthetic neutrality. We may judge falsely, we may judge unconsciously, but we cannot even bring the book to mind without judging its elements, seeing them as shaped into a given kind of thing. Even if we denied that the sequence of events has meaning in the sense of being truly sequential, that denial would itself be a judgment on the rightness of Stephen's actions and opinions at each stage: to decide that he is not growing is as much a judgment on his actions as to decide that he is becoming more and more mature. Actually everyone reads the book as some kind of progressive sequence, and to do so we judge succeeding actions and opinions to be more or less moral, sensitive, or intellectually mature than those they follow.[11] If we felt that the question of Joyce's precise attitude toward Stephen's vocation, his aesthetics, and his villanelle were irrelevant, we would hardly dispute with each other about them. Yet I count in a recent checklist at least fifteen articles and one full book disputing Joyce's attitude about the aesthetics alone.[12]

Like most modern critics, I would prefer to settle such disputes by using internal rather than external evidence. But the experts themselves give me little hope of finding answers to my three problems by rereading *Portrait* one more time. They all clutch happily at any wisp of comment or fragmentary document that might illuminate Joyce's intentions.[13] And who can blame them?

The truth seems to be that Joyce was always a bit uncertain about his attitude toward Stephen. Anyone who reads Ellmann's masterful biography with this problem in mind cannot help being struck by the many shifts and turns Joyce took as he worked through the various versions. There is nothing especially strange in that, of course. Most "autobiographical" novelists probably encounter difficulty in trying to decide just how heroic their heroes are to be. But Joyce's explorations came just at a time when the traditional devices for control of distance were being repudiated, when doctrines of objectivity were in the air, and when people were taking seriously the idea that to evoke "reality" was a sufficient aim in art; the artist need not concern himself with judging or with specifying whether the reader should approve or disapprove, laugh or cry.

Now the traditional forms had specified in their very conceptions a certain degree of clarity about distance. If an author chose to write comedy, for example, he knew that his characters must at least to some degree be "placed" at a distance from the spectator's norms. This predetermination did not, of course, settle all of his problems. To balance sympathy and antipathy, admiration and contempt was still a fundamental challenge, but it was a challenge for which there was considerable guidance in the practice of previous writers of comedy. If, on the other hand, he chose to write tragedy, or satire, or elegy, or celebration odes, or whatever, he could rely to some extent on conventions to guide him and his audience to a common attitude toward his characters.

The young Joyce had none of this to rely on, but he seems never to have sensed the full danger of his position. When, in his earliest years, he recorded his brief epiphanies—those bits of dialogue or description that were supposed to reveal the inner reality of things—there was always an implied identification of the recorder's norms and the reader's; both were spectators at the revealing moment, both shared in the vision of one moment of truth. Though some of the epiphanies are funny, some sad, and some mixed, the basic effect is always the same: an overwhelming sense—when they succeed—of what Joyce liked to call the "incarnation": Artistic Meaning has come to live in the world's body. The Poet has done his work.

Even in these early epiphanies there is difficulty with distance; the author inevitably expects the reader to share in his own preconceptions and interests sufficiently to catch, from each word or gesture, the precise mood or tone that they evoke for the author himself. But since complete identification with the author is a silent precondition for the success of such moments, the basic problem of distance is never a serious one. Even if the author and reader should differ in interpretation, they can share the sense of evoked reality.

It is only when Joyce places at the center of a long work a figure who experiences epiphanies, an epiphany-producing device, as it were, who is himself used by the real author as an object ambiguously distant from the norms of the work, that the complications of distance become incalculable. If he treats the author-figure satirically, as he does in much of *Stephen Hero*, that earlier, windier version of *Portrait*,[14] then what happens to the quality of the epiphanies that he describes? Are they still genuine epiphanies or only what the misguided, callow youth thinks are epiphanies? If, as Joyce's brother Stanislaus has revealed, the word "hero" is satiric, can we take seriously that antihero's vision? Yet if the satirical mode is dropped, if the hero is made into a real hero, and if the reader is made to see things entirely as he sees them, what then happens to objectivity? The portrait is no longer an objective rendering of reality, looked at from a respectable aesthetic distance, but rather a mere subjective indulgence.

Joyce can be seen, in Ellmann's account, wrestling with this problem throughout the revisions. Unlike writers before Flaubert, he had no guidance from convention or tradition or fellow artists. Neither Flaubert nor James had established any sure ground to stand on. Both of them had, in fact, encountered the same problems, and though each had on occasion surmounted the difficulties, Joyce was in no frame of mind to go beneath their claims as realists to the actual problems and lessons that were concealed by their evocative surfaces. A supreme egoist struggling to deal artistically with his own ego, a humorist who could not escape the comic consequences of his portrait of that inflated ego, he faced, in the completed *Stephen Hero*, what he had to recognize as a hodgepodge of irreconcilables. Is Stephen a pompous ass or not? Is his name deliberately ridiculous, as Stanislaus, who invented it, says? Or is it a serious act of symbolism? The way out seems inevitable, but it seems a retreat nonetheless: simply present the "reality" and let the reader judge. Cut all of the author's judgments cut all of the adjectives, produce one long, ambiguous epiphany.[15]

Purged of the author's explicit judgment, the resulting work was so brilliant and compelling, its hero's vision so scintillating that almost all readers overlooked the satiric and ironic content— except, of course, as the satire operated against other characters. So far as I know no one said anything about irony against Stephen until after *Ulysses* was published in 1922, with its opening in which Icarus-Stephen is shown with his wings clipped. Ironic readings did not become popular, in fact, until after the fragment of *Stephen Hero* was published in 1944. Readers of that work found, it is true, many authoritative confirmations of their exaltation of Stephen— for the most part in a form that might confirm anyone's prejudice against commentary. "When he [Stephen] wrote it was always a mature and reasoned emotion which urged him" (155). "This mood of indignation which was not guiltless of a certain superficiality was undoubtedly due to the excitement of release. . . . He acknowledged to himself in honest egoism that he could not take to heart the distress of a nation, the soul of which was antipathetic to his own, so bitterly as the indignity of a bad line of verse: but at the same time he was nothing in the world so little as an amateur artist" (130). "Stephen did not attach himself to art in any spirit of youthful dilettantism but strove to pierce to the significant heart of everything" (25). But readers were also faced with a good many denigrations of the hero. We can agree that *Portrait* is a better work because the immature author has been effaced; Joyce may indeed have found that effacing the commentary was the only way he could obtain an air of maturity.

But the fact remains that it is primarily to this immature commentary that we must go for evidence in deciphering the ironies of the later, purer work.

What we find in *Stephen Hero* is not a simple confirmation of any reading that we might have achieved on the basis of *Portrait* alone. Rather we find an extremely complicated view, combining irony and admiration in unpredictable mixtures. Thus the Thomist aesthetics "was in the main applied Aquinas and he set it forth plainly with a naif air of discovering novelties. This he did partly to satisfy his own taste for enigmatic roles and partly from a genuine predisposition in favour of all but the premises of scholasticism" (*SH* 64). No one ever inferred, before this passage was available, anything like this precise and complex judgment on Stephen. The combination of blame and approval, we may be sure, is different in the finished Portrait; the implied author no doubt often repudiates the explicit judgments of the younger narrator who intrudes into *Stephen Hero*. But we can also be sure that his judgment has not become less complex. Where do we find, in any criticism of Portrait based entirely on internal evidence, the following kind of juxtaposition of Stephen's views with the author's superior insight? "Having by this simple process established the literary form of art as the most excellent he proceeded to examine it in favour of his theory, or, as he rendered it, to establish the relations which must subsist between the literary image, the work of art itself, and that energy which had imagined and fashioned it, that center of conscious, re-acting, particular life, the artist" (*SH* 65; italics mine). Can we infer, from *Portrait*, that Joyce sees Stephen as simply rationalizing in favor of his theory? Did we guess that Joyce could refer to him mockingly as a "fiery-hearted revolutionary" and a "heaven-ascending essayist"?[16]

In *Stephen Hero*, the author's final evaluation of the aesthetics is favorable but qualified: "Except for the eloquent and arrogant peroration Stephen's essay was a careful exposition of a carefully meditated theory of esthetic" (68). Though it might be argued that in the finished book he has cut out some of the negative elements, such as the "eloquent and arrogant peroration," and has presented the pure theory in conversational form, it is clear that Joyce himself judged his hero's theory in greater detail than we could possibly infer from the final version alone.

Similar clarifications can be found in *Stephen Hero* of our other two crucial problems, his rejection of the priesthood and his poetic ability. For example, "He had swept the moment into his memory . . . and . . . had brought forth some pages of sorry verse" (57). Can the hero of *Portrait* be thought of as writing "sorry verse"? One would not think so, to read much of the commentary by Joyce's critics.

But who is to blame them? Whatever intelligence Joyce postulates in his reader—let us assume the unlikely case of its being comparable to his own—will not be sufficient for precise inference of a pattern of judgments which is, after all, private to Joyce. And this will be true regardless of how much distance from his own hero we believe him to have achieved by the time he concluded his final version. We simply cannot avoid the conclusion that to some extent the book itself is at fault, regardless of its great virtues. Unless we make the absurd assumption that Joyce had in reality purged himself of all judgment by the time he completed his final draft, unless we see him as having really come to look upon all of Stephen's actions as equally wise or equally foolish, equally sensitive or equally meaningless, we must conclude that many of the refinements he intended in his finished Portrait are, for most of us, permanently lost. Even if we were now to do our homework like dutiful students, even if we were to study all of Joyce's work, even if we were to spend the lifetime that Joyce playfully said his novels demand, presumably we should never come to as rich, as refined, and as varied a conception of the quality of Stephen's last days in Ireland as Joyce had in mind. For some of us the air of detachment and objectivity may still be worth the price, but we must never pretend that a price was not paid.

Notes

1. William Empson, "The Theme of *Ulysses*," *Kenyon Review* 18 (Winter 1956): 36, 31.

2. Lawrance Thompson, *A Comic Principle in Sterne—Meredith—Joyce* (Oslo: British Institute, University of Oslo, 1954), 22.

3. Harry Levin, *James Joyce* (Norfolk, Conn.: New Directions, 1941), 58–62.

4. Mark Schorer, "Technique as Discovery," *Hudson Review* (Spring 1948): 79–80.

5. Caroline Gordon, *How to Read a Novel* (New York: Viking, 1957), 213.

6. Grant Redford, "The Role of Structure in Joyce's 'Portrait,' " *Modern Fiction Studies* 4 (Spring 1958): 30. See also Herbert Gorman, *James Joyce* (London: John Lane, 1941), 96, and Stuart Gilbert, *James Joyce's Ulysses* (London: Faber and Faber, 1930), 20–22.

7. James Joyce, *A Portrait of the Artist as a Young Man*, edited by Chester G. Anderson (New York: Viking, 1964), 212; hereafter cited parenthetically in the text as *P*.

8. William T. Noon, *Joyce and Aquinas* (New Haven, Conn.: Yale University Press, 1957), 34, 35, 66, 67. See also Hugh Kenner, "The *Portrait* in Perspective," *Kenyon Review*, 10 (Summer 1948): 361–81.

9. Gilbert, *James Joyce's Ulysses*, 22.

10. Richard Ellmann concludes that whether we know it or not, "Joyce's court is, like Dante's or Tolstoy's, always in session" (*James Joyce* [New York: Oxford University Press, 1959], 3).

11. Norman Friedman considers it a "tribute to Joyce's dramatic genius that a Catholic can sympathize with the portrayal of Catholic values in the novel which the hero rejects" ("Point of View in Fiction," *Publication of the Modern Language Association* [December 1955]: 11–84). But this is not to say that the Catholic readers are right; or that we need not make up our minds about the question.

12. Maurice Beebe and Walton Litz, "Criticism of James Joyce: A Selected Checklist with an Index to Studies of Separate Works," *Modern Fiction Studies* 4 (Spring 1958): 71–99.

13. See, for example, J. Mitchell Morse's defense of a fairly "straight" reading of *Ulysses*, based largely on Gorman's reading of Joyce's *Notebooks* ("Augustine, *Ayenbite*, and *Ulysses*," *Publication of the Modern Language Association* (December 1955): 1147, n. 12.

14. James Joyce, *Stephen Hero*, edited by Theodore Spencer (New York:

New Directions, 1944); hereafter cited parenthetically in the text as *SH*. Only part of the manuscript survives.

15. See Denis Donoghue's "Joyce and the Finite Order," *Sewanee Review* 68 (Spring 1960): 256–73: "The objects [in *Portrait*] exist to provide a suitably piteous setting for Stephen as Sensitive Plant; they are meant to mark a sequence of experiences in the mode of pathos ... The lyric situation is insulated from probes, and there is far too much of this cosseting in the Portrait ... Drama or rhetoric should have warned Joyce that Stephen the aesthetic *alazon* needed nothing so urgently as a correspondingly deft *eiron*: lacking this, the book is blind in one eye" (258). Joyce would no doubt reply—I think unfairly—that he intended Stephen as both *alazon* and *eiron*.

16. One reviewer of *Stephen Hero* was puzzled to notice in it that the omniscient author, not yet purged in accordance with Joyce's theories of dramatic narration, frequently expresses biting criticism of the young Stephen. The earlier work thus seemed to him "much more cynical," and "much, much farther from the principles of detached classicism that had been formulated before either book was written." How could the man who wrote *Stephen Hero* go on and write, "in a mood of enraptured fervour," a work like *Portrait*? ("A Portrait in Two Mirrors," *Times Literary Supplement*, February 1, 1957, p. 64; review of *Stephen Hero*).

It is true that, once we have been alerted, signs of ironic intention come rushing to our view. Those of us who now believe that Joyce is not entirely serious in the passages on aesthetics must wonder, for example, how we ever read them straight. What did we make of passages like the following, in those old, benighted days before we saw what was going on? "The lore which he was believed to pass his days brooding upon so that it had rapt him from the companionship of youth was only a garner of slender sentences from Aristotle's Poetics and Psychology and a *Synopsis Philosophiæ Scholasticæ ad mentem divi Thomæ*. His thinking was a dusk of doubt and selfmistrust, lit up at moments by the lightnings of intuition" (*SH* 176–77). "In those moments the world perished about his feet as if it had been [with] fire consumed: and thereafter his tongue grew heavy and he met the eyes of others with unanswering eyes for he felt that the spirit of beauty had folded him round like a mantle and that in reverie at least he had been acquainted with nobility. But, when this brief pride of silence upheld him no longer, he was glad to find himself still in the midst of common lives, passing on his way amid the squalor and noise and sloth of the city fearlessly and with a light heart" (*SH* 177). If this is not mockery, however tender, it is fustian.

The Style of the Troubled Conscience

HÉLÈNE CIXOUS

◆　◆　◆

THE ALMOST COMPLETE BODILY TRANSPOSITION of a retreat sermon,[1] which breaks in upon Stephen's consciousness with its images of stereotyped terror, is a forerunner of episodes in *Ulysses*: the style is that of objective reality in order to mark its strangeness to—and difference from—the subject. By using a piece of completely foreign prose, Joyce suppresses the central awareness of Stephen's consciousness for the length of the sermon. This on the one hand gives Hell a much more autonomous (and thus more concrete) existence, and on the other confers upon this horrible world enough strength of its own for it to invade Stephen's consciousness and cause bewilderment and alienation. Joyce would cheerfully mock that vulnerability, which he shared with Stephen. He once wrote the following limerick in a letter to Ezra Pound (9 April 1917):

> There once was a lounger named Stephen
> Whose youth was most odd and uneven—
> He throve on the smell

Of a horrible hell
That a Hottentot wouldn't believe in.

Even though the Hottentot would not believe in it, Stephen
wished to do so—at least for the time it took to burn himself
sufficiently so that he might keep the image of it as both a proof
of the cruelty of the Church and a psychological stimulant for
himself. It is necessary to have been afraid if one is to know what
bravery is.

It has been said that *Portrait* can be read as a succession of
conflicts between dream and reality.[2] In fact there is no neat
dividing line between Stephen's dream experiences and his encounters with reality, but such a distinction exists in *Ulysses*, where
the "Circe" episode is definitely hallucinatory. There is only one
reality in *Portrait*, which is lived out on different levels by the
young man whose consciousness and imagination are undergoing
modifications ranging from the imperceptible to the violent as he
passes through the crises that mark his spiritual evolution. The
world outside seems more or less substantial as Stephen's own
state varies. It is important to point out that it is the effects of
sin and of the religious terror following it which break the boundaries of objective reality and the protection of subjectivity—and
to such an extent that reality, as Stephen transforms it into his
imaginary hell, overflows and invades the outer world. The ugliness of reality rose in its sordid tide within Stephen's soul, while
the ugliness of that soul seemed to him to contaminate the universe. This is all the more striking because the two movements
toward interpretation follow each other: at the end of chapter II,
Stephen has given up trying to introduce some order and beauty
into the chaotic life of his family and, as though impelled by a
need for vengeance and satisfaction, goes off to seek the desired
communion in the disorder of the senses. Being a stranger and
outcast in his own family, he is "adopted" by a prostitute; who
is, of course, part of the new communion.

"By day and by night he moved among distorted images of
the outer world."[3] He moves in a world which he distorts, and
the reader is moved into a reality which never gives any impres-

sion of being real. More exactly, the reader is ushered into the mental circumvolutions of an extremely subjective person. It is neither Life nor the City that Joyce describes through Stephen, but rather the claim that Stephen himself makes at the end of the book: "I go to encounter for the millionth time the reality of experience and to forge in the smithy of my soul the uncreated conscience of my race" (*P* 252–53). This may serve as the best definition of that "neorealism" of which *Portrait* is the subjective application. What Stephen encounters is reality as experience, and what he brings back to his "smithy" for the forging of the conscience of his race will be the negotiations of himself with this reality.

This is as much as to say that Joyce reconstitutes Dublin here, the Dublin of the *Portrait* being Stephen's Dublin, while the town in *Ulysses* is that of Bloom. The two towns may be superimposed, but they are quite different. Chapter III is thus doubly important, because on the one hand reality takes its revenge on the mind which had distorted it, and on the other it is already possible to see a fully developed technique of rendering the real as subjective and more inward, a technique which is used so completely in *Ulysses*; the author is adept at using language to move or change the center of reality to inner or outer regions of the consciousness.

At the beginning of chapter III Stephen is frequenting the world of sensual satisfactions, slipping under the ban of the Church. In this world, the body does the talking and gives the orders to such an extent that each part of Stephen's body seems possessed of a strange autonomy, while his soul is reduced to howling wordlessly like a beast. His feet carry him into the labyrinth of the forbidden district; his blood revolts; "the inarticulate cries and the unspoken brutal words rushed forth from his brain"; his lips refuse to bend down to a kiss; his belly counsels him to stuff himself full of stew.

Joyce gives us the portrait of a man possessed, and even if Stephen is not conscious of actual devils, he feels himself gripped by terrifying forces. He hears the buzzing of a crowd in his ears at strange times. When he undertakes the deconsecration of reality by means of the savage desires and monstrous lusts of his dreams, he believes himself to be acting with free will: "He bore cynically with the shameful details of his secret riots in which he exulted to defile with patience whatever image had attracted his eyes" (*P* 99). His response to the dirtiness of the real world is a taking of pleasure in foulness; he wallows in lechery that leaves no respite. What he had voluntarily begun escapes from his control before he realizes it, and he leads himself on with hopes of the encounter of which he dreamed—yet he is now separated from it by a horrible reality. Reality is already a totally subjective concept; he is a prey to "some dark presence moving irresistibly upon him from the darkness, a presence subtle and murmurous as a flood filling him wholly with itself" (*P* 100). The shifting, murmurous tide of the outside world (against which he had wanted to raise a dam of elegance and order) has become his very thought, and its uncontrollable proliferations surround and penetrate his inner world. This demonic infiltration is directly opposed to the blessed visitation of his soul by the angel of beauty. He is still beyond all clarity of conscience—he is always the product of the Church and of its system of threats and rewards. The Church has such a hold over him that it imposes its own vision upon Stephen while he is in a state of mortal sin. The hell described by Father Arnall (borrowed, as we have already seen, from the Italian Jesuits) is received into Stephen's soul, and he is carried back to his childhood by seeing "the figure of his old master, so strangely re-arisen" from the past. He remembers the ditch he fell in, the little cemetery where he had dreamed of being buried, the firelight on the walls of the infirmary, and the now-disappeared innocent boy also rises again, to be set by Father Arnall in his right place in the majestic order of Time as controlled by God. The events between the successive sermons and their various effects on Stephen are expressed by subtle modifications of the forms of language. "During these few days I intend to put before you some thoughts concerning the four last things. They are, as you know from your catechism, death, judgement, hell, and heaven" (*P* 109–10), says the preacher in giving the program of the retreat, accompanying it by many invocations of God, the saints, and the angels on behalf of all the sinners present.

For Stephen, this signals terror. A thick fog darkens his mind. Outside reality is dull, dark, and motionless—as though everything were already dead. "And that was life," thinks Stephen, meaning the life of a beast, of an inert body and materially oriented soul, congealing in thick grease. He who had until this very day been capable of sustaining a living relationship with words finds himself lost, and even incapable of coherence. "The letters of the name of Dublin lay heavily upon his mind" (*P* 111) for all is in decomposition.

The following day brings him death and judgment, and he is powerless; he no longer hears Father Arnall's words, but another voice, his own voice, whispers death and despair into his soul, repeating the sermon to him and imagining the death of the body. "Into the grave with it! Nail it down into a wooden box, the corpse" (*P* 112) This is himself, horrified with fear for his own safety. Suddenly his imagination outstrips the preacher's harsh tones, and in a frenzy of self-hatred continues, "Thrust it out of men's sight into a long hole in the ground . . . to rot, to feed the mass of its creeping worms and to be devoured by scuttling plump-bellied rats" (*P* 112). Then Stephen lets the supreme judge speak directly as he drives the unjust, the hypocrites, the accursed, far from him.

The preacher recalls to him that "death is the end of us all" and that "death and judgement . . . are the dark portals that close our earthly existence, the portals that open into the unknown and the unseen, portals through which every soul must pass, unaided save by its good works" (*P* 114). It seems to Stephen as though these portals of darkness leading to the unknown are opening for him. "Now it was God's turn" (*P* 112). All the great apparatus and the great solemn cry of the judge impress Stephen, and he is as captivated by the sonority of the phrase as by the epic evocation of Apocalypse. His soul responds to "the archangelical trumpet" that blows "the brazen death of time" (*P* 113). The wind of the last day blows and scatters the jewel-eyed harlots,

who flee before the hurricane, shrieking like mice; this is not in
the sermon, but it is the second response of Stephen's audio-
visual imagination, of that perpetual overflowing of creative force
which is—did he but realize it—the very sign of how impossible
it is for him to surrender his mind or soul to others.

These sermons, filling his soul with shame and terror, inspire
an extraordinary series of imaginary visions: he is soon to discover
that sin and fear are better spiritual stimulants for the poet's
imagination than are virtue and piety. One need only compare
Stephen repentant to Stephen terrified to realize that, for him,
hell is the monotony of good conscience. The world of dreams
and of created life pours all its strangeness into his humbled mind
and produces a weird vision, inspired perhaps by de Quincey's
dreams of Easter redemption. Stephen sees himself standing in a
wide landscape where sea and sky gently mingle, where God does
not exist because he is too severe and cannot pardon even the
error of two children, Stephen and Emma; but she, the Virgin,
who is not offended, unites the guilty children. It may be God's
turn now, but Stephen is manifestly trying to rid himself of the
shackles of this excessively great presence. He is already attempting to draw near the delicate sensual pleasures that emanate from
the musical, shining beauty of the Virgin. This vision is succeeded
by another in which a flood covers all the trees, houses, monuments, and mountains, rising as Stephen likes to imagine it, but
with a touch of the baroque about it in order to deprive God of
his conventional, ordinary flood. "All life would be choked off,
noiselessly: birds, men, elephants, pigs, children" (*P* 112).

It is, of course, possible not to stop at this one detail in the
mass of hallucinations recorded but it seems to be a sign from
Joyce, in this rapid foolish enumeration, that already the sinner
is beginning to fall back toward the pleasure of such baroque
sights and images, before he has even achieved redemption. Finally, Father Arnall devotes several minutes to the description of
the abode of the damned, with the slow precision of a mathe-
matics lesson in over seven long, rhythmical paragraphs. This hell
is a model of organization for physical and mental torture, a
model of order and elegance in sadism, and thus could not fail

to captivate Stephen's still rebellious mind. He is almost subjugated by the musical harmony, the dark glow, the balance between the parts and the whole which make that world an evil masterpiece. But, well proportioned as it is, and beautiful as a temple, this hell introduces Stephen to another with the sinister grace of a ballet. The one is a monument and the other a kind of pantomime, early predecessor of the hallucinations in the house of Circe; maddened, the inner speech acts out God's judgment for itself—for a moment—and the contrast between majesty and illusion makes the parody:

> God had called him. Yes? What? Yes? His flesh shrank together as it felt the approach of the ravenous tongues of flames, dried up as it felt about it the swirl of stifling air. He had died. Yes. He was judged. A wave of fire swept through his body: the first. Again a wave. His brain began to glow. Another. His brain was simmering and bubbling within the cracking tenement of his skull. Flames burst forth from his skull like a corolla, shrieking like voices. Hell! Hell! Hell! Hell! Hell! Hell! (P 125)

For Stephen, the return to banality is made very seriously: "He had not died." There is still time.

As time goes on, the irony grows heavier; this time the sermon deals with the extension, duration, and eternity of the torments of the damned. And now it is all over, and one has only to confess.

Stephen remains alone with his soul, or rather, alone with his chorus of demons; they enjoy the situation intensely, waiting, spying, amusing themselves by wondering what he will do about his confession. Stephen's hell is not far away; in fact it is his room, where he has committed so many imaginary sins. And all his sins are there, describing the most terrifying and sardonic spirals. Joyce used to say that Art has the gift of tongues, and it is true that everything in *Portrait*, as in *Ulysses*, speaks its own particular language; the language of Stephen's sins reels out its phrases as though trying to stifle him in their long coils. "We knew perfectly well of course that though it was bound to come to the light he would find considerable difficulty in endeavouring to try to induce himself to try to endeavour to ascertain the spiritual plenipotentiary and so we knew of course perfectly well . . ." (*P* 12). This is the voice of pride—which fear has not succeeded in reducing to silence. Stephen indeed denies his sins but cannot avoid hearing their language, which is a travesty of his own. He can escape from sadism but is unable to break loose from masochism; the soul, however free, is marked by the monstrous rhetoric of punishment. Agreed, the hell described is far too realistic not to exist, but Stephen is already transposing it into the personal key. Alone with his soul, like Virgil with Dante, he treads the steps that lead toward the tribunal of his room, "the dark shell of the cave." "He went up to his room after dinner in order to be alone with his soul, and at every step his soul seemed to sigh; at every step his soul mounted with his feet, sighing in the ascent, through a region of viscid gloom" (*P* 136)

For the artist believing in the evocative power of words, the sermons were more than a skillful piece of oratory designed to bring the sinner to his knees. They had an effect on the world outside and on the cave within, touching Stephen on the raw in his imagination, in his spoken language, and in the relationship between his reason and his words. They have affected his actual vision of the world. It is the artist in him that has been put to the torture, for he has been thrown into the appalling circle of Disfigurement, where the world grimaces and the tongue turns against itself, coiling serpentlike about words. Yet the thought that is bitten and writhes from the viper's poison is still alive and has not been alienated. In apparent delirium it is ironically triumphant, for we first think that the word really has been punished. As J.-J. Mayoux says, "The accused, guilty, condemned and terrified voice of Beckett's Lucky is heard here for the first stammering time."[4]

But, beyond the fever of language, his thought fights against delirium, for his entire life and work are at stake. The viper poisons all his sense connections with reality, punishing the flesh by inflicting delirium of the senses. Stephen loses contact with the perceptible world, no longer looking at that which is not himself from the heights of his former pride; his sin has smeared a film of dirt over his eyes and lips, and he sees everything through his own disgust. The first separation had been intellectual. At this crisis of spiritual terror, he feels that he is being attacked in his imagination, and out of respect for words he at first yields to the power that uses them. But the world that appears to him is a world of hallucination:

> He feared intensely in spirit and in flesh but, raising his head bravely, he strode into the room firmly. A doorway, a room, the same room, same window. He told himself calmly that those words had absolutely no sense which had seemed to rise murmurously from the dark. He told himself that it was simply his room with the door open. (*P* 136)

The world as seen by a guilty conscience is unrecognizable. Stephen has lost reality—irrecoverably, it seems. His ideas of identity are confused and changed, his memory and reason paralyzed, and his own room with the door open seems to him the yawning mouth of hell. Yet, paradoxically, the violence which has been done to the young man's imagination is the final step in its liberation, for the artist who has passed through the delirium and confusion can find beyond them another limitless reality. Until now the world had been like a path bordered by two hedges, but after the descent into hell, the boundaries disappear. Now there is no limit between reality and dream, between the law and the forbidden, between the language that is subject to the conventional grammar of communication and the free word.

The long, winding phrases are not meaningless, as Stephen tells himself that they are, but on the contrary form his first free sentence, his first sentence to take no account of tradition. Its meaning exists not only at the level of the words, but also in its movement and rhythm; it projects and develops its meaning in a new allusive dimension beyond what is actually said—a fresh and as yet untouched field of significance. The demons who wish to break up his thought and cloud his senses are in fact not those whom he has believed them to be. He is in the process of discovering that the world is not solely what it appears to be—that its meaning cannot be expressed logically—and this discovery costs him considerable mental anguish. Nietzsche used to say, "I fear that we cannot rid ourselves of the notion of God, because we still believe in grammar"; it is this belief in grammar that is slowly dying in these convulsions of language and of Stephen's mind. The sentence he has heard terrifies him, because it is so different, such a departure, from the act of contrition which he remembers from the recent service in the chapel. It has imprinted itself on his memory like a geometric line, its sincere repetition banishing all doubt:

—O my God!—
—O my God!—
—I am heartily sorry—
—I am heartily sorry—
—for having offended Thee—
—for having offended Thee—
—and I detest my sins—
—and I detest my sins—
—above every other evil—
—because they displease Thee, my God—
—because they displease Thee, my God—
—Who art so deserving—
—Who art so deserving—
—of all my love—
—of all my love—
—and I firmly purpose—
—and I firmly purpose—
—by Thy holy grace—
—by Thy holy grace—
—never more to offend Thee—
—never more to offend Thee—
—and to amend my life—
—and to amend my life— (*P* 135)

This beautiful regular construction of prayer that echoes itself is contrasted with the insinuating, horizontally proceeding thought that is still in search of its own way; here is born the language that secretes and bears in it its own meaning, which is to print that meaning upon reality. Language as reality recreates the world from its echo; it questions itself, and it answers. It *is* the same window, but it is also the other room and the other window, opening out onto the infinite spaces of creation.

Notes

1. See *L'Inferno Aperto* of Giovanni Pietro Pinamonti (first published 1688, first translated into English 1715); and Kevin Sullivan, *Joyce among the Jesuits* (New York: Columbia University Press, 1956), 125–28.

2. Hugh Kenner, *Dublin's Joyce* (New York: Columbia University Press, 1987), 123–25.

3. James Joyce, *A Portrait of the Artist as a Young Man*, edited by Chester G. Anderson (New York: Viking, 1964), 99; hereafter cited parenthetically in the text as *P*.

4. Jean-Jacques Mayoux, *Joyce* (Paris: Gallimard, 1965), 75.

A Portrait of the Artist

PATRICK PARRINDER

❖   ❖   ❖

The Portrait and the Artist

T HE TEXT OF *A Portrait of the Artist as a Young Man* is dated
"Dublin 1904 / Trieste 1914." 1904 was the year in which
Stephen Hero was written and Joyce left Dublin with Nora Barnacle
to become a language teacher on the Adriatic. Ten years later,
after some vicissitudes, he was still there. His life was about to be
transformed, thanks to the First World War (which would force
him to move to neutral Switzerland) and to a chance letter from
Ezra Pound in December 1913, which marked the beginnings of
his literary celebrity.[1] Pound arranged for serial publication of the
Portrait to begin in the *Egoist*, a small avant-garde literary and political magazine, in February 1914; in June of the same year the
London publisher Grant Richards at last brought out *Dubliners*.

The writing of *Portrait* thus spans ten years during which Joyce
kept rigorously to Stephen Dedalus's program of "silence exile
and cunning." His literary silence was broken only by *Chamber
Music* and by a small quantity of essays and journalism, some of

it written in Italian.[2] His exile, at first only temporary, was confirmed by his unhappy experiences in revisiting Ireland in 1909 and 1912. Cunning is evident in the far-reaching revisions with which he transformed *Stephen Hero*, a raw apprentice work, into *Portrait* with its eloquence of style and fastidious pursuit of artistic impersonality. Joyce makes Stephen Dedalus echo the famous passage in Flaubert's *Letters* which declares that the writer should stand aloof from his work: "The artist must stand to his work as God to his creation, invisible and all powerful; he must be everywhere felt but nowhere seen."[3] *A Portrait of the Artist* brings the doctrine of impersonality to bear in an area which Flaubert himself had never attempted. It sets out to be an impersonal or ironic autobiography.

The irony consists in Joyce's balancing of the different points of view it is possible to adopt toward the young Stephen. Stephen himself comes to believe he is following a predestined course and unfolds a fervently idealistic artistic creed. Through him Joyce is able both to affirm the romantic myth of artistic genius and to partially dissociate himself from the arrogance and self-conceit which follows from that myth. Irony is always implicit in the narrative, yet it cannot be too heavily underlined or it will destroy the basis of Joyce's—not merely Stephen's—claims for his writing. The book is uncertainly poised between mature reservation and an almost intoxicating sympathy with Stephen's experience. Finally, it may be, the artist-myth in *Portrait* taken on its own was too powerful, and Joyce's attempt to relive it burst the bounds of mature detachment. He then had to create a disillusioned sequel to his autobiographical novel, in the parts of *Ulysses* centered on Stephen.

Joyce started off, as few if any novelists before him had done, by sticking scrupulously to the ostensible facts of his own life. His rewriting of the main events of his life is as nothing compared with the melodramatic inventions to be found in even the most "confessional" of earlier novels. This is the main point of difference between *Portrait* and the *Bildungsromane* and *Künstlerromane* ("novels of education" and "artist-hero" novels) of the nineteenth century. *Portrait* is less close to books like *Wilhelm Meister, David Copperfield*, or Gissing's *New Grub Street* than it is to the genre of literary autobiography and memoirs. The pattern of destiny which Stephen discovers in the events of his own life suggests that one crucial source is the tradition of spiritual apology or confession, from St. Augustine to Newman. Stephen's destiny, however, bears witness to the religion of Art rather than of Christianity, and it is in the field of artistic memoirs and autobiographical sketches that we shall find the closest analogues to *Portrait*. One such memoir by an older contemporary—George Moore's *Confessions of a Young Man* (1888)—no doubt influenced Joyce's title.

Stephen's belief in the priestly role of the artist and his duty to "forge in the smithy of my soul the uncreated conscience of my race" (*P* 253) has its roots in the high romanticism of Wordsworth and Shelley. *Portrait* transmutes the stuff of actual experience into artistic myth as thoroughly as Wordsworth had done. In addition, it serves as a "prelude" in the Wordsworthian sense to the more comprehensive edifices of *Ulysses* and *Finnegans Wake*. Nevertheless, *Portrait* is not a straightforwardly romantic work. While Stephen remains ultimately committed to the Shelleyan notion of the artist as unacknowledged legislator of the world, his attention—unlike that of the Wordsworthian or Shelleyan hero—is devoted to disentangling himself from the external world and exploring the secrets and intricacies of his own art. His preoccupation with art as a sacred mystery links him to the aesthetic and decadent movements of the late nineteenth century. The reverence that the aesthetes and decadents felt for their romantic predecessors was tinged by the melancholy conviction that these poets had sought in the external world for "what is there in no satisfying measure or not at all" (*CW* 78). (These words, borrowed from Walter Pater, were used by Joyce himself in his essay on the Dublin romantic poet James Clarence Mangan.) The artist now turned, not to unspoiled nature, but in on himself to find a truly satisfying richness and beauty. Oscar Wilde went so far as to suggest that all artists are solipsists, whether they know it or not: "every portrait that is painted with feeling is a portrait of the artist," we read in *The Picture of Dorian Gray*.[4] It may have been a similar conviction that led Joyce to turn to autobiographical fiction in the first place.

Stephen Hero is written in the naturalistic manner and portrays Stephen, during his student years, as an Ibsenite. Early in 1904, however, Joyce had written a short essay called "A Portrait of the Artist," which contrasts sharply with *Stephen Hero* even though Joyce incorporated some passages from it into his novel. The "Portrait of the Artist" was—understandably—rejected by the editors of *Dana* as incomprehensible. Far from presenting the artist as a free-standing fictional character, through realistic description and dramatized dialogue, Joyce had written a tortuous, allusive, and contemplative essay modeled on the Walter Pater of *Imaginary Portraits* (1887). Such a portrait was, as he expressed it, "not an identificative paper but rather the curve of an emotion."[5] The artist portrayed is one who turns aside from his contemporaries to seek the "image of beauty"[6] in the byways of esoteric and occult learning. Though the essay concludes with a Shelleyan vision of social revolution, there is no suggestion here (as there is in the "epiphany" passage in *Stephen Hero*) that the artist might find beauty in the "commonest object" or among the people around him. Instead, "To those multitudes not as yet in the wombs of humanity but surely engenderable there, he would give the word."[7]

The artist, if he is to "give the word" to future humanity, must follow the image of beauty and free himself of all servitude to the words of those alien to him. That is equally the message of the 1904 "Portrait" and of its 1916 counterpart. In the mature *Portrait* the words of others are dramatized as external and internal voices. The book begins with the voice of Stephen's father and ends with Stephen's departure for the Continent at the behest of imaginary voices clamoring, "We are your kinsmen" (*P* 252). At this point he has rejected his father's voice in favor of voices he believes to be more "authentic" more "internal." They are at once the Sibylline voices of inspiration and prophecy and the voices of his fellow artists in the literary tradition. Nevertheless, Stephen's ability to discover such authentic voices remains unproven, since only in his career as a writer, which he has yet to begin, can he break his self-imposed silence and show that he, too, has it in him to "give the word." The proof of the oracle would be found in the writing.

Voice, Memory, and Discontinuity

"The past assuredly implies a fluid succession of presents, the development of an entity of which our actual present is a phase only" Joyce declares in his 1904 essay.[8] The "actual presents" out of which his successive attempts at autobiographical fiction were written included, of necessity, a strong autobiographical urge. The same urge is present at least incipiently in every earlier stage of Stephen's childhood and youth. We see him not only learning about and reacting to his environment but creating a sense of identity based on accumulated experience and feelings. His sense of identity is intimately connected with memory, and the *Portrait* begins, effectively, at the point where Stephen as an infant first exercises his powers as a memoirist. The description of him as "retaining nothing of all he read save that which seemed to him an echo or prophecy of his own state" (*P* 155) belongs to a particular phase of adolescence, yet it is also deeply characteristic of Stephen from the beginning. His inner knowledge of his own identity is ratified by his discovery of a series of prophecies, signs of a predestined outcome to his story, of which the principal one is his own name. The oddity of the name Dedalus is foregrounded very early in *Portrait*: eventually he realizes it is "a prophecy of the end he had been born to serve" (*P* 169), in other words, of artisthood. Joyce uses the twin themes of predestination and habitual autobiography to persuade us of the inevitability of Stephen's emergence as a writer, a career toward which he is seen to be innately predisposed. And, as an embryonic writer, he is ceaselessly rewriting the "book of himself" (*U* 187).

The narrative structure of *Portrait* is a "fluid succession of presents" (though each present is narrated in the past tense) linked by an evolutionary process, which shows the development of Stephen's identity and his accumulated memory. Each phase in the succession of presents is a tightly constructed narrative unit, which may seem sharply discontinuous with what comes before and after it. The discontinuity is textual and generic as well as temporal; in *Portrait* as in *Ulysses*, Joyce's method amounts to "one style per episode." Linking the episodes is a series of evolutionary chains of images and themes. It is helpful to enumerate these, and I shall do so in unsystematic fashion beginning with Stephen's understanding of his surname.

The epigraph of *Portrait* is from Ovid and denotes the Dedalian theme: "And he set his mind to work upon unknown arts" (*Et ignotas animum dimittit in artes*). Nasty Roche commences hostilities with his famous question to Stephen in the first Clongowes episode—"What kind of a name is that?" (*P* 9). The oddity of his name is further noticed by Athy and, much later, by Stephen's fellow student Davin, who asks whether it is Irish. Stephen's reply, offering to show Davin his family tree in the Office of Arms (*P* 201), is a brazen attempt by Joyce to naturalize the palpably fictional.[9] Earlier we have listened to Stephen trying out his name as it would look if he joined the priesthood—"The Reverend Stephen Dedalus, S.J." (*P* 161)—and finding it does not fit. His eventual discovery that the name Dedalus is emblematic of the artist, and that it betokens the artist's means of escape from the island of his birth and imprisonment, comes pat like the solution to a detective story which has been kept hidden by simply diverting the reader's attention.

Stephen's discovery of the significance of his name comes about as a result of his increasingly specialized involvement with language. The very first game that he plays is a language game, in which he turns Dante's proverbial (and rhyming) threat about eagles into a symmetrical pair of verses:

> Pull out his eyes,
> Apologise,
> Apologise,
> Pull out his eyes.

At Clongowes, the formal process of learning has begun, and Stephen spontaneously extends this to learning about language. He is fascinated by the different meanings of such "queer words" (*P* 11) as *belt* and *suck*, as well as by the correspondence between words and things, which allows cold and hot water to come out of taps marked cold and hot. In adolescence the secrets of his awakening sexuality and of his difference from his father are summed up in the shock of the word *fœtus* scratched on a desk. In the recognition scene on Dollymount beach, there is a famous (if slightly obscure) passage in which Stephen becomes conscious of his obsession with words:

> He drew forth a phrase from his treasure and spoke it softly to himself:
>
> A day of dappled seaborne clouds.
>
> The phrase and the day and the scene harmonised in a chord. Words. Was it their colours? He allowed them to glow and fade, hue after hue: sunrise gold, the russet and green of apple orchards, azure of waves, the greyfringed fleece of clouds. No, it was not their colours: it was the poise and balance of the period itself. Did he then love the rhythmic rise and fall of words better than their associations of legend and colour? Or was it that, being as weak of sight as he was shy of mind, he drew less pleasure from the reflection of the glowing sensible world through the prism of a language manycoloured and richly storied than from the contemplation of an inner world of individual emotions mirrored perfectly in a lucid supple periodic prose? (*P* 166–7)

The passage is at once argument and evocation. To the extent that it presents genuinely alternative views of language, they are the major doctrines held by nineteenth-and early twentieth-century romantic poets, spelled out one by one. Stephen appears to be rejecting Keatsian verbal associationism, Pure Sound, and Paterian or Conradian impressionism in favor of an expressionist model of language as the precise representation of an "inner world" of individual emotions, a view which should have found favor with T. S. Eliot. Language, molded by the genius of the artist, has then become a "perfect mirror." If this is the ideal toward which the young Stephen aspires, the fifth section of the *Portrait* suggest the sort of resistance in language he may be destined to encounter. For Stephen is a poet, the author of a villanelle full of "coloured" words, and not yet capable of "lucid supple periodic prose," such as we find in *Dubliners*. Moreover, the vocabulary which surrounds him is not individual or authentic but secondhand. Debating the word *tundish* with the dean of studies, he reflects:

> How different are the words *home, Christ, ale, master,* on his lips and on mine! I cannot speak or write these words without unrest of spirit. His language, so familiar and so foreign, will always be for me an acquired speech. I have not made or accepted its words. My voice holds them at bay. My soul frets in the shadow of his language. (*P* 189)

Stephen in *Portrait* is searching for an authentic language which he can voice. It is a typically romantic quest, inherited by the symbolists and decadents of the late nineteenth century and passed on to the early modernists. Arthur Symons's words in the peroration to *The Symbolist Movement in Literature* (1899) are representative:

> Here, then, in this revolt against exteriority, against rhetoric, against a materialistic tradition; in this endeavour to disengage the ultimate essence, the soul, of whatever exists and can be realised by the consciousness; in this dutiful waiting upon every symbol by which the soul of things can be made visible; literature, bowed down by so many burdens, may at last attain liberty, and its authentic speech.[10]

Stephen, as poet and aesthetic theorist, should have been in full agreement with Symons's exhortation. Symons's vocabulary is close to *Portrait* and, moreover, he had dedicated his book to Yeats,

whose verses from *The Countess Cathleen* are echoed by Stephen. B
that is not the whole story. It is fairly clear what direction
young Irish romantic, attracted by the decadents and chafing
against the "acquired speech" of his British rulers, might have
been expected to take around 1900. Among the leaders of the
1916 Easter Rising were at least two published poets, Pearse and
MacDonagh. It is the Irish nationalist in Stephen which makes
him reflect—of *home, Christ, ale,* and *master*—that "I cannot speak
or write these words without unrest of spirit." Yet he is too honest
to suppose that Gaelic, for him, would be any less of an acquired
and secondhand speech. As he became an international writer
Joyce tended more and more to represent the state of not being
at home in one's language as a universal condition, the fate of
fallen man after Babel rather than a product of the power structure of the British Empire. In *Finnegans Wake* there is no "authentic
speech" since everything comes at secondhand: the voices Joyce
creates emerge from his mental word processor and are in no
sense prior to, or more authentic than, the actual writing. In
Portrait there are one or two anticipations of Joyce's later comic
sense of the use, and inevitability, of borrowed speech. Stephen
takes over words and phrases of the Elizabethans, for example, to
serve as an erotic shorthand (*P* 176, 233). Cranly's absurd dog-
Latin does a good deal to enliven the dialogues of the final section.
Joyce's later work implies that all modern literary language is
bastardized and cut adrift from its roots—that language, in fact,
has become grotesque. The world thus demands an art which
reconciles Stephen's quest for a unique language with Cranly's
ebullient philistinism.

There are two further developing themes in *Portrait:* voices and
memory. To see how words, voice, and memory are intertwined,
we need only consider the cry which issues from Stephen's lips
as, possessed by the demon of lust, he wanders into the red-light
district of Dublin for the first time:

> It broke from him like a wail of despair from a hell of sufferers
> and died in a wail of furious entreaty, a cry for an iniquitous
> abandonment, a cry which was but the echo of an obscene

scrawl which he had read on the oozing wall of a urinal. (*P* 100)

Words inscribed on a urinal wall (comparable, no doubt, to the word *Fœtus* scratched on a desk) and then imprinted on his memory are "echoed" in a cry. Stephen's whole development could be expressed in terms of a vocal metabolism in which words and voices enter into his consciousness and are digested by the memory, before issuing forth as emotional statements of which the simplest form is the cry. The disjunction between outer and inner, between voices and cries, becomes obvious to Stephen in adolescence, when he feels it at first as a sickness interrupting normal digestion:

> His very brain was sick and powerless. He could scarcely interpret the letters of the signboards of the shops. By his monstrous way of life he seemed to have put himself beyond the limits of reality. Nothing moved him or spoke to him from the real world unless he heard in it an echo of the infuriated cries within him. He could respond to no earthly or human appeal, dumb and insensible to the call of summer and gladness and companionship, wearied and dejected by his father's voice. (*P* 92)

Though it may weary him at this moment, his father's voice plays a crucial part in the novel. *Portrait* begins (as we have seen) with his father's words and ends with a cry addressed to an imaginary father. Stephen's father's voice triumphs over Dante's voice in the Christmas dinner scene, though both are etched into the young boy's consciousness. When in adolescence he wearies of his actual father's voice, he is all the more vulnerable to those of the "spiritual fathers," the priests. Joyce, indeed, introduces a startling innovation which amounts to a scandalous breach of the rules of modern fictional construction. In the third chapter, the priest's voice takes over and dominates *Portrait*, through the series of sermons which occupies nearly thirty pages of text or almost one eighth of the whole book.

After the priest's voice, it is the turn of the voices of nature and the imagination, which Stephen hears on the beach as he decides that his destiny is to be an artist. Once that decision is made he is again haunted by the voices of his social environment, which are raised against him in reproach. Leaving his house on the way to the university, he hears the screech of a mad nun but "shook the sound out of his ears by an angry toss of his head":

> His father's whistle, his mother's mutterings, the screech of an unseen maniac were to him now so many voices offending and threatening to humble the pride of his youth.

Stephen "drove their echoes even out of his heart with an execration," but they are not to be dismissed so easily. Davin puts the claims of nationality, language, and religion to him. His mother's voice is emphasized toward the end of the novel, pleading with him not to desert his religion and praying, Stephen reports, "that I may learn in my own life and away from home and friends what the heart is and what it feels" (*P* 252). Nevertheless, he can summon up imaginary voices which assure him he is right. Just before his final walk with Cranly he gains strength in his fight with his mother from the cries of swallows returning from migration: "The inhuman clamour soothed his ears in which his mother's sobs and reproaches murmured insistently" (*P* 224). The birds, as Stephen tells himself by means of pedantic references to Swedenborg and Cornelius Agrippa, are age-old vehicles of augury. The final picture of Stephen is of one who is stubborn enough, by and large, to make the voices around him tell him what he wants to hear. But it is not always so, and in *Ulysses* the circumstances surrounding his mother's death will stretch his ability to rationalize the path he has taken to the utmost.

The role of memory in *Portrait* has already been touched upon. Unlike most protagonists in autobiography, Stephen's memory is active and is foregrounded even in childhood. In one respect this may seem no more than a compositional strategy: Stephen's first days at Clongowes are not narrated chronologically but by means of a series of flashbacks which betray the onset of fever, preventing him from routine absorption in such activities as the game of football. The term *flashback* suggests an automatic process, like that which goes on in the cutting room of a film studio. But Stephen's memory is not only episodic and repetitive but creative. For example, the train of references to the "square ditch" with its rats and cold slimy water in the first few pages helps to determine the kind of person Stephen becomes. Wells's action in shouldering him into the ditch is probably the cause of his lifelong aquaphobia, seen in the beach episode ("how his flesh dreaded the cold infrahuman odour of the sea" [P 167] and again in *Ulysses*. Memories of water at Clongowes—the ditch, the turf-colored bathwater, the "wettish" air—are so indelible that they can eventually be classed as instinctual and shown to influence the crucial decisions of his life. When Stephen is tempted to join the priesthood, memories of Clongowes cause his soul to revolt at the thought of collegiate life:

> He wondered how he would pass the first night in the novitiate and with what dismay he would wake the first morning in the dormitory. The troubling odour of the long corridors of Clongowes came back to him and he heard the discreet murmur of the burning gasflames. At once from every part of his being unrest began to irradiate. A feverish quickening of his pulses followed and a din of meaningless words drove his reasoned thoughts hither and thither confusedly. His lungs dilated and sank as if he were inhaling a warm moist unsustaining air and he smelt again the warm moist air which hung in the bath in Clongowes above the sluggish turfcoloured water.
>
> Some instinct, waking at these memories, stronger than education or piety, quickened within him at every near approach to that life, an instinct subtle and hostile, and armed him against acquiescence. (P 160–61)

Its reliance on "instinct" rather than reason makes this a remarkably original passage. Any nineteenth-century novelist could have shown Stephen arguing with himself over the pros and cons of the priestly life, but Joyce does not do this. The question is settled at a level of feeling "stronger than education or piety" and therefore prior to argument. Indeed, Stephen's decision is a bodily as much as a mental event. He is not conscious at this moment of the alternatives to a career in the Church; he is not yet ready to devote himself to art or to opt to go to university. He rejects the priesthood not because he wants to do something else, but because he knows he *is* something else, and that is the sum of his accumulated and remembered experiences, which "quickens" within him as if it were life itself. Toward the end of the *Portrait* the workings of Stephen's memory begin to be over-shadowed by his maturing intellect and imagination. To trace the growth of intellect, imagination, and memory together would be to describe *A Portrait of the Artist* as a whole.

Portrait is unified not only by the workings of its protagonist's memory, but by an unconscious textual memory or series of repetitions, which are most easily traced at the level of imagery. Hugh Kenner, in a 1948 article, pointed out that in *Portrait* "the first two pages, terminated by a row of asterisks, enact the entire action in microcosm."[11] From the first two pages we can trace "verbal leitmotivs," or image sets, which recur throughout the narrative. Stephen's impressions in infancy can be broken down (with some complications) into a series of binary oppositions. Thematically the most important of these may be tabulated as follows:

father	versus	mother
father and mother	versus	baby
his father and mother	versus	Eileen's father and mother
telling stories	versus	playing the piano
storytelling and playing the piano	versus	singing and dancing
the Michael Davitt brush (maroon)	versus	the Parnell brush (green)

Dante's rewards (the cachous)   versus   Dante's punishments (the
eagles)

In addition to these thematic oppositions, there are others that
seem purely imagistic:

wild rose blossoms	*versus*	*green wothe botheth*
warm urine	versus	cold urine
hiding under the table	versus	the coming of the eagles

It is open to any reader to trace these oppositions through the
book. Stephen's class at Clongowes is divided into rival teams,
York and Lancaster (the white rose and the red rose). He reflects
that you "could not have a green rose. But perhaps somewhere
in the world you could" (*P* 12). Maroon and green are the colors
of Davitt and Parnell, so that the red and green of Christmas
(holly and ivy, or the "great fire, banked high and red" and the
ivy [*P* 20, 27] betoken a political schism. When Stephen becomes
pious, the rosaries he says "transformed themselves into coronals
of flowers of such vague unearthly texture that they seemed to
him as hueless and odourless as they were nameless" (*P* 148). The
blankness and inanition of the religious life, "a heart of white
rose" (*P* 145), is then contrasted with the red rose of passion and
art, embodied both in the lotuslike apparition Stephen sees at the
end of the beach episode and in the "roselike glow" (*P* 217) he
senses as he writes his villanelle. The lotus speaks to him of "some
new world, fantastic, dim, uncertain as under sea, traversed by
cloudy shapes and beings. A world, a glimmer, or a flower?" Yet
Stephen's imaginary green rose retains a recognizable connection
with Ireland and Parnell. The one place where you could have a
green rose is, of course, in *A Portrait of the Artist*.

Image analysis of this sort will take us some way (though
certainly not all the way) into Joyce's novel. It is not always clear
that he exerts a very precise control over his images; often the
repetitions elude any unforced critical explanation by their very
frequency and diversity. For example, the Dedalian leitmotif of

flight is represented by various images of birds and bats that crop up in Stephen's consciousness. Plainly his interest in flight connects with his fear of water (aquaphobia). During his adolescent religious phase he feels himself "standing far away from the flood [of sexual desire] on a dry shore" (*P* 152). Stephen is not deeply attracted by the dryness of asceticism as manifested in the "pale loveless eyes" (*P* 186) of the Jesuit priest; he wants to feel superior to the element of water, rather than just safely dry-shod. Images of birds abound in *Portrait*, but it is only in the beach scene and the scene on the steps of the National Library that the bird images appear portentous or symbolic. The ancient hero whom Stephen adopts as his spiritual father is a "hawklike man flying sunward above the sea" and the cry that rises to Stephen's lips in this moment is the "cry of a hawk or eagle on high" (*P* 169). Girls and women, also, are compared to flying creatures. Stephen's girl on the beach "seemed like one whom magic had changed in the likeness of a strange and beautiful seabird" (*P* 171). Emma's life, he thinks, might be "simple and strange as a bird's life" (*P* 216). The birdlike girl is thus a transfigured version of the shadowy Emma, Stephen's "beloved," but in the final chapter there is added a rather different, though equally idealized image of womanhood. Davin, the clean-limbed Irish nationalist and Gaelic sports enthusiast, tells Stephen of the pregnant countrywoman who invited him to her bed. To Stephen such guileless sexuality stands for the awakening soul of Ireland, "a type of her race and his own, a batlike soul waking to the consciousness of itself in darkness and secrecy and loneliness" (*P* 183). (Why batlike? Presumably because bats are the quietest and most furtive of flying creatures.) The batlike soul is an image of much more than merely sexual promise; indeed it is abstracted from sex. Davin's woman is made to stand for Stephen's potential audience, the type of person for whom he is to go out and "forge in the smithy of my soul the uncreated conscience of my race."

The danger of the symbolic or imagistic reading of *Portrait* is that it overlooks, of necessity, the discontinuities, shifts of perspective, and changes of focus which fissure the narrative. When Mr. Dedalus describes the betrayers of Parnell as "rats in a sewer"

(*P* 34), the alert symbolic reader will recall the rat that Stephen saw at Clongowes and point to Stephen's identification with the victimized Irish leader. What we are witnessing, however, is a type of linguistic accident or coincidence in which the same semantic material has, in its new (and metaphorical) context, an utterly different value. Joyce himself was to become fascinated by such coincidences, but there is no sign that he gave deliberate attention to this particular example. The result of pursuing such chains of poetic association too far is to produce a *Portrait* very different from the one Joyce actually wrote.

The book is divided into five chapters, which exhibit a clear chronological, etiological, and stylistic progression. At the same time, each chapter roughly exhibits the same pattern of development. According to Kenner, the pattern is one of "dream nourished in contempt of reality, put into practice, and dashed by reality."[12] Kenner describes the movement of *Portrait* as a sort of vicious spiral, since "each chapter closes with a synthesis of triumph which in turn feeds the sausage-machine set up in the next chapter." The "synthesis of triumph," we might add, is in each case an approximation of the cry Stephen finally utters at the end of the book: "Welcome, O life!" Near the end of chapter 4 he exclaims, "To live, to err, to fall to triumph, to recreate life out of life!" (*P* 172). Chapter 3 ends with "Another life! A life of grace and virtue and happiness!" (*P* 146); chapter 2 with Stephen's first kiss which is a new awakening and an image of life; and chapter 1 with his successful appeal against injustice, which leaves him feeling "happy and free" and hearing the sound of cricket bats "like drops of water in a fountain falling softly in the brimming bowl" (*P* 59)—an image of plenty which is reminiscent of the psalmist's "My cup runneth over." When Stephen at the end of the book announces that he is going "to encounter for the millionth time the reality of experience" (*P* 252–3), it is (the structure implies) already the fifth in an exhilarating sequence of new starts.

This repeated rhythm in *Portrait* should not, however, be allowed to obscure the sense of disjointedness that the book conveys, especially on close reading. The surviving portion of *Stephen*

Hero presents a much more conventional, continuous progression than the finished version, which moves by leaps and jerks. It would be naive to pretend that Joyce's artistic control, as he revised his manuscript, was total or that the end product is altogether seamless. Stephen's younger brother Maurice, an important character in the earlier version, has been eliminated from *Portrait*—except that he does make a single unexplained appearance in chapter 2. ("—O, Holy Paul, I forgot about Maurice, said Mr Dedalus" [*P* 71]—words which Joyce might have echoed.) When we read at the beginning of the Cork episode that "Stephen was once again seated beside his father in the corner of a railway carriage at Kingsbridge," and a moment later find him recalling "his childish wonder of years before and every event of his first day at Clongowes" (*P* 86), it is not difficult to make out that Stephen's parents took him to Clongowes *by* train. The momentary flashback must refer to an earlier version of *Portrait* which—as Joyce told his brother on 15 December 1907—"began at a railway station like most college stories."[13] Joyce left traces of this beginning only in Stephen's memory—or did he, rather, forget to remove them?

The effect of *Portrait*'s many narrative suppressions is not only to highlight the faculty of memory but to produce a book that has to be negotiated warily. When Stephen felt sick and feverish in the refectory at Clongowes:

> He leaned his elbows on the table and shut and opened the flaps of his ears. Then he heard the noise of the refectory every time he opened the flaps of his ears. It made a roar like a train at night. And when he closed the flaps the roar was shut off like a train going into a tunnel. That night at Dalkey the train had roared like that and then, when it went into the tunnel, the roar stopped. He closed his eyes and the train went on, roaring and then stopping; roaring again, stopping. (*P* 13)

This passage once again feeds speculation about Stephen's first train journey, the source of the "childish wonder" he will eventually recall. Later that evening he imagines going home for the holidays in a "long long chocolate train with cream facings" (*P* 20)—an amusing phrase in its own right, but also one which supports the conclusion that he went to Clongowes by train. Here, however, we have an evening journey passing through Dalkey on the line from Bray (where the Dedalus family lives) to Dublin. A few pages later we see Stephen again remembering the tunnel, and at the same time learning to manipulate metaphor:

> First came the vacation and then the next term and then vacation again and then again another term and then again the vacation. It was like a train going in and out of tunnels and that was like the noise of the boys eating in the refectory when you opened and closed the flaps of the ears. Term, vacation; tunnel, out; noise, stop. (*P* 17)

This charming passage shows Stephen learning to understand his experience, by reducing it to a kind of imaginative order. The in and out of the tunnel, however, may serve as a metaphor for further alternations in the opening chapter, which Stephen cannot perceive; these are the alternations of narrative genre and of narrative units. The first two pages of infantile consciousness have a poetic, not a chronological form. (Chronologically they have no beginning or end, though there could be no stronger poetic beginning than "Once upon a time.") They give the effect of memories reassembled at a later date. The first Clongowes episode, however, shows Stephen actively using his imagination and memory, cut off as he is by fever from unreflecting participation in the life around him. This abruptly gives way to the Christmas dinner scene, a dramatized episode in which Stephen's time for reflection is reduced to a minimum. The second Clongowes episode is balanced between external event and inner reflection. Stephen, having broken his glasses, is set somewhat apart, though not as severely as when he was ill. His sensations of pain and fear as the pandybat hits him are described with extraordinary vividness. His inner consciousness remains paramount as he nerves himself up to complain to the rector and walks alone through the "low dark narrow corridor" not unlike a tunnel. Strength-ened by the legend of the Irish patriot Hamilton Rowan (who outwitted his pursuers in the same place), Stephen emerges from this narrative tunnel into the lucidity of his interview with the rector. These four discontinuous episodes make up chapter 1 of *Portrait*. Joyce's suppression of linking passages in the narrative has become commonplace in twentieth-century fictional technique, though it was not so when he was writing. The result is a com-promise between the linked collection of impressionistic stories or sketches (such as the first three stories in *Dubliners*) and the discursive continuity of the nineteenth-century novel.

As we read on in *Portrait*, there are further marked disconti-nuities. The sermons in the third chapter, the extended rhapsody on the beach in the fourth, and the aesthetic dialogues and jour-nal entries of the fifth are all an affront to conventional narrative decorum. Thanks to Joyce's extensive use of free indirect style, the book's vocabulary, syntax, and cadence tend to become more complex as Stephen grows older. *Portrait* for this reason is not a "well-made" novel in the nineteenth-century or the Jamesian sense, though it has often been acclaimed as an example, in Mark Schorer's phrase, of "technique as discovery."[14] The changes in technique reflect the stages in Stephen's mental evolution, the growth of his soul. Alternatively, we may wish to see the discon-tinuities of *Portrait* as an index of the changing pattern of voices surrounding and defining Stephen.

Phases of an Identity

Who is Stephen? The earliest episodes of *Portrait* show him learning the identity that is given him by family and school. In each case, there are indications of a primal unity which has already given place to division. Soon, with the repercussions of Parnell's fall, the larger divisions of church and state will forcibly enter his own history.

When in the fifth chapter Cranly tries to persuade Stephen to make his Easter duty, he tells him that "Whatever else is unsure in this stinking dunghill of a world a mother's love is not" (*P* 241–42). Stephen first knows his mother as someone with a nice smell, who plays the piano so that he can dance. Yet even in the brief opening section she is present at a mysterious incident when he has done something wrong, and is required to apologize. Why did he hide under the table? Was it perhaps because he had expressed a wish to marry Eileen, the next-door girl whose family were Protestants? We do not know, but we do know that Stephen is conscious of estrangement from his mother very soon after this, as a result of being sent to boarding school. (Would Cranly have been so certain of a mother's love if *he* had been sent to boarding school?) *Portrait* ends with Stephen saying goodbye to his mother and getting good advice from her, but the same thing also happens very close to the beginning. Even as a small child he has learned the importance of a stiff upper lip on these occasions—"he had pretended not to see that she was going to cry. She was a nice mother but she was not so nice when she cried" (*P* 9). That Stephen is adaptable enough to think of Clongowes as his home is emphasized by the deeply satisfying entry on the flyleaf of his geography book:

Stephen Dedalus
Class of Elements
Clongowes Wood College
Sallins
County Kildare
Ireland
Europe
The World
The Universe (*P* 15)

This is followed by a verse written by his schoolfellow Fleming "for a cod":

Stephen Dedalus is my name,
Ireland is my nation,

> Clongowes is my dwellingplace
> And heaven my expectation. (P 16)

Clongowes, unfortunately, is not the cosy place in a unified world that these inscriptions describe. Rody Kickham, the boy's-school-story hero, ignores Stephen; Wells and Nasty Roche subject him to unpleasant inquisitions; and Wells has impulsively shouldered him into the ditch. Wells wants to know if he kisses his mother, while Roche tries to convict him of social inferiority by asking who his father is. The other boys' fathers, or some of them, are country gentry and magistrates; Mr. Dedalus's decision to send his son to Clongowes, however, is an act of social pretension he will be unable to maintain for long. When Stephen, in the sickbay, fantasizes about going home for Christmas, one of his most telling pieces of wish fulfillment is that "His father was a marshal now: higher than a magistrate" (P 20). Stephen wants to go one better than the other boys, not merely to be like them. The only "marshal" he has encountered is a former inhabitant of the house at Clongowes, whose ghost still haunts the stairs. Soon Stephen is feeling sorry for his father, pitying him for not having reached the magistracy. He remembers his father's reasons for sending him to Clongowes—"his father had told him that he would be no stranger there because his grand-uncle had presented an address to the liberator there fifty years before" (P 26)—and perhaps dimly recognizes his family's doomed attempt to live up to past glories.

In dreaming that his father had become a marshal, Stephen is beginning that quest for a new and better father that will culminate in *Portrait* in his idolization of the Greek hero Daedalus—though Daedalus in turn will be discarded, and Stephen will continue his quest for a spiritual father in *Ulysses*. Stephen's search originates as a psychic manifestation of the kind which Freud termed a "family romance." In a family romance, Freud wrote, "The child's imagination becomes engaged in the task of getting free from the parents, of whom he has a low opinion, and of replacing them by others who, as a rule, are of higher social standing."[15] Stephen's family romance begins with the fantasy that his father's social standing has miraculously risen. Later he will come to the point of mentally disowning his family altogether: "He felt that he was hardly of the one blood with them but stood to them rather in the mystical kinship of fosterage, fosterchild and fosterbrother" (*P* 98). In an extended sense, the family romance with its burden of fantasy compensation for the inadequacies of the actual family is a pervading theme throughout Joyce's later work.

At home for Christmas, Stephen has been promoted from the nursery to the dignity of the family dining table for the first time. The famous Christmas dinner scene shows all pretense of family unity being shattered and, with it, Stephen's trust and confidence in his parents. The fall of Parnell, the Irish parliamentary leader, after the O'Shea divorce case in 1890 would have had legendary status in Irish history had Joyce never written, but *Portrait* is a powerful addition to the legend. Stephen is "for Ireland and Parnell and so was his father" (*P* 37). Parnell's fall coincides with a reversal in Simon Dedalus's fortunes, just as it did in the case of Joyce's own father. Simon invokes the authority of his ancestors, including a grandfather who was condemned to death as a "whiteboy," or rural insurrectionary; all these men, he claims, would have supported Parnell against the treacherous priests. The Catholic priests have betrayed Ireland before, reneging on Irish independence soon after the British government had passed the Catholic Emancipation Act of 1829. Simon encourages the blasphemies of his friend Mr. Casey and declares, "We are an unfortunate priestridden race and always were and always will be till the end of the chapter" (*P* 37). His attitude scandalizes Dante Riordan and opens a bitter conflict between the "patriarchy" and the "matriarchy" in Stephen's family.

The Christmas dinner is a powerfully dramatized episode in which we only intermittently share Stephen's thoughts. It is a miniature tragedy, carefully orchestrated by Joyce to include echoes of both Ibsen and Aristotle. At the end Mrs. Riordan sweeps out, slamming the door and leaving the menfolk prostrated behind her rather like Nora Helmer in *A Doll's House*. Then there is an Aristotelian catharsis of pity and fear as Stephen raises his "terrorstricken face" and sees that "his father's eyes were full of tears" (*P* 39). We must assume that the revolt of Dante, and his mother's ineffectual attempts as a peacemaker, leave Stephen's sympathies torn in two. He knows Mrs. Riordan was a Parnellite until recently. Simon moreover, is clearly to blame for letting the quarrel get out of hand and spoil the Christmas dinner. Stephen is shocked by his father's coarse and self-indulgent anticlerical outburst—after all, it is his father who has sent him to Clongowes, to be taught by the priests. Though he recognizes that Parnell is the victim of injustice, Stephen cannot yet understand how injustice can be laid at the door of the Church. However, the next episode, in which he is brutally punished by Father Dolan for accidentally breaking his glasses, will speed up his education a little on this point.

The final Clongowes section replaces political and family tragedy with a tragicomic episode which might have been modeled on the plot of the conventional boarding school story. The episode begins and ends with the "pick, pack, pock, puck" (*P* 41, 59) of ball on cricket bat, and within it we hear another all-too-familiar sound, that of corporal punishment. It is a measure of the extent to which both his father and the priests have fallen in his eyes that, by the end of this section, Stephen has become his own romantic hero. He is egged on by the indignant and mutinous voices of his schoolmates, but, in deciding to complain to the rector about his unjust punishment, he is essentially on his own. His imagination calls up whole series of mentors and father figures to sustain him in his resolve. Why did the prefect of studies have to ask twice what his name was? "The great men in history had names like that and nobody made fun of them" (*P* 55). As he passes along the deserted corridor leading to the rector's room he is aware of the ghosts of the Jesuit saints, of the old marshal, and of the patriot Hamilton Rowan (1751–1834), who escaped from the redcoats in this very house. Rowan and the marshal make an implicit link between the great men of history and the patriarchal tradition of the Dedalus family; we remember the great uncle who presented an address to the liberator (Daniel

O'Connell, the hero of Catholic emancipation) at Clongowes. History repeats itself, on a miniature scale. "The senate and the Roman people declared that Dedalus had been wrongly punished" (*P* 53), as another boy puts it. As he comes back from the rector's office he is cheered by his schoolmates in triumph. His naive trust in family and school have been shaken, but he has learned to believe in himself and has discovered, in the rector's magnanimity, a confirmation of the government of human life by an impartial court of appeal.

Stephen, however, is taken away from Clongowes, as his father cannot afford the fees. At the beginning of the second chapter, he is back in the patriarchal world in which Uncle Charles and his father rehearse the family legends. Feminine influence on Stephen seems to have departed once Mrs. Riordan abandoned the Christmas dinner table and swept out of the door. His mother means little to Stephen, and we see him as segregated from women, whether on his days with Uncle Charles, at his new school, Belvedere College (where boys take the female parts in the school play), or on his visit with his father to Cork. However, the male mentors who dominate this chapter come to seem both inadequate and fraudulent. Uncle Charles grows senile, Vincent Heron (Stephen's friend and rival at Belvedere) bullies him, and the rector of Clongowes comes down to earth so far as to share a joke with Simon about his son's pandying. Stephen finds himself beset by the pious exhortations and badgerings of male voices:

> While his mind had been pursuing its intangible phantoms and turning in irresolution from such pursuit he had heard about him the constant voices of his father and of his masters, urging him to be a gentleman above all things and urging him to be a good catholic above all things. These voices had now come to be hollowsounding in his ears. When the gymnasium had been opened he had heard another voice urging him to be strong and manly and healthy and when the movement towards national revival had begun to be felt in the college yet another voice had bidden him be true to his country and help to raise up her fallen language and tradition. In the profane

world, as he foresaw, a worldly voice would bid him raise up his father's fallen state by his labours and, meanwhile, the voice of his school comrades urged him to be a decent fellow, to shield others from blame or to beg them off and to do his best to get free days for the school. And it was the din of all these hollowsounding voices that made him halt irresolutely in the pursuit of phantoms. (*P* 83–84)

The *"phantoms"* that beckon Stephen to turn aside from the male world are, increasingly, those of real and imaginary women. Throughout the chapter Stephen is beset by sex. "He wanted to meet in the real world the unsubstantial image which his soul so constantly beheld" (*P* 65). The unsubstantial image is represented by Mercedes, the heroine of *The Count of Monte Cristo*, and Stephen's attempts to locate the image in the real world are seen in his two failed trysts with a girl of his own age called Emma, and later in his visit to a prostitute. The chapter balances the growth of imagination against the moral squalor Stephen detects in his family now that his father's fortunes are in decline. Simon's hypocrisy, which is extravagantly displayed on the visit to Cork to sell off his property there, destroys any remaining illusions Stephen has about his family and its traditions.

The property in Cork, which Simon has squandered in his attempts to keep up the family appearances, should have been Stephen's inheritance. Throughout the visit Simon superbly patronizes his son, as if he were indeed coming into an inheritance rather than being done out of one. Stephen needs all the detachment and bitter aloofness he can muster to cope with his father's incessant cock-and-bantam rivalry. A tongue-tied silence characterizes much of his behavior on the visit to Cork—an episode of interminable paternal monologues to which he listens without sympathy. In what one critic has called an "autobiography within an autobiography"[16] Simon is telling his son the story of his life and covering up his present failure with nostalgia for his cavalier youth. But for Stephen his torrent of self-indulgence is overshadowed by a single word cut on a desk in Queen's College—the word *Fœtus*, which seems to express all the "monstrous reveries" and "monstrous images" of his awakening consciousness of the body. Masturbation guilt sweeps over him. Yet the shock of the word *Fœtus*, unloosing the "infuriated cries within him" (*P* 92) and closing his ears to his father's wearisome voice, is a salutary one. The nameless and speechless fetus is a challenge to his own knowledge of origin and personal identity; and, in response to the challenge, Stephen speaks his name to himself:

> —I am Stephen Dedalus. I am walking beside my father whose name is Simon Dedalus. We are in Cork, in Ireland. Cork is a city. Our room is in the Victoria Hotel. Victoria and Stephen and Simon. Simon and Stephen and Victoria. Names. (*P* 92)

His memory of his childhood grows dim; all he can recall are the names. But then, cut off from the child that he once was, he begins to tell himself the story of that "little boy in a grey belted suit." For the space of a paragraph he becomes a deliberate autobiographer, recalling the geography lessons he had from Dante, his experiences at Clongowes, and his impressions and sensations in the infirmary. Notably absent from this miniautobiography is any mention of his immediate family. The omission makes his story that of one who, as Simon's friend Johnny Cashman hints, is "not his father's son" (*P* 94)—a small ex–boardingschool boy who was once a nameless fetus. In this mood he has, however, two new resources. One is a "cold and cruel and loveless lust" (*P* 96). The other is literature. Stephen is able to salve his bitterness and despair by repeating some lines of Shelley. And so this disturbing episode ends by confirming his ability to oppose the written word (his own and others') to the hollow-sounding voices around him.

Stephen, however, still has to cope with the explosion of consciousness represented by the word *Fœtus*. In giving way to his sexual desires he is unloosing the "cry that he had strangled for so long in his throat" (*P* 100). Degrading though it may be, his visit to the whore restores the human contact that he has missed ever since his knowledge of his father's failure began to impinge on his innocent days with Uncle Charles. Stephen is tongue-tied once again in the young woman's room, but it is her physical gestures more than her words—touching his arm, ruffling his hair, and undoing her gown—which bring him into a state of peace with his body. For the first time since childhood, he becomes aware of speech, not as disembodied admonition but as a vehicle of empathy with another person. With her kiss, he seems to pass beyond the world of "hollowsounding voices" to the root of speech:

> He closed his eyes, surrendering himself to her, body and mind, conscious of nothing in the world but the dark pressures of her softly parting lips. They pressed upon his brain as upon his lips as though they were the vehicle of a vague speech; and between them he felt an unknown and timid pressure, darker than the swoon of sin, softer than sound or odour. (P 101)

Stephen has been segregated from female influence during his adolescence; now the physical reality of the woman bursts on him like a revelation. Such a blissful escape from the realms of socially acceptable voice and speech cannot possibly be allowed to last.[17] He feels he has transgressed the social order and that the "squalor and insincerity" (P 67) he had felt around him have taken possession of his own mind. In a heightened version of the movement we have observed in *Dubliners*, the rapture of the kiss is succeeded by the sense of sin and the agonies of penitence. In the next chapter, the whore's penetration of Stephen's brain and soul is cauterized by Father Arnall's pungent sermons. Father Arnall's is a paternal voice far more compelling in its sway over the adolescent mind than that of Stephen's natural father. Through his eloquence, the text itself is pervaded by the crushing authority of the Church.

Catholic and Protestant readers alike have responded to this chapter in which Joyce—like such near-contemporaries as Dostoevsky and D. H. Lawrence—exposes traditional Christianity not as a religion of love but as one based on torture, fear, and self-mortification. Stephen's combination of imaginative power and newly awakened sensuality makes him an easy prey for the preacher's morbid evocation of physical disgust. His early sexual experience was an attempt to appease a sort of soul hunger, a longing to escape from the banalities of existence represented by his father and his schoolmates; but the Church is far better qualified than the red-light district to offer a genuine "other world" beyond theirs. Stephen's first sexual rapture has long faded when the retreat beings, and—echoing Shelley's fragment which he voiced in the previous chapter—he is again subject to "weariness" and the solitude of an empty, chaotic universe. Catholicism repopulates the universe with heaven and hell, reward and punishment, presided over by the Virgin "whose emblem is the morning star" (*P* 105). For Stephen, this revelation of the imaginative depths of the religion he has been brought up in since childhood is irresistible. There is nothing surprising about his agonies of penitence.

Father Arnall's sermons are the product of the literary tradition of "spiritual exercises" deriving from St. Ignatius Loyola, the founder of the Jesuit order. Their authority over Stephen, however, owes everything to oral delivery and can best be described in the phrase Joyce used for the artist's endeavor in his essay "A Portrait of the Artist": these are sermons which conclusively "give the word." Yet in writing them into his novel Joyce was embarking on a Swiftian or Voltairean philosophical exercise, designed to expose the contradictions and absurdity of the traditional view of the terrors of hell. In the measure that Stephen becomes enthralled by the voice of the priest, so should the reader become immune to it. Starting out from the commonplaces of Christian doctrine, the sermons tease out the implications of these doctrines with a literalness and realism which amount in the end to a grotesque perversion of reason. When Father Arnall discourses on eternity, for example, his purpose is to make the brain "reel dizzily" (*P* 132), in fact to torture it. The more vivid the listener's imagination, the more he is likely to be stunned and—given the social authority vested in the Church—inoculated against any further questioning of the eternal verities. Would not such a questioner, a potential heretic, be like the little bird coming to the mountain, "reaching from the earth to the farthest heavens" (*P* 132) for its grain of sand in the knowledge that the mountain will rise again and again even after his puny intellect has succeeded in demolishing it? Yet, from another point of view, the technique of the sermons is surprisingly crude and indiscriminate: for all their eloquence and ingenuity, in their resort to terrorizing the audience and in their deliberate confusion of literal and metaphorical statements, they come close to absurdity. So far as terror and intimidation are concerned, they invite the response of the English master, in a brief respite between sermons:

—I suppose he rubbed it into you well.
—You bet he did. He put us all into a blue funk.
—That's what you fellows want: and plenty of it to make you work. (*P* 125)

The master's healthy cynicism suggests that religion is no more than social cement, an "opium of the people." The priest's voice encourages the boys to get on with their work by discouraging idle speculation; it is an aversion therapy designed to make thinking for oneself seem painful and profitless. Stephen's reaction is an extreme example of such a conditioned reflex. Father Arnall says that, bad as are the physical punishments of the damned, their worst torments are mental and result from unappeasable remorse and from envy of the blessed from whose good fortune they are eternally excluded. Memory and imagination, the very faculties which distinguish Stephen from his fellows, thus become the most refined instruments of infernal torture.

Stephen confesses his sins, though not—significantly—to one of the priests at Belvedere College. Joyce uses the imagery of physical evacuation ("The last sins oozed forth, sluggish, filthy" [*P* 144]), but the sins sound paltry once they are put in words, and the "old and weary voice" (*P* 145) of the Capuchin priest betrays that he is too worldly wise to expect that the penitent will give up his sins—they will recur as inevitably as the body secretes fluids. This priest represents another face of the Church, not the inhuman rigor of spiritual exercises but the promise of communion and spiritual peace in exchange for penitence and submission to authority.

As he went through the back streets of Dublin in search of the chapel where he could make his anonymous confession, Stephen felt a brief reverence for the poor people around him. His communion, however, is taken within the privileged circle of Belvedere College. He goes to Mass with the comfortable thought that a substantial breakfast awaits him at home. Earlier in the chapter this would have been a sign of gluttony, one of the deadly sins into which he has fallen; now it is taken as a sign of grace:

> White pudding and eggs and sausages and cups of tea. How simple and beautiful was life after all! (*P* 146)

So Joyce's irony undercuts Stephen's penitence. Purged of the cries of self-assertion that arose within him, he has rejoined the Church and at the same time reestablished his right to enjoy his bourgeois comforts. He says "amen" to the words of the service and—in an ending which parallels the kiss of the previous chapter—raises the host to his lips.

The fourth chapter begins with Stephen's display of religious piety which, far from appeasing his soul hunger, leads to a "sensation of spiritual dryness" (*P* 151). Since Joyce will end this chapter with an epiphany on Dollymount Beach, it is notable that he begins by showing Stephen metaphorically stranded and beached. The "flood of temptation" (*P* 152) remains well away from his dry shore, but at the end of the chapter he will master his aquaphobia and walk out toward the passionate tides across the sands of Dublin Bay. He does so in obedience to a voice which is neither that of his father nor of the Church—a voice which we do not, perhaps, need the authority of a quotation from Newman to identify as the "voice of Nature" (*P* 164).

Nature, his sense of what is innate to him, is Stephen's chief reason for refusing to train for the priesthood. The words of the subtle and urbane director of Belvedere are unable to inspire him with a sense of vocation, a sense that he has been "called." We see both the inevitability of Stephen's refusal and his own limited understanding of the step he has taken. His decision to try to attend university pleases his father but confirms an unspoken breach with his mother. What he does not know is that he is about to receive another call and that his path will be determined by a spiritual experience as overwhelming as any call to the priesthood. The final section of the chapter is a sustained poetic rhapsody in which every prompting of the external world and of his own nature points toward his becoming an artist.

It is on Dollymount Beach that, as he would later put it, Stephen's "soul is born" (*P* 203). Whatever its earlier stirrings, only now can he say, "His soul had arisen from the grave of boyhood, spurning her graveclothes" (*P* 170). (The image is again reminiscent of Ibsen's *When We Dead Awaken*.) Joyce affirms the birth of the soul in a rich, vibrant, and sonorous prose, which marks the culmination of the romantic vision of artisthood expressed in *Portrait*. The section contains many mingled strains of poetic imagery: evocations of the sands and the sea, of clouds and flight, and of noises and names are interwoven to create a rapturous and spellbinding symphony in words. The verbal symphony attempts to give sound and substance to the single inarticulate "cry" which Stephen himself experiences—a cry which comes forth both from deep within himself and from the natural world around him:

> His throat ached with a desire to cry aloud, the cry of a hawk or eagle on high, to cry piercingly of his deliverance to the winds. This was the call of life to his soul not the dull gross voice of the world of duties and despair, not the inhuman voice that had called him to the pale service of the altar. An instant of wild flight had delivered him and the cry of triumph which his lips withheld cleft his brain. (*P* 169)

The references to voices in this extract are developed throughout the beach episode. The voice of the world of duties is represented by his father's "shrill whistle," which he expects to call him back (*P* 164), by the tramping of the squad of Christian Brothers whose names Stephen hears (or imagines hearing) on the bridge, and by the banter of his bathing schoolfellows. Set against these outer voices is the inner music which resounds in Stephen himself: an "elfin prelude" (*P* 165), a "chord" (*P* 166), "a confused music within him as of memories and names which he was almost conscious of but could not capture even for an instant" (*P* 167). The music, however, issues in words: "He felt his cheeks aflame and his throat throbbing with song" (*P* 170). Two symbols, the birdlike girl and the hawklike man, express the communion between Stephen's own nature and the wild nature around him. He is "crying to greet the advent of the life that had cried to him" (*P* 172), and his cry is summed up in words which suggest a transferred religious ecstasy, a "nature-worship" such as is found in the novels of Meredith and D. H. Lawrence:

—Heavenly God! cried Stephen's soul, in an outburst of profane joy. (*P* 171)

Stephen has rejected the priesthood but has by no means dispensed with broadly religious categories of experience.

The beach episode illustrates Matthew Arnold's influential contrast of Hebraism and Hellenism—of Christian revelation and artistic "sweetness and light"—and it is no accident that the voice of nature speaks partly through Greek symbols and emblems. Stephen's fellow students unwittingly introduce the Hellenistic motif when they offer back his name in a Greek form: "—Stephanos Dedalos! Bous Stephanoumenos! Bous Stephaneforos!" (*P* 168). Daedalus, the inventor of flight, manifests the artist's ability to create "a new soaring impalpable imperishable being" (*P* 169), akin to the "dappled seaborne clouds" (*P* 166), which can travel in reality where Stephen can only go in his imagination. The girl in midstream, who seems "like one whom magic had changed into the likeness of a strange and beautiful seabird" (*P* 171), is both a secular angel and a manifestation of the muse as she would appear to the Daedalian or winged artist. The chastity of Stephen's vision as he contemplates the girl in this annunciation scene is both wholly convincing and in sharp contrast to other visions of beach girls and girls with their skirts pinned up in Joyce: not only Gerty MacDowell, the modern Nausicaa whose self-display is watched by the tired businessman Leopold Bloom in *Ulysses*, but also the women conjured up earlier in this chapter by the rector's joke about bicycling priests (*P* 155).

Stephen at the end of the fourth chapter has, as it were, taken his vows and become an artist. Artisthood for him appears as a vocation or state, not as a process of achievement, so that he can glory in possessing it long before he has produced any artistic works. To artisthood as a vocation, he transfers the dedication and religious ardor that conventionally pertain to the priesthood. He has exchanged the spiritual dryness of his days as a neophyte Christian for the spiritual (and possibly physical) state of "dewy wetness" (*P* 217) in which he later prepares to compose his villanelle.

Stephen now tends to cast the Church as his enemy and rival. Particularly telling is his jealousy of Father Moran, the priest with whom he suspects his "beloved" of flirting in the Irish language class in the fifth chapter. The priest, Stephen contemptuously tells himself, is "but schooled in the discharging of a formal rite" whereas he, the artist, is a "priest of eternal imagination, transmuting the daily bread of experience into the radiant body of everliving life" (*P* 221). This is a very transparent conception, which reveals a veneration of eternity reminiscent of Father Arnall and his sermon. The stage of self-liberation that Stephen has reached at the end of *Portrait* (and the same may be said of Joyce at the age when he began to write) is that of staking everything on his sense of belonging to a heretical priesthood, the custodians of the "religion of art." At the same time he has begun the process of intellectual and emotional hardening destined to make him very different from the languorous fin-de-siècle poets who were his predecessors in turning art into an object of worship. The "Villanelle of the Temptress" that is Stephen's principal literary composition in the fifth chapter marks his homage to the decadent school. Many of the decadent poets, as is well known, recanted their aesthetic heresies and ended their days back in the bosom of the Church. By the end of *Portrait* we are beginning—

but no more than beginning—to perceive that Stephen may be made of sterner stuff.

The third and fourth chapters have taken place largely in the theater of Stephen's consciousness—a theater, however, which echoes with a few commanding voices from outside, notably the voice of Father Arnall. The presentation of Stephen's university life restores the sense of human variety and the breadth of social perspective which were absent from these chapters. For a time, Stephen listens acutely to the voices around him, though by the end he has withdrawn into diary keeping, and listening has given place to writing. It is hard to do justice to the variety and rich modulations of this chapter, which introduces a number of characters with the greatest economy of gesture and contains some of Joyce's liveliest and most memorable dialogues. Much as he may despise his fellow students Stephen tends to make them into larger-than-life figures, representatives of the major attitudes at work in the society around him. Of Davin, for example, Stephen reflects, "The gossip of his fellowstudents which strove to render the flat life of the college significant at any cost loved to think of him as a young fenian" (*P* 181). Stephen is as adept as any of his fellows at giving a legendary quality to the flat life of the college, at least to the extent that it impinges on him. It is true that this portrait is an unflattering one, which did not please everybody. Maud Gonne, the Irish revolutionary, wrote in 1917, "Those who know the young students in Dublin, the intensity and vividness of their lives . . . would find it hard to recognise the uncouth nonentities presented by Joyce."[18] Posterity, it must be confessed, tends to prefer Joyce's "uncouth nonentities" to Maud Gonne's brand of high-minded zealots.

Stephen begins the chapter by driving the voices of his father, his mother, and the mad nun out of his heart with an execration. For the time being these are supplanted by a new set of voices: those of his friends and also the silent voices (*silence* is a keyword in this chapter) of the literary tradition. Walking to college, he thinks in turn of the words of Gerhart Hauptmann, Newman, Cavalcanti, and Ibsen and one of Ben Jonson's songs—in itself a remarkable display of intellectual precocity on Stephen's part. Beyond this, there is the philosophical task he has given himself, that of deriving a theory of beauty from some sentences of Aristotle and Aquinas, even though their learning is "held no higher by the age he lived in than the subtle and curious jargons of heraldry and falconry" (P 180).

If literature and philosophy are portals of discovery, they can also serve as defense mechanisms, helping to shut out the noise of his environment. The same is true of his conspicuous adoption of the role of the poet: it forces him to justify himself and at the same time protects him against the claims of the more assertive of his fellow students. It is both amusing and, in the light of Ireland's subsequent history, deeply instructive to see how Stephen evades the challenges represented by three of these, MacCann, Davin, and MacAlister, by playing off each against the others. MacCann is collecting signatures for a universal disarmament petition, *"Pax super totum sanguinarium globum"* (P 198), as Cranly mockingly puts it. Stephen's refusal to sign is characteristic and yet not easy to justify (Joyce, after all, never wavered in his detestation of militarism and violence). He discredits the petition by remarking that Davin, the "fenian," has signed; Davin in his simplicity can find no contradiction between universal peace and armed rebellion in the cause of Ireland. Davin is the most likable of the student ideologists, but Stephen exposes him (and with him a whole strain of Irish nationalism) as incorrigibly sentimental and given to self-deception. Davin's well-meant confusion reflects ironically on the idealism of MacCann, who believes that the petition is a step on the road to a new millennium of universal altruism. MacAlister, the Ulster Catholic, is the least sympathetic of the three characters under consideration. His attitude to knowledge is crassly utilitarian, he accuses Stephen of intellectual crankery, and (worst of all) he has a grating Belfast accent. Stephen is irritated by him to the point of "bidding his mind think that the student's father would have done better had he sent his son to Belfast to study and have saved something on the train fare by so doing" (P 193). Another student, Moynihan, calls MacAlister "a devil for his pound of flesh" (P 193); and it is perhaps the self-righteousness implicit in this remark which persuades Stephen to swallow his own irritation. "Can you say with certitude by whom the soul of your race was bartered and its elect betrayed—by the questioner or by the mocker?" (*P* 193–94), he reflects.

Treachery, in Stephen's view, is an inescapable part of Ireland's heritage. The belief that the Irish invariably betray one another is one of his justifications for washing his hands of his native country. Later, the same belief sustained Joyce's own habitual cynicism about Irish politics. Parnell's fate, on this view, was both predictable in itself and a warning to all his potential successors. Moreover, the betrayers are not necessarily the utilitarian northerners, the West Britons, or those most infected by English values. Sentimental, self-righteous southern Republicans also have a history of treachery. Whatever we think of Stephen's (and Joyce's) political disenchantment, he cannot be accused of being pro-English. H. G. Wells, reading *Portrait* at much the same time as Maud Gonne (that is, within a year of the 1916 Easter Rising) noted, "Everyone in this story, every human being, accepts as a matter of course, as a thing in nature like the sky and the sea, that the English are to be hated."[19] But Stephen's attitudes grow out of his experiences in childhood and youth, which have taught him that the ideological voices of his fellow students, like the earlier voices of duty and moral exhortation, are so many snares and nets. He says to Davin, "You talk to me of nationality, language, religion. I shall try to fly by those nets" (*P* 203).

Stephen's search for spiritual freedom coexists with an extreme defensive anxiety to secure himself against the possibility of betrayal. This is the rationale behind his watchwords "silence, exile, and cunning" and also I suspect, behind his theory of aesthetic "stasis" in which the mind is "arrested and raised above desire and loathing" (*P* 205). The static work of art is by definition silent—eloquently silent, no doubt, like Keats's Grecian Urn—but still the opposite of a voice exhorting its hearer to take some action. Stephen's dedication to silence is not yet complete, since he still feels able to confess his feelings to friends such as Davin and Cranly. It is Cranly who first hears of his refusal to make his Easter duty, which opens a breach between him and his mother and is his first unequivocal act of rebellion. Cranly is a shrewd listener, telling Stephen how curiously his mind is "supersaturated with the religion in which you say you disbelieve" (*P* 240). Beneath his hardboiled exterior he shows considerable affection for Stephen and is vividly aware of the loneliness to which his rebellion will bring him. Yet Stephen also constructs an imaginary romance between Cranly and Emma, the shadowy girl from his adolescence to whom he still feels emotionally drawn. It is as if he has singled out Cranly from the other students only to force him into the mold of the betrayer.

Is he, then, perfecting himself as an artist at the (necessary) expense of the human relationships Dublin could offer? If so, the exhilarating cry of "Welcome, O life!" with which *Portrait* ends must be read as a triumphant announcement that Stephen has fulfilled his artistic novitiate. This would imply that artisthood is indeed the noblest of vocations and that—as with the priesthood—the world is well lost for it. There is, however, another less exalted and religiose view of the artist, which serves as an implicit corrective to Stephen's effusions and as a source of irony. (The irony, of course, is very much more patent when we think of Stephen as he appears in *Ulysses*.) A priest is judged by what he is—by the state of his soul—but an artist must earn his title by what he creates or produces. Stephen takes it for granted that he commands the privileges of the artist, though his title to them rests on a distinctly meager performance in the present and an unknown promise for the future.

In accordance with this ironic perspective, Stephen's actual development as a writer in *Portrait* is a mixture of real discoveries and false starts. In part we see him as an epiphanist, recording the manifestations of beauty he encounters. He collects a "garner of slender sentences" (*P* 176) from Aristotle and Aquinas and some less exalted phrases from the Elizabethan lutanists. Instructed by his dabblings in theosophy, he looks out for natural symbols, such as the returning swallows he sees and hears outside the National Library—creatures which are "in the order of their life and have not perverted that order by reason" (*P* 225). These are Yeatsian sentiments, and in turn they evoke the death speech from Yeats's play *The Countess Cathleen*, which Stephen has witnessed at the disastrous opening of the national theater:

> Bend down your faces, Oona and Aleel,
> I gaze upon them as the swallow gazes
> Upon the nest under the eave before
> He wander the loud waters.

> A soft liquid joy like the noise of many waters flowed over his
> memory and he felt in his heart the soft peace of silent spaces
> of fading tenuous sky above the waters, of oceanic silence, of
> swallows flying through the seadusk over the flowing waters.
> (*P* 225–26)

Like several other passages toward the end of *Portrait*, this has the
deliberate air of an epiphany. The "soft liquid joy"—wetness—is
reminiscent of the much more extended sequence in which he
is inspired to compose the villanelle. At the same time the imagery is almost identical with that of poem XXXV of *Chamber
Music*:

> All day I hear the noise of waters
>   Making moan
> Sad as the seabird is when going
>   Forth alone
> He hears the winds cry to the waters'
>   Monotone.

> The grey winds, the cold winds are blowing
>   Where I go.
> I hear the noise of many waters
>   Far below.
> All day, all night, I hear them flowing
>   To and fro.

This fine lyric, severely modeled on a verse form of Verlaine's, is
a much more genuine achievement than the self-conscious "symbol of departure or of loneliness" (*P* 226) in *Portrait*. In it the poet

is the seabird. In the prose passage, however, the lush word painting comes close to absurdity. "Oceanic silence" is an oxymoron, and the "soft liquid joy" seems to be produced, in the end, by no more than Stephen's intoxicated contemplation of his own words: "A soft liquid joy flowed through the words where the soft long vowels hurtled noiselessly and fell away, lapping and flowing back and ever shaking the white bells of their waves in mute chime and mute peal and soft low swooning cry" (*P* 226). But this is only one of the directions in which Stephen's precocious intelligence is turning.

Stephen's aesthetic theory both extends and distorts what has earlier been put forward in *Stephen Hero*. Once again Joyce sets it out with a curious blend of autobiography and fictional artifice. Speaking to Lynch, Stephen claims to be quoting from a "book at home" in which he has written down a series of questions (*P* 214). These questions may be found in the "Paris notebook" in which Joyce made signed and dated entries in 1903—a year *after* his graduation from University College. In *Portrait*, Stephen opposes "kinetic" to "static" art, redefines *integritas, consonantia,* and *clari²as,* and then distinguishes between the lyrical, epic, and dramatic forms of art. Stephen's definition of *claritas,* or radiance—the key to his theory of beauty—has a quite different emphasis from the one he offered in *Stephen Hero*. He starts by disavowing symbolism or idealism, in the ninetyish or Yeatsian sense of "the supreme quality of beauty being a light from some other world." That would, perhaps, be a too obviously mystical or religious view of art for Stephen to espouse. In its place, he offers a lyrical account of the experience of artistic inspiration. The supreme quality of beauty "is felt by the artist when the esthetic image is first conceived in his imagination" (*P* 213). Shelley's comparison of the mind in creation to a fading coal and the physiologist Galvani's description of a cardiac condition "called the enchantment of the heart," are thrown in by way of elaboration. All of this is profoundly evasive, a mystification of the artistic process which gives no indication of the sources of the all-important "esthetic image." Shelley, as a neoplatonist, *would* have believed that the image is a light from some other world. Aquinas likewise would argue that our ability to respond to earthly beauty is divinely inspired. Stephen can merely speak of an "enchantment of the heart" without saying by whom or what the poet is made open to enchantment. The answer is implicit in the following episode—in which he composes the "Villanelle of the Temptress"—but Stephen does not manage to formulate it theoretically. In the villanelle episode, the poet is enchanted by the "temptress," or muse, and she in turn is a figment of his own brain. Because his brain is still supersaturated with the Catholic religion, the "temptress" is also the Virgin Mary.[20] For the same reason, Stephen in *Portrait* is unable to evolve a satisfactory theory of artistic creation. One indication of its unsatisfactoriness is that he unceremoniously abandons it, in favor of a wholly different and much more materialistic approach, which he expounds (using Shakespeare as his text) in the Library chapter of *Ulysses*.

Stephen has more success in *Portrait* as a theorist of literary genres. Indeed, his distinction between the lyrical, epic, and dramatic forms has possibly attracted as much comment as the rest of the book put together. My interest at present is simply to read it as a commentary on Stephen's (and Joyce's) artistic development, which is clearly a progression from the lyrical to the dramatic. The lyrical form is "the simplest verbal vesture of an instant of emotion, a rhythmical cry such as ages ago cheered on the man who pulled at the oar or dragged stones up a slope. He who utters it is more conscious of the instant of emotion than of himself as feeling emotion" (*P* 214). Stephen has uttered many such cries in the course of his childhood and adolescence, and with the composition of the villanelle he shows himself capable of a highly sophisticated, verbally elaborate rhythmical cry. But also, "the simplest epical form is seen emerging out of lyrical literature when the artist prolongs and broods upon himself as the centre of an epical event and this form progresses till the centre of gravity is equidistant from the artist himself and from others" (*P* 214–15). Stephen from childhood has been shown constituting himself as an autobiographer, brooding upon his own development as the center of an epic event. The process involves detachment of the "personality of the artist," which "passes into the narration itself" and thus becomes separable from the character of the hero, though not always unambiguously so. Stephen's emergence as an autobiographical artist remains quite incomplete, since it can only be fulfilled by the writing of *Portrait* itself. The third stage—the dramatic form which is realized when "the vitality which has flowed and eddied round each person fills every person with such vital force that he or she assumes a proper and intangible esthetic life" (*P* 215)—is still more a prophecy for the future.

Read in this way, Stephen's theory of literary genres serves to rationalize Joyce's development, rendering a unique and perhaps fortuitous process as classical and inevitable. The symbols and prophecies which herald Stephen's emergence as an artist have the same effect. *Portrait* as a whole is the outcome of a long romantic tradition of special pleading on behalf of the artist. Joyce's absorbing and utterly convincing picture of Stephen's childhood and youth persuades us of the inevitability and poetic justice of his later specialization. At the same time, *Portrait* cuts itself off from the ideal of the fully rounded human personality. Karl Marx imagined a nonalienated society in which the fulfilled man would be able to hunt in the morning, fish in the afternoon, rear cattle in the evening, and be a critic after dinner. Such a life would be meaningless to Stephen, whose whole identity is founded on the idea of a predestined, priestlike vocation. It would, however, suit Leopold Bloom, who already lives a bourgeois version of the all-around life. *Portrait*, though one of the most brilliant of early twentieth-century novels, would seem distinctly one-sided did it not also serve as a prologue to *Ulysses*.

In *Portrait* two views of the artist—the Dedalian view that he is born and the more conventional view that he must prove himself by what he makes—are held in a subtle dialectic. The latter view, though unstated, is the basis of the narrator's ironic detachment. There is, however, an implied resolution of the dialectic in the notion that Stephen is the future author of an achieved work of art, *A Portrait of the Artist*, which largely vindicates the high claims he has made. Or can it be that the formative experiences that would show him how to *write about* his childhood belong in the future and are as yet unforeseen? The ending of *Portrait* is delicately balanced between these two interpretations. The final pages are in the form of a writer's notebook. The first entry is dated March 20 and is a memorandum of a talk with Cranly, the dramatized version of which we have already read. Here the bridge between Stephen as protagonist and Stephen as autobiographer is deliberately crossed. The three concluding notebook entries form a coda terminating the novel in exquisitely musical fashion, in which the dialectic of "voices" and "cries" is brought to a triumphant resolution. The restraining voice of his mother, reminding him "what the heart is and what it feels," is set against the "spell of arms and voices"—those of imaginary kinsmen, like the temptress he has conjured up in his villanelle, siren voices beckoning him away from home with their "tale of distant nations." Stephen resolves the conflict with a final invocation of his "Old father, old artificer"—primarily referring to his adopted mentor Daedalus but carrying an inevitable implied salute to the real father, whose stature has fallen steadily during the course of the narrative only to rise again, as the storyteller with whose voice it all began. "In my end is my beginning"—for, to begin his task as autobiographer, Stephen will have to write an opening paragraph in which he adopts his father's voice.

Such an interpretation is momentarily satisfying, presenting *Portrait* as a closed and circular narrative in the manner of *Finnegans Wake*. But it overlooks both the imminence of *Ulysses*, which in some respects is a genuine sequel to *Portrait*, and also the actual texture of the last few pages of notebook entries. Most of these are disparate, inconsequential, and inharmonious. Stephen's tone is frequently brittle, posturing, and unstable. Far from knowing what he is looking for, he is setting down "epiphanies" of a very varied kind, which just might be worked up into something substantial. Is this the artist who is ready to "forge in the smithy of my soul the uncreated conscience of my race"? The answer must be that he is still at the stage of life when his ambition outruns his capabilities. With Emma, for example, he makes "a sudden gesture of a revolutionary nature. I must have looked like a fellow throwing a handful of peas into the air" (*P* 252). The gesture is premature and out of place—but at least Stephen himself can see the irony of it. Emma, it is clear, regards him as something of an exhibitionist rather than revering him as an artist. His chapter-ending cry of "Welcome, O life!"—repeated, as we have seen, for the fifth time—does not of itself guarantee that Stephen will achieve the deliverance he seeks. In this sense *Portrait* is open-ended. The young artist's rejection of family and friends will lead him not to assured international fame but to the Martello Tower and the voices he will hear in *Ulysses*.

Notes

1. For Pound's role in establishing Joyce's literary reputation, see *Pound/Joyce*, ed. Forrest Read (London: Faber & Faber, 1968).

2. The Italian texts have been published as *Scritti Italiani*, ed. Gianfranco Corsini and Giorgio Melchiori (Milan: Mondadori, 1979).

3. Gustave Flaubert, *Letters*, ed. Richard Rumbold (London: Weidenfeld & Nicolson, 1950), 98.

4. Oscar Wilde, *The Picture of Dorian Gray* (Oxford: Oxford University Press, 1981), 5.

5. James Joyce, "A Portrait of the Artist," in *A Portrait of the Artist as a Young Man: Text, Criticism, and Notes*, ed. Chester G. Anderson (New York: Viking, 1968) 257–58.

6. Ibid., 260.

7. Ibid., 265.

8. Ibid., 257–58.

9. In 1907, Joyce, presumably finding the name "Dedalus" too artificial, had thought of changing it to Daly (see Richard Ellman, *James Joyce* [New York: Oxford University, Press, 1982], 264).

10. Arthur Symons, *The Symbolist Movement in Literature* (New York: Dutton, 1958), 5.

11. Hugh Kenner, "The Portrait in Perspective," in *James Joyce: Two Decades of Criticism*, 2d ed., ed. Seon Givens (New York: Vanguard, 1963), 137.

12. Ibid., 169.

13. Ellmann, *Joyce*, 264.

14. Mark Schorer, "Technique as Discovery," in *Forms of Modern Fiction*, ed. W. Van O'Connor (Minneapolis: University of Minnesota Press, 1948), 9ff.

15. Sigmund Freud, "Family Romances," in Freud, *On Sexuality* (Harmondsworth, England: Penguin, 1977), 222–23.

16. Maud Ellman, "Polytropic Man: Paternity, Identity, and Naming in *The Odyssey* and *A Portrait of the Artist as a Young Man*," in *James Joyce: New Perspectives*, edited by Colin MacCabe (Bloomington: Indiana University Press, 1982), 73–104.

17. See Richard Brown, "James Joyce: The Sexual Pretext," Ph.D. thesis, University of London, 1981, chap. 4.

18. Quoted in Samuel Levenson, *Maud Gonne* (London: Cassell, 1977), 308.

19. H. G. Wells, "James Joyce" in *H. G. Wells's Literary Criticism*, ed. Patrick Parrinder and Robert M. Philmus (New York: Barnes & Noble, 1980), 174.

20. For a full discussion of the villanelle, see, e.g., Robert Scholes, "Stephen Dedalus, Poet or Esthete?" in *A Portrait: Text, Criticism, and Notes*, ed. Anderson, 468–80.

The Challenge: *"ignotas animum"* (An Old-fashioned Close Guessing at a Borrowed Structure)

◆　◆　◆

I T   I S   S T R A N G E that a quaint device which Joyce used once, and only once—the selection of an epigraph—should have gone unnoticed all this time. The following remarks propose that *"Et ignotas animum dimittit in artes,"* coming right before *A Portrait* itself, is of import and worthy to be subjected to some minute epigraphic hieroglyphing (with deference to *U* 689.14).

The motto, to be sure, has been glossed—but not noticed. What commentators generally offer is the summary metamorphosis into myth and hasty symbolism, for which, naturally, there is excellent reason. But glossing over is not reading, the reading of a phrase in such a privileged pre-position, a phrase which itself exemplifies the auspicious hazards and retrospective comforts of the act of reading.

Joyce sets out in a foreign language. But he does not stipulate that his audience know Latin, aware, no doubt, that, as conditions change, even fewer readers would have benefited from a classical education. The first platitudinous observation is, tritely, that the opening already divides the readers into two broad groups: at one end of the spectrum, the (rare) erudite scholar who immediately recognizes the quotation and puts it into its proper context; at the other extreme, the reader for whom it is a complete blank. Most of us will figure somewhere halfway, able, at least, to spell out some message by holding on to the familiar roots. In any case, we are Janus-faced with a common enough situation: according to our background, the line changes its meaning, and rather radically, from zero to a rich bundle of associations. This is *part of* the meaning of the sentence. Imagine, in a similar instance, the opening scene of *Ulysses*, how it would appear to a Dubliner of 1900, or even a reluctant accomplice like Oliver Gogarty himself—and how essentially different it must strike a non-Irish student of the 1970s.

Commentaries are designed to provide welcome remedies. They tend to dispel ignorance with concise strokes, and with the attendant danger of wholesale skipping. To approach Joyce we may all need notes, at some stage. Notes (by the way, the exact opposite of "*ignotas*") unfortunately have to parcel out instant information which, when in print, can be taken for relevant truth. By their nature, notes are goal- and object-oriented, not toward the inquisitive endeavor (it's their aim to shortcut this). In our comprehensive wisdom we may underrate the motive force of ignorance (of the Socratic kind). If Odysseus had set out from Troy with a copy of *The Mediterranean on Five Drachmas a Day* he would have saved himself enormous trouble, but the *Odyssey* would have become a much more tedious epic or, more likely, none at all.[1] Commentators also like to think that a final, clinching gloss supersedes all the previous trials and errors when the best glosses, actually, can hardly be anything else.

In our case the best-intended notes go straight to the story of Daedalus and dismiss the words themselves in some synoptic translation. Quantitatively, the epigraph has been translated, many times over,[2] but the inherent quest is hardly translatable: any rendering into one of our modern European languages necessarily interferes with the word order, and this happens to a sentence introducing a novel which embodies the problematic triumphs of order. Translations stress the result and neglect the process; they make choices for us and prevent us from doing just this (for example, what is *"artes"*?). Reading (Latin *legere*, to gather, choose) has to do with selection.[3]

Notice how *"Et ignotas animum dimittit in artes"* does not name or state any subject. Glosses rectify this quickly by presenting the Greek inventor and treating us to highlights of his career. This is the way in which we have to transform much of what Joyce wrote down: we supply the implicit background. If we do it here, the cue is taken not from the words quoted but from the subsequent reference line which Joyce also offers, but afterward (Ovid, *Metamorphoses*, VIII.188). All that the predicate itself, without the appended bibliography, reveals is that the plot is about some one person, in the singular. Looking for antecedents, we might pick the most likely two that are present in the volume: (a) the artist mentioned in the title (especially because of the near-startling tautology), or (b) the artist-author whose name has also preceded. It is no secret that these two readings do in fact apply. The point here is merely that the search for identity, so prevalent in the happy Joycean hunting grounds, has set in already as a grammatical fact and is by no means over. For another possible candidate (adding up, with the referential Daedalus, to a startling grand total of four) might also be the only other person inevitably present at this juncture, the reader, who is indeed caught up in doing just what the sentence proclaims. The same application is useful for another intriguing first exposure, the name and title *Ulysses.*[4]

The sentence will now be examined in slow motion.

It gets underway in a typically modernist fashion: *"Et . . ."* This indicates continuity, that something has gone before; it presupposes a context yet to be discovered. The Daedalus story would tell us that it is a tight spot for the hero. The reader, who does not yet know this, is in a corresponding predicament.

And the first content word reinforces this: *"ignotas,"* our prime impression of the world, something unknown. And even more puzzling, we do not know *what* is unknown. The most expert Latin speaker would have to wait for direction: the adjective will come to be attached to something feminine, plural, and accusative, and so it has to be suspended in the mind. In the beginning there is ignorance, which may give way to knowledge (*i-gno-tus* is cognate with "know," "recognize," "cunning," "gnosis," "gnomon," and so on).[5]

No clarification comes with the next item: "animum" could mean a number of things (orginally related to "breath," it was a metaphor for the spiritual faculties, mind, but also soul, memory, character, courage, pride, will, desire, and so on). Grammatically, it is another, but unrelated, accusative. If, for some reason, the poet were to interrupt his declamation at this point, the audience would be at a total loss. No syntactical pattern is emerging. Imagine in how many combinations the first three words could conceivably be developed. The constellation *ignotas animum*, pre-presents the quintessential frustration of the Joycean reader. Our speculative and emotional faculties (animus) are confronted with something unknown and as yet wholly uncoordinated, with the implied hope that the near future may, somehow, sort things out.

The verb, when it comes at last, promises orientation: "dimittit" can be construed with the preceding noun (though, according to the practices of Latin poets, one would do well not to stake all one's money on it, for there's no telling what's yet to follow). *Dimittere animum* yields a metaphor: to send forth, to send out the questioning mind on a mission, to dispatch it—in different directions, all over the place (*di-*), for the goal has not been localized as yet.[6] The nineteenth-century concern with the historical growth of language has sharpened the view for the original images contained in composite verbs. It is here that translations will easily simplify the process by anticipating the perfective attainment at the cost of the inchoative groping.[7] Interestingly enough, Ovid uses a similar image in an almost parallel phrase for a near-parallel situation; Narcissus, when stupefied by the ubiquitous voice of the nymph Echo, glances around in all directions: *atque aciem partes dimittit in omnes*.[8] The Daedalus phrase sounds like an echo of this earlier one; the repetitive technique itself reminds us of *A Portrait*.

The procedure of *dimittere* entails a high percentage of abortive rummaging and false starts; the novel will be full of it. In fact the perfective fallacy may have led to so much discussion as to whether Stephen Dedalus ever deserves our official certificate as an acknowledged artist. Joyce's characters do a lot of tentative conjecturing. To let the inquisitive mind roam around has become the desperate and often random human strategy, which has gone by many names at disjointed times: speculation, stream-of-consciousness, the Joyce industry, are just some of them.

The little function word "in" adds nothing but the all-important direction (if it had come right at the beginning, it would have facilitated our syntactical navigation a lot). But it is not until "in artes" that the mind can be arrested and the disposition of the now-intelligible matter be perceived—from behind. "Ignotas" finds it retarded anchorage, the pieces fit together, the arrangement becomes clear. This is not a surprise for the circumspect interpreter of classical texts. The nature of Latin poetry makes it possible for a sentence to perform, verbally, what it says; the meaning comes about by just the mental search and postponed rearrangement which is also its theme. This is the kind of sentence—call it, say, expressive form—that Joyce liked to make up. In words not his own, but by his own judicious selection, he has warned his readers, given them a trial run. For only with the last element do the parts become adjusted and do we recognize that the sentence is that which it is. "Its soul, its whatness, leaps to us from the vestment of its appearance. The soul [*animus* also means soul] of the commonest object, the structure of which is so adjusted, seems to us radiant."[9]

The structure which Joyce pilfered telescopes quest and achievement as well as a whole cultural and technological aftermath, especially if *artes* is rightfully associated with invention, civilization, and the Artist in his Joycean exfoliations. Translations focus on that; they can hardly avoid rendering *artes* as "arts,"[10] thereby limiting themselves to the successful terminal stage. *Ars*, more modestly, had originally to do with fitting things together; it came to mean skill, dexterity, craft, cunning, craftsmanship, strategy, ways and means, even deceit, handicraft, science, and—finally—art. Indo-european etymologists traced it to a root, *ar-*, to fit, to join.

What Daedalus excelled in was all of this. He fitted things together: stones for a labyrinth, feathers for wings. Writers join words—some, like Ovid or Joyce, in exile with elaborate cunning. The readers, in their turn, try to fit the pieces together in their own agile minds.

Clearly the art of fitting disparate words together, by unhurried storage and retrospective arrangement, must have declined since Augustan times when the offspring languages began to dispense with their flexible endings and sentences had to comply to narrower syntactical rules. So, for all his extravagant modernity, Joyce also turns back to reinstitute an ancient technique to spell out meanings by sending the mind forward and backward. Ovid (who might have been surprised) has been enlisted to predict arts of joining that even Joyce, when he composed *A Portrait*, did not yet know. The quotation encapsules dynamic principles that were present only *in potentia*, and it exacts skills that we are still learning. It sets out with our common starting point, ignorance, and it suggests how, for lack of any better method, we might cope with it. The emphasis is not so much on the achievement, *artes* (allowing it here to mean the accomplished arts), for that remains doubtful always, but on the process. The prerequisites are not so much erudition, though that helps quite a bit, but curiosity and versatility. Homer called that quality, early in the game, *"polytropos."*[11] Unprecedented demands are made on the reader's agility. The one thing the reader must not be is the exact opposite of *ars*: inert (Skeat: "dull, inactive . . . L. *inert*, stem of *iners*, unskillful, inactive.—L. *in-*, not; and *ars*, art, skill"). We may choose to call the eventual joining "symbolism," but it might be instructive to realize that this is an act rather than a thing (it is unfortunate that "symbol" ever became immobilized in a noun and, in numerous studies, treated as something solid and clumsy)—the activity is "sym-ballein," a bringing together of separate pieces.

The dyschronicity of the Latin sentence has a Joycean ring too. It seems to bring together two distinct phases as one—the initial prolonged endeavor, and the final destination; these are super-imposed or, perhaps better, "entwined" (as *FW* has it at 259.7). Or, to rephrase it, the word *"ignotas,"* when mentally transferred to the end, will come to stand for *"notas"* then (for the *artes* have now been discovered). Metamorphoses of time are built into the sentence. Or—once more—the Ovidian micromodel illustrates the complementary facets of written language: a temporal di-mension on one's first experiencing it (literally, Lat. *ex*, and *periri*, to go through) in a process, and then, once recognized as a whole, a spatial perspective a structure whose properties can be studied. Remember our first perplexed struggle through *Ulysses* as against the later tranquil contemplation of its symmetries and structural devices or one of its schemas.

The events related conjure up a crucial moment in the past when the mind is projecting into the future, a favorite moment, too, of Joyce, who closes *Ulysses* with a memory of a past (or even two) when Molly envisages and plans the near future (volitional and otherwise): "I will." The first page of *FW* reiterates a period in the past when imminent events have not yet happened again: ". . . passencore . . . not yet . . ."

An extrinsic but fitting anachronism is that when Joyce copied the epigraph, the unknown art (when limited to the technology of flight) had become sensationally well known.

As predicted in its motto, *A Portrait* will evoke the gropings of a developing mind at crucial stages, often in almost paraphrases of the original pattern: "his mind had been pursuing its intangible phantoms," "his mind wound itself in and out of the curious questions," "his mind had struggled to find," "his mind, . . . wea-ried of its search, . . . turned . . . to" (*P* 83, 106, 154, 176). Very early a defective joining is arrived at which is as yet unknown: *"O, the geen wothe botheth"* (*P* 7.12).[12] A considerably more mature mind is later watched casting around for rhymes and words and images for the intricately fitted villanelle. "His mind was waking slowly to a tremulous morning knowledge" (*P* 217.4) is yet another var-iation on the thematic enactment of the epigraph.

Exploration into obscure areas is not always successful. In the beginning Stephen does a lot of wondering about things not known, called "strange" or "queer." "Suck was a queer word" (12.11), and investigation leads, somewhat aimlessly, to a lavatory in the Wicklow Hotel. "Tower of Ivory," as cryptic as anything could be, can somehow be related to Eileen's white and cold hands: "By thinking of things you could understand them" (*P* 43.9). About the transgression of the older students, one can only speculate. In the course of Joyce's development there will be more and more conjecture and less ready-made certainty.

At Stephen's climatic awareness of the portent of his own name, classical echoes conveniently cluster. The artist, in his new-found vocation, proceeds at once to transform the first real being available, the girl in the water, into a literary composition and even into the kind of event that is dealt with in the *Metamorphoses*: "one whom magic had changed into the likeness of a strange and beautiful seabird" (*P* 171.13).

It all began, really, long before *A Portrait*. In "The Sisters," a story full of guesses and empty of certainties (and with a delayed identity), the boy puzzled his "head to extract meaning from . . . unfinished sentences" (*D* 11.19). The first words spoken aloud in the whole opus, "—No, I wouldn't say he was exactly" (*D* 9.19), seem to have a prophetic ring, too. As Joyce went along, he had to devise new tools to stimulate the processes. A chapter in *Ulysses* like "Proteus" seems devoted to that. "Eumaeus" draws out another indefatigable struggle, for example: "in a quandary as he couldn't tell exactly what construction to put on belongs to" (*U* 645.20; note how this might describe someone grappling with a Latin text). Whether informed or not, Leopold Bloom is forever curious and wants to find out. With dimittent zeal he persists. The unknown may be something forgotten ("Black conducts, reflects [refracts, is it?], the heat" [*U* 57.10], or something never quite grasped: "Parallax. I never exactly understood . . . Par it's Greek: parallel, parallax" (*U* 154.6). Parallax, come to think of it, is an instance of sending the observant mind in two, or more, different positions and having it compare notes.

Ignorance and knowledge, error and truth, jumble incongruously in "Ithaca." It is fitting that Bloom should proceed "energetically from the unknown to the known through the incertitude of the void" (*U* 697.30). The shuttling to and fro between these two poles is meditated in different places; "there being no known method from the known to the unknown" is part of Bloom's "logical conclusion, having weighed the matter and allowing for possible error" (*U* 701.16–20)

The artefact of *Ulysses* is made up of parts fitted together, sometimes, as in "Wandering Rocks," conspicuously so. There was good reason why as the first of all modern works of literature, *Ulysses* should have been dismantled and alphabetically rearranged for handy reference, in Hanley's *Word Index*. The index helps us when we do not, as ideally we should, recall dispersed phrases from memory. But even an ideal memory does not always see us through. It takes patience as well. Out of Bantam Lyon's unintelligible "I'll risk it" at the end of "Lotus Eaters" (*U* 86.7), even the most perspicacious reader can make no sense, and fairly little out of "Potato I have" (*U* 57.2). Such items, like "ignotas," have to be kept in mind until further orders. That one central symbolic connection (by "throwing together") should be built around variations of "throw away," reveals something about the method of composition: nothing should ever be wasted in Joyce's ecological universe. A late paragraph in "Ithaca" recalls and assembles the various scattered elements in an exemplary nucleus of "previous intimations" and delayed "coincidences." That Bloom and the reader had been tantalized by "the language of prediction" (*U* 675–76) we learn as an *after*thought.

The best correspondence to dangling *"ignotas"* are the fragments in the overture of "Sirens," which demonstrates the artifactuality of composition. "Full tup. Full throb" (*U* 256.27) has to be suspended until a cluster of motifs on page 274 suggests a context.

The herarchitexture of *Finnegans Wake* celescalates the *artes* even further. A pragmatic list of clues to characterize it—inadequately—could be gleaned from Skeat's entry of the Indogermanic root:

AR, to fit. Skt. *ar-as*, spoke of a wheel; Gk. *har-menos*, fitted, *ar-thron*, joint; *ar-mos*, joint, shoulder; L. *ar-mus, ar-tus*, a limb; *ar-ma*, arms, *ar-s*, art; Goth. *ar-ms*, an arm. Ex. *harmony, arms, art, article, arm* (I).[13]

A detailed application of the above terminology would be tedious, but it would highlight some of the tectonic aspects of the *Wake* and hint at its "arthroposophia" (*FW* 394.19). In its frequent moments of partial self-revelation *Finnegans Wake* confesses itself as "doublejoynted . . . injoynted and unlatched . . . hubuljoynted" (*FW* 27.2, 244.29, 310.31). It is "the book of Doublends Jined" (*FW* 20.15). It is made up of "parts unknown" (*FW* 380.23). Its ends are riveted by the article "the," its ultimate joint. It articulates contradictions.

And it insults its readers with the obscure and the unfamiliar, reveals their ignorance and inertia, provokes them into the most desperate clutching at tenuous solutions; "the endknown" (*FW* 91.28), *interalia*, exemplifies and names the process leading to eventual recognition. The reader has to resort to an unknown degree of artful and animated dimitting—all over the library shelves and into recondite areas, a hither-and-thithering bustle that affords considerable amusement to innocent bystanders. The more *ignotum* a piece looks, the more hit or miss the procedure is likely to become. Daedalus too, one presumes in self-defense, must have tried out a few preposterous ideas before he could take off.

Perplexity is integrated into the *Wake*, the tentative interpretations of cryptic documents one of its themes. Shem's riddle triggers a series of far-flung guesses and one delayed correct, but not very helpful, solution. Much of chapter 4 consists of scientific investigation. The list of the names of ALP's mamafesta opens with the invocation of (also) HCE as Roman emperor Augustus (or Greek Sebastos): "The Augusta Augustissimost for Old Seabeastius' Salvation" (*FW* 104.6). This is what the *Metamorphoses* culminate in, the glorification of Augustus along with Jupiter, who share heaven and earth between them. Having ended his poem with "*Pater est et rector uterque*" (both appellation fit HCE as well; see "rector" at *FW* 126.10), Ovid then goes on to praise the emperor even more in his *invocatio*.

Ovid's epigraphic shorthand formula for the mystery novel

(body in the library—detective applying his wits—extensive investigation—tidy revelatory realignment of parts) or scientific procedure (problem—hypothesis and experimentation—theory) is borne out elaborately in Joyce's three prose works which followed, but, paradoxically, it is also invalidated by the lack of ultimate resolution. New *ignotas* are planted all along the way to instigate new searches.

Mysteries not revealing themselves before the end belong to the oldest tricks of literature. In *FW* the mystification is immanent in the microstructure. Understanding trails behind. Recognition comes to pass (D.V.) in the course of time, not on the spot. This commonplace affects the minutiae. "riverrun," at our first go off is disquieting but becomes a bit less so once we have negotiated the first sentence, and it gains momentum when we reach the final "a long the"—and somewhere along the journey we can also pick up overtones like "reverend." The process is what the word says, and does: a running. Which is what rivers do, or time does.

Finnegans Wake, as Latin and Greek could, postpones clarification. Different from classical usage, the *Wake* syntax generally adheres to the familiar patterns. Sentences reveal their drift, on the whole, right away, but their lexicologistics often depend on hindsight resemantification. The seasoned reader may instantly apprehend the two components of "The playgue" (*FW* 378.20). But when we stumble into "The finnecies of poetry," we may well have to grope around for "Finn?" "fin?" "fancies?" "phantasies?" (American pronunciation), "finesses?" and so on. The continuation of the phrase "wed music" (*FW* 377.16) can *then* suggest meanings like "fiancee" or "fiancailles." In this case there was also prospective conditioning. Signals like "hornemoonium" and "Mumblesome Wadding Murch" prepare the way. But, again, "Mumblesome" is retransformed into the composer's name not before the following two words have been adjusted.

No one, on first looking into "how the bouckaleens shout their roscan generally" (*FW* 42.11), can recognize the shape that this dominant motif will later take, just as it is wholly impossible to identify a still totally unknown HCE from the initial vestment

"Howth Castle and Environs" (and a newcomer who is told that this "is" H. C. Earwicker has a right to be outraged). Later, perhaps, the elements may fuse in the mind of the reader; the pieces can be re-membered, reassembled, and reordered. It is toward the end that "we have fused now orther" (*FW* 593.10).

No metamorphosis can occur in "raising hell" before we have reached some point of "while the sin was shining" (*FW* 385.10), when, miraculously, hell can turn into hay.[14] Notice how "comming nown from the asphalt" seems to acquire even more redundant solidity when the phrase moves on to "to the concrete" (*FW* 481.10), but that the sequence also allows the first part to click into its opposite and to give the whole sentence also a figurative and a grammatical twist.[15] Hesitant disclosure becomes a literal pass-time of the *Wake*.

PUBLIUS OVIDIUS NASO, a virtuoso of form, did not, for all we know, intend to compile reading exercise for verbal labyrinths two millennia away. Nor did Joyce, when he found a concise prologue, early along an unknown way, devise a freshman course in preparation of the vextremities of *Finnegans Wake*. The quote nevertheless is graven in the language of prediction. It so happens that Joyce reactivated some of the cognitive techniques (from *techne*, roughly the same as *ars*; skill, cunning, craftsmanship, resourcefulness, and art) that were required to combine sense out of the apparently random disposition of Latin or Greek words. And he brought reading back to what it once may have meant according to the terms that served to denote it. *Read* meant discern or advise and is cognate with *riddle*. German *lesen* and Latin *legere* denote a selective process. The Greek verb *anagignoskein* seems to evoke the chancy miracle most vividly, suggesting movement: *ana* (up, forward, or even backward, again) and cognition: gi-*gno*, which brings us back to "i-*gno*-tas," and so on; the ending marks it as an inchoative activity.[16]

In his *Epilogus*, Ovid celebrates reading in a less epistemological way. Proud of the opus just completed, he aspires to immortality: "*nomenque erit indelebile nostrum*"—his name will be indestructible. Stephen's vision—"He would create proudly . . . as the great artificer

whose name he bore, a living thing . . . imperishable" (*P* 170.3)—
may owe something to this line, and the line may tinge Shem's
malodorous ink (*FW* 185.25). The immortality will come about,
Ovid continues, "if ever the predictions of poets have any truth,"
by "the mouths of the people reading him":

> *Ore legar polui . . .*
>
> *. . . vivam*
> ["then will I live"]

A Berkleyan equation *legi* = *esse* might have appealed to Joyce
too. That to be read is the only way to remain alive is certainly
true, whatever else is not, of *Finnegans Wake* and all the written
arts.

Notes

1. Victor Berard proposed that the Phoenicians had been compiling
just some such volume for merchants and tourists and that it was later
translated and edited by the Greeks to become the *Odyssey,*

2. Some available versions:

"To arts unknowne he bends his wits." George Sandys, *Ovid's Meta-
morphosis Englished, Mythologized, and Represented in Figures*, ed. Karl K.
Hulley and Stanley V. Vandersall (Lincoln: University of Nebraska
Press, 1970), 359.

"He sets his mind to work upon unknown arts." Ovid, *Metamorphoses*, trans. Frank Justus Miller (London: Heinemann, 1960), 419.

"Applying his mind to obscure arts." *A Portrait of the Artist as a Young
Man*, ed. Chester G. Anderson (New York: Viking, 1968), 484 (ex-
planatory notes).

"And he devoted his mind to unknown arts." *A Portrait of the Artist
as a Young Man*, ed. J. S. Atherton (London: Heinemann, 1964), 239.

"To uncouth arts he bent the force of all his wits." Golding's
translation as quoted in Harvey Peter Sucksmith, *James Joyce. A*

Portrait of the Artist as a Young Man (London: Edward Arnold, 1973). 33.

"[Daedalus] turned his mind to subtle craft / An unknown art . . ." *Metamorphoses*, Trans. Horace Gregory (New York: Mentor; 1960), 220.

3. See, for example, the entry *legend* in Walter Skeat, *An Etymological Dictionary of the English Language* (Oxford: Clarendon, 1909). All the etymologies in this article are of course based on Skeat.

4. Cf. Marilyn French, *The Book as World* (Cambridge, Mass.: Harvard University Press, 1976), 3–22, and Fritz Senn's "Book of Many Turns," *JJQ* 10 (Fall 1972): 44.

5. Skeat, "GEN" (753).

6. The bulky *Thesaurus* or the *Lexicon Totius Latinitatis* (Patavii: Typis Seminarii, 1940) emphasize that, primarily, "dimittere est in diversas partes mittere."

7. The translations that use "apply" or "devote" suggest that the goal is already known.

8. *Metamorphoses*, ed. Miller, III.381.

9. *SH* 213.15n. And you all know what Stephen's next loaded term is, don't you?

10. Occasionally, however, a term like "invention" is used: "und richtend den Geist auf neue Erfindung," *Metamorphosis*, trans. Reinhard Suchier, ed. Philipp Reclam (Leipzig: Reclam, 1971), 206.

11. *Odyssey*, I.1. I dimitted my animum over this area in Senn, "Book of Many Turns," 36n.

12. I am following Hans Walter Gabler's emendation in *James Joyce's "Portrait,"* ed. Wilhelm Füger (München, Germany: Goldmann, 1972), 20. The imitation and conflation contains, coincidentally, the signal "bothe." "Geen wothe" does in fact mean *both* "wild rose" and "green place;" the inarticulate Stephen is a coauthor of *Finnegans Wake*.

13. Skeat, *Etymological Dictionary*, 752.

14. Cf. Fritz Senn, "A Reading Exercise in *FW*," in the "Joyce-Number" of *Levende Talen* (Groningen) 269 (June–July 1970): 472n.

15. Hugh Kenner supplied this example, in conversation.

16. Henry George Liddell and Robert Scott's *Greek Lexicon* (Oxford: Clarendon, 1968) arrives at the specific sense of reading via "perceiving, knowing well, knowing again, recognize." The point made here is not that Joyce knew this Greek verb, but that the ancients realized, painfully well, the precarious nature of the skills involved.

The Name and the Scar

Identity in The Odyssey and
A Portrait of the Artist
as a Young Man

MAUD ELLMANN

◆　◆　◆

and Rouse found they spoke of Elias
in telling the tales of Odysseus　　ΟΎ ΤΙΣ
　　　　　　　ΟΎ ΤΙΣ
"I am noman, my name is noman"
but Wanjina is, shall we say, Ouan Jin
or the man with an education
and whose mouth was removed by his father
　　　　　because he made too many things
whereby cluttered the bushman's baggage
vide the expedition of Frobenius' pupils about 1938
　　　　　　　　　to Auss'ralia
Ouan Jin spoke and thereby created the named
　　　　　　　thereby making clutter
　　　　　　　—Ezra Pound, Canto 74

According to australian aboriginal legend, the demigod Wondjina created the world of things by giving them names. Intoxicated with his power, he named and made so many things that the universe could not contain his nomenclature. His father "cut out his mouth" to stop the clutter. How does one cut out a mouth? Pictures of Wondjina show a holeless face, the mouth wiped out without a scar, but the eyes gape wide with horror.

The Pisan *Cantos* are haunted by the figure of this mouthless god, punished for the incontinence of his creations. At the time of their writing, Pound himself had been arrested for his crimes of speech, specifically his fascist propaganda broadcasts for Rome Radio. Caged by the Americans at Pisa at the end of World War II, he symbolically castrated his own mouth by taking a vow of silence. In Canto 74, Pound splits Wondjina's name into two halves—Ouan Jin—as if to re-inflict the mutilation of the namer on the name. The fact that "Ouan Jin" is a French transliteration of a Chinese ideogram meaning "man of letters" underlines the fallen deity's affinity to Pound—"the man with an education."[1] In the canto, the dismemberment of Ouan Jin is preceded—and apparently triggered—by the intrusion of another severed name into the text: ΟΎ ΤΙΣ, meaning "no man," which Pound misunderstood as a pun on Odysseus's name. Through this ruse, Odysseus slips into the *Cantos* under the same alias that baffled his ungracious host, the Cyclops: "I am noman, my name is noman."

By floating these broken names into the poem, Pound sets up a resonance between the silenced namer (Wondjina) and the nameless hero (noman), overleaping the centuries, continents, and cultural traditions that divide these figures. If such myth hopping seems implausible, Pound justifies it by reference to the scholar W. D. Rouse, who discovered when retracing Odysseus's itinerary through the Mediterranean that Greek islanders continued to retell the Odyssean legends but cast Elias in Odysseus's role. The excerpt from Canto 74 can therefore be read in two antithetical ways. On the one hand, Pound seems to be anticipating Lévi-Strauss's argument that myths thrive on alterity: While their recurrent elements testify to the permanence of human ideation, their constant renamings and respellings ensure their eternal renewal. Yet the canto also undermines this reassuring sentiment, for the movement from Odysseus to Elias to ΟΎ ΤΙΣ to Wondjina to Ouan Jin represents an odyssey to namelessness.

Joyce's story "Grace" in *Dubliners* presents an Irish version of Wondjina, but there is little grace in Mr. Kernan's fall from vocal power. Following in the slippery footsteps of Tim Finnegan, Kernan tumbles drunkenly downstairs and bites off a piece of his tongue in his descent. But verbal impotence in Joyce's fiction is not confined to oral injuries. Harder to diagnose are symptoms such as those of Dubliners who fail to write, like Little Chandler, Farrington, and Mr. Duffy, or the incriminating "hasitatense" of HCE, the stuttering patriarch of *Finnegans Wake*.[2] In spite of his much-vaunted credentials, Stephen Dedalus also figures throughout Joyce's work as the promise of a writing—and an exile—evermore about to be. To the very end of his fictional career, Stephen could have been a contender, but never took the risk of exile in language. In *A Portrait of the Artist*, words fall apart before his eyes, disintegrating into the primeval chaos of their elements:

> He could scarcely interpret the letters of the signboards of the shops.[3]

> He found himself glancing from one casual word to another on his right or left in stolid wonder that they had been so silently emptied of instantaneous sense. (*P* 178)

> The letters of the name of Dublin lay heavily upon his mind, pushing one another surlily hither and thither with slow boorish insistence. (*P* 111)

Squalid, disheveled, insubordinate to the regime of sense, the alphabet no longer seems constitutive of language but engaged in a guerrilla war against the word.

Why have letters grown so mutinous? Why do all these would-be writers fail or fall? Joyce's writing, like Pound's, belies the notion that creation could consist of the stark enunciation of the name. If language has no origin, no Adam, but a dumb Wondjina at its source, there is no power to bind names to things, or letters to names. In Joyce, it is the fall of the father that precipitates the fall of language: They represent the "lapse at the same slapse," in Wakean terms (*FW* 291:25). From the beginning, Joyce's work is driven by doubt about paternity: The absent fathers and prodigal sons of his early work foreshadow the broken patriarchs and fallen gods of *Finnegans Wake*.

Pound's version of the fall of Wondjina raises questions of naming and authorship that this essay explores in Homer's *Odyssey* and Joyce's *A Portrait of the Artist as a Young Man*. In these works, the name both marks and masks an act of mutilation that mocks the illusion of personal autonomy. While fathers and sons fight for possession of the name, the mother is associated with a nameless scar. Reversing the creative power of Wondjina's mouth, this scar devours all the words and things that issue from the lips of gods or artists. In the "Oxen of the Sun" episode of *Ulysses*, Stephen describes the birth of the artwork as the "postcreation," superior in majesty to childbirth: "In woman's womb word is made flesh but in the spirit of the maker all flesh that passes becomes the word that shall not pass away. This is the postcreation."[4] Flesh "passes," in the sense that it is mortal, passing, evanescent, but it also "passes" in the sense that it is passed out of the body, evacuated from the womb, excreted from the bowels. Stephen's notion of the artwork as the "word that shall not pass away" represents an aesthetic of constipation. But the maternal scar defies this aesthetic, dissolving the distinction between word and flesh while flushing both into the unnameable. This is the decreation.

"WHERE DID THOTS COME FROM?" a nameless voice demands in *Finnegans Wake* (*FW* 597:25). The portmanteau word "thots" fuses thoughts with tots, implicating the conceptions of the mind in the conceptions of the uterus. According to Freud, the reason children ask so many questions is that they cannot solve the fundamental riddle, "Where do babies come from?" The literary critic's overwhelming question, "Where do writings come from?" can be understood as a sublimation of the tot's insatiable demand.[5] With the fall of the father, the question of the origin of writings or babies, thoughts or tots, becomes insoluble. The word in search of a speaker—the letter in search of a scribe, the thought in search of a thinker, the son in search of a sire—these orphans roam through Joyce's fiction, never finding their way home to their origins. Their wanderings bear witness to convulsions in the order by which fathers beget sons, thinkers beget thoughts, and gods beget worlds.

One reason why modernists like Joyce and Pound are fascinated by *The Odyssey* is that it anticipates their doubts about paternity. In the famous scene where Athena asks Telemachus if he is really Odysseus's son, he replies:

> My mother says indeed I am his. I for my part
> do not know. Nobody really knows his own father.[6]

"Pater semper incertus est," Freud writes, quoting an old legal tag: Fatherhood is always uncertain. Motherhood, by contrast, is "certissima."[7] This is because maternity is guaranteed by the evidence of the senses, whereas paternity depends on verbal testimony: "My mother says . . ." In effect, the father is created by the mother's word. Elsewhere, Freud proclaims that a tremendous advance of civilization was achieved when the fact of maternity was subordinated to the fiction of paternity—but paradoxically, it is the mother's testimony that establishes that fiction in the first place.[8] When Stephen argues in *Ulysses* that the Roman Catholic Church is based on doubt about paternity, he also ignores the mother's crucial role:

> Fatherhood, in the sense of conscious begetting, is unknown to man. It is a mystical estate, an apostolic succession, from only begetter to only begotten. On that mystery and not on the Madonna which the cunning Italian intellect flung to the mob of Europe the church is founded and founded irremovably because founded, like the world, macro and microcosm, upon the void. Upon incertitude, upon unlikelihood. . . . Paternity may be a legal fiction. Who is the father of any son that any son should love him or he any son? (*U* 9:837–45)

This stirring piece of rhetoric belongs to Stephen's mission to be father to himself, self-made and self-begotten. To achieve this end, he repudiates the mother, dismissing the Madonna as a sentimental pretext to sugar the patriarchal pill. At the same time, he denies the father's sexual relation to the mother, replacing the bodily father with the "mystery" of paternity. Through this stratagem, he atones for the desire to castrate the father, to oust him from the mother's bed, by endowing him with the stupendous potency of fictionality. In Lacanian terms, he compensates the father for the penis by giving him the "phallus"—a "mystical estate" indeed.

The Odyssey also invokes the mystery of paternity while withholding the body of the father. With a kind of scrupulous meanness, Homer defers the introduction of Odysseus, diverting the reader through four books about his son. "Fit out a ship with twenty oars," Athena instructs Telemachus:

> and go out to ask about your father who is so long absent,
> on the chance some mortal man can tell you, who has
>   listened to Rumour
> sent by Zeus. She more than others spreads news among
>   people. (*O* 1:280–83)

Placed in a similar position to Telemachus, the reader finds out about the father through Rumour, or the legends of the poets, or the stories that Odysseus invents about himself. For Odysseus is "a praiser of his own past" (*P* 241)—like Stephen's father, Simon Dedalus—who navigates through memories as well as through enchanted isles. His epic consists not only of his trials at sea but of his exploits in autobiography. It is striking that most of the action of *The Odyssey* is reported after the event: When Odysseus regales the Phaiacians with the tale of his Great Wanderings, the reader also catches up with his adventures retrospectively, his words having substituted themselves for his deeds. In addition to this "authentic" story of his life, Odysseus adopts a series of counterfeit identities. In book 13, fending off Athena's questions about his name, birthplace, and genealogy, he claims he is a murderer from Crete, fleeing retribution for his crime (*O* 13:256–86). Later on, he attempts to deceive Eumaeus, Telemachus, Penelope's suitors, and even Penelope herself with bogus autobiographies.

He inflicts his tallest tale on the hospitable swineherd Eumaeus. Having returned to Ithaca incognito, Odysseus wishes to persuade Eumaeus to lend him a mantle, disguised in which he means to seize possession of his house and storm the suitors. But instead of asking directly for the garment, Odysseus invents a fib about Odysseus inventing a fib to acquire a mantle on behalf of the present fibber (*O* 14:459–506). These "tales within wheels" leave Eumaeus understandably perplexed (*FW* 247:3). Still, the gentle swineherd encourages his guest to wile away the night in storytelling:

> These nights are endless, and a man can sleep through them,
> or he can enjoy listening to stories, and you have no need
> to go to bed before it is time. Too much sleep is only
> a bore. . . .
> . . . we two, sitting here in the shelter, eating and drinking
> shall entertain each other remembering and retelling
> our sad sorrows. (*O* 15:392–400)

Much as Scheherezade stays alive by telling tales night after night, so Eumaeus and his unknown master reinvent themselves through "endless nights" of storytelling, "remembering and re-telling" their life histories. It is striking that Odysseus's fictional existence lasts only as long as he keeps lying. When he regains his true identity, having retrieved his wife, kingdom, and name, he vanishes with all his pseudonyms into the silence that is Ithaca.

Despite their convolutions, Odysseus's lies tend to avoid the monstrous and supernatural so that they seem more plausible than the truth. He presents himself, with variations, as a nobleman misused by fortune, condemned to wander from the land of his fathers. All his stories serve as answers to the question, spoken or unspoken, raised by his mysterious arrival: "Who are you and where do you come from?"[9] If his mouth tells lies about his name and origins, however, Odysseus also has a secret aperture that speaks only the truth. This is his famous scar, which is discovered by his old nurse, Eurycleia, when she washes his feet, little suspecting that the weary stranger is her master in disguise:

the old woman took up the shining basin
she used for foot washing, and poured in a great deal of water,
   the cold
first, and then she added the hot to it. Now Odysseus
was sitting close to the fire, but suddenly turned to the dark
   side;
for presently he thought in his heart that, as she handled him,
she might be aware of his scar, and all his story might come
   out. (*O* 19:386–91).

"She might be aware of his scar, and all his story might come
out"—the translation suggests that the story literally bleeds out
of the scar.[10] In fact, two fragments of Odysseus's story do "come
out," or issue, from the mention of this scar. A long digression
follows, recounting two apparently disjointed episodes from the
hero's infancy and youth. This flashback occupies almost a hun-
dred lines before the narrative returns to the present. It is as if
Odysseus's scar has scarred the narrative itself, which plunges into
memory and self-dismemberment.

The two events yoked together in the flashback concern two
signs that identify the subject: word and flesh, his name and scar.
In the first episode, the infant hero receives his name from his
maternal grandfather, Autolykos, who finds the kingdom of Ithaca "distasteful" and decides to call the child Odysseus, which
means "distasteful"—a curiously inauspicious name to bear (*O* 19:
399–409). That the name should be bequeathed by the maternal
grandfather displaces it from the paternal line, which possibly
diminishes its potency. This may be the reason why Odysseus
accedes to his position in society only when he is inflicted with
the wound that "makes his name." In the second story recounted
in the flashback, the youth Odysseus goes hunting with Autolykos and kills a wild boar, but not before the beast has gored his
thigh: "too quick for him the boar drove / over the knee, and
with his tusk gashed much of the flesh" (*O* 19:449–50).

Thus Odysseus's scar reopens to let his story out: The tale of
naming, closely followed by the tale of maiming, both emerge
from the rupture in the narrative produced by the disclosure of

the scar. Name, scar, and story propagate each other in the pattern mapped out in figure 1.

The first movement (reading clockwise from the top right) is from the *scar* to the *story* that "comes out" of it. This is the story of the naming of Odysseus, provoked by Eurycleia's recognition of the scar. And scarcely has Autolykos pronounced the name "Odysseus" when another story issues from the *name*: the story of the *scar* (the hunting accident). This *scar* in turn elicits one more *story* before the flashback ends, in which Odysseus triumphantly reports the escapade to his proud parents:

> his father and queenly mother
> were glad in his homecoming, and asked about all
>   that had happened,
> and how he came by his wound, and he told well his
>   story. (O 19:462–64)

In order to complete the process of identification, it is not enough for Odysseus's *name* to be inscribed into a *scar*: the *scar* must be reinscribed into a *story*. The flashback therefore culminates with the story of Odysseus's storytelling, in which he gives voice to his own wound. By telling his story, the hero kills the wild boar a second time, with language rather than with spears, impaling nature with culture.

Figure 1

This cycle of name, scar, and story is accompanied by a cycle of stage settings. The primal scene of naming takes place in domestic space and the scene of mutilation in the wilderness, but the scene of storytelling takes place in the public arena of the court, where Odysseus assumes his position in the social order by translating his wound into his words. Yet all these scenes of naming, scarring, and narrating are reconstructed in the present scene of foot washing, which turns the narrative full circle back to the original domestic setting, where Odysseus received his name. Thus a mini-nostos, or homecoming, has occurred. The flashback concludes by restaging the moment of recognition when Eurycleia sees the scar and realizes its owner's name. The restoration of the name seems to seal the wound within the narrative, filling in the fissure opened up by the eruption of the past within the present. All is explained.

This sequence implies that the scar is the generative principle of narrative, for it represents a breach in the symbolic fabric, which can only be repaired through storytelling. In this sense, the scar confirms the principle that "nothing can be sole or whole / That has not been rent" (in the words of Yeats's Crazy Jane).[11] It is important that the scar repeats: A living scar, it resurfaces in both the body of the hero and the corpus of the text. What is more, the scar secretes—in the double sense of letting stories out but also hoarding them in secrecy. Finally, the scar erupts into the narrative itself and breaks its continuity. Linear progression suddenly gives way to cycles of remembering and dismembering. Erich Auerbach has argued that Homer's style is "of the foreground," so that despite the use of flashbacks and anticipations, whatever is narrated appears to be "the only present, pure and without perspective."[12] Extending this insight, one could argue that the past inheres within the present of *The Odyssey* in the same way that the scar remains imprinted on Odysseus's flesh, hidden only in the sense that it is temporarily obscured by his disguises. At any moment, the scar can reappear, unleashing the hemorrhage of that-which-was.

Why does the scar intrude into the narrative so late, just before the final showdown with the suitors? It is strange that these stories of identification, which belong to the prehistory of the hero's fictional existence, should be reserved for this eleventh-hour revelation. Through this narrative procrastination, Odysseus eludes the reader, just as he eludes his mythical pursuers, by dropping his disguises only when his story is about to close. Yet this belatedness inheres within the scar itself, which presides over a logic of doubling, deferral, *déjà vu*. Like a psychic trauma, the scar makes its impact *après coup* in both the story and the storytelling, through the process Freud describes as "deferred action." As we have seen, Odysseus achieves identity through the double action of language and violence: First his grandfather speaks his name, then the wild boar tattoos his flesh. This is a movement from voice to writing— in effect, the scar is that which writes Odysseus's name. As a signature, the scar requires a reader to be recognized, and reading is a retrospective act. Without a reader, the scar could not discharge its story; sealed in silence on the body, it awaits a Eurycleia to unleash its meaning. Although Odysseus is its first interpreter, only the second instance, the return or re-cognition, can activate the scar and make it speak. With Eurycleia's cry of recognition, writing is restored to voice just as the hero is restored to his patrimony.

If naming involves mutilation, as this sequence of events suggests, the subject is threatened with extinction in the very sign through which he comes to be. For the scar dismembers that which it identifies. While it seems to seal the subject, it also represents a seam through which identity relentlessly escapes.

A FAN ONCE ACCOSTED JOYCE in Zurich and cried, "May I kiss the hand that wrote *Ulysses*?" Joyce refused his hand, replying, "No, it did lots of other things too."[13] In *A Portrait of the Artist as a Young Man*, it is Stephen's mouth which is tainted by the "other things" that it has done: The lips that chant Hail Marys are also lips that munch and suck and kiss and spew profanities:

> If ever his soul, reentering her dwelling shyly after the frenzy of his body's lust had spent itself, was turned towards her whose emblem is the morning star, *bright and musical, telling of*

heaven and infusing peace, it was when her names were murmured softly by lips whereon there still lingered foul and shameful words, the savour itself of a lewd kiss. (*P* 105)

Stephen is dismayed that the highest and the lowest sentiments are both expressed, or "pressed out," through the same bodily members: the hand, the mouth.[14] Whether spoken or written, language passes through the body, corrupted by the physicality that Stephen is struggling to transcend. Words can never purify the flesh, for they are fashioned by the flesh, tongued by the mouth, scrawled by the hand. Considering all the other things they do, these members cannot help but lie.

How can these members remember? Among the things the hand that wrote *Ulysses* did was write *A Portrait of the Artist as a Young Man*. In fact, it wrote three portraits of him: a brief essay of 1904, which was extended into *Stephen Hero*, which was then abandoned in favor of the novel regarded as the final text.[15] As for this last version, the indefinite article of its title suggests a Wordsworthian prelude to autobiography, rather than a definitive account: It is *a* portrait, not *the* portrait. If autobiography entails a repetition of the author's life, Joyce's portrait repeats itself, producing identity after identity. The process continues in Joyce's later works, where the figure of the artist splits into father and son—Bloom and Stephen in *Ulysses*, HCE and Shem the Penman in *Finnegans Wake* (although fatherhood in the first case is fictional rather than genetic). What is it about self-portraiture, for Joyce as for Wordsworth, which makes them so reluctant to conclude?

In the case of *The Prelude; or, The Growth of a Poet's Mind* (1805), Wordsworth must read his own life backward to understand how he became the poet that he is. But the past can be recovered only through the present work of memory. Autobiography therefore involves a paradoxical procedure whereby memory constructs the past in order to determine how the past constructed memory. As Gertude Stein puts it, "At any moment when you are you you are you without the memory of yourself because if you remember yourself while you are you you are not for purposes of creating you."[16] In "Scylla and Charybdis," Stephen speaks of the artist weaving and unweaving his own body, and the same could be said of the autobiographer, who must account for his existence in the present by unraveling the fabric woven by the past (*U* 9:376). In this sense, he decomposes what the past composed, unwrites the hand that wrote. Remembering entails dismembering or more precisely, "disremembering"—to borrow Davin's Irishism from *Portrait* (*P* 181).

If *Portrait* borrows from *The Prelude* any model of the poet's mind, it is not the metaphor of growth but the principle of "spots of time." Described by Wordsworth as "islands in the unnavigable depth of our departed time," these spots can be interpreted as snags in temporality, which act like scratches on a broken record, introducing a subversive logic of compulsive repetition into the teleology of growth. A spot can mean a point in space or time, but it can also mean a blemish, mark, or scar. As it happens, the passage in which Wordsworth introduces the idea of spots of time climaxes in the discovery of a scar in the shape of a name. In book XI of *The Prelude*, Wordsworth writes:

> There are in our existence spots of time
> That with distinct pre-eminence retain
> A renovating virtue.

This claim for the renovating virtue of the spot consorts oddly with the content of the episode, in which the young Wordsworth, rambling on horseback through the rough and stony moor, loses his companion and finds himself confronted by the name of a murderer, carved into the earth to mark the place where he was hanged:

> The gibbet-mast was mouldered down, the bones
> And iron case were gone; but on the turf,
> Hard by, soon after that fell deed was wrought,
> Some unknown hand had carved the murderer's name.

Neither the name, nor the hand that wrote it, is revealed. What fascinates the poet is the act of cutting the inscription and the uncanny "renovation" of its characters:

The monumental writing was engraven
In times long past; and still, from year to year,
By superstition of the neighbourhood,
The grass is cleared away, and to this hour
The letters are all fresh and visible.[17]

As we shall see, *Portrait* also presents identity as a scar without an author or an origin and, ultimately, without even a name. And this is a scar that constantly reopens, so that its letters may remain "all fresh and visible."

This scar emerges in chapter 2, when Stephen and his father take a sentimental journey to Simon Dedalus's origins in Cork. In this episode, it is Stephen's father who assumes the role of autobiographer: By praising his own past, he attempts to recapture the young man that he was by disremembering the failure that he is. His nostalgia draws him to the anatomy theater, where he carved his initials in a desk before giving up the study of medicine ("many human lives were saved," according to Joyce's brother Stanislaus, when their father abandoned medicine in 1867).[18] But another inscription precedes the discovery of these initials in the narrative—the word *Fœtus*, carved into the dark stained wood as violently as the murderer's name is carved into the earth in Wordsworth's *Prelude*. All fresh and visible, this graffito provokes a crisis of masculinity in Stephen, evoking "monstrous reveries" (*P* 89–90).

Does Joyce identify with Stephen's monstrous reveries, or does he portray them ironically? So much has been written on Joyce's supposed irony that the question needs to be addressed before moving on to the more interesting question of the scar. Irony assumes a firm distinction between creator and creation, which *Portrait* constantly subverts. To establish an ironic stance, the author must remain aloof and uncontaminated by the fiction he has brought to life, smiling at his younger self with the benefit of hindsight and experience. But this figure of Joyce-the-ironist is a phantom created by the text itself and by the reader's disbelief in Stephen Dedalus. How could Joyce—we ask ourselves—identify himself with Stephen's grossly inflated ambition, morbid narcissism, fin-de-siècle languor, dandyish attitudinizing, intellectual preciosity, prickly misogyny, guilt-ridden masturbation, "louse-eaten" body, filthy teeth, scatological obsessions, and betrayal of every personal attachment (*P* 234)? Could Joyce possibly take pride in the single feeble lyric that emerges out of Stephen's overblown aesthetic theory? Were it not for the spellbinding portrait of Stephen as a child, the artist as a young man would be unbearable, yet there is little consistency between the Stephens of these episodes: "Molecules all change. I am other I now," as yet another Stephen puts it in *Ulysses* (*U* 9:205).[19] A hostile early critic argued, "Samuel hewed Agag to pieces, but the pieces were not Agag; and the fragments here offered of the experience of Stephen Dedalus are no substitute for a 'portrait of the artist as a young man.' "[20] In subsequent criticism, however, "Joyce" has come to stand for all the unity and self-awareness that Stephen as a young man lacks. But this idea of Joyce is begotten by the text itself: There is no evidence that Joyce distinguishes himself from Stephen. On the contrary, the porosity of Stephen's consciousness belies the notion that the character could be distinguished from his author, or indeed from any of the other authors who pervade this text, in which quotations typically run to ten per page. With "so many voices offending and threatening to humble the pride of his youth," it is difficult to tell where Stephen ends and polylogue begins (*P* 175–76).

The critical reception of *Portrait* exemplifies Gertrude Stein's observations on the fate of classics. When a masterpiece is born, she argues, "for a very long time everybody refuses and then almost without a pause almost everybody accepts." All of a sudden, everybody realizes the work of art is beautiful, but "when it is still a thing irritating annoying stimulating the all quality of beauty is denied to it." "If everyone were not so indolent," Stein complains, "they would realize that beauty is beauty even when it is irritating and stimulating not only when it is accepted and classic."[21] In the case of *Portrait*, first reactions tell us more about the "irritating annoying stimulating" aspects of the novel than the sanitized reflections of later critics. Ever since the work has been accepted as a classic, critics have focused on the process of transcendence, arguing that Stephen transcends his squalor by means of art, while Joyce transcends his character by means of irony. But it was precisely the absence of transcendence that the first reviewers of the book deplored. H. G. Wells famously accused Joyce of a "cloacal obsession," and the same motif crops up repeatedly (Deming 86). One review, entitled "A Study in Garbage," describes *Portrait* as an "extraordinary dirty study," whose author would be better suited to writing "a treatise on drains," while the author of "A Dyspeptic Portrait" complains that Joyce "drags his readers after him into the slime of foul sewers" (Deming 85, 98). "Mr Joyce can never resist a dunghill," fulminates another critic, while yet another deplores the "privy-language" of *Portrait* (Deming 100, 97). Joyce's "preoccupation with the olfactory," particularly when it takes the form of Stephen's "passion for foul-smelling things," also comes in for much abuse (Deming 100, 93). More temperately, Clutton-Brock detects in Stephen a "conflict of beauty and disgust"—and one could argue that this conflict continues to be battled out by critics, with the disgusted lining up on one side and those enraptured with the novel's beauty on the other (Deming 90). Only Wyndham Lewis seems to find *Portrait* insufficiently disgusting, with "far too tenuous an elegance for my taste" (Deming 120). Other early critics point out that the novel has no plot, that Stephen Dedalus has "no continuum, no personality," and that "thoughts pass through his mind like good or bad smells. He has no control of them" (Deming 110, 90). The character is too "thin-skinned" to keep good thoughts in or bad thoughts out (Deming 97). In terms of style, Edward Garnett regrets the "longueurs" of *Portrait*, and Wells judges that Joyce has "failed to discredit the inverted comma," the dialogue flickering "blindingly" between dashes that confuse the speakers and their speech (Deming 81, 87).[22]

Despite their hostility, these criticisms provide important insights into the structure and imagery of the novel, particularly into the fragility of personal identity. For it is true that Stephen's character is inconsistent, porous, plural. Stephen leaks: He not only absorbs the voices, sights, and smells that assail his senses from without, but he excretes his own effluvia into the atmosphere. These discharges dissolve the boundary between body and language, for it is words as well as flesh that Stephen sweats, exhales, urinates, defecates, ejaculates, and vomits. The absence of quotation marks exacerbates the leakage of identity, confounding speech with speaker, dialogue with narrative. Early critics were also right in pointing out that the novel is obsessed with smell, particularly of the putrid or excremental kind. According to Freud, vision superseded smell in the hierarchy of the senses when the human animal began to stand upright, and beauty of appearance took the place of body odor as the dominant sexual stimulant.[23] Smell differs from vision in that it dissolves the distance between subject and object, for the nose imbibes the very substance of the smelled, while the smell rubs off on the smeller, causing him or her to smell in turn. This intimate two-way exchange differs drastically from the impact of sound waves on the ear or light waves on the eye, where subject and object remain discrete and uninfected by each other. In *Portrait*, the predominance of the nose implies that personal identity cannot be self-contained; instead, the subject functions as a conduit for the odors of the city, transforming Dublin into a smellscape. It is revealing that images of drainage, sewers, and cloaca reappear throughout the early criticism, for Joyce depicts the subject as a drainage system, absorbing and recycling the leftovers of others.

This system divides into three economies. The first is an economy of flow, in which the subject issues forth in verbal and bodily secretions:

> His sins trickled from his lips, one by one, trickled in shameful drops from his soul festering and oozing like a sore, a squalid stream of vice. The last sins oozed forth, sluggish, filthy. (*P* 144)

This account of Stephen's confession equates his words with blood, pus, urine, semen, excrement. Elsewhere, breath, money, and saliva also feature as currencies in the economy of flow. Throughout his adolescence, Stephen vacillates between two states—"unrest" and "weariness"—a cycle punctuated by "ejaculations," both verbal and corporeal, for the text persistently confuses these domains (*P* 96, 103, 176, 147):

> Such moments passed and the wasting fires of lust sprang up again. The verses passed from his lips and the inarticulate cries and the unspoken brutal words rushed forth from his brain to force a passage. (*P* 99)

The word "passed," used twice in these two sentences, together with "passage," turns up repeatedly in the economy of flow. In this case, passion has to pass through language, passing out of Stephen in the form of verse, while the wasting fires of lust spring up again to force a passage, whether visceral or verbal. If any of these flows is blocked, a devastating weariness results:

> The old restless moodiness had again filled his breast as it had done on the night of the party but had not found an outlet in verse. . . . and all day the stream of gloomy tenderness within him had started forth and returned upon itself in dark courses and eddies, wearying him in the end. (*P* 77)

This obstructed "stream" could consist of either verse or semen, for the metaphor conflates these categories. Everything that passes through Stephen's mind or body liquefies: Money "runs" through his fingers, confessions "trickle" from his lips, while poems ooze or stream or burst orgasmically:

> A soft liquid joy like the noise of many waters flowed over his memory. . . . A soft liquid joy flowed through the words where the soft long vowels hurtled noiselessly and fell away, lapping and flowing back. (*P* 97, 225–26)

Many bodily rhythms orchestrate these flows, from peristalsis to the beating of the heart. The rhythms of systole and diastole, inhalation and exhalation, tumescence and detumescence re-echo in Stephen's cycles of unrest and weariness, as well as in the paired words and phrases that punctuate the narrative: "opening, closing, locking, unlocking"; "click, click: click, click"; "passing, passing"; "pick, pack, pock, puck"; "term, vacation; tunnel, out; noise, stop"; "bucket and lamp and lamp and bucket"; "ever, never, ever, never" (*P* 20, 41, 59, 17, 187, 132). While regularity predominates, there are also jolts and interruptions in the orchestration, often produced by the epiphanies, which act like foreign bodies in the bloodstream of the narrative, causing cardiac arrests. "Tidal" phrasing also creeps into the "furious music" of evacuation (*P* 87):

> The sentiment of the opening bars, their languor and supple movement, evoked the incommunicable emotion which had been the cause of all his day's unrest and of his impatient movement of a moment before. His unrest issued from him in a wave of sound: and on the tide of flowing music the ark was journeying, trailing her cables of lanterns in her wake. (*P* 75)

The word "tide" associates this flow of sound with menstruation, flouting the difference between the sexes. Such terms reduce the orifices to equivalence: Mouth, nostrils, anus, genitals all serve as "outlets" for the economy of flow. Stephen's outpourings are verbal, respiratory, seminal, menstrual, urinary, fecal, salivary, vomitory, or all of these at the same time:

> He stretched out his arms in the street to hold fast the frail swooning form that eluded him and incited him: and the cry that he had strangled for so long in his throat issued from his lips. It broke from him like a wail of despair from a hell of sufferers and died in a wail of furious entreaty, a cry for an iniquitous abandonment, a cry which was but an echo of an obscene scrawl which he had read on the oozing wall of a urinal. (*P* 100)

This cry is literally a dirty word: It comes orgasmically or diarrhetically or spurts like blood from a reopened wound.

Notice that this spontaneous overflow is not original: Stephen's dirty word is merely the echo of "an obscene scrawl oozing on the wall of a urinal." This echo indicates that everything that issues out of Stephen's body has to have passed into it before. The economy of flow therefore depends on a reverse economy of influence. A major form of influence is food, including food for thought and transubstantial victuals in particular. In the ritual of Holy Communion, the Word of God is transformed into a totem feast, and *Portrait* imitates this recipe. Depending on the cooking, language can transform itself into a Eucharist or Irish stew. "Stuff it into you," Stephen's belly counsels him, and in his greed he gobbles words as eagerly as food (*P* 102). At other times, however, his rapacity is conquered by disgust, or by discriminations worthy of the aesthete Des Esseintes in Huysmans's *A Rebours*: "he tasted in the language of memory ambered wines, dying fallings of sweet airs" (*P* 233). Joyce's novel makes a meal of almost anything: Here Stephen literally eats his words, savoring the language of his memory. But he rarely gets the chance to sample anything so mellow. Most of the food and words that he consumes are old and stale, the rotting crumbs that other eaters, other speakers left behind:

> Mr Dedalus pushed his plate over to Stephen and bade him finish what was on it. (*P* 71)

> [Stephen] drained his third cup of watery tea to the dregs and set to chewing the crusts of fried bread that were scattered near him, staring into the dark pool of the jar. The yellow dripping had been scooped out like a boghole. (*P* 174)

Often the attention lavished on these scraps and dregs and pickings makes the narrative itself seem gluttonous:

> Tea was nearly over and only the last of the second watered tea remained in the bottom of the small glassjars and jampots which did service for teapots. Discarded crusts and lumps of sugared bread, turned brown by the tea which had been poured over them, lay scattered on the table. Little wells of

tea lay here and there on the board and a knife with a broken
ivory handle was stuck through the pith of a ravaged turnover.
(*P* 163)

Language also reaches Stephen half-devoured: "Old phrases, sweet
only with a disinterred sweetness like the figseeds Cranly rooted
out of his gleaming teeth" (*P* 233).

As far as food is concerned, Stephen exercises some free will
in deciding what he takes into his body. But he cannot resist the
influence of smell. In his ascetic exercises, he figures out ingenious
ways of mortifying all his sense-organs except his nose:

> To mortify his smell was more difficult as he found in himself
> no instinctive repugnance to bad odours, whether they were
> the odours of the outdoor world such as those of dung and
> tar or the odours of his own person among which he had
> made many curious comparisons and experiments. (*P* 151)

It is largely through pneumatic means that Stephen's precursors
disseminate their influence: "The spirit of Ibsen," for example,
blows through Stephen "like a keen wind" (*P* 176). Less clean and
less Norwegian, however, is the language that the artist is obliged
to breathe most frequently:

> A smell of molten tallow came up from the dean's candle
> butts and fused itself in Stephen's consciousness with the jingle
> of the words, bucket and lamp and lamp and bucket. (*P* 187)

> His last phrase, soursmelling as the smoke of charcoal and
> disheartening, excited Stephen's brain, over which its fumes
> seemed to brood. (*P* 246)

In the first passage, words that smell of molten tallow demoni-
cally repeat themselves in Stephen's mind; in the second, sour-
smelling phrases seep into his nostrils. Stephen's lungs provide a
rendezvous for the economies of flow and influence: The verbal
gases that he breathes condense into his flows of verse and re-

evaporate into the afflatus of influence. In a passage that looks forward to Anna Livia Plurabelle, the river that evaporates into a cloud in *Finnegans Wake*, the vapor of Stephen's sexual fantasy deliquesces into the wet dream of his villanelle:

> Conscious of his desire she was waking from odorous sleep, the temptress of his villanelle. . . . Her nakedness yielded to him, radiant, warm, odorous and lavishlimbed, enfolded him like a shining cloud, enfolded him like water with a liquid life: and like a cloud of vapour or like waters circumfluent in space the liquid letters of speech . . . flowed forth over his brain. (*P* 223)

Here, influence is converted into flow: The odorous vapors emitted by the temptress precipitate a waterfall of "liquid letters."

In most cases, however, Stephen finds it difficult to turn his influences into flows and to separate his air—or airs—from the breath of other speakers. Most of his verses are reported indirectly, but the few fragments recorded in the text are thickly sugarcoated with quotation. Ezra Pound described his own juvenile imitations of the decadents as "stale creampuffs," and the same epithet applies to Stephen's efforts. Even the word "weariness," which issues from Stephen's crises of "unrest," is recycled from Shelley and Ben Jonson (*P* 96, 176). When this quotation fails to come to his relief, the "soft speeches of Claude Melnotte" rise to his lips to "[ease] his unrest" (*P* 99). As we have seen, his dirty word is also a quotation, the "echo" of graffiti in a urinal, where writing— the "wake" of the word—is stained with urine, the wake of the flesh. On careful inspection, almost every word that passes in or out of Stephen derives from other people's writings. This means that the economies of influence and flow presuppose a third economy of literature.

—One difficulty, said Stephen, in esthetic discussion is to know whether words are being used according to the literary tradition or according to the tradition of the marketplace. I remember a sentence of Newman's in which he says that the

Blessed Virgin was detained in the full company of the saints. The use of the word in the marketplace is quite different. *I hope I am not detaining you.*

—Not in the least, said the dean politely.

—No, no, said Stephen, smiling, I mean. . . .

—Yes, yes: I see, said the dean, I quite catch the point: *detain.*

(*P* 188)

At the time of writing, Joyce could scarcely have predicted the modern usage of the term "detain" to denote the imprisonment without trial of suspected terrorists in Northern Ireland. When Newman uses it, "detain" carries no sense of being held by force: The Virgin is "detained" among the saints much as Burton in *The Anatomy of Melancholy* is "detained and allured with . . . grace and comeliness" (*OED*). In the dialogue quoted above, the word detain enters the economy of literature when Stephen withdraws it from the process of exchange. Literature "detains" language as parsimony detains money, or constipation feces; "detain" is also an antiquated term for constipation. In *Portrait*, the economy of literature consists of words and flesh detained, held back, occulted out of circulation; for as Stephen explains, words have one meaning in "the literary tradition" and quite another in the "marketplace" (*P* 213). Speech in storage, literature disrupts the interchange of flow and influence, producing blockage in the marketplace. To borrow a key term from *Dubliners*, literature is the "paralysis" of language.

By detaining words, literature introduces gaps into the narrative, aporias that obstruct the exchange of meaning:

He stood still and gazed up at the sombre porch of the morgue and from that to the dark cobbled laneway at its side. He saw the word *Lotts* on the wall of the lane and breathed slowly the rank heavy air. (*P* 86)

As a proper name, *"Lotts"* means nothing but refers to someone or something undisclosed. Opaque, detained, and paralyzed, the word presents itself within smelling distance of the morgue, evoking for Stephen the rank, heavy odor of "horse piss and rotted straw" (*P* 86). Of all the vapors that circulate through Stephen's nose, the smelliest are those that emanate from literature. Worse than the smell of speech is the stench of writing—dead speech stored in literature—whose miasma creeps into his lungs to splutter from his mouth as liquid speech.

But Stephen contributes to the stench of literature himself, writing dirty letters and leaving them to ambush blushing readers:

> The sordid details of his orgies stank under his very nostrils ... the foul long letters he had written in the joy of guilty confession and carried *secretly* for days and days only to throw them under cover of night among the grass in the corner of a field or beneath some hingeless door or in some niche in the hedges where a girl might come upon them as she walked by and read them *secretly*. (*P* 115–16; my emphases)

"Secretly ... secretly," these littered letters store the stinking details of Stephen's orgies, "secreting" both his verbal and his bodily abandonments. Like Odysseus's scar, these letters take deferred effect: They await a younger, Irish Eurycleia to read them and release their coffined fumes. While these letters reek of sex, the legends in shop windows stink of mortality:

> Diffusing in the air around him [was] a tenuous and deadly exhalation and he found himself glancing from one word to another on his right or left in stolid wonder that they had been so silently emptied of instantaneous sense until every mean shop legend bound his mind like the words of a spell and his soul shrivelled up, sighing with age as he walked on in a lane among heaps of dead language. His own consciousness of language was ebbing from his brain and trickling into the very words themselves which set to band and disband themselves in wayward rhythms:

> > *The ivy whines upon the wall*
> > *And whines and twines upon the wall*
> > *The ivy whines upon the wall*

> *The yellow ivy on the wall*
> *Ivy, ivy up the wall.*

Did anyone ever hear such drivel? Lord Almighty! Who ever heard of ivy whining on a wall? (*P* 178–79)

This "tenuous and deadly exhalation" arises from "dead language," in which words have been withdrawn from circulation, heaped up in "mean" shop legends and hoarded in the miserly economy of literature. Stephen cannot help but breathe these noxious vapors and pass them out again as "drivel." In this passage, the three economies take part in a complete transaction: The economy of literature releases deadly exhalations, which influence the artist's lungs and issue in the flow of poetaster's drivel.

OF ALL THE WORDS detained in literature, the most mysterious is the inscription *Fœtus*. This appears at the climax of the trip to Cork in chapter 2, where Stephen's father tries to cork his own identity (his son, by contrast, sees himself as a discarded cork bobbing on the filthy surface of the river Liffey, his heart dancing "like a cork upon a tide" [*P* 66, 69]). Simon, returning to his birthplace, remembers his past triumphs and rediscovers his engraved initials in a desk. But this self-affirmation is belied by the financial motive of this journey, for the fallen father returns to his origins only to auction his possessions, reducing his family to destitution. What is more, the rediscovery of his initials follows the eruption of the rune *Fœtus*, which casts a kind of spell over his son:

> They passed into the anatomy theatre where Mr Dedalus, the porter aiding him, searched the desks for his initials. Stephen remained in the background, depressed more than ever by the darkness and silence of the theatre and by the air it wore of jaded and formal study. On the desk before him he read the word *Fœtus* cut several times into the dark stained wood. The sudden legend startled his blood: he seemed to feel the absent students of the college about him and to shrink from their company. A vision of their life, which his father's

words had been powerless to evoke, sprang up before him out of the word cut in the desk. A broadshouldered student with a moustache was cutting in the letters with a jackknife, seriously. Other students stood or sat near him laughing at his handiwork. One jogged his elbow. The big student turned on him, frowning. He was dressed in loose grey clothes and had tan boots.

Stephen's name was called. He hurried down the steps of the theatre so as to be as far away from the vision as he could be and, peering closely at his father's initials, hid his flushed face. (*P* 89–90)

This passage, like the inscription itself, defies interpretation. Obstinately literal, the word *Fœtus* poses a granular resistance to metaphorization. What is emphasized is not the meaning of the word, but the murderous activity of cutting it: One can almost hear the scraping of the knives. Like Odysseus's scar, this word cuts through the thin skin of the present, opening invaginated layers of the past. Yet it requires a reader to release its story, and Stephen *misreads* the incision, performing what Harold Bloom would describe as a creative misprision of the trace:[24]

He read the word *Fœtus* cut several times in the dark stained wood. The sudden legend startled his blood.... A broadshouldered student ... was cutting in the letters with a jackknife.

What is puzzling here is the inconsistency of number. "Cut several times," the incision is plural, but among the rascals conjured up in Stephen's vision, only one is credited with authorship. Despite this multiplicity, Stephen incorporates these scars into the fiction of a single author—"from only begetter to only begotten"—and resurrects a father for the letter. The student—singular—who vandalized the desk leaps back into sadistic life, surrounded by his sniggering accomplices. His scratches startle Stephen's blood—a curious phrase, suggesting either a swoon or an erection. Seamus Deane has pointed out that Stephen swoons as frequently as a heroine in an eighteenth-century novel, but in this case his startled blood induces a hallucination of machismo—in the form of the broad-shouldered, moustached, knife-armed author flanked by his lieutenants—and causes Stephen to hide his "flushed face," engorged with blood.[25]

In at least four ways, then, the "word cut in the desk" encroaches on the father's power. First, it breaks out where the father's name should be. Second, it lets forth a vision of the past that Simon Dedalus's words are "powerless to evoke." Third, it rouses Stephen's sexuality, provoking a homoerotic fantasy of writing that flushes his face with guilty blood. Finally, the plurality of the inscription defies the notion of a singular paternity, "from only begetter to only begotten." How can a mark "cut several times" be pinned down to a single author? But it is crucial that the initials preempted by *Fœtus* stand not only for Simon but for Stephen Dedalus.

In a psychoanalytic frame of reference, it is not surprising that the father's name should be associated with an act of mutilation. In *Moses and Monotheism*, Freud associates the patronym with circumcision, while Lacan treats the "nom-du-père" as a synonym for castration. Yet this does not explain why another cut precedes the father's initials in the text, or why this cut spells *Fœtus*. The inscription itself, pointing backward to prenatal life, combined with its premature arrival in the text, stealing the thunder of the father's name, opens up a world before beginnings, a wounding anterior to naming. Both the timing and the meaning of the word suggest that *Fœtus* represents the navel of the novel: the founding scar that marks the primordial attachment of the fetus to the mother. Imprinted on both men and women, the navel testifies to the facticity of motherhood, rather than the mystery of fatherhood, mocking the "legal fiction" of paternity. Ambushed by this umbilical scar, Stephen erects his broad-shouldered author to defend himself against the threat of merger in the mother. Only when his father calls his name is he rescued from the gulf of the unnameable. If the "sudden legend" startles his blood, it is because the phallus has been overtaken by the omphalos.

In *Ulysses*, the navel is associated with the home: Both Bloom and Stephen live in omphalos symbols, and Stephen in "Proteus" imagines the "navelcord" as a vast telephonic network extending back to the Garden of Eden (3:37–40). "Put me on to Edenville," Stephen instructs an imaginary operator, giving the telephone number for creation from nothing: "Aleph, alpha: nought, nought, one." Yet the navel also signifies the exile of the body from its first home in the uterus. Although the birth scar knots the subject in a private skin, it also marks the spot at which identity dissolves into indebtedness: "the cords of all link back, standentwining cable of all flesh," Stephen ruminates in "Proteus" (*U* 3:37–40). In Joyce's work, moreover, the navel constantly re-opens, horrifically in his epiphany about the death of his brother Georgie:

> [Dublin: in the house in Glengariff Parade: evening]
> Mrs Joyce—(crimson, trembling, appears at the parlour door) . . . Jim!
>
> Joyce—(at the piano) . . . Yes?
>
> Mrs Joyce—Do you know anything about the body? . . . What ought I do? . . . There's some matter coming away from the hole in Georgie's stomach. . . . Did you ever hear of that happening?
>
> Joyce—(surprised) . . . I don't know. . . .
>
> Mrs Joyce—Ought I send for the doctor, do you think?
>
> Joyce—I don't know. . . . . What hole?
>
> Mrs Joyce—(impatient) . . . The hole we all have. . . . .here (points)
>
> Joyce—(stands up)[26]

In a few brisk strokes, this scene stages the collapse of symbolization. First the mother, crimson-faced, infused with blood, looms up at the parlor door, bursting through the membrane of Joyce's absorption in his music. She hails him—"Jim!"—demanding that he answer to his name, "the name that we are told is ours," in Stephen's words (*U* 9:928). What the mother has witnessed, beyond the frail enclosure of the mise-en-scène, is something literally unspeakable—a monstrous inversion of the process of gestation, the body vomiting its "matter" from the "hole" that feeds the fetus in the uterus. As Luke Thurston has pointed out, the mention of this "hole" opens up a hole in language, which sucks up meaning like the "umbilical vanishing-point" of the Freudian dream.[27]

In a famous footnote to *The Interpretation of Dreams*, Freud writes: "There is at least one spot in every dream at which it is unplumbable—a navel, as it were, that is its point of contact with the unknown" (SE 4:111n). It is appropriate that the navel of the dream should make its first appearance as a footnote, for the birth scar also functions as a footnote in the flesh, acknowledging an ineradicable debt to the lost mother. Later, Freud incorporates this umbilical footnote into the body of his text, redefining the navel as a "tangle of the dream-thoughts which cannot be unravelled and which moreover adds nothing to our knowledge of the content of the dream." A knot that adds nothing, this navel imposes an uninterpretable residue, a node or ganglion from which "the dream-thoughts branch out in every direction into the intricate network of our world of thought." It is where this "meshwork is particularly close" that the dream wish rises up "like a mushroom out of its mycelium" (SE 5:525). The navel could therefore be described as the "allwombing tomb" of dreams (to borrow Stephen's phrase from "Proteus" [*U* 3:402]), because it both engenders the dream wish and obliterates interpretable meaning. In the navel, the dream thoughts implode in their own density, opening a black hole at the center of the dream work.

Joyce's epiphany suggests that "the hole we all have . . . here," like the navel of the dream, cannot be named or symbolized in language. Mrs. Joyce, choking on her own euphemisms, finally resorts to pointing, her bodily gesture taking the place of the indicative function of the word. But what is she pointing at? The stage direction provides no index for this silent finger. Suspended without referent, the word "here" points back at itself, at the hole in writing opened up by speech and gesture. Only the speaking, pointing body can provide the "here" with a location; in the text, the deictic floats free of space or time. Thus the "hole . . .

here" can refer not only to the mother's navel, but to "the invisible and traumatic centre" of the text itself, the hole through which meanings hemorrhage.[28] In the drama sketched out in the epiphany, the mention of the "hole . . . here" rouses Joyce from the piano, producing a full-body erection—he "stands up." Yet this attempt to mime the phallus fails to fend off the collapse of the signifying function: Joyce's gesture, like his mother's, substitutes the matter of the body for the meaning of the word, which remains unspoken and unspeakable. Like the scene in the anatomy theater, this epiphany implies that "the hole we all have" precedes and ultimately overwhelms "the name that we are told is ours." If the subject is depicted as a plumbing system, pumping the currencies of flow and influence, the navel is the central plughole through which language and identity go down the drain.

One of the most memorable meditations of Stephen's schooldays concerns the sound of water going down a plughole, a train of thought provoked by the word "suck." "You are McGlade's suck," one schoolboy insults another. "Suck was a queer word," Stephen thinks:

> The fellow called Simon Moonan that name. . . . But the sound
> was ugly. Once he had washed his hands in the lavatory of
> the Wicklow Hotel and his father pulled the stopper up by the
> chain after and the dirty water went down through the hole
> in the basin. And when it had all gone down slowly the hole
> in the basin had made a sound like that: suck. Only louder.
> (*P* 11)

Here Stephen attempts to motivate the arbitrary signs of language by attributing an onomatopoeic origin to "suck." Yet the memory of the drain in Wicklow actually sucks the meaning out of suck, if the term is intended as an insult. "Only louder": The sucking noise does not explain the metaphorical fecundity of suck but drowns its polyvalency in sound (tellingly, it is the father who unplugs the drain and opens the abyss of literality). This passage suggests that language is mined with navels, self-sucking holes that siphon meaning out of circulation.

Joyce's epiphanies perform a similar function, in that they riddle the narrative with cavities where metaphor disintegrates in literality. In *Stephen Hero*, Joyce defines epiphany as "a sudden spiritual manifestation, whether in the vulgarity of speech or of gesture or in a memorable phase of the mind itself."[29] This exalted rhetoric contradicts the effect of the epiphanies, however, whose triviality often "borders on nonsense," as Catherine Millot has pointed out. Metonymic as opposed to metaphoric, the epiphanies present themselves as cinders, "obscure remainders of a silent conflagration. . . . blind and useless witnesses of the inexpressible."[30] In this sense they resemble psychic traumas, in which fragments of the real embed themselves within the mind, obstructing the curative effects of metaphor with stubborn literalism.[31] Joyce's epiphanies resemble navels in that they purport to refer directly to the real, resisting symbolization; most of them are also naveled with ellipses. The scenes that they evoke, moreover, tend to be umbiliform, in that they zero in on apertures where meaning drains away. In one of the epiphanies included in *Portrait*, a monkey's skull grins at Stephen from a doorway, while a whining voice calls out for Josephine, apparently mistaking Stephen for a female.[32] Never explained, this fragment gouges out a navel in the narrative, emptying meaning from the present while marking the eruption of the past in the form of the epiphany itself, which is resurrected out of Joyce's juvenilia. The scene floats free of context much as the monkey face floats free of body, its grin suspended like the Cheshire cat's. Is it a vision or a waking dream? We never know.

The motif of decapitation—or "decollation," as Stephen later calls it—reappears at other epiphanic moments in *Portrait*. Stephen is invited to consider entering the priesthood:

The director stood in the embrasure of the window, his back to the light, leaning an elbow on the brown crossblind and, as he spoke and smiled, slowly dangling and looping the cord of

the other blind. . . . The priest's face was in total shadow but
the waning daylight from behind him touched the deeply
grooved temples and the curves of the skull. (*P* 153–54)

This window sucks up light, much as the plughole sucks up
water, and the darkness virtually decapitates the priest, obliter-
ating everything but crevices of bone. The fact that the priest is
fingering a cord throughout the interview lends a further umbilical dimension to the window hole, although this cord also
evokes a noose, as Hugh Kenner has observed.[33] Later, Stephen
wonders why he can imagine Cranly only as a severed head dangling bodiless in front of curtained apertures:

> Why was it that when he thought of Cranly he could never
> raise before his mind the entire image of his body but only the
> image of the head and face? Even now against the grey curtain
> of the morning he saw it before him like the phantom of a
> dream, the face of a severed head or deathmask, crowned on
> the brows by its stiff black hair as by an iron crown. It was a
> priestlike face . . . in the shadowings before the eyes and along
> the jaws. (*P* 178)

In the following passage from Stephen's diary, it is hard to tell if
the severed head belongs to Cranly or to John the Baptist, the
"decollated precursor":

> Also, when thinking of him, saw always a stern severed head
> or deathmask as if outlined on a grey curtain or veronica.
> Decollation they call it in the fold. (*P* 284)

In the "fold" of the Church, Decollation, or the Beheading of
John the Baptist, is an ecclesiastical feast celebrated on 29 August.
Freud argues in his essay "Medusa's Head" that the severed head
serves an apotropaic purpose, warding off castration by giving it
symbolic form (SE 18: 273–74). In *Portrait*, however, the severed
head appears wherever navels, in the form of portals, threaten to
devour words or flesh.

In Greek tradition, the omphalos, or navel of the world, referred to the shrine of the Delphic oracle, specifically to its sacred mound-shaped stone. Plutarch, in an essay entitled "On the E at Delphi," known to Joyce, exuberantly overreads the Greek E supposedly engraved on this omphalic stone.[34] Greek Es play an important part in disguising the identity of Joyce's heroes: Bloom uses Greek Es to sign his pseudonymous letters to Martha Clifford, and the Greek **E**, turned over and walking on three feet, becomes the siglum of HCE, the fallen father in *Finnegans Wake*. (It is man who walks with three feet in the evening in Oedipus's answer to the riddle of the sphinx: **m**.) When HCE is "interred in the landscape," his **E** turns upside-down with its three feet in the air: **w**.[35] In addition to Plutarch's essay, Joyce might have come across the Greek E in Arthur Conan Doyle's story "The Sign of Four," where the use of Greek E enables Sherlock Holmes to detect the perpetrator of a forgery. " 'They are disguised hands, except the letter,' Holmes said, presently, 'but there can be no question as to the authorship. See how the irrepressible Greek *e* will break out.' "[36] This irrepressible letter also enabled Richard Ellmann to determine the authorship of Joyce's clandestine letters to Marthe Fleischmann, where the Greek Es intended to disguise Joyce's signature paradoxically ensured its authenticity.[37] These Greek Es, with their inaudible incursions on the patronym, hark back to the omphalos and hollow out a navel in the name, knotting the subject in his signature while flushing his identity away.

Both hole and button, both wound and seam, the navel separates the child's body from the mother's but also testifies to their original connectedness. As a sign of inescapable anteriority, the navel has always troubled believers in creation from nothing. Did the first man, Adam, begotten by God the Father, bear a navel? Thomas Browne said no, objecting to pictorial representations that dimple our first parents' bellies with navels. Why would God ordain "parts without use or office"? Navels are mere "superfluities," Browne remonstrates. Having no anatomical navel, Adam retained "an umbilicality even with God himself," an unbroken metaphorical connection to his maker.[38] In the nineteenth century, however, Philip Henry Gosse (father of the more-famous

Edmund) took issue with Browne's contemptuous dismissal of the navel. In *Omphalos* (1857), a bizarre defense of creationism, Gosse insists: "The Man would not have been a Man without a Navel."[39] Briefly summarized by Edmund Gosse, *Omphalos* contends that "there had been no gradual modification of the surface of the earth, or slow development of organic forms, but that when the catastrophic act of creation took place, the world presented, instantly, the structural appearance of a planet on which life had long existed." Much satirized by his contemporaries, Philip Henry Gosse's argument implies that God planted fossils in the earth to test our faith in the divine creation, "to tempt geologists into infidelity." For the same reason, God gave Adam a navel to provide him with the vestige of a past, even though he was created full-grown yesterday, without a mother or a navel cord.[40]

In "Proteus," Stephen takes sides with Thomas Browne against the omphalos, because it represents the debt to motherhood that Stephen refuses to repay. "Whatever else is unsure in this stinking dunghill of a world a mother's love is not," Cranly reminds him. "Your mother brings you into the world, carries you first in her body" (*P* 241–42). But it is precisely this bodily connection that Stephen is struggling to disremember. An emblem of his own belatedness, the navel belongs to the nightmare of history from which he is trying to awake. It reminds him that he is "made not begotten," unlike Adam, who was begotten not made (*U* 3: 45). But Stephen wishes to be self-begotten, to break free of the mycelium or Daedalean labyrinth of cords extending from his navel to prehistory ("the cords of all link back, strandentwining cable of all flesh"). Hence he attempts to erase the navel by invoking Eve's "belly without blemish, bulging big, a buckler of taut vellum," her skin as blank as an unwritten page (*U* 3:42). In this fantasy, the mother is reduced to a surface to be written on—"taut vellum"—rather than the writer of "a sign upon the flesh," the navel (*P* 171). Unnaveled and unmothered, Eve's power of maternity is neutralized, enabling Stephen to imagine an escape from her omphalic tentacles. Erasing the navel is Stephen's way of saying, "Woman, what have I to do with thee?" Lynch tells Stephen that a statue of a woman should always be draped, with one hand "feeling regretfully her own hinder parts," because she "remembers the past"—"all women do." Stephen, on the other hand, wishes to believe that "the past is consumed in the present," navel cords and all (*P* 250–51).

The obsessive recurrence of navels in Joyce's work implies a compulsion to return to origins in order to restage the trauma of separation from the past. In *Ulysses*, the navel takes the form of Bloom's home at 7 Eccles Street, where a picture of the nymph Calypso hangs over the marriage-bed, although it was Calypso who lured Odysseus away from marriage into a "little navel of the sea." The navel of *Finnegans Wake* is the middle of the sentence where the epic both begins and ends, as if in yearning for the unbroken circularity of the umbilical cord. In the *Wake*, as in the Freudian dream, there are no "definite endings," for every word links back to former texts (SE 5:525). When a critic of the *Wake* complained that it was "trivial" to write a book in puns, Joyce retorted that some of the puns were trivial, but others were quadrivial.[41] These quadrivial neologisms branch out like dream thoughts into the "intricate network" of the already written. "The last word in stolentelling," the *Wake* steals other people's words, flouting "copriright" and private property; it feeds upon the "stolen" as a fetus feeds upon its mother through the navel cord (*FW* 424:35, 185:30). To extend the analogy; the *Wake* could be seen as the literary uterus in which new possibilities of writing emerge out of the strandentwining cable of the past. In the allwombing world of *Finnegans Wake*, there is no clear separation between self and other, now and then, here and elsewhere. The psychoanalyst Michèle Montrelay describes the fantasy of uterine existence in similar terms: "a time when nothing was thinkable: then, the body and the world were confounded in one chaotic intimacy which was too present, too immediate—one continuous expanse of proximity or unbearable plenitude. What was lacking was lack."[42] In *Finnegans Wake*, what is lacking is a navel that could separate the corpus of a text from its progenitors—instead, all merge in one chaotic intimacy.

A Portrait of the Artist as a Young Man, on the contrary, compulsively repeats the rupture of the navel cord. If the *Wake* is a "commodius vicus of recirculation," with neither an end nor a beginning, *Portrait* is a series of false starts and dead ends, in which the interchange of flow and influence is constantly "detained" by putrefying lumps of literature and literality (*FW* 3:2). Several Stephens are engendered in the novel, but none of these is corked or self-contained. The moment of birth is constantly restaged: In Stephen's visions of transcendence of his origins; in his fantasies of flying by the "nets" of nationality, language, and religion; in his cycles of unrest and weariness, punctuated by his verbal and seminal "ejaculations"; in his ambition to give birth to the "soaring impalpable imperishable being" of his art: "O! In the virgin womb of the imagination the word was made flesh" (*P* 203, 169, 217). Both *Portrait* and the *Wake* are omphalocentripetal, but *Portrait* seeks the navel as a point of rupture, the *Wake* as a point of coalescence with the past. In *Portrait*, memory is disremembering; in *Finnegans Wake*, memory is mammary.

Notes

1. See Guy Davenport, "Pound and Frobenius," in *Motive and Method in the Cantos*, ed. Lewis Leary (New York: Columbia University Press, 1954), 49.

2. See James Joyce, *Finnegans Wake* (1939; reprint, New York: Viking, 1967), 296 n. 4: "Hasitatense?" See also p. 97, l. 26. These puns allude to Piggott's famous misspelling of "hesitancy," which unmasked his forgery when he tried to pass off as Parnell's a letter condoning the Phoenix Park murders of 1882. *Finnegans Wake* is henceforth cited as *FW*, followed by page and line numbers.

3. James Joyce, *A Portrait of the Artist as a Young Man* (1916; reprint, New York: Viking, 1964), 92. Henceforth cited as *P*.

4. James Joyce, *Ulysses* (1922; reprint, Harmondsworth, England: Penguin, 1986), ch. 14, ll. 292–94. Henceforth cited as *U*, followed by chapter and line numbers.

5. "On the Sexual Theories of Children" (1908), in *The Complete Psychological Works of Sigmund Freud*, trans. James Strachey (London: Hogarth, 1953–1974), 9:212. Henceforth cited as SE (Standard Edition), followed by volume and page numbers.

6. *The Odyssey*, trans. Richard Lattimore (New York: Harper, 1967), bk. 1, ll. 215–16. Henceforth cited as *O*, followed by book and line numbers.

7. Freud, "Family Romances" (1909), SE 9:238.

8. See Freud, *Moses and Monotheism* (1939), SE 23:114.

9. See Richard Lattimore, introduction to *The Odyssey*, 11.

10. The Greek original is less explicit, but the close conjunction of scar and story justifies Lattimore's translation.

11. "Crazy Jane Talks with the Bishop," in *The Collected Poems of W. B. Yeats*, edited by Richard J. Finneran, rev. 2d ed., 260.

12. Erich Auerbach, *Mimesis: The Representation of Reality in Western Literature*, trans. Willard R. Trask (Princeton, N.J.: Princeton University Press, 1953), 2.

13. Richard Ellmann, *James Joyce* (1959; rev. ed., New York: Oxford University Press, 1983), 110.

14. In Stephen's words, "to express, to press out again, from the gross earth . . . an image of the beauty we have come to understand—that is art" (*P* 207). See Maud Ellmann, "Disremembering Dedalus: *A Portrait of the Artist as a Young Man* (1981), in *James Joyce: "Ulysses" / "A Portrait of the Artist as a Young Man": A Reader's Guide to Essential Criticism*, ed. John Coyle, 103–19 (Duxford: Icon, 2000). The present essay revises and expands Ellmann, "Polytropic Man: Paternity, Identity, and Naming in *The Odyssey* and *A Portrait of the Artist as a Young Man*," in *James Joyce: New Perspectives*, ed. Colin MacCabe, 73–104 (1982; reprint, Bloomington: Indiana University Press, 1991).

15. "A Portrait of the Artist" (1904), in Robert Scholes and Richard M. Kain, eds., *The Workshop of Dedalus: James Joyce and the Materials for "A Portrait of the Artist as a Young Man"* (Evanston, Ill.: Northwestern University Press, 1965), 60–68; *Stephen Hero*, ed. Theodore Spencer, John J. Slocum, and Herbert Cahoon (New York: New Directions, 1963).

16. Gertrude Stein, "What Are Master-Pieces and Why Are There So Few of Them," in *Look at Me Now and Here I Am*, ed. Patricia Meyerowitz (Harmondsworth, England: Penguin, 1984), 149.

17. Wordsworth, *The Prelude* (1805), bk. XI, ll. 278–315 (Ithaca: Cornell University Press, 1985).

18. Cited in J. B. Lyons, *James Joyce and Medicine* (Dublin: Dolmen, 1973), 19.

19. Compare *P* 240, where Stephen says, "I was someone else then."

20. Unsigned review of *A Portrait of the Artist as a Young Man*, *New Age* (12 July 1917), reprinted in Robert H. Deming, ed., *James Joyce: The Critical*

Heritage (London: Routledge and Kegan Paul, 1970), 1:110. This volume is henceforth cited as Deming.

21. Stein, "Composition as Explanation," in *Look at Me Now*, 23.

22. Joyce told Grant Richards, the publisher of *Dubliners*, that quotation marks were an "eyesore" that gave "an impression of unreality"; see Richard Ellmann, *James Joyce*, 353.

23. Freud, *Civilization and Its Discontents* (1930), SE 21:99–100n, 106n.

24. Harold Bloom, *A Map of Misreading* (New York: Oxford University Press, 1975), 3–6.

25. Seamus Deane, introduction to Joyce, *A Portrait of the Artist as a Young Man* (Harmondsworth, England: Penguin, 2000), xxxviii.

26. "Epiphany 19" (1902), in Scholes and Kain, eds., *Workshop of Dedalus*, 29.

27. Luke Thurston, "Writing the Symptom: Lacan's Joycean Knot," Ph.D. thesis, University of Kent, 1997.

28. Ibid.

29. *Stephen Hero*, 211.

30. Catherine Millot, "On Epiphanies," in *James Joyce: The Augmented Ninth*, ed. Bernard Benstock (Syracuse, N.Y.: Syracuse University Press, 1988), 207–8.

31. For the literality of trauma, see Cathy Caruth, ed., *Trauma: Explorations in Memory* (Baltimore, Md.: Johns Hopkins University Press, 1995), 3–12.

32. *P* 68; see also "Epiphany 5," in Scholes and Kain, eds., *Workshop of Dedalus*, 15.

33. Hugh Kenner, *Dublin's Joyce* (London: Chatto and Windus, 1955), 113.

34. Plutarch, "On the E at Delphi," in *Plutarch's Morals: Theosophical Essays*, trans. C. R. King (London: Bell, 1882), 173–96.

35. See Richard Ellmann, *James Joyce*, 597.

36. Arthur Conan Doyle, *The Complete Sherlock Holmes* (Harmondsworth, England: Penguin, 1981), 96.

37. See Richard Ellmann, *James Joyce*, 449–50.

38. Sir Thomas Browne, *Pseudodoxia Epidemica* (1646), in *The Works of Sir Thomas Browne*, ed. G. Keynes (London: Faber and Faber, 1964), 2:345.

39. Philip Henry Gosse, *Omphalos: An Attempt to Untie the Geological Knot* (London: Van Voorst, 1857), 349.

40. Edmund Gosse, *Father and Son: A Study of Two Temperaments* (1907; reprint, Harmondsworth, England: Penguin, 1989), 104.

41. Eugene Jolas, "My Friend James Joyce," in *James Joyce: Two Decades of Criticism*, ed. Seon Given (New York: Vanguard, 1948), 24.

42. Michèle Montrelay, "Inquiry into Femininity" (1977), in *French Feminist Thought: A Reader*, ed. Toril Moi (Oxford: Blackwell, 1987), 233, cited in Elizabeth Bronfen, *The Knotted Subject: Hysteria and Its Discontents* (Princeton, N.J.: Princeton University Press, 1998), 20–21. For a lively study of the navel in modernity, see Fred Botting, *Sex, Machines and Navels: Fiction, Fantasy and History in the Future Present* (Manchester, England: Manchester University Press, 1999).

Stephen's Diary in Joyce's *Portrait*—The Shape of Life

MICHAEL LEVENSON

◆　◆　◆

DESPITE THE UNFLAGGING CONTROVERSY over the character of Stephen Dedalus, remarkably little attention has been paid to the ending of *A Portrait of the Artist as a Young Man*, where one might have supposed that the problem would become acute. The diary that concludes the novel has had the rare distinction of being a virtually unannotated specimen within the Joycean oeuvre,[1] and while it is tempting to keep it free from the endless profusion of inky scholia, it raises issues too important to leave unremarked. One of the most intricate mechanisms in an intricate novel, its workings bear directly on the problem of interpreting Stephen's development. Questions of characterization join with questions of genre, and the relationship between individual agency and impersonal form becomes vivid. In elaborate, though submerged, patterns the diary reinterprets the narrative that it will soon conclude and offers some trenchant answers to a question that governs the novel as it governs this essay: What is the shape of a life?

Those who have not neglected the conclusion of *A Portrait of the Artist* have typically mentioned it only to express their dismay. Edward Garnett, reporting on the manuscript for Duckworth, spoke of the ending as "a complete falling to bits; the pieces of writing and the thoughts are all in pieces and they fall like damp, ineffective rockets." More recently Kenneth Grose has called it a "flat ending" which contains "many trivialities and unexplained references." The few attempts to interpret this puzzling conclusion have usually tried to understand it by assimilating it—either to Stephen's own theory of genre or to the larger design of Joyce's career. Susan Lanser, for instance, holds that the diary is Stephen's lyric but Joyce's drama, while Anthony Burgess, addressing the problem biographically, writes that the diary entries "anticipate, in their clipped lyricism and impatient ellipsis, the interior monologue of *Ulysses.*" Both approaches have their merits, but in each case the novel's ending tends to disappear, lost in the configurations brought forth to explain it.[2] The method of proceeding here will be to acknowledge the diary as an independent genre with its own norms and ambiguities, and then to pay close attention to its particular manifestation in Joyce's novel, where it reveals technical virtuosity in the service of larger fictional concerns. Consequently, this essay will move from considerations of genre to textual niceties, since it is between genre and text that the character of Stephen Dedalus hangs suspended.

According to Robert Martin Adams, "the final pages [of *A Portrait of the Artist*] splinter into isolated and laconic entries in a diary, which is anticlimactic unless one estimates its purpose as the detachment of Stephen Dedalus from what has, after all, been the world of his past, and the preparation of his mind for a launch into the future."[3] Adams alludes here to what one might, without being invidious, call the sentimental view of the novel's ending, which regards the final pages as a decisive expression of revolt. The shift to the first person then appears as an assertion of individuality and a repudiation of public norms. Thus Marilyn French writes that "having searched among many kinds of linguistic structurings of experience, Stephen creates his own—his diary." In Lanser's terms, the "public self" finally gives way to the private self; narrative detachment yields to personal expression: Stephen begins to compose his life in his own language.[4] Moreover, within a novel that has only vaguely indicated the movement of time, the diary allows Stephen to engage with time, to measure his development in a precise way and so to complete the pattern of the *Bildungsroman*, which culminates in that break with the past and preparation for the future to which Adams refers. In this sense the diary is a new mode of writing for a new mode of living. The question, of course, is whether it is something else besides.

1

Sir Arthur Ponsonby, that indefatigable collector of English diaries, offered a useful working definition of the form as "the daily or periodic record of personal experience and impressions"—a characterization that succinctly identifies two leading features of the genre: intimacy and periodicity.[5] For if a first convention of the diary demands fidelity to the experience of its author, a second requires this fidelity to be sustained over time, and sustained in some regular way. But as we former diarists all know, personal experience and periodic accounting do not always consort well together, and the commitment to regularity can quickly become a burden and even a source of shame. The pages of diary keepers are full of self-recriminations and hopeful new resolves. "Hold fast to the diary from today on!" enjoins Kafka, "Write regularly! Don't surrender!" Fanny Burney regrets that she "let this month creep along unrecorded," because she "could not muster courage for a journal," and she promises "to avoid any future long arrears." Burney's economic image is telling; it indicates the element of compulsion built into a form in which the writer incurs a new debt every day. "I have so long accustomed myself to write a Diary," says Boswell, "that when I omit it the day seems to be lost." At the extreme, which Boswell wittily anticipates, the diary ceases merely to reflect one's life and begins to govern it: "Sometimes it has occurred to me that a man should not live longer than he can record, as a farmer should not have a larger crop than he can gather in."[6]

The rhythm of the form has a further and disquieting consequence: it makes ending difficult. Once begun, the diary silently imposes the obligation to continue. This is the tyranny of the genre: it makes no provision for an end. Indeed, in important respects it is incompatible with an aesthetically or morally satisfying culmination. One of the most rending aspects of the diary of Alice James is that after she has delivered a courageous moral summation she lives longer than she had expected and her diary continues past her eloquent valediction to become a record of confusion, regret, and pain. By its governing convention the diary must unfold as life unfolds, and any attempt to bring it to conclusion will always invite the question: Why stop here? Behind that question looms another: How can one be sure that one *has* stopped?

These questions have a direct bearing on *A Portrait of the Artist as a Young Man*. A novel on the point of reaching its end suddenly alters to a form that only uneasily accommodates an end. In careless paraphrases it is sometimes said that the novel concludes with Stephen's exile from Ireland; in fact, of course, it does no such thing. In the last scene before the diary begins, Stephen tells Cranly of his decision to leave, but a month later he is still in Dublin, writing in his journal. The entry of 16 April begins, "Away! Away!" and Stephen describes himself as "making ready to go."[7] However, ten days of silence pass before he announces a new resolve, "to forge in the smithy of my soul the uncreated conscience of my race" (253). This surely has the ring of finality, but Stephen lingers at least one more day, making his appeal to "Old father, old artificer" (253), and here the diary and the novel cease, before the exile-to-be has taken his first step.

Stephen's intention to break with the past is evident, but that intention, restated from day to day, acquires a past of its own; his romantic revolt threatens to become a tradition. Even as one grants Stephen's sincerity on each occasion, the repetitions create a cadence that risks turning the promised culmination into an ongoing sequence of culminations, with each trumping the one before until the spirit of revolt begins to languish. As the novel ends, the diary patiently awaits the next entry, and even the reader who shares the ardor of 27 April must begin to suspect that 28 April will bring not exile, only more ardor.

This is not just a difficulty for the reader, nor does it appear for the first time at the conclusion of the novel. Stephen himself has consistently worried over endings, from his early concern that "he did not know where the universe ended" (17) to his moment of anxiety during a late conversation with Cranly: "Stephen, struck by [Cranly's] tone of closure, reopened the discussion at once" (243). The refusal of closure represents a powerful motive for Stephen; his succession of rebellions can be seen as attempts to avoid closed forms, to "reopen discussion." The proud cry of the aspiring artist, "On and on and on and on!" (172) is a demand for a perpetual crossing of limits, a resolute march to the end of the universe. Yet, as Hugh Kenner has noticed, "on and on and on and on" carries an ominous undertone.[8] There is perhaps one "on" too many. The cry of romantic freedom begins to resemble the plaint of Sisyphus. When at the end of the novel Stephen makes his stirring vow "to encounter for the millionth time the reality of experience" (253), the magnitude of the number implies a deed equally grand, but it must not blind us to an unnerving implication. Either Stephen has *already* encountered experience many times, or many others have encountered it before him. In either case, his defiant act of individuality is only the latest instance, the millionth instance, of a persistently repeated gesture.

Thus a leading pattern in the novel is the *series*, which depends not on movement toward an end but on the recurrence of identities and similarities. Examples of serial form include several structural devices that have figured prominently in discussions of *A Portrait of the Artist*—for example, the repetition of motifs and Stephen's oscillation between achievement and decline—as well as such diverse manifestations as the villanelle, the many lists, and the frequent verbal alternations (for example, "First came the vacation and then the next term and then vacation again and then again another term and then again the vacation" [17]). The novel, in other words, relies heavily on a formal principle that challenges finality with repetition and that encourages a view of Stephen as bound within a perpetually unfolding series—as the sort of character, that is, who having done a thing once, would as soon do it a million times. Though not aimed at Stephen, a question in the hellfire sermon hits him squarely: "Why did you not, even after you had fallen the first or the second or the third or the fourth or the hundredth time, repent of your evil ways and turn to God?" (123). The threat is that obsessive repetition will turn the individual into something abstract and mechanical, and it should be clear that Joyce means to contemplate just such a threat.

After the ecstatic vision that leads to the writing of the villa-nelle, Stephen raises a pertinent question: "Was it an instant of enchantment only or long hours and days and years and ages?" (217). As in many other places, Stephen imagines the epiphanic moment stretching endlessly outward, unfolding into eternity, but this visionary prospect coincides in disturbing ways with the image of damnation as "an evil of boundless extension, of limitless duration" (130). Indeed, one of the most forbidding implications in the plotting of Stephen's character is precisely the suggestion that the revelatory moment may prolong itself through "hours and days and years and ages," and so prevent not only a satisfying culmination but even the consolations of catastrophe. The en-chanted instant that lasts forever has its mirror image in the prospect of Stephen "falling, falling but not yet fallen, still un-fallen but about to fall" (162).

It should be evident that the conventions of the *Bildungsroman* cannot be assimilated to the pattern of serial repetition. The *Bil-dungsroman* presupposes some principle of development, which in turn presupposes some concept of an end. To the extent that Joyce's novel depends on these conventions, the image of the exiled artist serves as its end, as the point against which devel-opment can be measured.[9] To our question—What is the shape of a life?—the upward curve of *Bildung* suggests one answer, the unswerving line of repetitions another. A first approach to the question of character in *A Portrait of the Artist* must acknowledge both formal principles and acknowledge, too, that they complete.

It is at the novel's conclusion that they compete most directly, and this is an initial reason for paying attention to Stephen's diary, part of whose force is that it confirms both patterns. The ambiguity between novelty and similarity inheres in the genre: on the one hand, the precisely dated entries ensure an advance through time; on the other hand, the unit of form is methodically reiterated. A harmless manifestation of this ambiguity can be found in Pepys where the sometimes harsh notes of change are muted by the gentle drumming of that "Up" which begins so many of his daily accounts. In *A Portrait of the Artist* the conflict is sharper and aligns with our earlier distinction between personality and periodicity. The diary places intimate conviction, certain that it has at last identified its purpose, in the context of an ongoing series of intimacies. It provides a record of development through the mode of repetition, creating the disturbingly ambiguous image of a young man finally becoming an artist for the millionth time.

Even this image, however, is too simple, and it does not yet lead to an interpretation of Stephen's character that departs significantly from certain prevailing views. But it establishes terms for the argument to follow, where it will be possible to bring forward some new evidence and to suggest some new conclusions. Here the analysis will become unavoidably more detailed, since it will be necessary to pursue Joyce to the level of composition where his secrets are better kept and their exposure is more satisfying.

II

A source for Stephen's diary was undoubtedly Turgenev's *The Diary of a Superfluous Man*. Joyce had read it by 1904 at the urging of Stanislaus, who records in *his* diary his elder brother's unilluminating opinion: "I asked him what he thought about it. He said he thought the man very like me. This was my idea too."[10] In a letter of 1905, Joyce wrote dismissively of Turgenev, whom he compared unfavorably to Lermontov;[11] on the other hand, we learn in *Stephen Hero* that young Dedalus "had read and admired certain translations of Turgeniéff's novels and stories." Joyce himself was sufficiently interested to acquire eleven volumes of the edition that Heinemann began to publish in 1910,[12] and whatever his final judgment of Turgenev, he did not hesitate to borrow from him.

Tchulkaturin, the protagonist of *The Diary of a Superfluous Man*, writes his diary in the last weeks of his life, beginning on 20 March. Stephen composes his diary in the final weeks of his Dublin life; he too begins on 20 March. This is the sort of superfine ligature that we have come to expect from Joyce, a scarcely perceptible stitch whose only contribution is to remind us that there is one more thread to follow. If we trace it back to Turgenev's novel, we discover first of all a number of rather slight anticipations of *A Portrait of the Artist*. It seems probable, for instance, that Tchulkaturin's maladroit appeal to his beloved Liza suggested an image for Stephen's final meeting with E———C———, and that the "Farewell, life!" of the superfluous man gave (by inversion) Stephen's roseate "Welcome, O Life!" (253). After a particularly bathetic piece of exposition, Tchulkaturin writes, "I have read over what I wrote yesterday, and was all but tearing up the whole manuscript. I think my story's too spun out and too sentimental."[13] In Stephen's leaner prose (leaner, that is, than the prose of Constance Garnett) this becomes, "Read what I wrote last night. Vague words for a vague emotion" (251).

This last example begins to raise a more substantial concern. As opposed to the memoir or the autobiography, which typically are written from a fixed standpoint, the diary must continually change its perspective. Its retrospective view is daily rendered obsolete as life outstrips the diary; each entry brings a new retrospect, inviting a restless process of self-correction and self-revision. In this aspect of the genre, it is *reversal* not repetition that challenges the prospect of uninterrupted individual development. "Could his mind then not trust itself?" (233) Stephen had wondered, and the diary reveals a mind increasingly suspicious of its own habits. The entry of 30 March concludes with a fanciful *mot*—"Then into Nilemud with it!"—and the next day's account consists only of the observation, "Disapprove of this last phrase" (250). When Cranly had pressed him to admit that he was happy in his early religious conviction, Stephen had responded, "I was someone else then" (240), and one of the effects of the diary is to make this self-obsolescence more rapid, opening the possibility that Stephen will reverse himself from sentence to sentence. He risks becoming "someone else" at every new utterance, as in the account of his final meeting with E—— C——, where he contemplates a "new feeling": "Then, in that case, all the rest, all that I thought I thought and all that I felt I felt, all the rest before now, in fact . . . O, give it up, old chap! Sleep it off!" (252).

This problem becomes still more severe when the diary is situated in relation to the third-person narrative that precedes it. For perhaps the most telling idea that Joyce derived from *The Diary of a Superfluous Man* was that an intimate account of the present could become an involuntary record of the past, and that the self could never know how much of its life history it might inadvertently disclose. As Tchulkaturin nears the end of his life, an old romantic misadventure comes to dominate his thoughts, and even as his death approaches he adverts to his old failure rather than to his impending fate. Joyce, too, turns Stephen's present reflections into a commentary on the past, but his methods are characteristically more athletic. The diary's "events and conversations which baffle us by their incongruity and seeming unimportance"[14] possess an active underlife where they are neither incongruous nor unimportant.

The record of 25 March recalls a "troubled night of dreams," the first of which Stephen describes in this way:

A long curving gallery. From the floor ascend pillars of dark vapours. It is peopled by the images of fabulous kings, set in stone. Their hands are folded upon their knees, in token of weariness and their eyes are darkened for the errors of men go up before them for ever as dark vapours. (249–50)

The dream receives no commentary; it is placed in no context, but it constructs its own context through a cipher that we must learn to read. The "errors of men" had been at issue before in the novel, in the third chapter during the period of Stephen's crippling guilt, relieved at last when he confesses his sins. At that culminating moment he feels that "his prayers *ascended* to heaven from his purified heart like perfume streaming upwards from a heart of white rose" (145; my emphasis); in his dream there "ascend pillars of dark vapours."[15] If the verbal parallel stopped here, one could dismiss it as incidental. But the word "vapours" immediately secures another connection, appearing twice in the diary and twice during the scene at the church where the sound of a penitent floats "in vaporous cloudlets out of the box," a "soft whispering vapour" (142). Furthermore and decisively, the "token of weariness" in Stephen's dream recalls the "token of forgiveness" that he had received from the priest (145). The dream, that is, glances back to the confession through a set of masked references which, however, invoke the earlier event only to recast its implications. In place of the joyous ascent of prayers (from "a heart of white rose"), Stephen envisions the ascent of dark vapors; the token of forgiveness becomes a token of weariness; and the priest, with hand "raised above" Stephen, gives way to those dark-eyed kings with hands "folded upon their knees," heedless of the "errors of men." Through a series of linguistic transpositions, the triumph of the confession is overturned, and we are left with the bleak dreamscape where human sins ("the errors of men") win no remission but pass before dark eyes in stony faces.

Stephen himself betrays no awareness of the connection between the dream and the earlier incident, but the startling method of the diary is to look past conscious recognitions in favor of subterranean relations established among words themselves. Stephen had regarded language, together with nationality and religion, as a collective form that inhibited the freedom of the artist, and as will become clear, the final movement of the novel plays out a drama between the individual speaker and the speech of the tribe. His language knows what Stephen may not. Here is the entry of 5 April:

Wild spring. Scudding clouds. O life! Dark stream of swirling
bogwater on which appletrees have cast down their delicate
flowers. Eyes of girls among leaves. Girls demure and romping.
All fair or auburn: no dark ones. They blush better. Houp-la!
(250–51)

The word "wild" should itself be enough to send us back to the
epiphany on Dublin Bay, to a sequence such as this: "He was
unheeded, happy and near to the *wild* heart of life. He was alone
and young and wilful and *wild*hearted, alone amid a waste of *wild*
air and brackish waters" (171; my emphases). The word and its
variants appear a dozen times in the few pages of the scene. The
second phrase from the diary, "scudding clouds," calls to mind
the phrase that arouses Stephen's artistic piety: "A day of dappled
seaborne clouds" (166). "O life!" returns us to his euphoric pledge:
"To live, to err, to fall, to triumph, to recreate life out of life"
(172). The "swirling bogwater" had been anticipated in "shallow
swirling water" (166), "appletrees" in "apple orchards" (166). At
this point the diary, like the epiphany that it recalls, turns to
Stephen's contemplation of young girls, but in keeping with the
altered mood, the later vision displays none of the romantic reverence of the earlier scene. The girl Stephen had admired on the
bay had "long fair hair" and thighs "softhued as ivory" (171),
while in the later description he offers a jaunty appraisal of not
one fair girl but several. "All fair or auburn: no dark ones," and
his Paterian metaphor—"a faint flame trembled on her cheek"
(171)—now becomes rudely literal: "They blush better." The sacred aura of the epiphany yields to the levity of the diary, a
transformation well emphasized in the final link between the
scenes. In the last lines of chapter 4, Stephen compares the rim
of the moon to "the rim of a silver hoop" (173). And how does
that entry of 5 April conclude?[16] Look for yourself.
    The diary abounds with such echoes of earlier passages, repe-
titions of key words, puns, verbal substitutions. Long sequences
from the earlier narrative reappear in a form of symbolic notation
that allows Joyce to compress events and implications. Beneath
the casual surface of Stephen's personal record, there is an ex-

traordinary linguistic density, and here, as elsewhere in Joyce, one might speak of a linguistic unconscious which carries meanings that do not depend on the intentions of the speaker. It scarcely needs saying that this cunning technique violates one of the most familiar assumptions about the diary form: that it aspires to be a perfect transparency, that it is indeed the sincere literary form par excellence. Sincere Stephen may be, but it is plain that his diary is a mocking and duplicitous thing. Quite apart from Stephen's own perceptions, his language itself establishes connections, sees resemblances, marks differences. A space opens between the self and its form of representation. Stephen has high romantic intentions, but his language has intentions of its own.

Kenner has pointed out that the first two pages of *A Portrait of the Artist* "enact the entire action in microcosm";[17] as will become increasingly clear, the diary serves as an epilogue that does not merely conclude the action of the novel but recapitulates it through an elaborate set of veiled references.

22 *March*: In company with Lynch followed a sizable hospital nurse. Lynch's idea. Dislike it. Two lean hungry greyhounds walking after a heifer. (248)

It was with Lynch that Stephen had pursued the theory of aesthetics, offering his definition of art, drawing distinctions between static and kinetic emotions, characterizing pity and terror, describing the rhythm of beauty, until Lynch impatiently interrupts, "But what is beauty?" "Let us take woman," suggests Stephen. "Let us take her!" says Lynch "fervently" (208). The diary, that is, exploits the link between aesthetics and erotics; the pursuit of beauty becomes the pursuit of a "sizable hospital nurse" (during their conversation, Lynch and Stephen had walked past "the corner of sir Patrick Dun's hospital" [209]). The rarefied principles of Aquinas fall heavily to earth and Stephen, who had venerated that "static" emotion in which the "mind is arrested and raised above desire and loathing," succumbs to the "kinetic" emotion that "urges us to possess, to go to something." "We are all animals," Stephen had confessed, "I also am an animal." "You are," agrees Lynch (205–6). Within the diary, accordingly, both young men metamorphose into greyhounds, and beauty, having been a hospital nurse, becomes a heifer. Please recall that during the earlier conversation Lynch admits to having eaten "pieces of dried cowdung" (205); that Stephen poses the question, *"If a man hacking in fury at a block of wood . . . make there an image of a cow, is that image a work of art?"* (214),[18] and that when he defines *integritas* Lynch responds, "Bull's eye!" (212).

In each of these examples, as telling as the submerged references to a past scene is the rhetorical inflection that the new context provides. The exultation of the confession becomes the troubled dream, much as the romantic euphoria on the bay passes into an almost jaded sensualism, and the rather ponderous disquisition on art transforms into a sexual prowl. In looking for a way to characterize these changes, we might consider the second of the dreams that Stephen records on the morning of 25 March:

> Strange figures advance from a cave. They are not as tall as men. One does not seem to stand quite apart from another. Their faces are phosphorescent, with darker streaks. They peer at me and their eyes seem to ask me something. They do not speak. (250)

Once the general pattern has been recognized, this reference can be quickly identified. It points back to Stephen's horrific vision after the hellfire sermon, when he returns to his room, terror-stricken, too shaken at first to pass through the door: "He waited still at the threshold as at the entrance to some dark cave. Faces were there; eyes: they waited and watched" (136). In another page these become "goatish creatures," "lightly bearded," lit by "marshlight" (137); in the dream they are "not as tall as men," with "darker streaks" on their "phosphorescent" faces.

At present, more significant than this connection is a suggestion that might be drawn from it. It should be clear, first of all, that the "lecherous goatish fiends" with their "human faces," who move "hither and thither trailing their long tails behind them" (137–38), are satyrs, who appear during Stephen's crisis to taunt him for his fall into sensuality. Their reappearance in his dream suggests a way to regard the series of reversals at the novel's conclusion. For in one of its aspects Stephen's diary follows the precedent of the Greek satyr play, which concluded a tetralogy by replacing tragic gravity with comedy and parody. Much like a satyr play, the diary recalls motifs that had been treated seriously and casts them in a comic light, tweaking the solemnity that precedes it. Through the set of concealed references that we have been considering, decisive moments in the main narrative are invoked—the vision of hell, the confession, the affirmation of art, the meditation on beauty—but the tone has thoroughly changed, with the result that events which Stephen had regarded with grave earnestness now appear within a deft parody, almost a burlesque. Without disturbing the thematic surface which dutifully records Stephen's emotions and aspirations, Joyce dexterously suggests competing modes of interpretation. In the first implication pursued in this essay, the diary enforced a principle of serial repetition that challenged Stephen's confident advance, but here the challenge has become both more fundamental and better disguised. The quietly shifting mode intimates that while Stephen strikes heroic poses, his language plays a comedy.

III

This diary, which had seemed a harmless fizzle, an elusive whimsy, or an ill-motivated contrivance, discloses itself as a precise instrument of many and ingenious purposes. Its methods will ultimately need to be weighed against other methods in the novel, but already it seems fair to say that the provocations of the diary, coming as they do at such a sensitive moment, have a special privilege and oblige us to take them into account in any interpretation of the whole.

To this point, the considerations offered here would seem to lend more weight to that already weighty body of opinion that regards *A Portrait of the Artist* as preeminently an ironic novel. Certainly, the submerged references to the past and the recasting of momentous incidents in a parodic mode make it impossible to take Stephen's concluding pronouncements at their own valuation. He emits a tone of intrepid temerity, but other, less-heroic tones sound in muffled counterpoint. He marches into the future, surrounded by jeering echoes of the past, and when he makes his impetuous promise "to forge in the smithy of my soul the uncreated conscience of my race" (253), one must suspect that his own conscience has already been forged. He has vowed to "fly by those nets" of nationality, language, and religion (203), but at least one of those nets, the fine mesh of language, continues to trammel the artist who would be free. And yet, before drawing an ironic conclusion from these disturbing facts, we ought to consider one last flourish of Joycean virtuosity.

A Portrait of the Artist concludes with the apostrophe of 27 April—"old father, old artificer, stand me now and ever in good stead" (253)—and it is common to say that Stephen is speaking here not of his biographical father but of his mythical parent, the "hawklike man," "the fabulous artificer" whose name is "a symbol of the artist" (169). Certainly, the mythical reference is pertinent. But it is worth recalling that Simon Dedalus makes his first appearance precisely as an artificer who recounts the story of the "moocow" and "baby tuckoo." The novel, that is, begins with the father as storyteller and ends by invoking him as "old artificer."

The *second* person in the novel to tend Stephen is also the *second to last*, his mother, whose tasks have only nominally changed. When young Stephen wet the bed, "his mother put on the oilsheet" (7), and when an older Stephen prepares to leave Ireland, he describes her as "putting my new secondhand clothes in order" (252). Between an oil sheet and new secondhand clothes there is perhaps less to choose than an ambitious young artist would hope.

The preceding entry, 16 April, is a slightly revised version of one of Joyce's early epiphanies, which had also appeared in *Stephen Hero* and which contains the following passage:

> The spell of arms and voices: the white arms of roads, their promise of close embraces and the black arms of tall ships that

stand against the moon, their tale of distant nations. They are
held out to say: We are alone. Come. And the voices say with
them: We are your kinsmen. (252)

The original version of the epiphany had "people" where we now
find "kinsmen," and that change, together with the placement,
connects this *third-to-last* passage with the *third* sequence in the
prologue, in which Charles and Dante, Stephen's "kinsmen,"
make their first appearance as the ones who clap during the
singing and dancing. In the diary, this becomes the "spell of arms
and voices."

The next event in the prologue involves Stephen's early fantasy
of marrying Eileen Vance, while the *previous* entry in the diary, 15
April, describes the awkward final meeting with his current romantic avatar, E——C——. In the childhood incident, the idea
of marrying Eileen, a Protestant, provokes a threat of punishment.
In Joyce's original epiphany, the threat had been attributed to Mr.
Vance, but in *A Portrait of the Artist* it is assigned to "Aunt" Dante,
a decision that prepares for another cunning link between prologue and epilogue. For when Stephen feels "sorry and mean"
over his treatment of E——C—— he checks himself by suddenly
invoking "the spiritual-heroic refrigerating apparatus, invented
and patented in all countries by *Dante* Alighieri" (252; my emphasis).

Finally, the specific threat that concludes the prologue should
be recalled: if Stephen does not apologize, "the eagles will come
and pull out his eyes" (8). In the mysterious entry of 14 April,
Stephen records a description of an old man from the west of
Ireland, as it has been reported to him by John Alphonsus Mulrennan. Mulrennan quotes the old man as saying, "Ah, there
must be terrible queer creatures at the latter end of the world."
"I fear him," writes Stephen of the old man, "It is with him I
must struggle all through this night till day come, till he or I lie
dead" (252). In itself, this response to a man he has never met
appears thoroughly mysterious, but in light of the broader pattern, there is reason to believe—is there not?—that "the terrible
queer creatures" revive a memory of those eagles bringing retri-

bution, as does the old man himself, who in his "mountain cabin" (his aerie?), with his "short pipe" (beak?), his "redrimmed horny eyes," and "his sinewy throat" seems more bird than man.

Allow me, then, to register an implication that may already be evident. The novel begins with the sequence: father telling a story, mother putting on the oil sheet, Charles and Dante, the fantasy of marrying Eileen, Dante's threat, the eagles. It concludes with "terrible queer creatures," E———C——— and Dante Alighieri, the "kinsmen," mother putting his clothes in order, old father, old artificer. With unfailing verbal dexterity, Joyce concludes the novel by alluding to its beginning and, what is more, by inverting the initial order of events. In an elegantly disguised chiasmus, *A Portrait of the Artist* ends by reversing its opening.[19] It retraces its own steps and concludes where it began.

This last thrust not only wounds an aspiring artist; it constitutes a final assault upon the diary as a genre and, by extension, upon time itself. On its surface the diary lays claim to an unambiguous temporal progression, a resolute march into the future, duly measured and duly chronicled. It therefore encourages that sentimental view of the conclusion that regards Stephen as advancing steadily toward his new life. Within this view the distant past has ceased to matter; the artist ministers to the present in service of the future. Or, as Stephen himself puts it on 6 April, "The past is consumed in the present and the present is living only because it brings forth the future" (251). When Cranly had asked about his early life, Stephen had responded that he was not then "myself as I am now, as I had to become" (240), and he later wonders whether he "was ever a child" (251). He willfully orients himself toward an unformed future, dismissing the importunity of the past: "Michael Robartes remembers forgotten beauty and, when his arms wrap her round, he presses in his arms the loveliness which has long faded from the world. Not this. Not at all. I desire to press in my arms the loveliness which has not yet come into the world" (251).

The burden of this essay, of course, has been that the past is most important in this novel when it is least respected and that the diary, committed to the sentiments of the present as they prepare the future, is haunted with echoes of early life, which recur with a mocking persistence. Indeed, as the most recent example shows, the past does not merely echo in the present; it threatens to govern the future. The submerged pattern of events suggests that Stephen's bright promise is no more than "new secondhand clothes."

At the opening of the third chapter, Stephen had watched as the "equation on the page of his scribbler began to spread out a widening tail" and then "began slowly to fold itself together again." He imagines the equation as "his own soul going forth to experience, unfolding itself sin by sin, spreading abroad the balefire of its burning stars and folding back upon itself, fading slowly, quenching its own lights and fires" (103). The phrase "going forth to experience" anticipates the climactic promise to "encounter for the millionth time the reality of experience," but the further notion of a soul "folding back upon itself" gives us another way to regard that promise. It provides a compelling image for the chiastic inversions at the novel's close and suggests the darkest of answers to our question: What is the shape of a life? Moreover, it broadens the import of Joyce's allusions to Turgenev, for in terms of this conceit Stephen appears as just that "superfluous man" whose life folds back upon itself in a long retrogression. Just as he means to begin the future, the form suggests that he is receding into his past, that he is boldly advancing— toward his origins.

The individual artist who seeks "to discover the mode of life or of art whereby [his] spirit could express itself in unfettered freedom" (246) participates, in spite of himself, in a meticulously contrived form that silently contests this possibility. The novel, at the last, establishes a severe and unsettling disjunction between what Stephen means and what he says, between freedom and form.

The question of irony thus returns with a sharp force. If Stephen—who means to soar into the future—is last seen descending into the past, if the verbal echoes suggest that he is confined to the history he has disowned, and if the pattern of events intimates that what he takes to be progress may only be movement around a circle, then it is impossible to read the conclusion in the terms that Stephen himself offers. It would seem, on the contrary, that we must disregard the literal surface and, as in so many recent readings of the novel, assume an ironic standpoint putatively congruent with Joyce's own. Seen in such terms the diary would represent the severe conclusion of Joyce's spurning of his own protagonist, in which the arrangement of words and events opens a widening distance between what Stephen intends and what Joyce intends for him.

However, the provocation offered at the novel's conclusion is so great that it not only disturbs the literal surface; it stirs the ironic depths. In one of its implications, as I began by noting, the diary seems to herald a sequence of endless repetitions in which Stephen, always on the point of freedom and therefore never free, will ceaselessly reenact past events and reexperience past emotions. At the same time, it suggests a series of reversals in which incidents and emotions recur in debased form, the serious rendered comic, the grave made playful. Finally, the last paragraphs of the novel subtly intimate that Stephen will revert to his original condition and that what he takes as exile will be a return.

All of these possibilities, it is true, challenge a simple pattern of artistic maturity, but it is worth stressing that they constitute not one but many assaults. Much like sentimentality, irony has its variants, and before settling upon an ironic reading one must surely ask: Which irony? As with the historical and mythological parallels that link Stephen to Parnell, Christ, Daedalus, Icarus, and James Joyce (among others), the several ironies do not coincide, and we must avoid assuming that all departures from the literal surface arrive at the same figural destination. Indeed, in an important sense, the multiple ironies restore the integrity of a literal reading, because they prevent the simplicity of a yea or nay.[20] Repetition and reversal certainly challenge the ideal of undisturbed personal development, but they also challenge one another. At the end of the novel, we confront at least four forms of the individual life: a pattern of *Bildung* (Stephen will become the artist he has aspired to be); a pattern of repetition (he will remain where he has arrived); a pattern of reversal (he will rehearse serious events in a comic mode); and a pattern of regression (he will return to where he began). To those who would object that these diverse alternatives discourage judgment of Stephen's character, the question might be put: What judgment is more appropriate for youth than to connect its ambition to all its possible issues?[21]

In another context, John Gross has bluntly formulated the question that has dominated interpretation of Stephen's character: "How exactly are we to take all this?"[22] But in a sense the critical locution is itself a source of the problem. The reader does not need to "take" Stephen—to wrench him from the dense web that surrounds him, to appropriate him to a single mode, to assimilate him to a controlling myth—but to *place* him, to situate him within a set of concurrent possibilities and to embed him in several modes. The persistent contention over the novel's irony threatens to obscure its workings. Joyce is less concerned to submit sentiment to the astringencies of irony than to conjoin all pertinent implications and to disclose the copresence of incongruous designs. Stronger than the attraction of irony is the allure of the pun, which depends not upon a collision but upon a union of meanings and which functions at every level of Joyce's work. Stephen's diary represents an elaborate narrative pun in which one sequence of events yields several lines of development, and Stephen himself exists as both romantic personality and modern *paronomasia*. He is more than his qualities: he is all those forms in which his life inheres, the myths which enclose him, the past which begot him, the prospects which await him. This is the heavy burden that Joycean character must bear; it must be all that it has been and all that it might become.

Notes

1. Exceptions include Zack R. Bowen. "Epiphanies, Stephen's Diary, and the Narrative Perspective of *A Portrait of the Artist as a Young Man,"* *James Joyce Quarterly* 16 (Summer 1979): 485–88; Susan Sniader Lanser, "Ste-

phen's Diary: The Hero Unveiled," *James Joyce Quarterly* 16 (Summer 1979) 417–24: John Paul Riquelme, *Teller and Tale* (Baltimore, Md.: Johns Hopkins University Press, 1983).

2. Edward Garnett, quoted in Richard Ellmann, *James Joyce* (New York: Oxford University Press, 1959), 417; Kenneth Grose, *James Joyce* (London: Evans, 1975), 39; Lanser, "Stephen's Diary," 418–19; Anthony Burgess, *Re Joyce* (New York: Norton, 1965), 68.

3. Robert Martin Adams, *Afterjoyce* (New York: Oxford University Press, 1977), 21.

4. Marilyn French, "Joyce and Language," *James Joyce Quarterly* 19 (Spring 1982): 250; Lanser, "Stephen's Diary," 420.

5. Arthur Ponsonby, *English Diaries* (London: Methuen, 1923), 1.

6. Franz Kafka, *Diaries 1900–1913*, trans. Joseph Kresh, ed. Max Brod (New York: Schocken, 1965), 233; Fanny Burney, *The Diary and Letters*, vol. 2, ed. Sarah Chauncey Woolsey (Boston: Little, Brown, 1902), 172; James Boswell, "The Hypochondriack," no. 66 (March 1783), in *The Hypochondriack*, ed. Margery Bailey (Stanford, Calif.: Stanford University Press, 1928), 266, 259.

7. James Joyce, *A Portrait of the Artist as a Young Man* (Harmondsworth, England: Penguin, 1976), 252. Subsequent references to this edition will be cited parenthetically within the text.

8. Hugh Kenner, *Dublin's Joyce* (Boston: Beacon, 1962), 132.

9. It is worth observing that the end toward which the *Bildungsroman* points need not appear within the fiction itself. It can exist as the implied *telos* that organizes the whole. Jerome Hamilton Buckley has offered the firmest argument for the pertinence of these conventions: "the *Portrait* is developed within the recognizable general framework of the Bildungsroman. It is an autobiographical novel of 'education,' tracing the growth of the hero from infancy to young manhood, describing his slowly decreased dependence on father and mother, his schooldays, his adolescent fantasies, his choice of a career, and his ultimate approach to his maturity or at least to his legal majority" (*Season of Youth* [Cambridge, Mass.: Harvard University Press, 1971], 230).

10. Stanislaus Joyce, *The Complete Dublin Diary of Stanislaus Joyce* (Ithaca, N.Y.: Cornell University Press, 1971), 62. In his reminiscences written years later Stanislaus still had Turgenev's novella on his mind: "The conclusion of the *Diary*, with the man's face drawn on the blank space at the foot of the last page, and the aimless scribbling by someone who had found and read the diary after the unfortunate Tchulkaturin's

death, seemed to me a masterstroke in the expression of futility. Jim was interested; he said he would read it again" (Stanislaus Joyce, *My Brother's Keeper*, ed. Richard Ellmann [New York: Viking, 1958], 167–68). No doubt he did. Joyce was never one to defer to the masterstroke of a predecessor.

11. Letter to Stanislaus Joyce in *Letters of James Joyce*, vol. 2, ed. Richard Ellmann (New York: Viking, 1966), 111.

12. James Joyce, *Stephen Hero*, ed. Theodore Spencer, rev. ed. John J. Slocum and Herbert Cahoon (London: Jonathan Cape, 1969), 47. On Joyce's acquisition of Turgenev's works see the list of books Joyce left behind in Trieste, in Richard Ellmann, *The Consciousness of Joyce* (London: Faber & Faber, 1977), 131.

13. Ivan Turgenev, *The Diary of a Superfluous Man*, trans. Constance Garnett (London: Heinemann, 1906), 95. For the similarity of the romantic confrontations compare, for instance, the two disruptive physical gestures. Tchulkaturin: "suddenly, without awaiting her reply, I gave my features an extraordinarily cheerful and free-and-easy expression with a set grin, passed my hand above my head in the direction of the ceiling. . . . Liza failed absolutely to understand me; she looked in my face with amazement, gave a hasty smile, as though she wanted to get rid of me as quickly as possible" (36). Stephen: "In the midst of it unluckily I made a sudden gesture of a revolutionary nature. I must have looked like a fellow throwing a handful of peas into the air. . . . She shook hands a moment after and, in going away, said she hoped I would do what I said" (252).

14. Bowen, "Epiphanies," 487.

15. In the original version of the epiphany, Joyce wrote "arise" rather than "ascend" (*The Workshop of Dedalus*, ed. Robert Scholes and Richard M. Kain [Evanston, Northwestern University Press, 1963], 29). It should become clear as we proceed that in drawing on his store of epiphanies Joyce adjusted them to the text (and the text to them) in order to secure connections between the first-person diary and the third-person narrative.

16. In "Circe," which stands to *Ulysses* much as the diary stands to *A Portrait of the Artist* and which frequently recalls the earlier novel even as it recalls its own beginning, the English "hoop" and the Frenchified "houp-la" meet in Lynch's "Hoopla" (James Joyce, *Ulysses* [New York: Random House, 1961], 557).

17. Kenner, *Dublin's Joyce*, 114.

18. I have James Soderholm to thank for calling my attention to this sculptor hacking in fury.

19. Hans Walter Gabler has astutely identified another chiastic relation between the novel's opening and its close: "In its four-part structure, the fifth chapter of *A Portrait of the Artist* is the exact symmetrical counterpart of the first. The childhood overture and the two Clongowes episodes, separated by the Christmas dinner scene, are the mirror image of the two movements of Stephen's wanderings through Dublin, separated by the villanelle episode, and the diary finale. In both chapters, bibliographical and textual evidence reveals that the final organization of their parts was established by intercalation of a contrasting episode into a homogenous stretch of narrative" ("The Seven Lost Years of *A Portrait of the Artist as a Young Man*," in *Approaches to Joyce's Portrait*, ed. Thomas F. Staley and Bernard Benstock [Pittsburgh; Pa.: University of Pittsburgh Press 1976], 50).

20. Hugh Kenner has justly observed that "the sharpest exegetical instrument we can bring to the work of Joyce is Aristotle's great conception of potency and act.... [In] the mind of Joyce there hung a radiant field of multiple possibilities" ("The Cubist Portrait," in *Approaches to Joyce's Portrait*, ed. Staley and Benstock, 179).

21. Wayne Booth has posed the problem of judgment forcefully in *The Rhetoric of Fiction* (Chicago: University of Chicago Press, 1961), 323–26.

22. John Gross, *James Joyce* (New York: Viking, 1970), 34.

Framing, Being Framed,
and the Janus Faces of Authority

VICKI MAHAFFEY

◆　◆　◆

IN *A Portrait of the Artist as a Young Man*, Stephen Dedalus is represented as a sensitive reader of cultural signs, trying to forge
an identity for himself consistent with his patrimony. What he
shows through his erratic behavior is that his fathers have bequeathed him not one but two mutually incompatible models of
responding to righteous authority, and as the book progresses, we
watch Stephen alternating helplessly between an obedient and a
scornfully defiant response to the imperative to sacrifice himself
for a communal cause. The reason that Stephen is powerless to
detach himself from the pendulum swing of these two responses
is that he never questions the major premise of authority: its
idealization of ultimate transcendence.[1] Stephen's aim is to establish for himself an authority comparable to the authority he ad-
mires and resists, to see himself raised above his peers, and to
resist any awareness of the universality—the commonness—of
his feelings. Stephen fails to realize not only that his own reaction
to authority is ambivalent, but also that the authority he would
appropriate is itself split: its "head," or consciousness, is divided

from its body, or sensual apprehensions. Christian morality has denominated these two bases of authority as "good" and "evil," respectively, thereby delegitimating sensory perception as an important part of what it means to be human. It is difficult for Stephen to see that, when he periodically defies the injunction to become a martyred hero, he is not rejecting Christian morality so much as responding to another authority, that of the senses, which awakens him poetically to the color and music of language. Stephen remains bound to his confusion not only because he accepts the view that mental and sensual impulses are antithetical but also because he upholds a view of authority as something that transcends its human and social context. His salvation and temptation are mapped onto the "higher" and "lower" regions of an individual being; by focusing on the singularity of that being, he is able to disregard the social and linguistic traditions and conventions that to some extent frame every individual. *A Portrait of the Artist* urges readers to recognize the kind of contextual frames that Stephen himself disregards; while remembering the real if not unlimited capacity of a narrator to frame personal experience, in turn.

Portrait, like *Ulysses, Finnegans Wake*, and even *Dubliners*, explores the similarity and the tension between mental and sensory authorities. The authority Stephen initially prefers is the authority of deliberate intention, which produces cultural and religious heroes. Such authority, in its consciousness and rationality, works better in theory (and in crises) than in everyday practice, when it is easily undermined by less conscious desires. Stephen's language repeatedly reveals the conflict between will and hidden desire, between his intended meaning and the meaning that his metaphors imply. Joyce prompts us to hear, in the underlying figures that shape language less obtrusively than do conventionally determined meanings and logic, the clusters of puns that trace what James Merrill once called "the hidden wish of words."[2]

In *Portrait*, Stephen's model for sovereign authority—the authority of heroic self-sacrifice—is the head, which he associates with Christ. His metaphor for sensory authority and for rebellious uprising in his penis, which serves as an intimate embodiment of

Lucifer and of the romantic poets. In the end Stephen tries to reconcile mind and body by becoming an author, by appealing to words as authorities that combine meaning and sensuality, but, although Stephen is finally able to balance the rival claims of mind and body through language, he is not a self-conscious enough reader to understand the complex dialogical relation between words or texts, on the one hand, and the human, social contexts that both define and are explained by them, on the other.

Stephen's subconscious sensitivity to the "unauthorized," figurative, or poetic dimension of language is the source of the book's subtle humor. When, for example, the priest at the end of the third chapter tells him, "As long as you commit that sin, my poor child, you will never be worth one farthing to God" (*P*, 145), Stephen's conscious interpretation of the sentence acknowledges the priest's benevolent intention: he knows that the priest is urging him to reform so that his soul may regain its value in God's eyes. Unconsciously, however, he registers the economic nature of the metaphor very sharply, as we can see three pages later, when he pictures his devotion as a heavenly "sale": "[H]e seemed to feel his soul in devotion pressing like fingers the keyboard of a great cash register and to see the amount of his purchase start forth immediately in heaven, not as a number but as a frail column of incense or as a slender flower" (*P*, 148). Stephen has intuited the underlying materialism of what he believes to be a purely spiritual order, and he expresses his unauthorized knowledge through figures, illustrating his determination to ensure that he will be worth much more than one farthing to God. Like Issy in *Finnegans Wake*, who will "confess it by her figure and . . . deny it to your face,"[3] Stephen "knows" two faces of verbal meaning at any one time, one conventional and intentional, the other sensual and figurative. Stephen's approach to language is as concrete as his approach to materiality is abstract, but he lacks conscious awareness of the doubleness of his response. As a result, his two kinds of knowledge are frequently in conflict in a way that makes him unable to sustain either.

It is the conflict between the authorities Stephen consciously embraces and those that he unconsciously, but demonstrably, hears and responds to that makes the first four chapters of *Portrait* difficult to read.[4] Stephen's receptivity to conflicting authorities causes the reader to react to him with ambivalence: his acute sensitivity to the latent metaphoricity of language evokes sympathy from similarly "artistic" readers, but his willful insensitivity to the discrepancy between his intuitive knowledge and his rational determinations prompts sharply analytical readers to regard him ironically. Stephen's growing power to articulate and encompass his experience is similarly double-edged. As *Portrait* progresses, Stephen learns to double and redouble his story, which is itself a doubling of "history," producing a gradual enrichment of text and context. At first we may be tempted to see Stephen as an ever-widening frame who manages to recapitulate, in his mind and verse, the stylistic evolution of the nineteenth century from Byron through Pater. By the last chapter, however, it has become apparent that Stephen's very ability to appropriate various styles constitutes an artistic failure: his poetic productions are doubly derivative of his reading and of his adolescent emotions. It is at this point, when we see that Stephen himself has been "framed," that we are in a position to appreciate the way Joyce's language has succeeded in overspilling the boundaries of Stephen's consciousness. The power of Joyce's language to frame Stephen illuminates the power of Stephen's own language to surpass as well as contain his thought. Stephen's discoveries can never be more than recoveries as long as he refuses to see that authority has not one but two faces, and that those faces are always partially framed by the changing forces of history and language.

Authority as Double Bind

Joyce poses the problem of the double bind in both the first and last chapters of *Portrait*, bracketing the book with the dilemma it is meant to reproduce and leave behind. The first major event to leave its mark on Stephen's consciousness is the experience of being bullied—first by Wells, then by Father Dolan. When Wells

shoulders him into the square ditch, Stephen retaliates physio-
logically, by getting sick, and imaginatively, by intertwining his
story with history, envisioning himself as Little and Parnell, dead:
"And Wells would be sorry then for what he had done" (*P*, 24).
Stephen actively implements the same strategy when he is later
bullied by Father Dolan: in his effort to become a hero, he models
himself after a head—"some great person whose head was in the
books of history"—and in particular the great men mentioned
in Peter Parley's tales about Greece and Rome, whose names re-
sembled his own (*P*, 53, 55). He places his trust in heads or leaders
and in names, a trust that ultimately seems justified when the
rector fulfills the promise of his name and position by rectifying
Stephen's wrong.

The glory of Stephen's double triumph, imaginative and active—a triumph that transforms him in his own eyes into "Stephen Hero"—tends to overshadow the fact that Wells bullies him
twice, verbally as well as physically, and that Stephen fails to
understand the more subtle taunting that mocks his own habits
of mind. When Wells asks Stephen whether or not he kisses his
mother before he goes to bed, he implicitly limits the range of
responses to two mutually exclusive possibilities, so that, whether
Stephen answers yes or no, he is still bound by the configuration
of the question. The questioner retains his authority and reaffirms
his superiority as long as the respondent accepts the terms of the
question, a situation that bewilders Stephen when Wells and his
friends laugh at him: "Stephen tried to laugh with them. He felt
his whole body hot and confused in a moment. What was the
right answer to the question? He had given two and still Wells
laughed. But Wells must know the right answer for he was in
the third of grammar" (*P*, 14). What Stephen fails to see is that
Wells's question encapsulates the dilemma of distance that has
baffled not only Stephen but many of his readers as well. The
only way to escape ridicule is to reject not the gesture of kissing
and the love that gesture represents but the simplistic model of
relationship as something that is either neurotically close or unnaturally distant. Stephen never succeeds in escaping the domination of that question: his responses to his mother at the begin-

ning and end of the book—naive identification and insensitive independence—are his two answers to Wells writ large.

When Cranly asks Stephen a version of Wells's question near the end of the book—"Do you love your mother?"—Stephen answers, "I don't know what your words mean" (*P*, 240). By that point Stephen has learned to escape laughter but not the rhetorical tines of a two-pronged question. Ten days later, Cranly, who alone among Stephen's friends seems sympathetically interested in the dilemma, propounds the problem in an altered form to Dixon and to Emma's brother, as Stephen records in his diary: "A mother let her child fall into the Nile. Still harping on the mother. A crocodile seized the child. Mother asked it back. Crocodile said all right if she told him what he was going to do with the child, eat it or not eat it" (*P*, 250). The tone of easy familiarity that Stephen assumes in retelling the story is misleading in one sense but absolutely appropriate in another: the story of the mother and the crocodile exemplifies in an almost scholastic form the comic hopelessness of unnaturally limited alternatives, a trap that Stephen, despite his knowledgeable air, has never been able to elude. Like the mother who cannot save her child by giving the crocodile either of the answers he suggests, Stephen stands to lose no matter how he responds to the riddle of relationship as traditionally formulated. He has tried both answers (with Wells) and no answer (with Cranly), but neither his eagerness to give the appropriate answer nor his refusal to respond at all constitutes an effective challenge to the question.

Readers of *Portrait* who accept the model of relationship imposed by the questions of Wells, Cranly, and the crocodile are themselves caught in a cognitive trap that resembles Stephen's. Readers who choose to sympathize with Stephen without balancing such sympathy with a more detached analysis of Stephen's shortcomings may see a reflection of their propensity to identify with a superior figure when Stephen chooses to identify himself with a literary or historical "hero," such as Parnell Byron or Daedalus. As Stephen shows, such proclivities, while evidencing imagination and feeling, leave those who indulge them vulnerable to ridicule. If, on the other hand, the reader goes to the other extreme and reads everything ironically, the Stephen of chapter V again reflects the reader's own hauteur. An ironic reading must inevitably condemn Stephen for not knowing "what the heart is and what it feels" (*P*, 252) as he jauntily escapes to Paris, but readers who eschew sympathy altogether become guilty of the same dismissiveness they are criticizing.

Stephen continues to regard his attachment and vulnerability to others as a problem that must be categorically affirmed or denied, but elsewhere in the first chapter Joyce presents him with an alternative approach to the dilemma of relationship: he could restructure the question. When Stephen is in the infirmary suffering the consequences of Wells's bullying, Athy gives him a breezy reading lesson that takes his own name as its text. Having told Stephen that Athy is the name of a town, he asks him a riddle: "Why is the county Kildare like the leg of a fellow's breeches?" When Stephen gives up, Athy answers the riddle— "Because there is a thigh in it" (*P*, 25). He then challenges Stephen to ask the riddle another way, but when Stephen declares himself unable to reriddle the question, Athy refuses to help him. The reader, like Stephen, is being asked to reformulate old riddles ("That's an old riddle, he said" [*P*, 25]), to structure them in new ways. In the infirmary Athy presents to Stephen a way to get well (and to get Wells), but Stephen is still entranced with the old riddle of heroism and betrayal, as his subsequent vision of Parnell's death shows. When readers in the 1960s debated the question of our aesthetic distance from Stephen, they reenacted Stephen's own dilemma about authority. Whether defending or attacking Stephen's character, the reader is trapped by a single question and for that reason vulnerable to the laughter of more experienced schoolfellows. As we now know, both responses and neither response are appropriate. The "old" riddle of mutually exclusive possibilities must be analyzed and reformulated.

Athy's riddle has a significant structural feature: It does not explicitly recognize either the speaker's or the listener's investment in the riddle of naming. Although the riddle forges a relation between a town and a part of the leg, it fails to indicate that it is Athy's own name that makes such a pattern of relationship significant. The structure of the question makes it possible for the listener to separate the riddle from the context that makes it personally meaningful—its relation to the person recounting it, as well as its relevance to the person listening to it ("You have a queer name, Dedalus, and I have a queer name too, Athy" [*P*, 25]). The riddle allows us to bypass teller and auditor as named entities importantly implicated in the network of language and to focus instead on more coincidental and remote symmetries of sound. Finally, the riddle challenges us to link two different contexts that enclose a common sound—trousers containing a thigh, and a county that includes the town of Athy—and thus celebrates the power of auditory correspondence by presenting perceived incongruities as a problem that language solves. We are reminded of the power of names not only to represent but to integrate objective experience.

The only way to reformulate Athy's riddle is by challenging habitual assumptions about what it means to read. Our automatic reading practices allow us to abstract authors from their puzzles, honoring them as the operators of language and not as those upon whom language operates, an exemption that we can then extend to ourselves as readers. The curtaining off of authors and readers from the textual performance facilitates a denial of the ways that the text reflects not only the observer but also the author and the sociohistorical context. Instead of splitting ourselves off from the text, on the one hand, and the author, on the other, *Portrait* urges us recognize the many possible doubles that language offers us. "Doubling" is not only a process of recognizing our own potential reactions within a text—seeing our own features in different aspects of Joyce's portrait—but it also, like "Athy," echoes the name of an Irish town that geographically situates and silently authorizes the author's riddles.

In order to ask Athy's riddle "the other way," Stephen would have to revise his assumptions about language, seeing it as something that overflows the boundaries of any one of its formulations, its authority more capacious and capricious than that of the person or structure that gives it a momentary shape, but meaningless without a shape to exceed.[5] Moreover, he would have to be more consciously aware of the way that a text must interact with a variable context to produce meaning. He would have to recognize language as the sham double that makes reflection possible. *Ulysses* forces its readers toward such realizations: its willful opacity compels the reader to look *at* language, as well as trying to peer through it, and its disorienting panoply of changing styles forces us, finally, to regard and use language as the ever-varying constant that allows us to plot and evaluate temporal and spatial change. In *Portrait*, however, language plays its uncanny role more subtly: it acts as a complex frame of reference for the perceptions of author, character, and reader without compelling any recognition that it *is* the dominant system of reference.

If language is the dominant *frame* of reference, Stephen acts as a *point* of reference within that frame that enables us to plot the variable relationship between the author and the reader, the living and the dead, with greater precision. Our challenge is to position, somewhere between Joyce's and our own, Stephen's growing ability to balance imaginative engagement and critical detachment, and his increasing facility in interweaving and disentangling his story and history. Stephen's value is precisely that he, unlike Joyce, is not a "finished artist," despite his drunken assertion to the contrary in "Circe."[6] He represents not the artist but the dialogical process of verbal recreation that we tend to split into reading and writing.[7]

When writer and reader are exposed as imaginatively intermingled in a shared text that has the power to reflect both, the illusion of authorial privilege is shattered. Language emerges as the shared domain of reader, author, and character, the place where all "multiplicity is focused."[8] It becomes more difficult for the author and reader to disguise the relationship between their own identities and the answers to the riddles they contemplate, as Athy did by memorably emphasizing the link between a town and a part of the body, rather than the link between the names of both and his own. Language, so conceived, acts as an interface that, like a portrait, gives back a compound image that both resembles and fails to resemble the perceiver. Joyce's *Portrait* has this capacity: it changes as the artist changes, but it also changes as its reader changes, acting as a stylistic equivalent to what Oscar Wilde used as subject rather than medium, the picture of Dorian Gray.[9]

In *Portrait*, then, the opposite positions of artist and reader often run together in relation to the fiction they share. Reading and writing mirror each other as contradictory and interdependent processes. For years, readers have argued over whether Stephen actually becomes an artist in *Portrait*, focusing attention on the two instances wherein his verbal productions are presented directly to us so that we may evaluate them: the aesthetic theories that he propounds to Lynch in the last chapter and the villanelle that he composes in the section that follows (*P*, 204–16, 217–24). Ironically, however, the determination of whether or not Stephen has a right to the title of artist tends to be made independently of an equally important determination that is intimately related to the first: What kind of a *reader* do Stephen's productions reveal him to be?

Stephen's theory of reading should be measured against his reading practice, and his theory and practice compared to that of the book's author and readers. Such an approach produces a more complex practical awareness of the book's reflexivity, its emphasis on the parallels between Stephen's attempts to read his world and our attempts to read Stephen. To the extent that our activity reproduces Stephen's, the text contextualizes us; if we accurately identify a representation of our mode of reading within the novel, we can then supplement that methodology with alternatives that are also represented within the fiction. By applying strategies represented in the novel to our own way of reading the novel, we allow the text to teach us more sophisticated ways of framing it and in that way regain momentary interpretive control over the "portrait" that has framed us, and will do so again—in different ways—on subsequent readings. If we then repeat the process, it is with the awareness that we are using the interplay between text and context to multiply the number of available interpretive frames. Event and context, reader and character, story and history repeatedly exchange positions as a condition of their mutual development. The condition that makes development possible but never finite is the imbalance between the employment of a word and the multiple possibilities for meaning that such employment excludes between an individual story and the panoply of history.

The tension between a realized network of meaning and potential networks of meaning, between the precision of definition and its ultimate inadequacy, is the central conflict in *Portrait*, a conflict that is dramatized in both social and linguistic terms. In the first chapter, Stephen's attempt to realize a relation to his name, to his schoolfellows, to his country, and to history itself is intermingled with his desire to define the meanings of words and phrases that puzzle him: God, politics, "tower of ivory." Comparably, his growing isolation in the second chapter presents itself as an evaporation of the meanings he has succeeded in attaching to language, and he watches words and names lapse back into a meaningless sensuality that reflects his own: when he tries to recall some of the vivid moments of his childhood, he remembers only names, dissociated from the images and events that gave them significance—Dante, Parnell, Clane, Clongowes (*P*, 93). The ability to read, to attach significance—quite literally—to signs, deserts him: "He could scarcely interpret the letters of the signboards of the shops" (*P*, 92). When language loses meaning, the speaking subject also dissolves, and the capability of speech is assumed by the sensual organs that convey it, the tongue and the lips.[10] When Stephen encounters the prostitute at the end of the second chapter, "his lips parted though they would not speak," and when Stephen surrenders to her, "body and mind," he is "conscious of nothing in the world but the dark pressure of her softly parting lips. They pressed upon his brain as upon his lips as though they were the vehicle of a vague speech," but what issues from between them is not speech but the sensual reality of her tongue, its pressure "softer than sound" (*P*, 101).

The theory of reading that Stephen outlines in the last chapter, although complicated, is surprisingly illuminating when applied to the reading of *Portrait* itself. According to Stephen, the apparent capriciousness of language as it gathers up and then empties itself of meaning produces a "rhythm of beauty" that he attempts to describe to Lynch (*P*, 206). Stephen argues that such a rhythm has the power to prolong and finally dissolve a state of mind that he describes as "esthetic stasis." "Stasis" is a moment of integration that temporarily satisfies the intellect or the imagination, an achieved construct that must repeatedly be dissolved and reconstituted as the relationship between individual events and their narrative contexts change.

What Stephen experiences as the achievement and dissolution of relation, and what he describes more analytically as the rhythms of beauty and truth, is a structural rhythm in which individuals may participate but not initiate or control. What individuals can control are the stages of apprehension, an understanding of which allows us to initiate and accelerate the rhythms of imaginative and intellectual comprehension. Three words from Aquinas provide the text for Stephen's commentary—*integritas, consonantia,* and *claritas*—but the arrangement of these prerequisites for beauty into a dialectic of apprehension that can be learned and applied is Stephen's. Stephen's formula for apprehending the uniqueness of any perceived object is simply to separate it from its immediate context and then to analyze its structure and significance. The synthesis of this process of separation and integration is the "enchantment," or stasis, that is born of the momentary balance of two forces—forces such as illumination and darkness, which reach equilibrium in the image of a "fading coal" that Shelley used to describe the mind in creation (*P*, 213).

Stephen uses the term *apprehension* to designate the appreciation of the structural relationships that comprise any whole. Stephen's theory is therefore a theory of reading, and if we consciously apply it to our reading of *Portrait*, it allows us to evaluate Stephen's own reading in a more balanced way. If, for example, we detach ourselves from Stephen when he is puzzling out the meaning of a word or phrase and perform the same activity independently as well as vicariously, we can arrest and contemplate the point where Stephen's strengths meet his limitations, generating a "balanced" view that should in turn produce an ambivalent response. In the first chapter, Stephen is repeatedly troubled by a phrase from the litany of the Virgin Mary, "Tower of Ivory." He connects it in his mind with Eileen because she is a Protestant and "protestants used to make fun of the litany of the Blessed Virgin. *Tower of Ivory*, they used to say, *House of Gold!* How could a woman be a tower of ivory or a house of gold? Who was right then?" (*P*, 35). Stephen solves the problem by linking Eileen with the Virgin: he calls up an image of Eileen's hands, "long and white and thin and cold and soft" and thinks, "That was ivory: a cold white thing. That was the meaning of *Tower of Ivory*" (*P*, 36).

Stephen's "definition" of "Tower of Ivory" is ingeniously economical: he furnishes the Holy Virgin with attributes of the virgin who lives on his street. However, if we take the phrase out of its immediate context (appreciating its *integritas*), "apprehend it as complex, multiple, divisible, separable, made up of its parts, the results of its parts and their sum, harmonious" (Stephen identifies the structural complexity of an individual unit as its *consonantia*), and then "make the only synthesis which is logically and esthetically permissible" (*P*, 212, 213), we can see that "Tower of Ivory" is also "ivory tower," an encoded commentary on Stephen's habits of mind. For all of his ingeniousness, Stephen lives in a many-storied ivory tower. He has written himself into a fairy tale that begins, "Once upon a time and a very good time it was," a tale that takes place in Clongowes castle, site of heroic deeds that he hopes to imitate, a tale passed down to him by his father, a gentleman who, he fondly believes, may one day be a magistrate.

Our experience of Stephen's aesthetic theory allows us to re-define and recontextualize Stephen's experience at Clongowes as his storied rendition of a lived experience that is itself an uncon-scious response to the stories of childhood, in particular, to the fairy tale. That this story antedates Stephen himself is clear from the opening of the novel: the book begins with a story, but not until the third sentence do we learn that "he" is the subject of that story. The story is told before its subject is identified, before the life story of the subject has even begun. Like a reader whose knowledge of language precedes specific knowledge of an individ-ual text, Stephen's experience of language and narrative antici-pates and shapes his experience of the world; but knowledge of the world and the text forces both the reader and Stephen to redefine the meaning of language as it was first conceived.

Chapter I traces the impress of the fairy tale on Stephen's mind, a narrative that Joyce prompts us to connect with the Gospels. The Gospels, like the fairy tale, present a fable of identity motivated and shaped by a desire for self-definition that is partly realized through the definition of human doubles—words. The last of the four New Testament Gospels (the nonsynoptic gospel) explicitly affirms the primacy of the word over the world. St. John proclaims, "In the beginning was the Word," a word that precedes its own definition: "and the Word was God." The movement from word to reality to a more complex understanding of the word is the movement of the Christian Bible from Word to Incarnation ("And the Word was made flesh") to the Crucifixion that makes ultimate Revelation possible.

As an account of the crucifixion and resurrection of the Word, the gospel can be read as one of the most powerful narrative illustrations of the rhythm of truth that Stephen analyzes more abstractly in the last chapter: the human referent must be lost in the flesh in order to be regained through the word, a process that must be periodically repeated if our dual consciousness of word and flesh, and their reciprocity, is to be kept alive. In the first chapter, Stephen establishes, almost unconsciously, a meaning for both his Christian name and his patronym by identifying himself with Christ and Christ's doubles in the twin realms of Church and State: St. Stephen, on the one hand, and Parnell together with the Greek and Roman national heroes recalled by Stephen's classical surname, on the other. However, the principle of connection that binds the various narratives is not allegorical, which would place history in the service of this story, but verbal, which equalizes the relationships among the narratives and allows them to illuminate each other.[11]

If we apply Stephen's formula to "Tower of Ivory," its reconstitution as "ivory tower," when supported by the fairytale structure of the chapter, presents us with an instantaneous double image of the beauty and limitation of a sensitive child's vision. When, in the midst of the discussion of the mysterious sin committed by Simon Moonan, Tusker Boyle, and the others, Stephen comforts himself by remembering his triumph of definition, reflecting with satisfaction, "By thinking of things you could understand them" (*P*, 43), his connection should prompt the reader to rethink and reevaluate the possible relation between his attempt to imagine the Virgin Mary and his desire to realize the meaning of punishment by proxy. This relation is apparent through verbal links that show how concretely Stephen makes the transition from an image of the Virgin to the story of Christ's martyrdom; in this case, it is hands that draw Mary, Christ, and Stephen together when Stephen is pandied in retaliation for the sexual misconduct of his schoolfellows.

Stephen's memory of Eileen's ivory hands is sparked by his recollection of Lady Boyle paring his nails. Unconsciously, Stephen sees these two pairs of hands as linking the puzzle of virginity with the enigma of sexual transgression and punishment. If we apply Stephen's formula for insightful apprehension to his description of the hands of Mr. Gleeson and Lady Boyle, the inner narrative that motivates Stephen, turning him into his schoolfellows' savior, becomes clear. The word *nails*, detached from the referent that its immediate context dictates, attaches itself to different hands and to an older narrative that serves not as an allegorical equivalent to but as a critical commentary on this one. The focus of Stephen's concern has shifted from the Virgin to the Son, from the puzzle of purity to that of sin and symbolic atonement. Sharp nails can excruciate as well as extend and beautify a hand, and Stephen's unconscious understanding of this is reflected in his concentration on Mr. Gleeson's hands as an image of the paradox of gentleness and pain, implicated in the sin as well as in its punishment:

> He had rolled up his sleeves to show how Mr Gleeson would roll up his sleeves. But Mr Gleeson had round shiny cuffs and clean white wrists and fattish white hands and the nails of them were long and pointed. Perhaps he pared them too like Lady Boyle. But they were terribly long and pointed nails. So long and cruel they were though the white fattish hands were not cruel but gentle. And though he trembled with cold and fright to think of the cruel long nails and of the high whistling

sound of the cane and of the chill you felt at the end of your
shirt when you undressed yourself yet he felt a feeling of queer
quiet pleasure inside him to think of the white fattish hands,
clean and strong and gentle. (*P*, 45)

When Stephen is cast in the role of scapegoat, "punished," as
Fleming anticipated, "for what other fellows did" (*P*, 43), when
his own hands are made to burn, tremble, and crumple "like a
leaf in the fire" (*P*, 50) for the sin of Tusker Boyle's long white
hands and Mr. Gleeson's fattish ones, he takes it upon himself to
complete the narrative by interceding with the Father, the "rector" whose name promises rectification of wrongs, on behalf of
himself and his schoolfellows. In the process he constructs a glo-
rious and recognizable meaning for his own name, translating it,
in his own mind, into "Stephen Hero." As Stephen Hero, he
realizes the meaning of his "Christian" name, which in that of
the first Christian martyr, St. Stephen, at the same time that he
extends his earlier identification with Parnell, the national martyr.

In the first chapter of *Portrait*, readers, like Stephen, are confronted with problems of definition: specifically, they are asked to
define Stephen's relationship to a world of words by contrasting
the fantasies that he uses to define mysterious words, phrases,
and songs with the more complex meanings and associations that
Stephen does not yet understand. Such definition show not only
what Stephen has read—the Bible and fairy tales—but *how* he
reads them, vicariously and not critically. He positions himself
within them and never outside them, a strategy that makes heroes but not authors or critical readers. What he does manage to
do is to assimilate, in his own life story heroic figures that history
has set in opposition to one another: Christ and the Romans,
Christ and Parnell. He has constructed "the most satisfying relations of the intelligible"—what is intelligible to him as a hopeful, obedient, and naive child—and in the process has defined for
himself a cluster of puzzlingly attractive words. To the extent
that we can appreciate those definitions, our reading is sympathetic, whereas more ironic possibilities emerge when we focus
on the larger contexts of Stephen's definitions, the contexts that

he ignores. As Stephen will later understand in theory, the only balanced reading is a double one that can appreciate, in rhythmic alternation, both the triumph and the inadequacy of definition.

Night Worship: Heavenly Bodies

In chapter I, Stephen gradually defines a heroic identity for himself by constantly interrogating individual words and by unconsciously exploring his relationship to the Word. By juxtaposing Stephen's unconscious identification with Christ with an account of Stephen's repeated attempts to understand the meaning of language, Joyce emphasizes the extent to which the New Testament presents itself as an allegory of communication, as a history of a creative Word moving toward a Revelation expressed as a final sentence, or judgment. The larger contours of the New Testament are, according to such a view, reproduced in miniature in the life of one man, conceived as a divine word penetrating the tympanum of a woman's ear, his corpus/corpse a literal embodiment of human communication, represented by the eucharistic bread and wine. Such an allegory represents and promulgates an idealistic view of reading as a transcendent communion made possible through communication, which is always, by definition, a sacramental act. The story of Christ suggests that the sensual incarnation of the abstract Word is significant primarily because it makes ultimate transcendence possible, a transcendence effected through atonement and symbolic communication. Christian scripture celebrates the power of language to abstract itself—eventually—from its sensual referents, its mesh of defining circumstances, and to reunite itself with the will of-its-creator. A Christian ideology, as its constitutive language suggests, celebrates oneness: atonement is literally a compound of the words "at one"; atonement, by implication, is a way of being "at one" with the will of another, an experience that, in Christian Scripture, defines communication.[12]

Stephen's initial response to the problems posed by language and identity is primed by a literal, if unconscious, reading of the

Gospels as a parable of how communication works. Identity must be defined through language, and language incarnated in experience so that it may be abstracted and reassimilated. Stephen's struggle to equate language and sensual experience—to understand "tower of ivory" as Eileen's hands, "suck" as the sound of draining water (*P*, 11), Leicester Abbey as the lights of Clongowes castle (*P*, 10)—is an effort to give flesh to words, to effect their incarnation. These words have life but no meaning for Stephen, like the vivid words that pass between Dante and Mr. Casey over Christmas dinner. Stephen responds physically, even mimetically, to the passionate words—the glow of anger on Mr. Casey's face rises in his own as "the spoken words thrilled him" (*P*, 38)—but he knows no larger context to play the words against, so he can neither assimilate perspectives nor produce a meaning that can help him bridge the distance between himself and the scene he is witnessing. It is not until Stephen inadvertently atones for the sins of Tusker Boyle and Simon Moonan that he discovers a way of being "at one" with the worlds from which he had been alienated through his relative youth and ignorance: with the community at Clongowes and with his divided family. His punishment allows him to seal the rift separating him from his immediate environment, as well as the rift that divided his family, by playing the role of savior, a role that reconciles the narratives of Parnell and Christ, allowing him to live out and join the meanings of two abstract words that had puzzled him—God and politics.

Christian Scripture, when considered as a commentary upon language, takes as its ideal the transcendent power of imaginative integration. But, as Joyce suggests in the second and fourth chapters, the language of Scripture can be interpreted imagistically as well as literally, as an exploration not of the word but of the body. This more romantic interpretation reads Christ and Lucifer as representations of heavenly bodies, Lucifer as falling star and Christ as rising sun, as well as rising Son (see "Was Jesus a Sun Myth?" in "Circe," *U*, 15.1579). Stephen's formula for apprehension, when applied to key words in Christian Scripture, shows how coherently its language supports such an interpretation, unveiling "East-er" as the time (place) where the Son (sun) rises in order to compensate for the fall of Eve (eve)—the coming of evil. So interpreted, Christian narratives, like pagan ones, are anthropomorphic accounts of heavenly bodies that differ from their Greek counterparts in focusing not on constellations and their genesis but on the dramatic opposition between day and night, the perpetual revolution in the heavens.

If, as a parable of reading, Scripture idealizes the value of communion through a transcendence of meaning, it reverses that emphasis when read poetically, in terms of the images that the sounds of its words imply. Whereas the philosophical idealist represents the ideal as a heavenly abstraction, the sensual idealist pays romantic homage to heavenly bodies, the moon or the stars, thereby idealizing distance rather than "at-one-ment." If Christ sheds his mortal body to live eternally as an abstract and transcendent Word, Lucifer takes two forms, both of which are physical. In his prelapsarian state, he takes the form of a heavenly body, the morning star, a traditional symbol of pride of the intellect, having the power to enlighten (*Lucifer* means "light bringer") but doomed to fall. In his fallen state he takes the form of a snake, a representation of the sexual part of a male body that, like the intellect, is marked by rise and fall. Lucifer, in his duality and in the relative weakness of the light he brings, is inferior to a greater heavenly body, the Son (sun), who must fall in order to re-arise into heaven in the morning/during mourning. The counterpart of Lucifer-Satan in his opposition to the Son is woman, who also takes two forms—Mary and Eve, virgin and temptress. Mary, like the unfallen Lucifer, is represented by the morning star, harbinger of the sun; not only does she take the form of the same heavenly body as Lucifer but her mortal body is made heavenly as well: she is impregnated when God's Word passes the membrane of her ear, not by the rupturing of a "lower" membrane. The fallen Eve, Satan's lure and victim, sins by listening not to God's Word but to the blandishments of the body and promises of divine knowledge offered suggestively to her by a snake. The stories of Lucifer-Satan and his female counterparts facilitate not an imaginative transcendence of the body but a particularization of the symmetry of mental and sexual processes, fraught with a directive to privilege thought and communication over sexuality.

In *Portrait*, Stephen learns to see the transcendent desires of childhood as unrealistic and escapist by replaying his story, in chapter II, in the "anatomical" theater of troubled adolescence. The readings that frame Stephen shift accordingly: the classical heroes of *Peter Parley's Tales* (*P*, 53) are replaced by romantic poets, particularly Byron and Shelley; the fairy tale yields to tales of adventure; Christ as portrayed in the Gospels is displaced by a Miltonic Satan, romantically interpreted. Stephen's heroes are no longer saviors but heretics; his drive is not toward atonement but toward separation and exile—what, from an orthodox point of view, is called "sin." Exiled from the fairy tale, he discovers adventure, a narrative different in mood and in the nature of its resolution, but identical in its movement from isolation to reconciliation. Stephen exiles himself from the spiritual world he had built in chapter I through the painstaking accretion of sensual definitions and gravitates instead toward a physical one, where communion is private and sensual rather than public and symbolic, and the desire to consume the body is subsumed by the desire to experience its sensual particulars. Whereas the first chapter celebrated a triumph of social and historical at-one-ment, the second represents the pleasures of critical deconstruction, the process by which human and written characters shed their more symbolic significations and display their hidden sensuality.

In chapter II, Stephen's growing sense of alienation is most frequently expressed in his own mind as a process of fading. What is fading away in the second chapter is the network of self-defining associations that Stephen had constructed in the first. His removal from Clongowes and the physical dislocation of his family from Blackrock to Dublin has the effect of eroding all of the heroic fantasies that he had shored around himself in childhood. As in the first chapter, Stephen longs to shed "weakness and timidity and inexperience" (*P*, 65), but, initially, in his proud and rebellious phase, what he actually shuns is the consciousness of his own body, an awareness that his idealistic yearnings are shadowed by sexual drives. Stephen's fantasies are repeatedly interrupted by reminders of the ineluctable physicality of existence, reminders from which he recoils in horror. When he is watching the firelight, listening to an old woman's pathetic reports about "Ellen," he focuses his attention on "the words," "following the ways of adventure that lay open in the coals," until Ellen herself actually appears in the doorway (*P*, 68). Stephen sees Ellen as a grotesque reminder of the feeble animality of the body; he describes her as a "skull," a feeble, whining, monkey-like creature whose silly laughter exposes the silliness of his own idealizations. Similarly, the word *fœtus* that Stephen discovers carved into a desk in the anatomy theater in Cork mocks him with its semantic specificity, its horrifying power to bring the dead and the unborn to life and to challenge, with uncompromising realism, the attenuated sensuality of romantic desire.

Stephen's desire to fade out of existence manifests itself verbally as the desire to divest word and narrative of any personal or worldly meaning. When he writes his Byronic poem to E——C—— he strips the account of their shared tram ride of all of its noncelestial characteristics: all the "elements which he deemed common and insignificant fell out of the scene. There remained no trace of the tram itself nor of the trammen nor of the horses: nor did he and she appear vividly. The verses told only of the night and the balmy breeze and the maiden lustre of the moon" (*P*, 70). As Stephen's carefully constructed myth of himself lapses, his definitions of words and names undergo a similar divestment. The first chapter illustrated ways in which words accrued meaning, and, as Stephen learned to define words and phrases sensually, the reader was prodded to resituate those phrases in other well-known narrative contexts. In the second chapter, Stephen concentrates on the art of dissociating words from contexts to create a soothing, rhythmic music, as he does when he "prays" on the night mail to Cork: "His prayer, addressed neither to God nor saint, . . . ended in a trail of foolish words which he made to fit the insistent rhythm of the train" (*P*, 87). The sensual sounds of words also console him when gathered into the less furious music of poetry or song: Shelley's fragment on the moon or the "come-all-you" that his father sings about exile and the fading of love (*P*, 96, 88).

Stephen's physiological changes have exiled him from the theater of his mind, forcing him to look for a new part to play in a different theater, an anatomical one that will allow him first to displace and eventually to act out his physical desires. Stephen's weary sense of fading and being stripped, along with the language that mimics his state of mind, prepares him for the experience of physical contact, anticipating his observation of the prostitute as "she undid her gown" (*P*, 100). The desire for familial reconciliation that drew him to the "family romance" of Christian Scripture and fairy tale has been ousted by the desire for sexual union that draws him from family romance to romanticism, from the general and mythic to the particular and physical, from a respect for the power of symbolic communication and revelation to an appreciation of the sibilant and sensual activity of the tongue. Memories of his family and his childhood fade in preparation for his initiation into "another world" (*P*, 100), a "fallen," "evening" world of darkness and abandonment, in which other, softer ties replace familial ones, and other lips press their story upon his brain.

Stephen's yearnings for a higher existence, his lyrical preoccupation with "the maiden lustre of the moon" (*P*, 71), "wandering companionless" (*P*, 96), are bound to his fierce physical desires, which he identifies as "the tides within him" (*P*, 98). The moon governs these tides, as it governs those of the sea; his identification with a heavenly body both masks and represents a new awareness of his physical body: both bodies induct him, subtly, into the rituals of night worship, although he fails to appreciate their interdependence. Not until the opening of the third chapter does he begin to betray an unconscious awareness that heavenly and earthly bodies may be equated and that the prototype for such an equation is Christ's counterpart, Lucifer.

Lucifer, as the sermon will remind Stephen, is a star turned snake, a "son of the morning" who "took the shape of a serpent" (*P*, 118). In these two forms he represents intellectual and physical assertiveness, the double pride that sharply contrasts with Christ's humility. In the third chapter, Stephen is most aware of himself as a snake, whose mind winds itself in and out of curious questions of "spiritual and bodily sloth" (*P*, 106), whose soul sickens "at the thought of a torpid snaky life feeding itself out of the tender marrow of his life and fattening upon the slime of lust" (*P*, 140); his archetype is his penis, "the most subtle beast of the field" that "feels and understands and desires" (*P*, 139). If Stephen sees his body as serpentine, he sees his soul as Luciferian, "stars being born and being quenched" (*P*, 103). At the beginning of the chapter, the stars begin to crumble, "and a cloud of fine stardust" falls through space (*P*, 103), a simultaneous idealization and liberalization of a Luciferian fall.

Viewed in one way, Stephen's experiences in the first and second chapters are as different as day and night; viewed in another way, they illustrate complementary phases of the same experience. In the first chapter, he is alienated from family and peers through youth and ignorance; in the second chapter, he wills such a separation, finally objectifying his sense of difference through sin. In both cases he is punished for his detachment: in the first chapter, he is pandied for breaking his glasses, for his helpless inability to see what is nearest him; in the second chapter, he is twice chastised for a more calculated and critical detachment—for his written affirmation of the soul's inalterable distance from the Creator, which Mr. Tate condemns as "heresy" (*P*, 79), and for the detachment from conventional morality reflected in his preference for Byron over Tennyson. As in the first chapter, he is again cast in the role of a scapegoat: he is whipped with Heron's cane, pummeled with a knotty cabbage stump, and pushed into barbed wire for his defense of Byron's "heresies." Both at Clongowes and at Belvedere, in both his Christian and his Luciferian incarnations, Stephen is brought to book for differing from his fellows. At Clongowes, Stephen used his chastisement to bridge that difference, whereas at Belvedere his treatment at the hands of his friends confirms the apprehension of difference that Stephen has learned to savor: "He chronicled with patience what he saw, detaching himself from it and testing its mortifying flavour in secret" (*P*, 67). However, even his critical detachment leads him back to the world he had scorned, not through social communion or verbal communication but through the private pleasures of physical contact.

Sexual sin brings its own sense of at-one-ment, a physical oneness that Christianity defines as the opposite of spiritual atonement. Joyce defined sin as a separation that is paradoxically inseparable from atonement, arguing, in his essay on Oscar Wilde, that "the truth inherent in the soul of Catholicism" is the understanding "that man cannot reach the divine heart except through that sense of separation and loss called sin."[13] The "sin" of sexuality and the "virtue" of atonement are evaluative interpretations of the same paradox, the coincidence of identity and difference. Christ's atonement is portrayed as a reconciliation with the heavens, but it is also an excruciating separation from the earth; comparably, sexual sin may sunder an individual from the community, but it also constitutes the most intimate form of contact. Lucifer's "fall" from the heavens is also a "rise"—a rising against God that takes as its alternative form a rising of the flesh.

If a fall interpreted one way constitutes a rise when interpreted another, then the very separability of opposites when divorced from the contexts that authorize them must be called into question. Joyce's methodologies not only emphasize the importance of contexts, they also generate new interpretations for the narrative contexts they recall. Both Lucifer and Christ participate, in complementary ways, in a single rhythm, the rhythm of separation and integration that multiplies and individuates language and experience. Scripture—and language—can only be understood as a double experience, as allegory and poetry, meaning and sense, just as human life is equally dependent upon the vitality of mind and body. The last half of *Portrait* illustrates Stephen's unusual sensitivity to both kinds of experience and his comic blindness to their interrelationship. If we read not only with Stephen but against him, reading imagistically when he reads literally, and literally when he reads imagistically, playing his story off against the history that informs and shapes it, then the humorous possibilities of that interdependence become apparent.

Retreat

The atonement that climaxes the third chapter of *Portrait* is also, as the event that prompts it suggests, a retreat. The Church uses the strategy of "retreat" to simulate the "withdrawal," or separation, that can inspire a desire for its counterpart, atonement. This is how the rector, another righter of wrongs, defines it (*P*, 109). But Stephen's formula for apprehension, which is basically a strategy for gaining a more distanced perspective on language and narrative, allows us to appreciate the relevance of its other meanings—a retreat is also a recession, a retrogression, a place of safety or refuge (*OED*). This is the effect of the retreat on Stephen: he regresses to a childlike piety and simplicity, reestablishing his imaginative association with obedient goodness and purity. Stephen's retreat to the world of childhood innocence is precipitated by the unexpected resurgence of the past: he notices his old master, Father Arnall, seated at the left of the altar, and the narrator explains, "The figure of his old master, so strangely rearisen, brought back to Stephen's mind his life at Clongowes. . . . His soul, as these memories came back to him, became again a child's soul" (*P*, 108–9). He reenacts, in response to the words of the sermon, the highlights of his experience at Clongowes: instead of a burning hand, he is given a "burning ear," a fire that spreads through his body and brain (*P*, 115, 125). As at Clongowes, he longs to "be at one with others and with God," a longing that leads him toward the renewed experience of communication and communion that the Eucharist represents for him (*P*, 143, 146).

Christ's separation from authority through incarnation mirrors Lucifer's separation from authority through insurrection, as His refusal to plead with his Roman captors mirrors and reverses Lucifer's successful persuasion of Adam and Eve. Joyce's treatment of Stephen in the contexts of both narratives suggests that the conflicts of "scripture" are representations of different attitudes toward language, attitudes that have also defined the alternating tendencies of literary history—the classical and the romantic tempers, which Joyce associates with Christ and Lucifer, respectively. Joyce presents these tendencies as structurally identical, their apparent differences merely differences of accent. In *Portrait*, Joyce portrays classicism, usually characterized as a predominantly rational attitude, as a triumph of imaginative integration, and romanticism, frequently portrayed as irrational, as a triumph of critical deconstruction.[14] The emphasis of classicism is upon truth, but the road to its apprehension is imaginative, not critical, and the emphasis of romanticism is upon beauty, apprehended through uncompromising criticism. Both individually and together, classicism and romanticism reproduce the rhythms of beauty and truth.

When Stephen tries to model himself on an ideal, his language reasserts his—and its—ineluctable materiality; when he revels in his own sensuality, the structure of his experiences and his accounts of them betray his indebtedness to ideas. When, in the fourth chapter, Stephen is attempting to transform himself into a hero of the early Church, beginning each day "with an heroic offering of its every moment," imagining himself "kneeling at mass in the catacombs," and believing that he can mortify his senses (*P*, 147, 150–51), the sensuality of his own response to language betrays him. Sensitive to the hidden rose in "rosary," he relates without conscious irony, "The rosaries too which he said constantly—for he carried his beads loose in his trousers' pockets that he might tell them as he walked the streets—transformed themselves into coronals of flowers of such vague unearthly texture that they seemed to him as hueless and odourless as they were nameless" (*P*, 148). Stephen thinks of the flowers as "nameless" because their names—roses—would prompt him to realize that a sensual referent is coloring his response to a sacred practice.

When Stephen attempts to turn words, and himself, into abstract outlines of an ideal meaning, the sensuality of the body and of the word reasserts itself, exposing the comic naiveté of Stephen's project. In counterpoint, it is when Stephen would affect an appreciation of purely carnal or sensual knowledge that his expressions become most chaste and chastened. His account

of the prostitute's caresses is as transparently reverent as his ecstasy in the presence of the bird girl. Stephen's desire for flight—
realized in his imagination, reflected in his high-flown prose, and
projected onto the vision of a wading girl—is an attempt to deny
the limitations of the body that the "pitiable nakedness" of his
adolescent friends so clearly exposes. Stephen, "remembering in
what dread he stood of the mystery of his own body," casts himself as a triumphant Daedalus, with the result that "the body he
knew was purified in a breath and delivered of incertitude and
made radiant and commingled with the element of the spirit" (*P*,
168, 169). Listening to "a voice from beyond the world," he shuts
out the voices from the world that call him a garlanded ox: "Bous
Stephanoumenous! Bous Stephaneforos!" (*P*, 168). Dreaming of
Daedalus, the "hawklike man flying sunward above the sea," Stephen ignores the voices from the sea that remind us of Icarus's
fall: "O cripes, I'm drownded! . . . Stephaneforos!" (*P*, 169). He fancies himself a classical hero and a risen Christ, whose "soul had
arisen from the grave of boyhood, spurning her graveclothes" (*P*,
170), when in reality he has only separated himself once more
from the "dull gross voice of the world of duties and despair" (*P*,
169).

In his epiphany of the bird girl, Stephen has found another
deity ("Heavenly God!" [*P*, 171]), has "felt the strange light of some
new world" (*P*, 172), and has surrendered himself to the embrace
of yet another breast, that of the earth. He thinks that he has
discovered a new vocation, when he has simply combined the
calls of the older ones. His "discovery" is an imaginative retreat
into religious ecstasy, but it is also a sensual surrender to the
romantic blandishments of language. He sees himself as Daedalus,
but with "his cheeks aflame and his throat throbbing with song"
(*P*, 170) he is also, without realizing it, Shelley's skylark. Stephen's
song, like that of the lark, derives its beauty from "ignorance of
pain"; like the unseen bird, his is the "shrill delight" of a "scorner
of the ground." Stephen's aim is still to transcend his human
limits. By the end of the fourth chapter, Stephen has drawn together his classical and his romantic yearnings, but only in the

world of his own mind. What is most palpably lacking is an understanding of the social context that partially frames him— an awareness of Dublin.

Dublin as Frame: Text and Context

The delusion that inspires Stephen more often than any other is the conviction that he can transcend the meanness of his environment. The euphoria that accompanies his anticipations of transcendence is expressed in many ways—in the literal uplift that raises him above his fellows at the end of the first chapter, as he is carried along in "a cradle of their locked hands" (*P*, 58); in his expectation that he will be transfigured when he encounters his Mercedes, that "weakness and timidity and inexperience would fall from him in that magic moment" (*P*, 65); in the ascent of prayers from his purified heart (*P*, 145); in the idealized flights that conclude both the fourth and the fifth chapters. The most celebrated passage in *A Portrait of the Artist* is one in which Stephen directly expresses his determination to elude the claims of his environment: "When the soul of man is born in this country there are nets flung at it to hold it back from flight. You talk to me of nationality, language, religion. I shall try to fly by those nets" (*P*, 203). It is Stephen's commitment to transcendence that makes him heroic in *both* a classical and a romantic sense, yet the continuity of life and narrative impedes any real transcendence, which would be possible only through death. Any reader of *Portrait* whose reading is impelled by a transcendent ideal, by a desire to escape the "nets" of language, religion, and nationality will experience the resistance the book offers to such flightiness. The only lecture Stephen attends in the last chapter is on the subject of electrical resistance, which should alert us to the importance not only of sympathizing with Stephen's desire-driven narratives but of resisting their illusions of ultimate triumph or escape as well.

In *Portrait*, as in *Dubliners*, *Ulysses*, and *Finnegans Wake*, the last chapter recomplicates the context in which the book has been read up to that point. Chapter V makes it clear that Stephen's struggle is the struggle between an individual and his context, a struggle that also shapes the process of reading. The end of the chapter, in particular, is not only a diary of a young man preparing for flight, his entries alternately callow and full of hope—dismissive of the past, contemptuous of the present, and in love with the "wild spring" of the future—but also a compressed casebook of the problems posed by language, nationality, and religion, bringing them into shared focus as representative problems of context: the pressure of a collective, past-laden present on the future-oriented individual. Stephen's "nets" are the nets of context (from *contextus*, woven together), nets that can and must be unwoven and rewoven but can never be left behind, as the comic ironies of the first four chapters demonstrate.

Stephen's vision of Ireland actually is what Yeats's *The Countess Cathleen* was loudly accused of being: a view of Ireland as a country that would sell her soul. Stephen famously spurns Ireland as a devouring mother—"the old sow that eats her farrow" (*P*, 203)—a judgment that he uses (along with condescension toward his real mother) to justify his desire for flight. However, the jaunty optimism with which the book ends exposes itself as uncharacteristically poor reading, which in turn highlights the sharpness of the theory of reading presented earlier in the chapter. Stephen shows himself in this last chapter to be both a theoretically precise reader and an emotionally limited one, but both his strengths and his limitations map out avenues through which the reader can enter Joyce's *Portrait* and his Dublin. Unlike the undisciplined Temple—the Rousseau of University College—Stephen trains himself to bear "the unspoken speech behind . . . words" (*P*, 242), which is how he comes to realize a crucial difference between himself and Cranly. Whereas Stephen must idealize or crassly dismiss the feelings of women, Cranly is capable of empathy for them. Stephen thinks that Cranly "felt then the sufferings of women, the weaknesses of their bodies and souls: and would shield them with a strong and resolute arm and bow his mind to them" (*P*, 245). Stephen, in sharp contrast, is almost immune to the pity and terror aroused by a sympathetic contemplation of the other; he only feels the moral power of empathy briefly, when he is "thrilled by [Cranly's] touch" and touched by the revelation of Cranly's "cold sadness" (*P*, 247).

Immediately after the account of Stephen's momentary intimacy with Cranly, the narrative is interrupted by Stephen's diary. The diary is significant partly because it is a record of Stephen's "final" interpretations, a record that he himself makes. It shows that Stephen's reading, like his experience, is not extensive; as he notes, "have read little and understood less" (*P*, 248). However, the diary can also be seen as a compendium of various interpretive possibilities that the rest of the book enables us to evaluate. Read against the context of the first four chapters, Stephen's "readings" all emerge as different techniques for framing his perceptions, and these techniques are as relevant to our way of reading Stephen as they are to his way of reading his peers.[15]

Stephen's diary begins with a grossly reductive reading of Cranly that is all the more repulsive in contrast to the eloquent scene that precedes and inspires it. For a moment Stephen understands Cranly's sympathy for women as a product of his loneliness and fear, but in his diary entry for that day he distances himself from his feeling for Cranly by using a particular exegetical strategy: he isolates a single fact to "explain" Cranly difference in perspective—the age of his mother. Stephen frames Cranly through his imaginative reconstruction of the circumstances of Cranly's life, dismissing his "despair of soul" as that of a "child of exhausted loins" (*P*, 248). Stephen's first "reading" is almost a parody of the biographical fallacy, an exposé of the distortion caused by oversimplifying the contexts of interpretation.

The next morning, Stephen elaborates on his reading of Cranly by identifying him with a figure from the Bible—John the Baptist. Not only is his reading allegorically reductive but it is clearly self-serving as well: he subordinates Cranly to himself by casting Cranly as his precursor, which makes Stephen Christ. Again, Stephen's ploy exposes, through caricature, the distortion caused by reading through only one frame of reference, a distortion often motivated by the desire to see in someone else's situation a prophecy of one's own. The one-sidedness of Stephen's interpretation of Cranly acts as a warning against methodologies that link a character with a single precursor, whether that precursor be Christ, Satan, Daedalus, or Icarus. By implication, the contexts of interpretation must be as complex and variable as Dublin itself.

When Stephen quotes a portion of Blake's "William Bond" as an expression of his fear that Emma might die, his error is again to ignore the context of the excerpt. Stephen makes fun of the pathos of the poem—"Alas, poor William"—and in so doing violates the spirit of the poem as a whole, which implores its readers to "Seek Love in the Pity of other's Woe." Insensitivity to context does not increase sensitivity to the individual; on the contrary, it stifles it. It is only when Stephen glimpses the inadequacy of his prior readings, the reductiveness of his interpretive tendencies, that he begins to appreciate and even to enjoy his experience of others. When he records his meeting with Emma in Grafton Street, he caricatures his own posturings, and for a moment he approaches genuine liking for her and a consciousness of his own limitations: "Yes, I liked her today. A little or much? Don't know. I liked her and it seems a new feeling to me. Then, in that case, all the rest, all that I thought I thought and all that I felt I felt, all the rest before now, in fact . . . O, give it up, old chap! Sleep it off!" (*P*, 252).

What Stephen lacks is not an awareness of his own contradictory nature but an acceptance of it. This is apparent throughout the last chapter, where Stephen's omissions help to create the very context by which he can be evaluated. What he omits in his theoretical discussion with Lynch is consistent with what is lacking in each of the other climactic scenes of the last chapter. He tells Lynch, "When we come to the phenomena of artistic conception, artistic gestation and artistic reproduction I require a new terminology and a new personal experience," and Lynch replies, "But you will tell me about the new personal experience and new terminology some other day" (*P*, 209–10). Similarly, in the scene with Cranly, Stephen is unable to answer when Cranly asks him if he has ever loved anyone (*P*, 240); during his composition of the villanelle, Stephen's onanism suggests that his artistic creations are as pleasurable and fruitless as his solitary, physical ejaculation. Artistic conception, gestation, and reproduction result from a union of opposites in the act of love, a doubling that, together with Dublin, Stephen elects to escape. What he fails to understand is not only the double construction of authority, an awareness that would make him an "artist" as well as a portrayed subject, but also the social, geographical, and historical contexts that both define authority and allow it to change. What Stephen does not yet see, in the words of Jeremy Lane, is that there is "no final authorisation, no simple authority, no single author; but a relative authorisation, the sanction of relation whose dual principle seeds plurality, admitting and containing its contrary."[16]

To paraphrase Wordsworth's famous statement, an author differs from other characters in degree, but not in kind. What differentiates authors—and readers—of a fiction from the characters within a fiction is, potentially, a more disturbing awareness of the nets that no individual can elude, and that all must attempt to elude, a sensitivity to the complex interdependence of all human and verbal contexts, and an acceptance of the multiplicity and sameness of all characters participating in an interactive system. With such an awareness, an "author" can recreate and interpret such systems through imaginative doubling, whereas without such an awareness, the "character" will reenact prior narratives in unintentional and unproductive—repetitive— ways. However, this distinction between author and character is itself, like all oppositions, a heuristic one, since it is impossible to be permanently inside or outside a system so long as that system and our awareness of it are subject to change. Every author is necessarily a character, or subject, and every character an author—and authority—in a dialogical process that produces no final synthesis. Joyce is, alternately, both within and outside the book, as are other authors, such as Shelley and Byron, and all of its readers, including ourselves. In this respect, as in several others, the language of the book defines a community not unlike the community Stephen is attempting to escape at the end, as he goes "to encounter for the millionth time the reality of experience" (*P*, 252–53). Ironically, the book ends with Stephen asking his father, and author, to direct him by his precedent: "Old father, old artificer, stand me now and ever in good stead" (*P*, 253). Stephen is recording his hope that his father will continue to do what he was doing for Stephen when the book opened: authoring and authorizing the story of Stephen's youth. What Stephen needs, however, is not the continued authorization of men but more of the emotional responsiveness he associates with women.

The Stephen that Joyce portrays is unfinished; his lack of completeness is a consequence of his identification with a Janus-faced authority whose faces are both male. In *Portrait* Stephen has no understanding of female experience whatsoever, as Joyce shows by highlighting Stephen's insensitivity to his mother, his alternation of "brutal anger" and unworldly homage for E—— C—— (*P*, 220), and his surprise mixed with contempt when he realizes that Cranly "[h]ad felt then the sufferings of women . . . and would . . . bow his mind to them" (*P*, 245). Stephen smiles when Moynihan scorns MacCann's agenda to win "votes for the bitches" (*P*, 195); women engender in him an admixture of terror and incomprehension. He sees them as seductively blood sucking and faithless, as he sees the peasant woman whom he describes as "a batlike soul waking to the consciousness of itself in darkness and secrecy and loneliness and, through the eyes and voice and gesture of a woman without guile, calling the stranger to her bed" (*P*, 183). Women are not quite human: instead, they are marsupials (as Stephen suggests in *Stephen Hero*), birds (such as the bird girl at the end of chapter IV), bats, or progeny-devouring pigs, like Ireland, "the old sow that eats her farrow" (*P*, 203).

Stephen's thoughtless misogyny is still apparent in *Ulysses*, but in the later book Joyce introduces Molly as the carnal counterpart of Stephen, whose ramifying language and flesh expose and fulfill the emptiness of his ideal abstractions. Through its three-part structure, in which Stephen and Molly oppose and complete each other on either side of Bloom, *Ulysses* silently suggests that Stephen's concern with the two male faces of moral authority calls up as a necessary supplement the burgeoning of a weblike textuality associated with women. Stephen's attention to male rationality contributes only the plot of the human story; its poetry and music, unexpectedly enough, emerge from subconscious memory, in the rhythmic interconnectedness and discontinuity of images that in *Ulysses* is orchestrated by women. In *Portrait* Cranly is the John the Baptist who prophesies what *Ulysses* will later show, even if Stephen never consciously understands it: "Your mother brings you into the world, carries you first in her body. What do we know about what she feels? But whatever she feels, it, at least, must be real. It must be. What are our ideas or ambitions? Play. Ideas! Why, that bloody bleating goat Temple has ideas. MacCann has ideas too. Every jackass going the road thinks he has ideas" (*P*, 242). *Ulysses* is not, like *Portrait*, a discovery of ideas but an exploration of the unknown experience of the Other, a quest not only for a spiritual father but for the buried reality of the mother.

Notes

1. One of the most concrete examples of the claim that authority promises transcendence is provided by an analysis of the relation of God, Christ, and Lucifer to transcendence. God—at least after the last Old Testament revelations—is detached by virtue of not being apprehensible to the senses (and Stephen sees His detachment as being extreme; He "remains within or behind or beyond or above his handiwork, invisible, refined out of existence, indifferent, paring his fingernails"; James Joyce, *Portrait of the Artist as a Young Man* [New York: Viking, 1968], 215; hereafter cited in the text as *P*). Christ is promised transcendence in return for forgoing it on earth; if He submits Himself totally to the will of God, he will achieve an at-one-ment that atones for the sins of others, and His reward will be that he will be restored to heaven as part of the Godhead. Lucifer wants to achieve detachment (or independence) by a less circuitous and painful route; he would claim his equality with God at the outset, and he is punished through the hopeless transcendence of banishment and exile.

2. James Merrill, "Object Lessons," review, *New York Review of Books* 19 (November 30, 1972), 31–34. Cited by Judith Moffett, *James Merrill: An Introduction to His Poetry* (New York: Columbia University Press, 1984), 118.

3. James Joyce, *Finnegans Wake* (New York: Viking, 1939), 271.14–15; hereafter cited in the text as *FW*.

4. The first spurt of sustained critical interest in *Portrait* was a belated one: not until the 1950s and early 1960s did the critical dialectic grow to its polemical crescendo, taking Stephen as its issue. Those who read Stephen as "Stephen Hero" faced off against Hugh Kenner, Stephen's wittiest detractor. Constituting, as it did, a critical Scylla and Charybdis, *Portrait* attracted an impressive array of minds to map its dangers, including Wayne Booth, Caroline Gordon, Robert Scholes, Maurice Beebe, and S. L. Goldberg. Then, in 1966, Arnold Goldman articulated an acute synthesis in his often neglected study *The Joyce Paradox* (Evanston, Ill.: Northwestern University Press, 1966). His solution is, essentially, not a solution at all but a sharp definition of the problem that gives it both a name (paradox) and a philosophical legitimacy (via Sartre, Ibsen, and Kierkegaard). The doubleness of the concept of doubling locked the readers of *Portrait* in a classical double bind, until the name *paradox* gave us a means of distancing ourselves from a reading experience that, in its wild fluctuations between appreciation and contempt, reproduced Stephen's own experience.

5. The other way to ask Athy's riddle is buried in the darkness of *Finnegans Wake*: it is Shem's "first riddle of the universe." Shem asks, "When is a man not a man?" "All were wrong, so Shem himself, the dictator, took the cake, the correct solution being—all give it up?—; when he is a—yours till the rending of the rocks,—Sham" (*FW*, 170.5, 170.21–24). Athy might have answered, "when he is a thigh," or a more general respondent, "when he is a name" (*Shem* means "name" in Hebrew). A name is a sham, and "sham" is here a variation of the teller's name, a teller inevitably implicated in the riddle of naming he or she contemplates.

6. James Joyce, *Ulysses*, edited by Hans Walter Gabler with Wolfhard Steppe and Claus Melchior (New York: Random House, 1986), 15.2508; hereafter cited in the text as *U*.

7. Derrida's attack on the desire to freeze and thereby contain meaning in "The End of the Book and the Beginning of Writing," *Of Grammatology* (Baltimore: Johns Hopkins University Press, 1976), 6–26, is relevant here.

8. Barthes argues that the reader is where all multiplicity is focused ("The Death of the Author," in Barthes, *Image-Music-Text*, translated by Stephen Heath [New York: Hill and Wang, 1977], 142–48).

9. In *The Picture of Dorian Gray* (New York: Oxford University Press, 1974), Basil Hallward tells Harry that "every portrait that is painted with

feeling is a portrait of the artist, not that of the sitter" (5). Basil knows that the beauty and corruption in his picture of Dorian is his own— that in painting it, he has exposed himself. What Basil had no way of knowing is that his portrait is also a portrait of the man observing it, Lord Henry; it is their dual participation in Dorian's life that the portrait will monstrously come to reflect. The first five words of Joyce's title, when considered in relation to their context in *The Picture of Dorian Gray*, suggest that Joyce's portrait, like Basil's, is a composite portrait of artist, character, and observer with an uncanny power to adapt its features to reflect our own. The distinction between writing and reading is, for someone engaged in either, a misleading one, since artists are always readers, and readers are always artists with the power to paint verbal portraits anew through the inevitable selectivity of observation and memory.

10. See Derek Attridge's excellent account of this phenomenon in the "Sirens" episode of *Ulysses*: "Joyce's Lipspeech: Syntax and the Subject in 'Sirens,'" in *James Joyce: The Centennial Symposium*, ed. Morris Beja et al. (Urbana: University of Illinois Press, 1986), 59–66.

11. The assumption that Joyce's allusions have an allegorical significance is responsible for many of the more rigid and less credible interpretations of both *Portrait* and *Ulysses*. Some of the allegorical grids have been classical, but most have been Christian.

12. At the end of *Portrait*, Stephen can understand love and communication only in these terms, as a humiliating at-one-ment. When Cranly asks him if he has ever loved anyone or anything, Stephen replies that he has tried to love God, which he defines as uniting his will "with the will of God instant by instant" (*P*, 240).

13. James Joyce, *The Critical Writings of James Joyce* (*CW*), edited by Ellsworth Mason and Richard Ellmann (New York: Viking, 1959), 205; Yeats, "Tables of the Law," in Yeats, *Mythologies* (New York: Macmillan, 1959), which, according to Ellmann and Mason, Joyce knew by heart.

14. Joyce's distinction between the classical and romantic tempers is first presented in his 1902 essay on "James Clarence Mangan" (*CW*, 73–83) and is presented again in Joyce, *Stephen Hero* (New York: New Directions, 1944), 78–79.

15. Although not concerned primarily with the reading process, Michael Levenson's essay on Stephen's diary is an excellent, full treatment:

"Stephen's Diary in Joyce's *Portrait*—The Shape of Life," *English Literary History* 52 (1985): 1017–35.

16. Jeremy Lane, "His Master's Voice? The Questioning of Authority in Literature," in *The Modern English Novel: The Reader, the Writer and the Work*, ed. Gabriel Josipovici (New York: Harper and Row, 1976), 126.

Thrilled by His Touch

The Aestheticizing of Homosexual Panic in
A Portrait of the Artist as a Young Man

JOSEPH VALENTE

◆　◆　◆

IN HIS LETTERS AND ESSAYS, Joyce alludes repeatedly to the homoerotic activities supposedly rife in English or Anglo-Saxon boarding schools and implicit in their representative social and athletic customs.[1] In the process, he not only displays a familiarity with the burgeoning *scientia sexualis* of his day, he flaunts a facility with the subcultural argot, dropping arcane phrases like "captain of fifty's regime" in the manner of a cognoscente (*SL* 136). Yet he does so by way of disclaiming any and all knowledge or awareness of such things. The dynamic that Freud called denegation, admitting to consciousness by way of a qualifying refusal, is instinct in virtually every one of these references.[2] At the same time, Joyce seems to have scrupulously avoided the use of terms that name same-sex desires and relations directly, preferring the sort of euphemisms that punctuate Stephen's discussion of Shakespeare in "Scylla and Charybdis": "brothers in love" (*U* 9.1046), "tame essence of Wilde" (*U* 9.532), "play the giddy ox" (*U* 1.171), "cities of the plain" (*SL* 86), "captain of fifty" (*SL* 136), "lady highkickers" (*SL* 74), and so forth. To paraphrase yet another of these prevalent euphemisms, Joyce does not speak the name of homosexuality so much as he names the absence of such speech. Nowhere is this lack of plain speaking any plainer than in Joyce's essay on Oscar Wilde, in which he refuses to give Wilde's "strange problem" or "crime" a name, even as he judges it "the logical and inescapable product of the Anglo-Saxon college and university system, with its secrecy and restrictions" (*CW* 204).[3] What could account for this unwonted circumspection from a man long since resigned to offending hypocritical sensibilities with his writing (*SL* 83)?

When one considers Joyce's own educational career at an elite, all-male boarding school, Clongowes Wood College, it becomes apparent that he has constructed homoeroticism along the lines of what Jonathan Dollimore has called "the proximate."[4] Being socially adjacent to the self, the proximate is that which can be most effectively dissociated from the self. Because it is right *here*, I can see or grasp it, and so it cannot be *right* here; the near-me can only be the not-me. And yet, owing to this adjacency, the essential reality of the proximate—the full extent of its relations to the self—always remains to be discovered; it can always be turned back upon the self, *à vous*, or even accommodated by the self in other guises and contexts. Like the colonial forms of ethnoracial affiliation (English versus Irish), like the socially marked idioms of a given language (slang versus "standard"), homo- and heterosexual affect are at once constituted symbiotically and defined disjunctively, the perfect ideological condition for the concept of proximate-ness to emerge. In Joyce's case, his critical and epistolary allusions to homosexuality insist upon a disjunctive definition, asserting almost gratuitously his heterosexual identity through a professed ignorance of its designated Other, and yet their enunciative context and performance repeatedly belie his intent, pointing to the fundamental imbrication of these erotic tendencies.

What makes the proximate at once ineluctable and dangerous, of course, is also what gives it a specific shape, valence, and site of operations—the existence of normative power relations. In the

modern world of male entitlement, the proximate-ness of homo-
and heterosexuality has taken on a particularly explosive form to
which Eve Sedgwick has given the name "homosexual panic."[5]
Sedgwick summarizes patriarchy itself as a "set of relations between men which have a material base and which, though hi-
erarchical, establish or create interdependence and solidarity
among men that enable them to dominate women."[6] Patriarchal
institutions, accordingly, like the elite male boarding school, be
it Anglo-Saxon or Irish Catholic, serve to promote what Sedgwick
calls male homosocial desires: a chain of fellowship, affection,
boosterism, and engagement, competitive and otherwise, of which
the conventional misogynistic *heterosexual* relationship can be seen
as a defining articulation. Appropriated by, circulated among, and
situated between men as objects of contest, rivalry, and reconciliation, women have traditionally been conscripted as the vehicles
of a homosocial desire that excludes and devalues them. That is,
the "intense and potent bonds" that women share with men work
to enforce the deep, structural complicity of men in preserving
their own privilege.[7] The heterosexual imperative functions as the
handmaiden of the law of the father.

But precisely because homosocial desire is consolidated by the
putative Otherness of heterosexuality, which opens the space of
gender inequity, homosocial desire finds itself rent by the putative
sameness of homosexuality, which, by short-circuiting the ap-
proved wiring of desire, threatens to upset the homosocial flows
of power. And yet, Sedgwick notes, male homosexuality emerges
from these same patriarchal institutions as a particular form of
male homosociality:

> The continuum of male homosocial bonds has been brutally
> structured by a secularized psychologized homophobia, which
> has excluded certain shiftingly and *arbitrarily* defined segments
> of the [same] continuum from participating in the overarching
> male entitlement, in the complex web of male power over the
> production, reproduction and exchange of goods, persons and
> meanings.[8]

And yet, no bright line can be drawn separating homosocial affects and intimacies and homosexual ones. Quoting Sedgwick once more:

> Because the paths of male entitlement required certain intense male bonds that were not readily distinguishable from the most reprobated bonds, an endemic and ineradicable state of . . . male homosexual panic [anxiety over what is, what is not, who is, who is not] became the normal condition of male heterosexual entitlement.[9]

The modern educational system in general and the elite boarding school in particular, where boys learn the ways of male entitlement under the pressure of powerful and labile erotic pulsions, have afforded a prototypical arena for the experience of homosexual panic.

Joyce not only betrays just this sort of sexual unease in his private correspondence, but, I will be arguing, he transfers these attitudes to his fictive alter ego, Stephen Dedalus, in a more extreme, explicitly panicky mode, which systematically shapes the most crucial decisions that Stephen enacts: his appeal to Conmee, his refusal of the priesthood, his assumption of an aesthetic vocation, his self-exile. A number of critics have, over the years, pointed to the operation of homoerotic energies in *Portrait*—for example, in the smuggling episode or in Stephen's final interview with Cranly—and a couple have even asserted the importance of these same energies as a component of Stephen's psychology.[10] What I would like to demonstrate is that these homosexual energies are indissociable from Stephen's phobic denial of them, that this denial constitutes a *fundamental determinant* of the novel's basic narrative structure and hence of Stephen's destiny, and that in his elaboration of Stephen's denial, Joyce *stages and thereby transvalues* his own disavowal of the homoerotic.

By taking this approach, I do not mean to imply any simple autobiographical identification of the figure of Dedalus with that of Joyce; the panic and denial that Stephen displays are not synonymous with Joyce's unease and disavowal but are heuristic parodies or exaggerations thereof, in keeping with what Hugh Kenner has called Joyce's cubist method of self-portraiture. I do mean to propose, however, that the combination of projection, misrecognition, and self-awareness connecting author and alter ego comprises a certain homoerotic ambivalence whose operation in the text helps to demystify Stephen's strongest claim to being Joyce's surrogate: his will to artistry.

I

The very title of the novel invokes fin-de-siècle homoeroticism, and does so in a characteristically Joycean fashion, by establishing, at the outset, the text as intertext. As Vicki Mahaffey has suggested, the phrase "a portrait of the artist" is a quite peculiar locution, which makes its derivation from one work in particular, Oscar Wilde's *The Picture of Dorian Gray*, that much more assured, especially since Dorian's portrait *keeps* him at the age of a young man. During the opening scene of Wilde's famous novel, Basil tells Henry, "Every portrait that is painted with feeling is a portrait of the artist, not the sitter. The sitter is merely the accident, the occasion. It is not he who is revealed by the painter; it is rather the painter ... who reveals himself."[11] In this light, Stephen can be taken either as a self-portrait in the ordinary sense or as a self-portrait strictly by virtue of being a portrait "painted with feeling," a condition likely to disfigure the ordinary self-portrait with a certain self-indulgence. Stephen must, therefore, not only be seen as both Joyce and not Joyce; he must also be seen as revealing Joyce precisely to the extent that he is not a self-depiction (being instead merely a portrait painted with feeling) and disfiguring Joyce to the extent that he is a self-depiction, altered by that feeling.

But Joyce's interest in the intercourse between revelation and representation in Wilde exceeded questions of the pragmatics of self-portraiture. It had a nakedly ethicopolitical edge as well. Joyce's primary response to *The Picture of Dorian Gray* was disappointment that Wilde had dissembled in presenting the homosexual charge binding Dorian, Basil, and Henry, that Wilde's own complex self-representation had not been more of a (sexual) revelation:

> I can imagine the capital which Wilde's prosecuting counsel made out of certain parts of it. It is not very difficult to read between the lines. Wilde seems to have had some good intentions in writing it—some wish to put himself before the world—but the book is rather crowded with lies and epigrams. If he had had the courage to develop the allusions in the book it might have been better. I suspect he has done this in some privately-printed books. (*SL* 96)

Like this letter, however, which conspicuously declines to develop "the allusions in the book" any more than Wilde does, leaving the homosexuality therein an "open secret,"[12] Joyce's title repeats the gesture of circumspection, leaving the homotextual relations between his novel and Wilde's at the level of "epigram." Or perhaps it would be truer to say that Joyce's title answers Wilde's deliberate circumspection with an unconscious disavowal; it simultaneously reveals and conceals the intense homotextual relation between his *Bildungsroman* and his precursor, revealing the "textual" affinity, in its most Derridean sense, while concealing or eliding the "homo." Whereas the feeling that makes Dorian's portrait a "portrait of the artist" involves Basil's homoerotic attraction to his sitter, as Joyce recognizes, Joyce's feeling for his sitter could only be construed as narcissistic, a modality of desire properly understood as the precondition for any object relation, homo or hetero. By remaining at the level of epigram, the title *A Portrait of the Artist* translates the open secret of *Dorian Gray*'s sexual economy into an open option or open possibility. That is to say, whereas *Dorian Gray* veils its specific erotic "truth" in order to betray it selectively, enacting a classic economy of repression and desire, *Portrait* announces but does not specify its erotic truth, entertaining a *jouissance* of suspension and volatility—a point to which I will return in my conclusion.

By the same token, the improbable Greek surname of Joyce's

alter ego, the marker of his prospective artistic identity, would inevitably be construed, in the aftermath of the entire Wilde controversy, as invoking the Hellenistic cultural movement that the name Dorian Gray had served to sensationalize. But here again, the name Dorian alludes specifically to the homoerotic component of that late Victorian cult of aestheticist self-development, the Dorians being regarded as the prototypical exponents of "Greek love." The name Dedalus, by contrast, carries far less determinate sexual connotations: The "old artificer" (*P* 253) not only fathered Icarus on a slave girl, he mentored and then murdered Perdix, and he pandered to the unnatural lusts of Pasiphaë, the queen of the Cretans, who were themselves generally reputed to have introduced the institution of *paiderastia* into Greece (a belief built into the etymology of the word itself).[13]

A similarly displaced homotextual relation presents itself in the symbol of Stephen's Irish art (no, not the cracked mirror [*U* 1.143–44], though it is telling that Wilde presides there as well): the impossible green rose. Stephen's aesthetic career begins on a significant pun, significantly repeated:

O, the *wild* rose blossoms
On the little green place.
He sang that song. That was his song. (*P* 7; emphasis added)

And again:

Perhaps a *wild* rose might be like those colors. And he remembered the song about the *wild* rose blossoms on the little green place. (*P* 12; emphases added)

Joyce underlines and clarifies the pun in *Finnegans Wake*, where it serves to stake the process of history itself on the wages of illicit sexuality:

has not the levy of black mail from the times the finish were in it, and fain for *wilde* erthe blossoms followed and impressive private reputation for whispered sins? (*FW* 69.2–4; emphasis added)

With this in mind, Stephen's subsequent musing—"But you could not have a green rose. But perhaps somewhere in the world you could" (*P* 12)—unmistakably recalls Wilde's famous "green carnation," which was an aestheticist emblem of imaginative artifice (the conventional reading of Stephen's rose) and a badge of the homosexual subculture of fin-de-siècle England,[14] a sense that Stephen's flower intimates sotto voce. By deploying this symbolic nexus in this fashion, Joyce puts Stephen in the position of registering, "owning" in some sense, the emergent cultural identification of artistry and homoeroticism that the aestheticist movement had adumbrated, but Joyce simultaneously avoids any suggestion that Stephen could himself be aware of, or even subliminally invested in, that identification. Joyce thereby sets up a recursive dynamic wherein Stephen's preordained vocation will have been grounded in an inarticulate homoeroticism once, and only once, his exposure to the taboos informing compulsory heterosexuality has catalyzed same-sex desire as a dread of the unspeakable, something to be expressed only in the negative form of a denial. So even before Stephen's homosexual panic begins to condition the contents of his life narrative, its genesis works a significant complication in the form of that narrative. Instead of unfolding on the latency model, which neatly conforms with the linear, quasi-organic development typical of the *Künstlerroman*, Stephen's homoerotic affects emerge in a knot or fold known, in Freudian parlance, as a "deferred action," in this case the retroactive generation of a subsequently phobic desire. To speak of Stephen's homoerotic cathexes, accordingly, is always to speak of his simultaneous denial and diversion of them, galvanized in his Clongowes education.

Stephen's thoughts on the green rose immediately follow his reflections on the widely suspect Simon Moonan. The homoerotic overtones of this interlude nicely encapsulate the temporal knot of deferred action, for they reveal both a naiveté too complete to be inhibited and a knowingness too acute to be innocent:

—We all know why you speak. You are McGlade's suck.

Suck was a queer word. The fellow called Simon Moonan that name because Simon Moonan used to tie the prefect's false sleeves behind his back and the prefect used to let on to be angry. But the sound was ugly. Once he had washed his hands in the lavatory of the Wicklow Hotel and his father pulled the stopper up by the chain after and the dirty water went down through the hole in the basin. And when it had all gone down slowly the hole in the basin had made a sound like that: suck. Only louder.... There were two cocks that you turned and water came out: cold and hot.... [A]nd he could see the names printed on the cocks. That was a very queer thing. (*P* 11)

I have quoted this passage at length because

1. Through the repeated use of terms like *suck, queer, cocks*, and so forth,[15] it lays down psychosymbolic associations among Stephen's developing fever, his ongoing fascination with—and aversion to—standing water and waste, and a retroactive homosexual panic.
2. As a link in the reversible chain of Stephen's psychic development, it puts an erotic spin on the sort of homosocial roughhousing that lands him in the square ditch and causes his fever. Stephen, remember, a designated mama's boy, will not trade his dandyish "little snuffbox" for Wells's macho "hacking chestnut, the conqueror of forty" (*P* 10); the box and the nut function as genital symbols for the respectively feminized and masculinized positions of Stephen and Wells. Since the incident exemplifies the sexualized aggression that Joyce attributed to English boardingschool activities, and since Joyce was likewise shouldered into the ditch, with similarly febrile consequences (*JJII* 28), it is worth noting that the square ditch runs along the perimeter of Clongowes and forms its boundary with the old English pale.[16] It is, in other words, a border zone where the masculinized Anglo-Saxon "conqueror" and the feminized Irish conquered meet and,

partly as an effect of the conquest itself, where their ethnoracial differences are both marked, even exaggerated, and
overridden, even erased. With respect to Joyce's cherished
distinction between the rampant homoeroticism of English
public-school life and the comparative innocence of its Irish
counterpart, the square ditch constitutes an objectified instance of the proximate itself, that is, a thin margin of dis-
sociation into which the subject might always land or be
pushed and his kinship with the Other be uncomfortably
reaffirmed.[17]

3. In light of points 1 and 2, it establishes a basis on which to
overcome an inveterate critical assumption that because Stephen does not fully grasp the implications of the "smugging" scandal until later on, he is not really party to the
homosexual energies circulating among the Clongowes students as they remember or recount the "crime" and anticipate the similarly titillating punishment. The mode of Stephen's knowledge is unconscious, which is to say it unfolds
in the *futur antérieur*.

As it turns out, these three narrative functions are strictly
correlative. For what most powerfully eroticizes the Clongowes
scene for Stephen is not the prosaic specification of Moonan and
Boyle's offense (smugging), nor even the poetic rehearsal of their
punishment ("It can't be helped / It must be done / So down
with your breeches / And out with your bum" [*P* 44]). It is rather
the way the taboo on their activity (that is, a prohibition enforc-
ing secrecy and enforced by shame) molds Stephen's private elaboration of these accounts and the way his elaboration, in turn,
interacts with other environmental cues, like the sound of the
cricket bats.

As Stephen speculates on the offense, his effort to exculpate
Moonan in his own mind lends a distinctly libidinal complexion
to his memories of the boy, as if the sense of transgression itself,
any transgression, carries its own highly labile erotic current:

What did that mean about the smugging in the square.... It
was a joke, he thought. Simon Moonan had nice clothes and

one night he had *shown him a ball of creamy sweets* that the fellows
of the football fifteen had rolled down to him along the carpet.
. . . It was the night of the *match against the Bective Rangers* and the
ball was made just like a red and green apple only it opened
and it *was full of the creamy sweets.* (*P* 42; emphases added)

Stephen's earlier fantasy about leaving on vacation already incorporated his experience with Moonan in a plainly, if unconsciously,
homoerotic fashion: "The train was full of fellows: a *long, long
chocolate train* with *cream facings*" (*P* 20; emphases added). This is a
classic instance in which commonplace homosocial reinforce-
ment, highlighted by the affiliation with team sports, merges almost seamlessly with the "most reprobated" sexual imagery and
investments. Once again, Stephen undergoes the panic this double
bind arouses as an "agony in the watercloset" (*U* 15.2643), a dread
associated with waste and standing urine:

But why in the square? You went there when you wanted to
do something. It was all thick slabs of slate and water trickled
all day out of tiny pinholes and there was a queer smell of
stale water there. (*P* 43)

Being the site of a certain mutual genital exposure, the male
lavatory space always carries some homoerotic potential; as a result, the introduction of a more explicitly sexual element, tapping
as it does Stephen's existing fear and confusion, renders the excremental function itself "queer" and therefore unspeakable for
him. One went to the lavatory to "do something" that apparently
dares not be named.

Regarding the punishment, his dread and his desire come simultaneously into view.[18] He imagines the prospect of being caned
less in terms of pain than in terms of "chill": "It made him shivery
to think of it and cold. . . . it made him shivery" (*P* 45). That this
chill bespeaks a sexualized frisson becomes immediately evident
in Stephen's focus on the ceremonial unveiling of the "vital spot"
(*P* 44): "He wondered who had to let them [the trousers] down,
the master or the boy himself" (*P* 45). Stephen's consideration of
the protocol involved suggests a mutuality of participation in the

act of undressing that bares the sexual energy animating the exemplary discipline. His subsequent vision of the caning itself implies a literalized dialectic or reciprocity between beater and beaten that issues in a sense of positive and implicitly homoerotic pleasure:

> [Athy] had rolled up his sleeves to show how Mr. Gleeson would roll up his sleeves. But Mr. Gleeson had round shiny cuffs and clean white wrists and fattish white hands and the nails of them were long and pointed. Perhaps he pared them too like Lady Boyle. . . . And though he trembled with . . . fright to think of the cruel long nails . . . and of the chill you felt at the end of your shirt when you undressed yourself yet he felt a feeling of queer quiet pleasure inside him to think of the white fattish hands, clean and strong and gentle. (*P* 45)

As the passage mushrooms into a full-blown if displaced sexual fantasy, Stephen takes center stage as the subject of warring sensations, an outer chill and an inner glow, an anticipated pain and an experienced pleasure, an involuntary engagement but a voluntary imagining, a sexual affect at once savored and denied. Indeed, Joyce exploits the equivocality of the word *queer* in this passage in order to mark not only the homoerotic nature of Stephen's ambivalence, but also to mark the ambivalent, uncanny impact of the homoerotic upon Stephen, his mixture of fear and fascination, attraction and repulsion, which is the recipe for a panic born of proximate-ness.

This proximate-ness, in turn, with its ambivalent affect, gives a sharply ironic twist to Stephen's subsequent pandying. It is not just that Stephen receives punishment for something he never did—scheme to break his glasses—nor even that he is made the scapegoat for a sexual scandal he imperfectly comprehends, which is how he comes to interpret the matter (*P* 54); no, what is ironic is that in the unconscious, where the thought or wish can stand for the deed and carry the same transgressive force,[19] there is indeed a recursive symmetry, if not equity, to Stephen's chastisement. If, as Stephen and the other boys suspect, the pandyings actually respond to the homoerotic indulgences of the smugging "ring," then Stephen can be seen as an accomplice after the fact, participating vicariously in these indulgences through his fantasy construction of Mr. Gleeson's discipline. In fact, the imagined caning and the real pandying communicate with one another precisely through Stephen's erotic preoccupation with his masters' hands. Having taken a "queer quiet pleasure" from the contemplation of Mr. Gleeson's "white fattish hands, clean and strong and gentle," Stephen seems to expect something of the same gratification from the prefect's fingers, in which he initially discerns a like quality, and Stephen finds Father Dolan's betrayal of this sensual promise to be, in some respects, the most galling aspect of the whole episode. His mind returns to it obsessively in the aftermath:

[H]e thought of the hands which he had held out in the air with the palms up and of the firm touch of the prefect of studies when he had steadied the shaking fingers. (*P* 51)

He felt the touch of the prefect's fingers as they had steadied his hand and at first he had thought he was going to shake hands with him because the fingers were soft and firm: but then in an instant he had heard the swish of the soutane sleeve and the crash. (*P* 52)

And his whitegrey face and the nocoloured eyes behind the steelrimmed spectacles were cruel looking *because* he had steadied the hand first with his firm soft fingers and that was to hit it better and louder. (*P* 52; emphasis added)

Since we are dealing with Stephen's perception of the scene, the insistent, fetishistic repetition of "soft," "firm," "fingers," "touch," and "steadied," along with the bizarre causal priority accorded Dolan's duplicitous touch, must be seen as recalling some sort of baffled desire as well as trauma or, rather, an overlapping of the two psychic movements. Stephen's trauma at the pandying fixates upon the master's touch because that is where Stephen's unconscious wishes insert themselves into both the smuggling scandal and the larger homosocial/homosexual economy of Clongowes. It is the point at which he has eroticized, and so from a certain point of view merited, the priests' brutal sanctions on such eroticism.

Stephen's subsequent protest at the injustice of his thrashing likewise belies his fascination with the male body, which is, of course, the impulse being disciplined:

> [A]nd the fifth was big Corrigan who was going to be flogged by Mr. Gleeson. That was why the prefect of studies had called him a schemer and pandied him for nothing. . . . But he [Corrigan] had done something and besides Mr. Gleeson would not flog him hard: and he [Stephen] remembered how big Corrigan looked in the bath. He had skin the same colour as the turf-coloured bogwater in the shallow end of the bath and when he walked along the side his feet slapped loudly on the wet tiles and at every step his thighs shook a little because he was fat. (P 54)

Stephen wants to assert a distinction between guilty, robust Corrigan and poor, little, innocent Dedalus. But in doing so, he discloses a familiarity with Corrigan's physique apparently gleaned from watching his "every step" in the bath, and the desire such familiarity would suggest seems further corroborated by the way Corrigan's bodily image simply takes over Stephen's juridical meditation. At the same time, his comparison of Corrigan's pigmentation to the dirty water in the bath recalls his own immersion in the square ditch and so indicates how profoundly this desire interfuses with dread.

Far from resolving this double bind, Conmee's vindication of Stephen and his schoolmates' ensuing homage only cements it. After his interview with the rector, Stephen is "hoisted" and "carried . . . along" (P 58) in a homosocial bonding ritual that obviously makes him quite uncomfortable, for he immediately struggles to extricate his body from their grasp. And it is only once "[h]e was alone" that "[h]e was happy and free" (P 59). He then proceeds to dissociate himself in a categorical fashion from any sense of triumph over the prefect and so, by extension, from the celebratory fellowship of his peers. The reason is not far to seek. The very image in which his sense of gratification crystallizes, a sound "like drops of water in a fountain falling softly in a brimming bowl" (*P* 59), is but the inverse of his image of the dreaded smugging square, "all thick slabs of slate and water trickled all day out of tiny pinholes." The aestheticized emblem of personal fulfillment thus encodes and carries forward the cloacal image of taboo sexual longing. Just as the prospect of painful social humiliation—being singled out for a caning—triggers in Stephen a "queer quiet pleasure" amid his anxiety, owing to its homoerotic undercurrents, so the fruits of Stephen's social victory trigger an unconscious anxiety amid validation, an anxiety registered along the associative chains of Stephen's mental imagery.

In this regard, the fact that this ambivalent water rhapsody actually emanates from a game of cricket, a sport exported from the elite playing fields of England to those of Ireland, implicates the author's unconscious as well in the structure of homoerotic disavowal. As Trevor Williams has argued, Joyce frames Stephen's success with a motif of colonial-cultural hegemony as a way of qualifying or undercutting its ultimate meaningfulness, in keeping with the alternating elevation-deflation mechanism of the narrative as a whole.[20] But in the process, Joyce necessarily undermines his own cherished distinction between the athletic customs of English and Irish boarding schools at precisely the moment when the sexual anxiety that distinction was designed to forestall infiltrates the crowning symbol of Stephen's young life— the brimming bowl.

Stephen's failure to resolve his homosexual panic, in spite of his social triumph, presages Joyce's treatment of the issue through the remainder of the novel, beginning with Stephen's entry into officially heterosexual activity, from courtship rituals to whoring excursions. Joyce consistently surrounds Stephen's participation in these practices with conspicuous forms and indices of sexual/ gender inversion, which, by the end of the century, was the dominant model of homosexuality in both the popular imagination and in the work of such prominent psychosexologists as Ellis, Symonds, Carpenter, Freud, Krafft-Ebing, and Burton (all of whom Joyce read).[21] Joyce's deployment of this received idea, however, as with so many others, works to reverse or disrupt its received social force. Interwoven as they are with distinctively masculine, heterosexual rites of passage, the inversion motifs in *Portrait* situate homoeroticism neither as a simple alternative to nor an anomalous deviation from some naturalized heteroerotic incitement but as an element uncannily symbiotic with that incitement and menacing to its normalization.

First, just before the Harold's Cross children's party—Stephen's "coming out" as a heterosexual male—an old woman mistakes him for a female, repeating the phrase "I thought you were Josephine" several times (*P* 68). Often treated as an isolated epiphany, this incident has little if any pertinence to the rest of the narrative, other than being the first of several instances in which gender inversion attaches specifically to Stephen. As such, it can be read as one of those incompletely processed "lumps" in which the subterranean concerns of a text concentrate themselves in a nearly illegible form. In support of this thesis, I would note that just after the party, Stephen actually bears out this gender (mis)identification in terms of the standard Victorian sexual typology. On the tram ride home with E.C., he assumes what was thought to be the essentially, even definitively feminine role of sexual passivity and withdrawal, receiving without responding to her perceived sexual advances.[22]

Once again, just before her attendance at Stephen's Whitsuntide performance, their first encounter since the party, a significant instance of gender misidentification supervenes. There appears backstage "a pinkdressed figure, wearing a curly golden wig and an oldfashioned straw sunbonnet, with black pencilled eyebrows and cheeks delicately rouged and powdered" (*P* 74). The presiding prefect asks facetiously, "Is this a beautiful young lady or a doll that you have here, Mrs. Tallon?" It turns out, of course, to be the "girlish figure" of a boy, "little Bertie Tallon," a circumstance that provokes "a murmur of curiosity" and then "a murmur of admiration" from the other boys. In Stephen, however, this transvestite spectacle precipitates a telling "movement of impatience. . . . He let the edge of the blind fall . . . and walked out of the chapel" (*P* 74). Why would Stephen react or overreact in this fashion? Perhaps because the superimposition of the signifiers of feminine desirability upon a schoolboy's already "girlish figure," the accompanying expression of the other schoolboys' admiration, and the disingenuous participation of the prefect combine to tap the ambivalence at the heart of Stephen's sexual desire, by recalling the roots of that ambivalence in his own school experience as the "little" boy, the mama's boy, the feminized boy. A subsequent passage, however, indicates that still more is at stake:

> All day he had thought of nothing but their leavetaking on the steps of the tram at Harold's Cross. . . . All day he had imagined a new meeting with her for he knew that she was to come to the play. The old restless moodiness had again filled his breast as it had done on the night of the party but had not found an outlet in verse. The growth and knowledge of two years of boyhood stood between then and now, forbidding such an outlet: and all day the stream of gloomy tenderness within him had started forth and returned upon itself in dark courses and eddies, wearying him in the end until the pleasantry of the prefect and the painted little boy had drawn from him a movement of impatience. (*P* 77)

Why do the moodiness attached to Stephen's sexual "growth and knowledge," not to mention the restlessness accumulated over his day of brooding on Harold's Cross, vent themselves specifically in response to a schoolboy's drag performance? Perhaps because Stephen's sexual ambivalence, tapped by this transvestite scenario, persists in such a way as to disturb the ease of his enlistment in the roles of compulsory heterosexuality, his dalliance with E.C. being a critical step in this process. Notice, in this respect, that Stephen figures his feelings for E.C. as a "stream of gloomy tenderness" moving "in dark courses and eddies," a metaphor that unmistakably keys into and recirculates the homoerotic valences and associations of Stephen's past experiences with dark or eddying courses of water: the square ditch, the sink at the Wicklow Hotel, the shallow end of the bath at Clongowes. Given this commingling of the "streams" of heterosexual affect with the "courses" of (water-)closeted homosexual desire, Stephen's prescription for calming his heart after he misses E.C., the "odour" of "horse piss and rotted straw" (*P* 86), seems a recognizable displacement.

Finally, Stephen's venture into the brothel district is characterized by a literal and symbolic inversion of the phallic mode of heterosexual activity. He serves as the object or locus rather than the agent of penetration. First, "subtle streams" of sound "penetrated his being" (*P* 100). Then, "his hands clenched convulsively and his teeth set together as he suffered the agony of . . . penetration" (*P* 100). Upon entering the prostitute's room, it is Stephen who becomes "hysterical," Stephen who is "surrendering himself," and Stephen who is passively penetrated by "the dark pressure of her softly parting lips" (*P* 101). Moreover, Joyce frames Stephen's long-anticipated (hetero)sexual transfiguration with lavatory motifs familiar from Clongowes. He depicts Stephen prowling "dark, slimy streets," penetrated by "subtle streams" of sound, and issuing "a cry which was but the echo of an obscene scrawl which he had read on the oozing wall of a urinal" (*P* 99–100). In this way, Joyce unsettles the popular *Bildungsmythos* of a young man's self-conscious graduation from homosexual play to heterosexual maturity and (re)productivity, and he replaces it with an ambivalent complication, a progressive overlapping and interfolding of sexual preferences that is registered at one level of self-narration only to be denied or externalized at another. Such interfolding even extends to Stephen's repentance for these sexual excesses at the religious retreat. For his nominally heterosexual sins, he imagines an eternal punishment expressive of his profound dread at his unacknowledged homosexual desires: a weedy field of "solid excrement" populated by bestial creatures with long phallic tails and faces whose similarity to and contact with the weedy field give them an anal cast (*P* 137). By the same token, Stephen envisions the regained innocence that confession and repentance promise to yield in terms of an ingenuous heterosexual marriage ceremony:

> She placed their hands together, hand in hand, and said, speaking to their hearts:
> —Take hands, Stephen and Emma. It is a beautiful evening now in heaven. You have erred but you are always my children. It is one heart that loves another heart. Take hands together, my dear children, and you will be happy together and your hearts will love each other. (*P* 116)

Keeping this sexual ambivalence at bay (what we might call the normative working through of homosexual panic) exerts a subtle yet potent pressure on the subsequent course of Stephen's development. On the one hand, his unconscious anxiety about the homoerotic component of his sexual drives can be seen as fueling his repentance and renunciation of their illicit enactment. On the other hand, and more important, a gradual accretion of images and associations of sexual inversion and memories of the homosocial interplay at Clongowes work to hold Stephen back from the logical terminus of his recovered piety, turning his consideration of the religious life toward a relieved demurral.

The latter point becomes evident over the course of his vocational interview with the director of Belvedere. The director opens the interview with a comment on "the friendship between saint Thomas and saint Bonaventure" and goes on to criticize the feminine design of "the capuchin dress" known as *les jupes* (*P* 154–55).[23] Stephen's silent, embarrassed response is a meditation upon the "soft and delicate stuffs" of women's clothing followed by a meditation on the Jesuit body, in both senses of the term:

> His masters, even when they had not attracted him, had seemed to him always intelligent and serious priests, athletic and highspirited prefects. He thought of them as men who washed their bodies briskly with cold water and wore clean cold linen. (*P* 155–56)

In a context thus informed by questions of homosocial affection and institutionalized cross-dressing, the director's ensuing gesture of suddenly releasing the blind's cord cannot but trigger, in both Stephen and the reader, the unconscious memory of Bertie Tallon in drag and Stephen's own impatient response: letting the edge of the blind fall.

As Stephen leaves the director, he begins to envisage his daily life as a priest in more concrete detail, and the (homo)eroticized traces of the past gather more thickly and affect Stephen more intensely:

> The troubling odour of the long corridor of Clongowes came back to him. . . . At once from every part of his being and unrest began to irradiate. A feverish quickening of his pulses followed. (*P* 160)

An olfactory cue, always the strongest for Stephen, puts him in the grip of an excitement that cannot be explained on a purely nonsexual basis or in terms of simple attraction or repulsion, but only by way of the annihilating proximate-ness of a taboo desire, its alien and alienating intimacy. The memory of the bathhouse atmosphere at Clongowes returns to Stephen with precisely this quality, being *in* and yet not *of* him:

> His lungs dilated and sank as if he were inhaling a warm moist unsustaining air . . . which hung in the bath in Clongowes above the sluggish turfcoloured water. (*P* 161)

The last phrase, it should be noted, substantially repeats Stephen's mesmerized description of big Corrigan's naked body. So when Stephen goes on to ground his refusal of the clerical life on "the pride of his spirit which had always made him conceive himself as a being apart in every order" (*P* 161), he represses one of his libidinal aims in the service of the larger economy of desire that feeds his panic. Stephen does not, as he later thinks, refuse the priesthood simply by obedience to a "wayward instinct" (*P* 165) but also out of fear of yet another "wayward instinct," which is implicated in his possible acceptance. This misprision resonates specifically in the odd, ambiguous phrase "apart in [not from] every order." To be "apart in" an order, after all, is also to be "a part in" that order; it is to find oneself in a situation of belonging and estrangement simultaneously, the condition of the proximate. It is precisely at this moment of proximate-ness that the text locates the first, decisive mental stirrings of Stephen's refusal: "Some instinct, waking at these memories, stronger than education or piety, quickened within him at every near approach of that life, an instinct subtle and hostile, and armed him against acquiescence" (*P* 161).

That Stephen's professedly homosocial discomfort cannot be dissociated from homosexual anxiety grows even clearer during the climactic scene on the strand, where Stephen receives his "true" calling. His fetishistic (which is to say, implicitly misogynistic) overvaluation of the bird girl's physical presence follows a correspondingly aversive overreaction to the physical presence of his unclothed schoolmates:

> It was a pain to see them and a swordlike pain to see the signs of adolescence that made repellent their pitiable nakedness. Perhaps they had taken refuge in number and noise from the secret dread of their souls. But he, apart from them and in silence, remembered in what dread he stood of the mystery of his own body. (*P* 168)

The phallic ("swordlike") nature of Stephen's pain, his confounding of his dread of others with a dread of self, and, finally, the now-familiar solace he takes in a fantasy of dignified solitude, all indicate a recurrence of Stephen's homosexual panic. The representation of his state of being upon removing himself from the spectacle of his naked classmates even recalls the description of his state of mind upon extricating himself from his classmates' celebratory embrace at Clongowes:

> He was alone. He was unheeded, happy and near to the wild heart of life. (*P* 171)

He was alone. He was happy and free. (*P* 59)

The crucial development on this occasion is that Stephen is able to legitimate his resource of splendid isolation through the romantic myth of the artist.

The bird girl can serve as Stephen's muse only insofar as she confirms this phantasmatic self-conception and thus delivers him from the embarrassments of censored and ambivalent sexual impulses. This function would go some way toward accounting for the extraordinary rapture she incites in him.[24] Stephen might be seen as placing her in a transferential position between himself and his naked peers, in much the same way that individual women, according to Sedgwick, are consistently being enlisted as eroticized points of mediation "between men" in order to forestall the "panic" that arises with the arbitrary, institutionalized disjunction between homosocial and homosexual practice.[25] At the same time, in order to perform this function, the bird girl must appeal to the braided homo- and heterocathexes motivating Stephen's gaze—and on apparently straightforward heterosexual grounds. That is, she must enable a simplification and sublimation of Stephen's perverse desire, which is where the aesthetic framework becomes crucial. In this regard, it is important that she is not a bird woman but a bird girl, poised in her incipient physical maturity between complete and incomplete gender differentiation. The repeated description of her look as "girlish" stresses as much by connecting her with that other "girlish figure," little Bertie Tallon. In fact, Joyce sets up a sort of textual ratio between the performances of Bertie and the bird girl, each of which constitutes a species of drag in that

1. each induces in its respective audience an admiration entirely bound up with some kind of aestheticized semblance: Bertie's garish overlay of feminine cues, the bird girl's concealed displacement of masculine ones; and
2. each induces in its respective audience an admiration that is itself in disguise, its homoerotic component hidden from consciousness.

Understood in these terms, the bird girl fits into Stephen's psychic economy in much the same way that Sybil Vane initially fits into Dorian's, as an objective correlative of a straightforward heterosexual investment that only exists "on stage," through aesthetic misrecognition. That is to say, in keeping with his reading of *Dorian Gray*, Joyce associates Wilde's brand of aestheticism not with his sodomite inclinations but with his dissimulation of them. For this reason, Joyce has Stephen's soaring inspiration express itself in what amounts to a broad stylistic parody of Wilde and Walter Pater, and he thereby establishes a subtle link between the sublimity of Stephen's aesthetic delirium and the repression and displaced release of the homosocial affect aroused by the swimmers (a dramatic irony perfectly in keeping with the cultural identification of art and same-sex desire fostered by Pater and consolidated by Wilde). It is remarkable, in fact, the extent to which the entire episode unfolds under (a pun on) the name of Wilde. Stephen's "ecstasy of flight made . . . wild his breath and . . . wild and radiant his windswept limbs," and "an instant of wild flight had delivered him" (*P* 169). "A new wild life was singing in his veins" (*P* 170). "He was . . . near to the wild heart of life . . . willful and wildhearted, alone amid a waste of wild air" (*P* 171). "He strode . . . singing wildly to the sea" (*P* 172). Once "her image had passed into his soul," the bird girl is figured as a "wild angel" (*P* 172). Just as the first signature song of baby Stephen touches punningly and significantly on Wilde, focusing upon a "wild rose" (*P* 7), later to transmogrify into the impossible "green rose" (*P* 12), so Stephen's first moments as a self-proclaimed artist have Wilde written all over them—over his flight, his song, his aesthetic object. From its flowering back to its roots, the narrative of Stephen's aesthetic destiny is staked upon his obsessive encrypting of homoerotic desire, that is, his encoding of this desire and his laying it to rest. And the name of Wilde, always there and not quite there, remarks this mechanism of denial.

Much the same structure characterizes Stephen's theoretical colloquium with Lynch. Sexualized byplay, such as Lynch's rubbing of his groin, is mediated by reference to an aesthetic ideal of female beauty, the Venus of Praxiteles, and routed through her

mutual appropriation by the interlocutors. When Stephen introduces the question of body with the exhortation, "Let us take
woman," and Lynch fervently responds, "Let us take her!" (*P* 208),
they align themselves in an aestheticized version of the erotic
triangle that Sedgwick takes to be the paradigmatic figure of hom-
osociality/homophobia. It is important to recognize in this regard
that notions of triangulated same-sex desire much like Sedgwick's
were already abroad in the late nineteenth century and were
readily available to Joyce. In *The Renaissance*, for example, Walter
Pater, whose prose we saw parodied in the decidedly homosocial
beach episode, advanced an equally homosocial interpretation of
Chaucer's *The Knight's Tale*, opining that "one knows not whether
the love of both Palimon and Arcite for Emelya, or of those two
for each other, is the chiefer subject"—a reading that seeks to
place an ideal of male love at the heart of the aesthetic experience.[26] For Stephen, of course, the aesthetic is the discursive mode
that raises the mind "above desire and loathing" (*P* 205), and yet
it is precisely this nominal status that makes art the perfect cover
for the taboo, which is itself defined by the cooperation of what
"the flesh shrinks from" and "what it desires" (*P* 206). Stephen's
sense of the aesthetic as being properly sequestered "in a mental
world" (*P* 206) is what allows it to facilitate covertly the discharge
of homosexual libido. Witness, for example, the sublime culmination of his theoretical communiqué. The vision of the arche-
typal artist, God, "paring his fingernails" (*P* 215) harnesses and
transforms the desire attached to Stephen's memories of the sexually ambivalent hands of Tusker (Lady) Boyle and the punishing
yet pleasure-giving hands of Mr. Gleeson.

Here we have then the erotic hinge on which the *Künstlerroman*
aspect of the narrative can be said to turn. Whereas the religious
life figures for Stephen the perilous slide of homosocial relations
toward homosexual exposure, prompting his flight, the aesthetic
vocation figures the sublimation of homosocial ties through the
elaboration of a heteroerotic ideal. It thus serves him as a kind
of supplement to the heterosexual imperative, a subsidiary distancing or mediating agency of homosocial bonds. That the het-

erosexual imperative should need the supplement of aesthetic transformation, however, is a sign of its ultimate vulnerability.

Such vulnerability is borne out in Stephen's friendship with Cranly, which features the closest thing *Portrait* has to a French triangle: Stephen projects upon Cranly a mutual competitive interest in E.C. This triangle is modeled in turn into an Oedipal triangle, in which the paternalistic Cranly remonstrates with Stephen over the proper devotion to be paid his mother. We seem, in other words, to be moving toward what Sedgwick would see as a normative heterosexual/homophobic resolution. But it does not work. For if Stephen requires a heteroerotic ideal to sublimate his stubborn homoerotic ambivalence, his rarefaction of E.C. paradoxically renders her too shadowy and insubstantial a figure to mediate his powerful homosocial relationship with Cranly. Stephen's fleeting sense of romantic rivalry notwithstanding, Cranly increasingly comes to take over the place of E.C. as Stephen's object of affection. True to the terms of the novel outlined thus far, this transfer of erotic intensity and intimacy to a male figure passes through the register of religious intercourse.

Shortly before Stephen's initial thoughts of Cranly, there occurs a moment of gender misidentification of the sort that occurs prior to Stephen's first date with E.C. Stephen's father refers to him as a "lazy bitch" (*P* 175). Joyce hereby intimates a structural parallel between Stephen's relations with E.C. and with Cranly, a sort of dueling courtship. Stephen's thoughts themselves are fairly bursting with a barely repressed homoeroticism. He begins by wondering:

> Why was it when he thought of Cranly he could never raise before his mind the entire image of his body but only the image of his head and face? (*P* 178)

The habit of mind Stephen observes would seem to locate Cranly, like the aestheticized image of Venus, exclusively "in a mental world," in this case by substantially blotting out his bodily existence. But the mental world in which Stephen would cloister his friend is sacerdotal rather than aesthetic, and as the following passage indicates, Stephen's identification of the clerical orders with marked homosocial/homosexual bonding has survived his rejection of them:

> The forms of the community emerged from the gustblown vestments. . . . They came ambling and stumbling, tumbling and capering, kilting their gowns for leap frog, holding one another back . . . smacking one another behind . . . calling to one another by familiar nicknames . . . whispering two and two behind their hands. (*P* 192)

The largely confessional nature of Stephen's mental intercourse with Cranly, in which he recounts "all the tumults and unrest and longings of his soul" (*P* 178), plugs directly into this homo-erotic fantasy of church life—too directly to escape Stephen's notice altogether. Even as he contemplates Cranly's "priestlike face," Stephen is brought up short remembering "the gaze of its dark womanish eyes," and "through this image" of gender inversion, "he had a glimpse of a strange dark cavern of speculation" (*P* 178)—the very cavern, I would submit, that the present essay has traversed.

Stephen does not really explore this "cavern" until his last interview with Cranly, when he announces his imminent departure from Ireland. Most readers of this scene have followed Richard Ellmann in taking the homosexual implications to emanate largely, if not entirely, from Cranly—"Stephen's friend is as interested in Stephen as in Stephen's girl" (*JJII* 117).[27] But Stephen is the one taken with Cranly's "large dark eyes" (*P* 245), which he earlier found "womanish"; Stephen is the one who inquires, with significant double entendre, "Are you trying to make a convert of me or a pervert of yourself?" (*P* 242); and Stephen is the one whose sexual interests are left most ambiguous:

> Yes. His face was handsome: and his body was strong and hard. . . . He felt then the sufferings of women, the weaknesses of

their bodies and souls: and would shield them with a strong and resolute arm and bow his mind to them.

Away then: it is time to go. A voice spoke softly . . . bidding him go and telling him that his friendship was coming to an end. (*P* 245)

Stephen here follows the cultural script of placing the figure of woman between himself and his homosocial counterpart, just as he did with the swimmers and with Lynch, but beside Cranly, she disappears into a vapid generality. By the end of the passage, it is hard not to see Cranly as Stephen's real object of sexual desire rather than as a rival for the favor of another. As if to emphasize this reversal, when an actual woman appears further on, mediating "the strife of their minds," Stephen perceives her in transgendered terms; he sees her "small and slender as a boy" and hears her voice "frail and high as a boy's" (*P* 244). That the transferential woman now figures in Stephen's mind as boyish, a Bertie Tallon in reverse, reflects the preeminence of Cranly in his affections.

Finally, if Cranly initiates the physical contact in this encounter, Stephen responds positively to it. Moreover, having eroticized the priestly office since his time at Clongowes, Stephen insistently positions Cranly as a cleric manqué, a priest without portfolio or "the power to absolve" (*P* 178). In this way, Stephen can experience sexual frisson without institutional subordination. This may be the key to Stephen's relationship with Cranly. In order that Stephen may resolve the trauma of the doubtful or duplicitous touch of his masters, such as Father Dolan, he enlists Cranly to extend to him the "touch" of a doubtful mastery, a touch that elicits a less immediate sense of dread. But precisely because Stephen can be so "thrilled by his touch" (*P* 247), Cranly embodies the most profound danger yet to Stephen's heterosexual self-conception. He not only represents the persistence of Stephen's religious sensibility in, and despite, his apostasy ("Your mind," he says, "is supersaturated with the religion in which you say you disbelieve" [*P* 240]); he also represents the persistence of its homoerotic attractions in and despite Stephen's aggressively hetero-sexual aesthetics.

As the vessel of this persistence, I would suggest, Cranly plays *the* decisive role in motivating Stephen's self-exile. For at this point, Stephen can only reconstruct the aesthetic mission as a safely heterosexual adventure by making its completion somehow contingent upon separating himself from the "one person . . . who would be more than a friend" (*P* 247), however much Stephen would like to project that sentiment onto Cranly alone. Surely it is no coincidence that this pivotal conversation with Cranly breaks off, assuring Stephen's departure, just when the possibility of homosexual attraction and involvement, which has been di-verted, displaced, and misrecognized throughout the novel, is fi-nally, if inconclusively, broached. Stephen's last unanswered ques-tion, "Of whom are you speaking" (*P* 247), epitomizes homosexual panic as a neurotic obsession with the identity, status, and loca-tion of homo-hetero difference and virtually defines Stephen as its captive.

II

Can we extend this diagnosis to Joyce and to his leave taking? This question cannot but return us to the pragmatic riddles con-cerning self-revelation and fictional representation introduced at the outset of this essay. The unstable differential equation be-tween Stephen and Joyce, wherein the portrait necessarily distorts or disguises the author in the process of portraying him, means that fictional self-exposure is by its nature a refuge as well, a way of confessing, as Stanislaus Joyce said, "in a foreign language."[28] Such self-portraiture requires no deliberate forms of secrecy, none of the lies or evasions with which Joyce charged Wilde, for it disrupts the logic of the closet itself, insofar as any space or practice of concealment is predicated on some minimal decid-able difference between the speaking and the spoken subject.[29] The generic hybridity of *Portrait* (fictive autobiography/"factive" *Bildungsroman*) works to inmix these textual positions, and so too does the novel's peculiarly claustrophobic *style indirect libre*, which persistently confounds, without wholly conflating the perspectives of narrator and protagonist. As a result of these formal and rhetorical innovations, any disclosure Joyce might have packed or wished to pack into his depiction of Stephen, including the stirrings of homoerotic desire and discomfort, ultimately prove indistinguishable from the exercise of poetic license as a mode of denial—which is not to say that denial is necessarily all, or even a part, of what such disclosures in fact amount to. By the same logic, Joyce's anatomy of Stephen's defensive or self-closeting strategies, particularly those involving homosexual panic and artistry, remains indeterminably an act of self-exposure, based on the implied correlation between author and alter ego, and an act of self-mystification, based on the generic incertitude surrounding the nature, degree, currency, and reliability of that correlation. In either case, the (epistemological) indeterminacies of Joyce's sexual self-representation encode a certain (ontological) instability of authorial selfhood as their originating condition, a slippage between ego and alter ego that implies the alterity of the ego itself.

From an epistemological standpoint, the distinctive generic modality of Joyce's novel—detailed, accurate, yet decisively fictional self-portraiture—makes the sexual candor that Joyce demanded of other writers easier, less risky, because it makes the credulity of the reader impossible. *A portrait of the artist is an open closet.* But from an ontological standpoint, the generic modality of *Portrait* shows the sexual candor that Joyce recommended to be harder, more problematic, because it altogether subverts the imaginary author, the illusion of a unitary identity, whose authentic, interior core can be alternately expressed or occulted. *An open closet betokens a liminal subject construction, one that lives both within and beyond psychic enclosure.*

This last thesis is perhaps best illustrated by drawing the contrast between my concept of the open closet and D. A. Miller's famous construct of the open secret. Defining the *open secret*, Miller writes, "In a mechanism reminiscent of Freudian disavowal, we know perfectly well that the secret is known, but we nevertheless must persist, however ineptly, in guarding it."[30] We do not simply hide a given piece of intelligence, in other words, we conceal our collective knowledge of that intelligence, allowing the secret to pass in a paradoxically unsecreted state.

In *A Portrait of the Artist*, Joyce reverses the terms of this discursive economy. Instead of a rhetorical form, the open secret, which establishes the subject's essential truths in the act of pretending to disguise them, Joyce fashions a rhetorical form, the open closet, which suspends or undermines such truths in the act of pretending to divulge them. Whereas the former mode centers the subject in terms of its unspoken desire, the immanent signified of its sexuality, the latter decenters the subject across a chain of signifying positions in which its desire is articulated. In the first case, the subject harbors a profound mystery to be exposed; in the second, the subject instances a radical uncertainty that remains flush with the text of its exposition—hidden, if you will, in plain sight. To illustrate the open secret in literary practice, Miller observes that Dickens, having "abandoned autobiography for the Novel," "encrypts" his secrets in the figure of David Copperfield.[31] Joyce, by contrast, having reclaimed autobiography for the novel, uses Dedalus to "screen," in both contradictory senses of the word, his own sexual desire and anxiety. *Dedalus's sexual ambivalences veil Joyce's while putting them on display and display them while putting them under a veil of doubt.* The open closet consists precisely in this practice of double inscription, and, as such, it orchestrates what in Lacanian parlance might be called a sexuality of the "not all,"[32] that is, a sexuality that defeats the categories of identity on which it continues to depend or, to turn things around, a sexuality that is framed by categories that cannot finally contain it.

On the one hand, this "not all" is the enabling condition of *jouissance*, the extreme verge of erotic intensity which, far from consolidating subjectivity, effracts it.[33] On the other hand, it is structurally homologous with the proximate, the rigid enabling condition of Joyce's sexual unease and Stephen's homosexual panic. Both the proximate and the "not all" figure border zones where the fundamental psycho-symbolic difference, the difference between sameness and Otherness, collapses. *Jouissance* registers this interval as a site of ecstasy; the proximate registers it as a site of anxiety. The distinction between them is purely evaluative, and it hinges on the relative affective priority accorded the jointly compelling aims of finding oneself and losing oneself, of solidifying one's social identity and of escaping that identity to engage some form of alterity.

A Portrait of the Artist does not so much reflect as enact an ideological slide along this continuum. At the narrative level, Joyce caricatures his already exaggerated concerns about his own status (sexual, artistic, class, and so on) in a figure ambiguously "identified" with himself. At the narrational level, through his distinctive use of the free indirect style, he continues to participate in the perspective being caricatured. To use the familiar terms of Joyce criticism, by maintaining a certain stylistic "sympathy" with his self-portrait, Joyce becomes subject to the very "irony" he directs at Dedalus. He thereby challenges, while continuing to acknowledge, his egoistic obsession, and in this process, he shifts from the more defensive address of his letters and essays to a more expansive one. For the subject of self-portraiture that he winds up projecting is not at all a closed, coherent identity but an ongoing transference between painter and sitter, authorial and alter ego, voice and image—a subject in whom there is perpetually something of the "not all." In a very real sense, then, Joyce is "thrilled"—his subjectivity made to quiver or tremble—by the "touch" of his own self-portrait. Stephen's narcissistic anxiety proves essential to Joyce's narcissistic *jouissance*; Stephen's homosexual panic is indispensable to Joyce's open closet. Joyce's strategy of disavowal, with which this essay began, is not so much dissolved or transcended in *Portrait* as it is internalized and sublated. Instead of disavowing the homoerotic as an intimate threat or disturbance to his identity, Joyce disavows the identity so disturbed and threatened, owning and disowning Stephen Dedalus in the same literary motion.

Notes

1. Richard Ellmann notes Joyce's association of homosexuality with public-school education; James Joyce, *Selected Letters of James Joyce*, ed. Richard Ellmann (New York: Viking, 1975), 74, 96, 136, hereafter cited par-

enthetically in the text as *SL*. See also James Joyce, *The Critical Writings of James Joyce*, ed. Ellsworth Mason and Richard Ellmann (New York: Viking, 1959), 201–2, hereafter cited parenthetically in the text as *CW*. Consonant with the standard abbreviations used by *James Joyce Quarterly*, subsequent references to Richard Ellmann, *James Joyce* (New York: Oxford University Press, 1982), will be cited parenthetically in the text as *JJII*. Joyce's opinion that English public schools were an incubator of homoerotic passion and practice conformed both with the popular sense of things—as described by Ed Cohen in *Talk on the Wilde Side: Toward a Genealogy of a Discourse on Male Sexualities* (New York: Routledge, 1993), 38—and with the writings of prominent contemporary sexologists and commentators, including Ellis, Symonds, Carpenter, Stead, Benson, and Jerome. See Havelock Ellis and J. A. Symonds, *Sexual Inversion* (London: Wilson and Macmillan, 1897), 37, 138, 141, 267 (where they cite Ulrichs, the father of the inversion model, to the same effect); J. A. Symonds, "A Problem in Modern Ethics," in his *Studies in Sexual Inversion* (privately printed, 1931), 112; Edward Carpenter, *The Intermediate Sex* (1896; reprint, London: Mitchell Kennedy, 1912), 85. Joyce apparently read all of these books. See Richard Brown, *James Joyce and Sexuality* (Cambridge: Cambridge University Press, 1985), 78–107. For Stead, Benson, and Jerome, see Alan Sinfield, *The Wilde Century* (New York: Columbia University Press, 1994), 65.

2. "Negation," in *The Standard Edition of the Complete Psychological Works of Sigmund Freud*, ed. and trans. James Strachey, 24 vols. (London: Hogarth Press and the Institute of Psycho-Analysis, 1953–1974), 19:235–39.

3. Here again, Joyce's attitude is consistent with contemporary sexual studies, echoing in particular Carpenter, *Intermediate Sex*, 90–91. See also Richard Dellamora, *Masculine Desire* (Chapel Hill: University of North Carolina Press, 1990), 208: "As male homosexuality became visible in public and in texts during the 1890's 'the emphasis on gender construction of the British male' that characterized the schools began to be perceived as problematic."

4. Jonathan Dollimore, *Sexual Dissidence* (New York: Oxford University Press, 1991), 14–17.

5. Eve Kosofsky Sedgwick, *Epistemology of the Closet* (Berkeley and Los Angeles: University of California Press, 1990), 182–212, and *Between Men* (New York: Columbia University Press, 1985), 83–96. On p. 195 of *Epistemology*, Sedgwick doubts whether the "arguably homosexual" objects of her own analysis properly bear out or embody the experience of homosexual panic, which "is proportioned to the non-homosexual identified elements of . . . men's character." Accordingly, she continues, "if

Barrie and James are obvious authors with whom to begin an analysis of male homosexual panic, the analysis I am offering here must be inadequate to the degree that it does not eventually work just as well—even better—for Joyce, Faulkner, Lawrence, Yeats, etc." In this respect, my essay can be seen as a continuation of Sedgwick's project, an attempt not only to explore Joyce's writing by way of her conception but also to demonstrate the adequacy of her conception by way of Joyce's writing.

6. Sedgwick, *Epistemology*, 184.

7. Sedgwick, *Between Men*, 25–26.

8. Sedgwick, *Epistemology*, 185.

9. Ibid.

10. These critics include James F. Carens, "A Portrait of the Artist as a Young Man," in *A Companion to Joyce Studies*, ed. Zack Bowen and James F. Carens (Westport, Conn.: Greenwood, 1984), 255–359; Jean Kimball, "Freud, Leonardo, and Joyce," in *The Seventh of Joyce*, ed. Bernard Benstock (Bloomington: Indiana University Press, 1982), 57–73; Chester Anderson, "Baby Tuckoo: Joyce's Features of Infancy," in *Approaches to Joyce's Portrait: Ten Essays*, ed. Thomas Staley (Pittsburgh, Pa.: University of Pittsburgh Press, 1970), 136–42; and Sheldon Brivic, *Joyce between Freud and Jung* (Port Washington, Wash.: Kennikat, 1980), 28–29, 47.

11. Oscar Wilde, *The Picture of Dorian Gray*, in *The First Collected Edition of the Works of Oscar Wilde*, ed. Robert Ross (1908; reprint, London: Dawsons, 1969), 12:8.

12. I will be treating D. A. Miller's concept of the open secret at length later in the essay. See Miller, *The Novel and the Police* (Berkeley and Los Angeles: University of California Press, 1988), 192–220.

13. For the Dorians and Greek love, see J. A. Symonds, "A Problem in Greek Ethics," in Ellis and Symonds, *Sexual Inversion*, 179–86. For a history of the Cretans and *paiderastia*, see p. 183. For a history and anatomy of the Hellenistic movement in its divers phases—sociopolitical, aesthetic, and erotic—see Linda Dowling, *Hellenism and Homosexuality* (Ithaca, N.Y.: Cornell University Press, 1994). For Daedalus's checkered career, see Mark Morford, *Classical Mythology*, 2d ed. (New York: McKay, 1977), 394–96.

14. In his own words, Wilde "invented that magnificent flower," the green carnation, as a "work of art." Richard Ellmann, *Oscar Wilde* (New York: Vintage, 1987), 424–25. The green carnation became a symbol of aestheticism memorialized in Robert Hichens, *The Green Carnation* (New York: Dover, 1970). According to Alan Sinfield, with *The Green Carnation*,

"the consolidation of queer identity began to take shape around Wilde" (*Wilde Century*, 118).

15. Elaine Showalter correctly contends that the term *queer* had homosexual connotations before the yellow 1890s; see her *Sexual Anarchy* (New York: Viking, 1990), 112. All subsequent references to and uses of the term will assume a distinct homosexual valence. For the homoerotic resonance of the above passage, see also Leonard Albert, "Gnomonology: Joyce's 'The Sisters,' " *James Joyce Quarterly* 27 (Winter 1990): 360–61; Brivic, *Joyce between Freud and Jung*, 24; Kimball, "Freud, Leonardo, and Joyce," 66.

16. For this information, I am grateful to Vicki Mahaffey, who gathered it on a visit to Clongowes in 1992.

17. This dynamic of proximate-ness played itself out quite humorously in Joyce's indirect dialogue with H. G. Wells. Wells objected to the "cloacal obsession" of *Portrait*. Joyce's reply to Frank Budgen reveals the kind of ethnoracial dichotomy that we have been adducing: "Why it's Wells' countrymen who build waterclosets wherever they go." But in a private comment to another friend, Joyce acknowledged, "How right Wells was" (*JJII* 414).

18. Carens speaks of the Clongowes episode as denoting an element of sexual ambivalence in Stephen; see "A Portrait of the Artist as a Young Man," 319.

19. This is what Freud means by the omnipotence of the unconscious wish, a crucial motif everywhere in his work. See, in particular, "Totem and Taboo," in *Complete Psychological Works*, 13:94–124.

20. Trevor L. Williams, "Dominant Ideologies: The Production of Stephen Dedalus," in *The Augmented Ninth*, ed. Bernard Benstock (Syracuse, N.Y.: Syracuse University Press, 1988), 316.

21. Carl Westphal is quoted in Christopher Craft, *Another Kind of Love* (Berkeley: University of California Press, 1994), 35. See Ellis and Symonds, *Sexual Inversion*; Carpenter, *Intermediate Sex*; Sigmund Freud, "Three Essays on Sexuality," in *Complete Psychological Works*, 7:136–48; Richard von Krafft-Ebing, *Psychopathia Sexualis* (1892; reprint, New York: Stern and Day, 1965), 186–294. The sex/gender inversion model is also espoused by somewhat lesser known sexologists, such as Tarnowsky, who differentiated inborn from acquired inversion; Gley, who "suggested that a female brain was combined with masculine glands"; and Magnan, who "hypothesized a woman's brain in a man's body." See Symonds, *Studies in Sexual Inversion*, 126, 135–36. For Joyce's reading in this area, see Brown, *James Joyce and Sexuality*, 78–107. Brown claims that Joyce's sexological views most closely

approximated those of Havelock Ellis, perhaps the most comprehensive exponent of sex/gender inversion. One notorious incident in particular confirms Joyce's subscription to the gender inversion model. According to Ellmann, he "scandalized a homosexual poet," Siegfried Lang, "by placing two fingers in [a pair of miniature ladies'] drawers and walking them towards the unhappy poet" (*JJII* 438), a taunt that recalls the phrase "lady highkickers" (*SL* 74).

22. For Ellis and Symonds, to feel as a man toward an object of affection means taking the active role in sexual relations; to feel as a woman means taking the passive role (*Sexual Inversion*, 63). Freud identifies male inversion with sexual passivity in "Leonardo Da Vinci and a Memory of His Childhood" (1910), *Complete Psychological Works*, 11:86–87. Later, Freud actually declared of the Wolf Man, "he understood now that active was the same as masculine, while passive was the same as feminine." "The History of an Infantile Neurosis," *Complete Psychological Works*, 17:47.

23. Kimberly Devlin reads the director's elliptical swipe at the Capuchin dress as a "test" intended to ascertain whether Stephen's interest in holy orders might be motivated by homosexual or transvestite impulses, a gambit that is "scandalously reinterpreted" in the Butt and Taff episode of the *Wake* dream as a sexual overture on the part of the father. "In the *Wake*," she concludes, "the patriarch's flaws are located not in any mere intellectual limitations, as they are in *Portrait* (see *P* 156), but rather in . . . his repressed and unacknowledged interest in the sexually taboo." But the director is, in fact, uncertain as to whether Stephen has any interest in the clerical life at all, so that as a test his unspoken stricture on *les jupes* seems premature. Moreover, as I will presently demonstrate, the patriarch's flaws are only restricted to "mere intellectual limitations" in *Portrait* insofar as Stephen's conscious mind is concerned; unconsciously, Stephen registers and reacts to intimations of homoeroticism in the priest's words. The interview, in other words, is not just "scandalously reinterpreted" as a sexual overture in the *Wake*, it is scandalously interpreted as such all along. See Kimberly Devlin, *Wandering and Return in "Finnegans Wake"* (Princeton, N.J.: Princeton University Press, 1991), 23.

24. Speaking more generally, Brivic contends that "it is because heterosexuality is a reaction against homosexuality in our artist that it is held so intensely" (*Joyce between Freud and Jung*, 47).

25. Sedgwick, *Epistemology*, 184–85.

26. Elsewhere in *The Renaissance*, Pater treats Abelard's nominally heterosexual desire for Eloise as a cover for same-sex desire, prompting Wilde to comment, in "The Critic as Artist," "we have whispered the secret of our love beneath the cowl of Abelard" (The Critic as Artist [Los Angeles: Sun and Moon Press, 1997], 105). The "cowl" that E.C. is wearing during the previously discussed tram episode (*P* 70, 222) may well owe something to the "cowl of Abelard," especially since Stephen makes a cowl of his blanket during the composition of his villanelle to E.C., which confesses "the secret of [his] love," under the cover(s) of a feminine identification (*P* 221–22). See Dellamora, *Masculine Desire*, 152–53, for all relevant quotations. Another crucial articulation of triangulated same-sex desire that Joyce certainly read is Stoker's *Dracula*. This Irish novel is organized from start to finish around the homosocial/homophobic relations between the count and his adversaries (Jonathan Harker, Seward, Van Helsing, and so on) as mediated by the novel's two women, Mina Harker and Lucy Westenra. Bram Stoker, *Dracula*, in *The Essential Dracula*, ed. Leonard Wolf (New York: Plume, 1993).

27. An outstanding exception is Carens, who takes specific issue with Ellmann, arguing that Stephen is "drawn" to Cranly and partakes of "the current of latent homosexuality in the scene" ("A Portrait of the Artist," 304, 323).

28. Stanislaus Joyce, *The Complete Dublin Diary of Stanislaus Joyce*, ed. George H. Healey (Ithaca, N.Y.: Cornell University Press, 1971), 103.

29. Reading this essay in its earlier, shorter version, Tim Dean construed my formulation of the open closet as "a form of evasion or hypocrisy," a not unreasonable interpretation, which I try to correct here. I am, accordingly, obligated to him for pressing me to clarify my argument and thus helping to instigate a rather extensive revision/expansion of the essay's concluding movement.

30. Miller, *Novel and the Police*, 207.

31. Ibid., 199.

32. For Jacques Lacan's concept of the "not all," see his essay "God and the *Jouissance* of the Woman," in *Feminine Sexuality*, ed. Juliet Mitchell and Jacqueline Rose (New York: Norton, 1982), 134–48.

33. I am indebted for this thread of the argument to Tim Dean, "Hart Crane's Poetics of Privacy," *American Literary History* 8 (Spring 1996): 83–109.

Portrait of an Aesthete

EMER NOLAN

◆ ◆ ◆

Y EATS'S EMBRACE of an exotic orientalism in his Celtic Twilight phase proved very attractive to the young Joyce. Yeats's characters Ahern and Robartes, heroes of *The Tables of the Law and The Adoration of the Magi* (1897), provide suitable heretic precursors for the Daedalus of *Stephen Hero*, who desires to cast off every social constraint, and to seek for himself another, secret lineage. Stephen enthuses about Yeats's stories:

Their speeches were like the enigmas of a disdainful Jesus; their morality was infrahuman or superhuman: the ritual they laid such store by was so incoherent and heterogeneous, so strange a mixture of trivialities and sacred practices that it could be recognised as the ritual of men who had received from the hands of high priests, [who had been] anciently guilty of some arrogance of the spirit, a confused and dehumanized tradition, a mysterious ordination. . . . These inhabit a church apart; they lift their thuribles wearily before their deserted altars; they live

beyond the region of mortality, having chosen to fulfil the law
of their being.[1]

Like Yeats himself, Stephen is searching for an alternative and
heterodox tradition with which to identify. In typically modernist
fashion, Yeats is here engaged in creating through art a tradition
to which his own art might then belong; insofar as he employs
materials as distant from Joyce's own inherited cultural traditions
as they are from his own, the latter is at liberty to respond to
and use these in his own writing. There is little trace in Joyce of
the specifically Irish or folkloric elements in Yeats's tales: for Yeats,
"Irishness" is an aspect of the identity he desires to create; for
Stephen, it is the identity he wishes to escape. In this way Yeats's
characters, as they appear in *Stephen Hero*, prefigure for Joyce the
great paternal exemplar invoked by *A Portrait of the Artist as a Young
Man*: the mythical forebear who summons Stephen both to fidelity and to absolute originality and individuality:

> His soul had arisen from the grave of boyhood, spurning her
> graveclothes. Yes! Yes! Yes! He would create proudly out of the
> freedom and power of his soul, as the great artificer whose
> name he bore, a living thing, new and soaring and beautiful,
> impalpable, imperishable.[2]

This ideal forerunner and begetter represents a "metafather" who
replaces the actual and inadequate paternal figures—Simon Dedalus, priests, teachers, and professors—represented in the text.
Joyce's "family romance," his elaboration of an alternative myth
of origin, solves what David Lloyd describes as the perennial autobiographical problem of reconciling "the tension between the
desire for self-origination, to produce oneself as if without a father, and the awkward knowledge of indebtedness to what precedes and influences the subject." For it is an awareness of such
indebtedness that this form reveals above any other in its depiction of the evolution of the self in response to external forces.[3]
Lloyd also remarks on the centrality of the autobiographical form
in cultural nationalist discourse, which he attributes to their mu-

tual participation in this narrative structure of Freudian family romance. Typically, according to Lloyd, the story of the nationalist hero—who disavows his actual roots—tells of his struggle to discover and identify with "the spirit of the nation"; as cultural exemplar, or as artist, he then comes to embody this essential spirit, thus prefiguring in himself the national unity which is promised for all.

In its representation of Dedalus's struggle toward a self-authored identity through art, *A Portrait of the Artist* seems to offer a fine example of this form of autobiography. However, in relation to Irish nationalism, Dedalus is engaged on a diametrically opposed family romance and is indeed devoted to the elaboration of a narrative which distances him from the religious, political, and "national" identifications already established in his biological family. While the content of his quest is in complete contrast to the aspirations of contemporary cultural nationalism—a project which was effectively dominant in the cultural milieu of Joyce's youth—nonetheless the aestheticist self-creation pursued by Dedalus offers a structural homology to the artistic mission to which it is ostensibly opposed. In his resolutely individualistic self-fashioning, Dedalus ironically reenacts the self-making and self-discovery of the nationalist cultural project. Here I will pursue the implications of this in the light of the reemergence of the concept of "the conscience of the race" at the conclusion of Joyce's text.

As critics of *A Portrait of the Artist as a Young Man* have often observed, Stephen's aspiration toward a fully autonomous and self-created identity is nowhere securely achieved in that text. Instead, Dedalus is presented as a subject forever in process, and the projected moment of his ultimate self-fulfillment in art is postponed beyond the limit of the narrative. Maud Ellmann indeed proposes that *A Portrait of the Artist* illustrates the impossibility of any such program and instead "presents a Stephen Dedalus who is dismembering, not developing but devolving, not achieving an identity but dissolving into a nameless scar."[4] She here addresses the inevitable erosion of any transcendental perspective by the experience of the biological body and of the materiality of language. In the perpetual contagion between word and flesh, body and language, which *A Portrait of the Artist* enacts, the individual is finally revealed not as a pure, self-identical entity but as the site of endless libidinal flux and interchange. The omnipotent, secluded artist can hold everything except his own body in aesthetic stasis: he is powerless, as it were, to stop his fingernails sprouting. As Ellmann implies, there can be no pure disembodied realm of art when, in psychoanalytic terms, the aesthetic signifies for Dedalus merely an aspect of an "economy of hoarding" or the place where he stores "the transcendentalized retentions of epiphany."[5] Literature is what is kept back, "*detained*," as Stephen puts it, from "the tradition of the marketplace" (*P*, 192) and "the chaos of unremembered writing" (*SH*, 82).

We must add to this account, however, that the bodily experience of this adolescent and unstable organism is inescapably social and political as well. The regulation of the body is at the center of the system of religious morality that Stephen seeks to challenge, but his own body denies to him the position of detached, rational, and scientific observer, which he needs in order to attack religious orthodoxy.[6] In this text, therefore, to attend in poststructuralist fashion to the dismantling of the stable, centered subject is paradoxically also to observe the protagonist yielding to already ideologically charged claims of inheritance and blood relation on the individual organism. Individuality collapses, that is to say, into an already established collective and historical tradition. When Joyce's friend, the nationalist Tom Kettle, writes in 1912—"Your very physical body is not your own. It consists of an initial legacy from your ancestors, and a daily plagiarism from the earth"[7]—he merely testifies to the irrelevance of liberal individualism to the society from which he comes. The respective analyses of Lloyd and Maud Ellmann, I would propose, can be read as significantly complicating, in a number of ways, a conventional reading of Stephen Dedalus's desire to leap out of a stagnating provincialism into a liberating, postnationalist modernity. In the first place, the text produces a highly complex notion of "tradition." It is both the dreary biological backdrop against which Stephen's individuality must be displayed, in the context of his immediate familial and social environment, and it is a tool borrowed from a cultural movement devoted to transforming that environment. To the extent that Catholic Irish nationalism is at odds with a more consistently secularizing and individualist nationalism, it seems to figure for Stephen as the undifferentiated background into which his subjectivity threatens to disappear. The irony in which he is caught is that his attempts to submit this context to a liberalizing critique reflect the ambitions of the Anglo-Irish cultural nationalism from which he is otherwise estranged. At the least, I consider that Dedalus's commitment to "escape" "flight," or exile should not be appropriated too quickly for a familiar depoliticized individualism; and in the Irish context the alternative to such individualism is not only the libidinally decentered subject, but (as with Gabriel Conroy) the subject decentered into the broader collectivity of political tradition.

Chief among the religious strictures to which Stephen is subjected is the demand for sexual continence. It is also, as he confides to his friend MacCann, the one to which he is most notoriously unequal (*SH*, 56). Stephen's oscillations between self-loss and self-containment are played out in the intimacy of the brothel or the confessional; in this sense at least Stephen is, in spite of what his friend Davin tells him, a terrible man who is *never* alone (*P*, 206). Stephen wishes to subvert these constraints on sexuality by the exercise of reason. He challenges MacCann's right to legislate for "normal human natures": does MacCann have the right to call himself "normal" if he has no need for sexual contact with women? If MacCann is normal then is it normal to be tone-deaf and shortsighted? This line of self-defense is in perfect accord with Stephen's general belief in the importance of bringing scientific rationality to bear on all aspects of human life, in harmony with the principles of the "modern method":

> The modern spirit is vivisective. Vivisection itself is the most modern process one can conceive. The ancient spirit accepted phenomena with a bad grace. The ancient method investigated the law with the lantern of justice, morality with the lantern

of revelation, art with the lantern of tradition. But all these
lanterns have magical properties: they transform and disfigure.
The modern method examines its territory by the light of day.
(*SH*, 190)

Stephen's blithe deconstruction of normality runs aground when
it comes to aesthetic discussion. In *A Portrait of the Artist*, when his
theory of the static nature of aesthetic experience is refuted by
Lynch's writing his name on the backside of the Venus of Praxiteles, Stephen is obliged to qualify his pronouncements with the
proviso that he is speaking only of "normal natures" (205). He
tells Lynch that he profoundly disdains the association his friend
makes between sex and art; he dislikes arguments which assert
that, for example, men perceive women's bodies as attractive because of the necessity for the propagation of the species. Such
arguments, he alleges, lead "to eugenics rather than to esthetic"
(*P*, 208). However, to his discomfort, some of his own arguments
begin to lead him also in that same worrying direction. The political and the ethical questions which Stephen faces, when
couched in the terms of scientific materialism, become inflected
by a grosser materialism of blood and genetics. In this we can
recognize a modernism not merely of rationalist demystification,
but one which has truck with ideas of biological determinism and
even of race consciousness, which would elsewhere appear to be
quite foreign to Joyce's fiction.

In *A Portrait of the Artist*, MacCann accuses Dedalus, after a dispute about the signing of a petition for universal peace: "I believe
you're a good fellow but you have yet to learn the dignity of
altruism and the responsibility of the human individual" (198–
99). However, this charge is first made in *Stephen Hero* in the characteristically fin-de-siècle context of a discussion of heredity and
degeneration. There, MacCann claims that sexual license is "a sin
against the future" and to the Ibsenite Stephen's horror produces
this moral from *Ghosts*. Stephen retorts that MacCann treats the
play as if it were a scientific document, but he has already made
clear his own aspiration that art should approach precisely this
condition. Dedalus announces his artistic mission to the president

of his college as "an examination of corruption" (*SH*, 96). The living subject of Stephen's investigation of corruption, of his "vivisection," is his own body, whose physical waywardness and instability taunt his pubescent pride and fastidiousness. Corruption in the examining subject himself upsets the objectivity of the project: "It shocked him to find in the outer world a trace of what he had deemed till then a brutish and individual malady of his own mind" (*P*, 90). Moreover, the very individuality and discreteness of his body is vulnerable to scientific consideration. "Do you believe in heredity?" his fellow students inquire, using his own skeptical rationalist beliefs against him. They continually assert that Stephen is held to his native traditions not by some easily refuted and spurned mystical tie but by genetic inheritance; as his mother tells him, "None of your people, neither your father's or mine, have a drop of anything but Catholic blood in their veins" (*SH*, 139). In his uncomfortable awareness of this, Stephen is challenged:

> Living in an age which professes to have discovered evolution, can you be fatuous enough to think that simply by being wrong-headed you can recreate entirely your mind and temper or can clear your blood of what you may call the Catholic infection? (*SH*, 211)

To his dismay, scientific rationality begins to confirm the claims not of modern enlightenment, but of tradition itself. Stephen accepts this quasi-materialist imagery to the extent of fearing, in the Catholic Eucharist, "the *chemical* action which would be set up in my soul by a false homage to a symbol behind which are massed twenty centuries of authority and veneration" (*P*, 243, my emphasis).

Stephen seems to associate his bodily insecurity primarily with his mother's physical weakness and insubstantiality. As his sister bleeds to death through her navel—never having separated herself from her mother successfully or established an independent identity—Mrs. Dedalus pleads with her undergraduate son: "Do you know anything about the body?" (*SH*, 168). She looks to the scientist to help her to supplement her own inadequate maternal instincts. His sister's death coincides with Stephen's darkest reflections on his life and art:

> He laid a finger upon every falsehood it contained: [an] egoism which proceeded bravely before men to be frighted by the least challenge of the conscience, freedom which would dress the world anew in [the] vestments and usages begotten of enslavement, mastery of an art understood by few which owed its very delicacy to a physical decrepitude, itself the brand and sign of vulgar ardours. (*SH*, 167)

Here, acknowledgment of oppression and of the demand for responsibility, together with the blatant exhibition of the mechanism by means of which these conditions are transcended in art, coincide with the artist's sense of the insufficiency of the body's own inherited constitution. Stephen continuously stresses that the demands of the patriots on him are physical: threats to his time, energy, strength, and, ultimately, in the person of Old Gummy Granny of *Ulysses* chapter 15, his survival; he is asked to become the living vessel of tradition. This awareness of tradition and the vocabulary of race which it involves is illustrated as Stephen gazes from the street at members of the Ascendancy at ease in their Kildare Street club:

> The name of the hotel, a colourless polished wood, and its colourless quiet front stung him like a glance of polite disdain. He stared angrily back at the softly-lit drawing-room of the hotel in which he imagined the sleek lives of the patricians of Ireland housed in calm. They thought of army commissions and land agents: peasants greeted them along the roads in the country: they knew the names of certain French dishes and gave orders to jarvies in highpitched provincial voices which pierced through their skintight accents.
>
> How could he hit their conscience or how cast his shadow over the imaginations of their daughters, before their squires begat upon them, that they might breed a race less ignoble than their own? And under the deepened dusk he felt the

thoughts and desires of the race to which he belonged flitting like bats, across the dark country lanes, under trees by the edges of streams and near the poolmottled bogs. A woman had waited in the doorway as Davin had passed by at night and, offering him a cup of milk, had all but wooed him to her bed; for Davin had the mild eyes of one who could be secret. But him no woman's eyes had wooed. (*P*, 237–38)

Here, the sense of physical or material inheritance and that of moral responsibility blend into each other. It is of course the latter which Dedalus ultimately embraces in his ambition to create "the conscience of the race," but here we see his earlier apprehension of the link between his individual existence and "the race to which he belonged." The Joyce who is too often identified simply as an apologist for spiritual transcendence reveals in these passages, and elsewhere in his work, a quasi-materialist consciousness of kinship, race, and inheritance. "Borrowed styles are no good" was Joyce's apparently unlikely advice to a young Irish writer in the 1930s, "you must write what's in your blood and not what is in your brain."[8]

Joyce's representation of Stephen's development in this precise cultural context also lends to the Dublin of *A Portrait of the Artist* a very different atmosphere from that which pervades *Dubliners*. In place of urban anonymity, one encounters here a world of intense, claustrophobic intimacy resonant with the clamor of a variety of social styles and voices. As Bakhtin points out, this is the kind of social environment which is so essential to the form of the *Bildungsroman*:

> The importance of struggling with another's discourse, its influence in the history of an individual's coming to ideological consciousness is enormous. . . . The process is made more complex by the fact that a variety of alien voices enter into the struggle for influence in the individual's consciousness (just as they struggle with one another in surrounding social reality).[9]

Bakhtin, as we have seen, suggests that the modern nation is the privileged site of such discursive interplay and heteroglossia. Elie

Kedourie attacks nationalism for its very valorization of social conflict and self-determination in this way. It is always, he argues, productive of strife to take autonomy as the highest moral and political good, as it is never "a condition achieved here and now, once and for all, it is rather to be struggled for ceaselessly, perhaps never to be attained or permanently secured."[10] *A Portrait of the Artist*'s depiction of Dedalus's supposed rejection of the ideology of cultural nationalism, then, remains complicit, to this extent, with the terms of nation building. However disgusted Stephen is with "the compact body of Irish revivalists" (*SH*, 43) in his college, he is never entirely disengaged; he is alienated rather than isolated. He is afforded the opportunity to define and redefine his artistic credo in the face of the Church's own "ambassadors" (*SH*, 210–11); he is sought out for personal interview by the president of the college, and his views are notorious among his peers. Stephen is present at the opening of the Irish Literary Theatre and witnesses the furore over Yeats's *The Countess Cathleen*; later, during the *Playboy* controversy, Joyce confessed his disappointment at missing the excitement of the riots to his brother Stanislaus: "I feel like a man in a house who hears a row in the street and voices he knows shouting but can't get out to see what the hell is going on."[11] This is a neat reversal of the image Joyce later employs to describe Shem the Penman's writerly withdrawal and domestic seclusion—"kuskykorked . . . up tight in his inkbattle house"[12]—sheltering from all the wars. Stephen's intimacy with the emergent forces in Irish society is suggested by the fact that one Hughes (apparently Joyce's fictional name for Patrick Pearse, whose Irish classes he attended) stands up to refute the artist after he delivers his paper on "Drama and Life" to the College Literary and Historical Society. Ireland's renegade artist may be roundly denounced by its future revolutionary leader, but he is, for all that, addressed and acknowledged by him. Hughes proclaims:

> Mr. Daedalus was himself a renegade from the Nationalist ranks: he professed cosmopolitism. But a man that was of all countries was of no country—you must first have a nation

before you have art. Mr. Daedalus might do as he pleased, kneel at the shrine of Art (with a capital A), and rave about obscure authors. In spite of any hypocritical use of the name of a great doctor of the Church Ireland would be on her guard against the insidious theory that art can be separated from morality. If they were to have art let it be moral art, art that elevated, above all, national art. (*SH*, 108)[13]

In this society, Stephen's refusal of political commitment in art becomes the subject of general comment and controversy. His assertion of artistic autonomy is assailed and defended, continually thematized and understood as politically charged from the outset. The gesture therefore carries a resonance and an importance here that it could not have sustained in an equivalent English social situation. Even the question of exile is publicly discussed, with the opinions of the author's mother duly canvassed and reported. This distinguishes Stephen's (and Joyce's) decision to leave Ireland from that of a long tradition of Irish expatriate writers: here it is consistently foregrounded as the content of the writing and not just as its context.

Joyce, then, professes aestheticism, but does not write aestheticist literature. Rather, he writes not so much as, but *about* an aesthete. In Bakhtin's terms, the language of aestheticism does not function so much as a primary means of representation but as the *object* of representation, parodied and stylized, as is the fate of all discourses when they are incorporated into the novel form:

> Thus when an aesthete undertakes to write a novel, his aestheticism is not revealed in the novel's formal construction, but exclusively in the fact that in the novel there is represented a speaking person who happens to be an ideologue for aestheticism, who exposes convictions that are then subjected in the novel to contest.[14]

The Ireland Joyce knew, it should be emphasized, lacked virtually any tradition of bourgeois, liberal, or individualistic dissent. Such calls for a common, disinterested cultural program as have been issued in Ireland arise consistently from within the Protestant community, which historically has been viewed by the great majority of people as the ally and beneficiary of a repressive colonial administration. They have tended to arise, moreover, as a cultural solution to that community's religious and political isolation, and at times when it was faced with new political threats from majority movements. Joyce's apparent taking up of the cause of disinterestedness, along with that of the autonomy of the artist, from within the Catholic community must thus be distinguished from both an Anglo-Irish and an English liberalism. It comes, that is to say, from a society in which such questions as whether Jesus was the only man who ever had pure auburn hair or who was exactly six feet tall (*SH*, 139) are a topic of serious discussion—a far cry, indeed, from literary London and Coole Park. This distinction ought also to be signaled by Stephen's evident discomfort with English liberalism itself. As he reluctantly tells the well-meaning Englishman, Haines, in *Ulysses*: "You behold in me, Stephen said, with grim displeasure, a horrible example of free thought."[15] In a culture lacking a dominant liberal tradition, Stephen experiences his own agnosticism as a painful anomaly.

When we view *A Portrait of the Artist* in this context, the conventional wisdom that regards Stephen as an individual who manages to "escape from ideology"[16] becomes even more difficult to sustain. The English liberal Haines in *Ulysses* advises him helpfully: "After all, I should think you are able to free yourself. You are your own master, it seems to me" Stephen knows all too well, as *A Portrait of the Artist* as a whole demonstrates at a formal level, that such a belief in the possibility of individual liberation is always already ideological. H. G. Wells's review of *A Portrait of the Artist*, in which he praises the book for the "convincing revelation it makes of the great limitations of a great mass of Irishmen," surely owes its trenchancy to Wells's fear that the English reader might otherwise be deceived or confused by what appears to be a liberalistic dimension in Stephen Dedalus's thought. Wells sees fit to warn:

> everyone in this Dublin story, every human being, accepts as
> a matter of course, as a thing in nature like the sky and the

sea, that the English are to be hated. There is no discrimination in that hatred, there is no gleam of recognition that a considerable number of Englishmen have displayed a very earnest disposition to put matters right with Ireland, there is an absolute absence of any idea of a discussed settlement, any notion of helping the slow-witted Englishman in his three-cornered puzzle between North and South. It is just hate, a cant cultivated to the pitch of monomania, an ungenerous, violent direction of the mind. . . . these bright-green young people across the Channel are something quite different to the liberal English in training and education, and absolutely set against helping them.[17]

The specific political detail of Wells's interpretation is all the more extraordinary in view of the fact that England is scarcely mentioned in Joyce's novel. The very possibility of such contemporary accounts of the book renders it all the more surprising that Art—"with a capital A"—as a place beyond ideology, the vision of an arena of perfect disinterestedness, individuality, and freedom is still advanced as the political message of *A Portrait of the Artist*. Dominic Manganiello, for example, provides a contemporary restatement of this position:

> The emancipation made possible through literature transcended those notions of freedom embraced by nationalists and socialists. . . . Enthusiasms must be tempered in the crucible of art, and must be judged in perspective. . . . Although Ireland's political hopes were buried with Parnell, Stephen's mission of ennobling his country holds a new promise of freedom, since the artist asserts that the individual is more important than institutions such as Church and State.[18]

Nevertheless, Manganiello's general case in *Joyce's Politics* does address an important paradox in Joyce's aesthetics: the absolute rejection of a didactic function for art, together with the retention of a confidence in the salutary effect of representative art. The latter provides a place where the people of Ireland might apprehend a negative image of themselves in Joyce's "nicely polished looking glass," and an ultimately positive one in the artist's image of "the uncreated conscience of the race." Paradoxically, Joyce's commitment to European naturalism continually pushes him back into the petit-bourgeois milieu of his youth. Naturalistic fidelity to a degraded reality and aestheticism become strange allies in his early fiction, in which paralytic banality is relieved only by the fineness of its depiction in language. The petit-bourgeois social group at the center of such Irish naturalism, however, is also one which will make the political revolution itself, which can scarcely, for example, be asserted of the characters of Arnold Bennett. It is, therefore, as Manganiello correctly identifies, around the question of the representation of the Irish people that Joyce's project again appears to betray an affinity with Yeats's. Here, Joyce again demonstrates a kinship with cultural nationalism, if this term is appreciated as encompassing a much more varied and complex set of propositions than the notion that—as, for example, Manganiello proposes—Irish patriots held that it was much better to die in Ireland, for Ireland, than to live anywhere else.[19] When David Cairns and Shaun Richards, in a similar vein, conclude of Joyce's *Dubliners*—"The reality, however, was that Joyce was holding to the principle of liberation of self and nation through loyalty to individual truth rather than in obeisance to short-term nationalist shibboleths"[20]—it should be remembered that even in Ireland in the first decade of the twentieth century, nationalism and "short-term shibboleths" are not synonymous. Recent attempts to interpret Joyce as a kind of elevated, more sophisticated form of Irish nationalist neglect the fact that nationalism tends anyway to see itself as a sophisticated cultural movement. In its romantic, European guise, it is an ideology devoted to self-creation and self-expression, education and art—a lonely project, in advance of the creation of the ideal national community, in a projected future and a collective freedom.

Notes

1. James Joyce, *Stephen Hero* (London: Jonathan Cape, 1956), 183; hereafter cited parenthetically in the text as *SH*.

2. James Joyce, *A Portrait of the Artist as a Young Man*, edited by Chester G. Anderson (New York: Viking, 1964), 170; hereafter cited parenthetically in the text as *P*.

3. David Lloyd, *Nationalism and Minor Literature: James Clarence Mangan and the Emergence of Irish Cultural Nationalism* (Berkeley: University of California Press, 1988), 162.

4. Foreword to Maud Ellmann, "Disremembering Dedalus: *A Portrait of the Artist as a Young Man*," in *Untying the Text: A Post-Structuralist Reader*, ed. Robert Young (London: Routledge & Kegan Paul, 1981), 189.

5. Ibid., 194.

6. R. B. Kershner discusses Stephen's paradoxical devotion to scientific positivism in his essay "Genius, Degeneration and the Panopticon," in *A Portrait of the Artist as a Young Man*, ed. R. B. Kershner (Boston: Bedford, 1993), 373–90.

7. Tom Kettle, "The Future of Private Property" (1912), quoted in J. B. Lyons, *The Enigma of Tom Kettle* (Dublin: Glendale, 1983), 17.

8. See Richard Ellmann, *James Joyce* (New York: Oxford University Press, 1982), 505.

9. M. M. Bakhtin, "Discourse in the Novel," in *The Dialogic Imagination*, edited by Michael Holquist and translated by Caryl Emerson and Michael Holquist (Austin: University of Texas Press, 1981), 348.

10. Elie Kedourie, *Nationalism* (London: Hutchinson, 1961), 32, 54.

11. Quoted by Ellmann, *James Joyce*, 239.

12. James Joyce, *Finnegans Wake* (New York: Viking, 1939), 176.30–31.

13. I am not aware whether any record exists of Pearse's presence at the lecture. Richard Ellmann makes no mention of Pearse and ascribes some of the sentiments expressed by Hughes to Arthur Clery and to other university students. See Ellmann, *James Joyce*, 93.

14. See Bakhtin, "Discourse in the Novel," 333.

15. James Joyce, *Ulysses*, edited by Hans Walter Gabler with Wolfhard Steppe and Claus Melchior (New York: Random House, 1986), 17; hereafter cited parenthetically in the text as *U*.

16. See, for example, Trevor L. Williams, "Dominant Ideologies: The Production of Stephen Dedalus," in *James Joyce: The Augmented Ninth*, ed. Bernard Benstock (Syracuse, N.Y.: University of Syracuse Press, 1988), 312–22.

17. H. G. Wells, review of *A Portrait of the Artist*, in *James Joyce: The Critical Heritage*, vol. 1, ed. Robert H. Deming (London: Routledge & Kegan Paul, 1970), 87, 88.

18. See Dominic Manganiello, *Joyce's Politics* (London: Routledge & Kegan Paul, 1980), 38–39, 33, 41.

19. See ibid., 138.

20. David Cairns and Shaun Richards, *Writing Ireland: Colonialism, Nationalism and Culture* (Manchester, England: Manchester University Press, 1988), 84.

The Woman of the Ballyhoura Hills

James Joyce and the Politics of Creativity

MARIAN EIDE

◆　◆　◆

THE IRISH REVIVAL was in its ascendancy when James Joyce embarked on his career as a writer. And while there is increasing evidence that he had sympathy with the movement's expression of revolutionary Irish politics and its attempt to re-create an Irish national culture,[1] his differences with specific positions and attitudes represented by proponents of Irish nationalism are dramatized throughout his writings. In *A Portrait of the Artist as a Young Man*, Joyce addresses the nationalist personification of Ireland as either an idealized woman (Mother Ireland or the beautiful queen) or a degraded seductress (the woman who invites a stranger into her bed) by creating his own, resistant personification of Ireland in the woman of the Ballyhoura hills. This Irish peasant woman presents a brief though complexly realized figure of the nation. In rendering her portrait, Joyce indicates his strong commitment to an aesthetic practice grounded both in an Irish national identity and in a progressive sexual politics. Joyce's version of national identity demands full consciousness as the basis for a morality composed of equal parts responsibility and desire, without the bonds of repression or hypocrisy. Joyce, then, counters a stereotypical morality that would equate responsibility and repression. In *Portrait*, his Irish national artist models full consciousness in the act of creativity.

Readers might recognize Joyce's investment in the connection between an artist's sexual experience and the aesthetics that would express a nation's identity emerging in a notebook Joyce kept in Trieste while revising *Portrait*. In one entry he expresses concern over the prevalence of sexual repression in Irish culture: "One effect of the resurgence of the Irish nation would be the entry into the field of Europe of the Irish artist and thinker, a being without sexual education" (*Portrait* 295). This entry records Joyce's belief that Irish writing will have a separate and particularly national identity and that it will have to compete in the field of European thought. The idea of a sexually inexperienced Irish artist concerns Joyce, and he counters this type through the variety of sexual encounters Stephen Dedalus experiences. Through Stephen's sexual preoccupations Joyce associates sexual and intellectual expression. Aesthetics, national politics, and sexuality are for Joyce mutually informing forces that Irish national literature must address.

Mary Reynolds has pointed out that the inception of Joyce's career was marked by his competition with the more idealist writers of the Irish Revival, and with Yeats and Synge specifically. The substance of that competition was to be his rival representation of the Irish nation. In "The Day of the Rabblement," Joyce writes that the Irish Literary Theatre had succumbed to the popular, unthinking nationalism of the crowd and to "the contagion of its fetishism and deliberate self-deception" (*Critical Writings* 71). In "The Holy Office," he rehearses his role in Irish art as a counter to the idealism of his predecessors, a role that makes him "the sewer of their clique./ That they may dream their dreamy dreams / I carry off their filthy streams" (*Critical Writings* 151). In *Finnegans Wake*, Joyce takes direct aim at the movement by calling it the "cultic twalette" (344.12), a phrase that both parodies Yeats's book *The Celtic Twilight* and names Joyce's role as the sewer of an idealist movement.[2] In *Portrait*, his critique is more indirect. Resisting the idealism of the revival, *Portrait* responds with a myriad of representations that express an ambivalent view of the emerging nation. Several emblems of creativity preoccupy Stephen and, as I will argue, inform the political dimension of his developing aesthetic theory in the fifth part of *Portrait*. The first emblem is the ambiguous image of a pregnant woman, who stands in the doorway of her lighted cottage inviting a stranger into her bed. The second recalls Shelley's idea of a fading coal brought partially to light by an inconstant wind. These images, in turn, ground Joyce's aesthetics in both national and sexual politics.

While Joyce's objections to the politics of the Irish Revival led some contemporary readers to label him an aestheticist (placing art above the quotidian concerns of politics or morality), Joyce actually dramatizes both the nationalist and the aestheticist points of view in his draft version of the novel, *Stephen Hero*, and in *Portrait* itself, in such a way as to declare his subtle differences from both and to mark out a national politics that informs his aesthetic approach.

In *Stephen Hero*, Stephen argues than an artist might not be apolitical but neither can the responsible artist adopt reactive or simplistic political views. Deciding to take Irish lessons in order to be more often in Emma Clery's company, Stephen discusses the matter with a Gaelic League member, Madden. Readers familiar with this period in Irish history will anticipate the positions that divide these two characters. As a member of the Gaelic League, Madden pairs the revival of the Irish language (which, as Stephen meditates in *Portrait*, was eradicated by English imperial culture) with the revival of a national identity that accompanies the struggle for Irish independence. Stephen's desire to take language lessons to pursue the pleasures of a love affair would seem to mark him as an aestheticist, but his position is actually slightly more complicated. In the course of their discussion, Madden tries to badger Stephen into adopting a recognizable political position. He argues, in brief, that the Irish in their "natural" state are more moral than other Europeans and especially the English, and that they ought to speak their own language to guard them from exterior influences.

Initially, Stephen plays devil's advocate without taking a clear stand on the issues Madden introduces. When Madden asks Stephen more directly if they do not "as a race" have a right to be free, Stephen demurs, saying he cannot use "these phrases of the platform." Madden presses him for political opinions and Stephen responds, "—I am going to think them out, I am an artist, don't you see?" (*Stephen Hero* 56). Stephen's response indicates that an artist's political views must be complexly conceived, not composed of the slogans that form casual conversation. His amorous motivation in taking the course suggests a possible difference with Madden's idealized Irish morality and initiates a connection between sexual desire and politics. Stephen's investment suggests that the liberation of the Irish nation must bring with it a liberation from the more oppressive and hypocritical strictures imposed by traditional Irish morality and exemplified by the Catholic church's positions on sexuality. Stephen negotiates an ambiguous balance that counters the traditional link between the church and its support of the independence movement with a desire for a different kind of liberation that encompasses not only national but also personal and moral expression.[3] In keeping with this ambiguous position, Stephen takes classes with the Gaelic League but refuses to wear its badge. In the language course itself, the teacher and sometime poet, Hughes, presents standard nationalist dogma by saying that English is the "language of commerce and . . . Irish the speech of the soul" (*Stephen Hero* 58). Stephen's differences with this dogma are later made apparent by Hughes's vitriolic response to Stephen's aesthetic theory.

Joyce is not, however, completely dismissing the claims of the Gaelic League by representing Stephen's difficult relations with its program. He is sympathetic, though not ultimately in agreement, with its rebellion against the imposition of the English language in Ireland. Stephen's aesthetic objectives encompass a complex desire for liberation (both erotic and political) that must be based on a coherent and independent identity for the Irish nation. In Stephen's view it is the responsibility of the Irish artist to "forge" a "conscience" for the Irish nation. In other words, the Irish artist creates a way for the Irish to understand themselves as separate from the double colonizing forces of Roman Catholicism and British imperial rule.[4] The artist must also imagine an independent morality that is not constrained by the dominant paradigms created by these two institutions. In forging such a conscience, Stephen uses the English language as his medium. Yet he is aware that this language is itself a symptom of external controls. In creating an aesthetic theory compatible with his national conscience, Stephen must consider the problem of language: how does an artist write in the language of the master without acceding to the colonial influence of the master's own aesthetic?

In a conversation that introduces and informs Stephen's discussion of aesthetics, Joyce dramatizes the loss of the Irish language as a loss to the nation and the national artist. Talking with the dean in the physics theater before class,[5] Stephen discovers that they use different words to refer to an instrument for filling lamps. The dean calls it a funnel while Stephen calls it a tundish, a word that the dean, who is English, assumes to be Irish. Stephen notes their different relations to the English language and is troubled by the implications:

—The language in which we are speaking is his before it is mine. How different are the words *home, Christ, ale, master,* on his lips and on mine! I cannot speak or write these words without unrest of spirit. His language, so familiar and so foreign, will always be for me an acquired speech. I have not made or accepted its words. My voice holds them at bay. My soul frets in the shadow of his language. (*Portrait* 189)

Recognizing English as a colonial language and one in which his particularly Irish thoughts might not easily be spoken, Stephen nonetheless realizes that this language is his "native" tongue, the first he learned to speak. Like many Irish, he does not speak what Madden might call his "own language." The result is that the medium of Stephen's aesthetic expression will always be foreign for him; he speaks in an acquired speech and writes in an acquired script.

Even the possibility of an Irish influence within the English language is minimized by Stephen's later realization:

> That tundish has been on my mind for a long time. I looked it up and find it English and good old blunt English too. Damn the dean of studies and his funnel! What did he come here for to teach us his own language or to learn it from us? (*Portrait* 251)

Stephen's realization of the loss of his national language and his initial thoughts about the effect of this loss on his writing, however, do not spark an attendant nationalist politics. He presents the issue of lost language in conversation with his friend Davin in the context of his refusal to serve a nationalist cause: "My ancestors threw off their language and took another. . . . They allowed a handful of foreigners to subject them. Do you fancy I am going to pay in my own life and person debts they made?" (*Portrait* 203). Yet Stephen's attempt to create an Irish art that will forge a national conscience is a version of the sacrifice he refuses at this moment.

In *Stephen Hero*, while Stephen argues privately for a complexly realized politics, his public essay for the Literary and Historical Society at his university seems nearly apolitical. Though the actual essay is not presented in this draft, we might infer a version of it through reader and audience responses. The university president, who considers censoring the essay, accuses Stephen of taking an aestheticist position:

> This theory you have—if pushed to its logical conclusion— would emancipate the poet from all moral laws. I notice too that in your essay you allude satirically to what you call the antique theory—the theory, namely, that the drama should have special ethical aims, that it should instruct, elevate and amuse. I suppose you mean Art for Art's sake. (*Stephen Hero* 95)

Though Stephen's aesthetic relies on St. Thomas Aquinas's definition of the beautiful as "that which satisfies esthetic appetite and nothing more" (*Stephen Hero* 95), Joyce (by placing him in discussion with the university president) suggests the possibility that art is responsible for more than aesthetic pleasure. At its extreme this responsibility is dramatized by Hughes's vilification of Stephen's paper. The narrator summarizes his remarks:

> The moral welfare of the Irish people was menaced by such theories. They wanted no foreign filth. Mr. Daedalus might read what authors he liked, of course, but the Irish people had their own glorious literature where they could always find fresh ideals to spur them on to new patriotic endeavors. Mr. Daedalus was himself a renegade from the Nationalist ranks: he professed cosmopolitanism. But a man that was of all countries was of no country—you must first have a nation before you have an art. (*Stephen Hero* 103)

Hughe's attack on Stephen dramatizes Joyce's differences with nationalist art, its moralism and provincialism. Joyce incorporates Hughes's perspective in an inverted form at the end of *Portrait*, when Stephen claims for an artist the task of creating the conscience of his race. Joyce's position implies that while the artist might not first need a nation, the nation does first need an art. Or as Stephen puts it to Leopold Bloom in *Ulysses*, "—You suspect . . . that I may be important because I belong to the *faubourg Saint Patrice* called Ireland for short . . . But I suspect . . . that Ireland may be important because it belongs to me" (16:1160–65).

In *Portrait*, Joyce presents Stephen's aesthetic theory in a private conversation with one sympathetic though distracted listener. Lynch admits to eating dung as a child, swears in "yellow," and rubs his groin when amused. Readers might initially wonder why Joyce chooses this crass character (rather than the more cerebral Cranly, for example) as a respondent to Stephen's ideas on the apprehension of the beautiful. Yet Lynch asks the pivotal question that reveals Joyce's difference from aestheticism and suggests Stephen's national and political investments:

—What do you mean, Lynch asked surlily, by prating about beauty and the imagination in this miserable Godforsaken island? No wonder the artist retired within or behind his handiwork after having perpetrated this country. (*Portrait* 215)

Lynch's witty heresy temporarily masks his significant contribution to the discussion by suggesting that art must take into account its context: "this miserable Godforsaken island." While God may have absented himself after the creation of the universe, the more earthly artist must create within and in response to those conditions.

Stephen realizes this necessity most concretely in concerns about his audience. It is clear that he wants to write for Irish readers and to have a measurable effect on their thought, and through his recollection of Davin's story he links this responsibility with sexual experience:

How could he hit their conscience or how cast his shadow over the imaginations of their daughters, before their squires begat upon them, that they might breed a race less ignoble then their own? And under the deepened dusk he felt the thoughts and desires of the race to which he belonged flitting like bats, across the dark country lanes, under trees by the edges of streams and near the poolmottled bogs. A woman had waited in the doorway as Davin had passed by at night and, offering him a cup of milk, had all but wooed him to her bed; for Davin had the mild eyes of one who could be secret. But him no woman's eyes had wooed. (*Portrait* 183)

Given his spotty record in romance, Stephen despairs of the influence he might have through creativity in parenting. But he demands of his art a greater influence, that it might parent an altered Irish race. Stephen thinks about his art and its audience in immediate association with Davin's encounter with a woman in the Ballyhoura hills. For Stephen, she represents a troubling yet auspicious alternative view of the nation he is writing for and about. This woman acts from a conscience that is freed from the

repressive demands of traditional morality and that also metaphorically addresses the status of Ireland as a colony that demands
its independence. In her figure and her choices, Stephen finds a
model for his national aesthetics as a coming into consciousness
by way of an altered understanding of morality. The woman of
the Ballyhoura hills is neither the Irish temptress who betrays
her nation by bedding the English stranger, nor the devouring
Irish mother who demands a blood sacrifice of her children and
then betrays them to the conqueror, the "old sow that eats her
farrow" (*Portrait* 203). Stephen's "Mother Ireland" is a figure of the
plenitude and excess of creativity; hers is an erotic abundance
that a nationalist might reject but Joyce clearly embraces.

While walking through Dublin streets to the university one
morning, Stephen remembers the story about the Ballyhoura
woman that Davin confided only to him. One night, stranded
after a late-ending hurley match, Davin chose to walk the entire
way home. On his way he grew thirsty and stopped at a lighted
cottage to ask for a drink. Stephen recollects Davin's account of
what followed:

> I spied a little cottage with a light in the window. I went up
> and knocked at the door. A voice asked who was there and I
> answered. . . . After a while a young woman opened the door.
> . . . She was half undressed as if she was going to bed when I
> knocked and she had her hair hanging; and I thought by her
> figure and by something in the look of her eyes that she must
> be carrying a child. She kept me in talk a long while at the
> door and I thought it strange because her breast and her shoul-
> ders were bare. She asked me was I tired and would I like to
> stop the night there. She said she was all alone in the house
> that her husband had gone that morning to Queenstown with
> his sister to see her off. And all the time she was talking, Stevie,
> she had her eyes fixed on my face and she stood so close to
> me I could hear her breathing. . . . at last she took my hand
> to draw me in over the threshold and said: *Come in and stay the
> night here. You've no call to be frightened. There's no one in it but ourselves.*
> . . . I didn't go in, Stevie. I thanked her and went on my way

again all in a fever. At the first bend of the road I looked back
and she was standing at the door. (*Portrait* 183)

Davin's recollection is marked by a wistful ambivalence. His gaze
returns to the woman even as he walks away into the night. He
describes the woman as pregnant, though his evidence is slight.
He shores up the equivocal testimony of her figure with the more
ambiguous observation of the "look of her eyes." It is as though
he must guard against his own sexual longings by transforming
this woman into the erotically inaccessible ideal of Irish motherhood. The simultaneous belief in her pregnancy and in the
sexual intentions underlying her invitation drive Davin's account.
Stephen's recollection of the incident highlights these two elements and by doing so reminds us of his own varying and con-
flicted reactions to women. The peasant woman emerges in *Portrait*
as a fantasized projection that reveals more about Davin and Stephen than about the woman herself. It is precisely the conflict
and ambivalence through which Joyce recounts the incident that
becomes the vehicle for a reworking of traditional myths about
Irish colonization. The woman of the Ballyhoura hills presents
an altered version of the conventional representation of Ireland
as a woman who invites the colonizing stranger into her bed.

In 1152, Devorgilla, the wife of nobleman MacMurrough, deserted her husband to join her lover, the rival lord O'Rourke.
MacMurrough, furious at her adulterous defection and unwilling
to allow her release from their marriage, decided to attack his
rival. But to ensure his military victory, he needed aid. He called
on the famous English soldier Strongbow. Unfortunately for Ireland, Strongbow took as his spoils a portion of Irish territory, and
that, as some of Joyce's characters theorize, was the opportunity
that facilitated English colonization of the island.[6] From this historical event grew the legend that attributed to Devorgilla's de-
sertion the invasion of foreign forces. That early legend initiated
the clichéd image of Ireland as a betraying woman, an image that
has endured as a mythical explanation for Ireland's colonial history under English rule.

There are several characters in Joyce's oeuvre who are proponents of this theory. The citizen in *Ulysses*, for instance, lays

responsibility for years of colonial oppression at the doorstep of this faithless wife: "—The strangers, says the citizen. Our own fault. We let them in. We brought them in. The adulteress and her paramour brought the Saxon robbers here. . . . A dishonored wife, . . . that's what's the cause of all our misfortunes" (12.1156–65). Joyce inserts his own critique of this simplistic view by recording the citizen's inconsistency in first blaming the entire Irish people ("Our own fault") for colonial rule and then blaming a single Irish woman ("the adulteress") who left her husband for reasons erased by history.

Deasy, in "Nestor," rehearses an expanded version of the same argument:

> A woman brought sin into the world. For a woman who was no better than she should be, Helen, the runaway wife of Menelaus, ten years the Greeks made war on Troy. A faithless wife first brought the strangers to our shore here. Mac-Murrough's wife and her leman, O'Rourke, prince of Breffni. A woman too brought Parnell low. (2:390–94)

Deasy, a grass widower, or deserted husband, filters the entire arc of history and mythology through the lens of his particular disappointment and produces a consistently misogynist version of historical defeat. Recognizing the way in which individuals filter political philosophies through the pleasures and disappointments of private experience, Joyce resists Deasy's disillusioned clichés, and through the woman of the Ballyhoura hills he emphasizes instead a set of mythologies that celebrates the subversion and resistance to authority that infidelity can also represent.

Through Davin's experience, Joyce's narration debunks this misogynist explanation of Ireland's colonization. In *Portrait*, the stranger to whom the Irish woman opens her door is, of course, not a stranger. Rather, Davin is depicted as a particularly Irish figure; his proficiency in Gaelic, his dedication to Irish nationalist politics, and his rural past mark him significantly as a native:

> The young peasant worshipped the sorrowful legend of Ireland. The gossip of his fellowstudents which strove to render

the flat life of the college significant at any cost loved to think
of him as a young fenian. His nurse had taught him Irish and
shaped his rude imagination by the broken lights of Irish myth.
(*Portrait* 181)

Davin is distrustful of foreign ideas and influences, and especially
of the English. In fact, Stephen has discovered a cache of violent
nationalist literature in Davin's room and taunts him with excerpts: "Long pace, fianna! Right incline, fianna! Fianna, by numbers, salute, one two!" In his defense, Davin describes himself as
an Irish nationalist "first and foremost" (*Portrait* 202). Davin, assuming the role of the foreign invader in the paradigmatic encounter with the native woman, inverts the structure because he
is so clearly a compatriot.

Davin's national politics are paired with sexual purism, and so
his friendship with the more sexually adventurous and politically
ambiguous Stephen is a challenge for the patriot. When Davin
questions Stephen's allegiances, his argument is based in part on
his politics but almost equally on his unorthodox sexual history.
Davin admits that the thought of Stephen's sexual experiences
temporarily prevented him from eating and sleeping. Stephen's
response is unexpected; he defends himself by claiming, "This race
and this country and this life produced me" (*Portrait* 203). In other
words, it is not only personal experience that structures political
vision; the national political situation shapes even the most personal experiences. Understanding this claustrophobic arrangement, in which the moral hypocrisy of the Irish nation produces
a sexual underclass and prevents the honest expression to which
his art aspires, Stephen protests:

> When the soul of a man is born in this country there are nets
> flung at it to hold it back from flight. You talk to me of
> nationality, language, and religion. I shall try to fly by those
> nets. (*Portrait* 230)

The nationalist vision of Ireland, as represented in *Portrait* by Davin
and in Joyce's life by the writers of the Irish Revival, was a vision

that both Stephen and Joyce saw as typical of Irish repression, a restraint from flight. It is possible to interpret Stephen's comment, "I shall try to fly by those nets," as an indication of his objective "to fly by" or beyond the constraints that the Irish nation places on his creativity. But it is also possible to understand Stephen's metaphor to mean that he will use the very restraints presented by Irish culture as the means for his flight; he will fly by means of those nets. Such a choice is figured by the exile that Joyce chose, an exile that always returned his gaze to Ireland. Just as his reading of the repressive accusation against Ireland's prostitution became the opportunity for him to read subversive potential into the actions of the woman of the Ballyhoura hills, the nets that his nation places on him become the means for a subversion of both imperialist and nationalist politics.

The sexual relations that Deasy and the citizen load with political implications do not map out accurately on Davin's experience either. This pregnant Helen of the Ballyhoura hills does not cross national boundaries or incite war. Insofar as sexual activity is limited within the confines of her Catholic culture to the goal of reproduction, her putative pregnancy renders the erotic invitation she extends to Davin a sort of redundancy, an excess. Because another (marital) sexual encounter has apparently already taken place, she simultaneously plays the roles of Ireland as mother and as whore, undermining the validity of each of these familiar types with her doubled gesture. While I am tempted to read the woman's invitation as a gesture of abundance and eroticism, Stephen's memory is not explicit in this way. Her erotic gesture could just as easily be motivated by loneliness or revenge. Whatever the unnamed catalyst, her actions introduce an excess into the expected economy of a monogamous Catholic marriage; her desire is inherently subversive of the institution by which she is bound.

The woman's erotic impulse also serves to remind us that occupation (marital or colonial) does not promise either control or permanence. The marriage laws that have promised her absent husband ownership of his bride are easily broken. Even while the mark of that ownership lies on her body, even as her pregnancy provides a visible sign of occupation by his seed and their progeny, her actions exceed the control of ownership or occupation. She can repeat the sexual act that promised her husband dominion over her body. By initiating that act with another she ensures that neither man will have permanent control. Her promiscuity gives new meaning to the traditional notion of Ireland as a prostitute who invites the stranger into her bed. The very prostitution that seduces the stranger also promises the impermanence of his reign and ultimately guarantees her own sovereignty. The pregnant woman's sexual invitation recalls the multiple colonial-occupations whose progeny became the hybrid nation of modern Ireland. In *Finnegans Wake*, for example, Joyce describes Ireland as a nation of "miscegenations upon miscegenations" (10).

If Davin had chosen to occupy this woman's bed, he would have filled that role only temporarily. The seduction and its outcome are limited by evidence that this occupation is only the most recent in a series.[7] Nor does the woman's pregnancy give primacy to her husband's previous occupation of her bed. On the contrary, impregnation facilitates her adulterous longing as it makes her new erotic encounter safe from the worry of procreative repercussions.

When Davin declines the woman's invitation, the myth is displaced once more, and emphasis is shifted from the blame placed on a promiscuous woman to the burden of choice that devolves on her suitor. It is not that her pregnancy makes the woman seem more virtuous. Perhaps the opposite is true. Rather, as we understand the experience mediated through Davin's perspective, we are made aware of his responsibility in the thwarted coupling. While characters such as Deasy and the citizen blame women from Eve to Kitty O'Shea for the deleterious results of their sexual desire, Davin's refusal indicates his shared responsibility. Davin is specifically presented as an Irish nationalist, highlighting a rarely noted aspect of Devorgilla's mythic betrayal. Her erotic pursuits did not lead her to the bed of an Englishman but to a rival Irish leader. It is her husband who made a strange bedfellow of the English by inviting Strongbow to aid in his revenge.

Colbert Kearney indicates another context through which Davin's encounter with the woman of the Ballyhoura hills may be read. Kearney associates this encounter with the aisling tradition, which he defines as

> a species of visionary poem with a clear political allegory. . . . In a typical *aisling*, the poet is lost in the mist or twilight when he is confronted by a woman of superhuman beauty. He asks if she is one of the fairy spirits or one of the classical goddesses or one of the legendary beauties. She replies . . . that she is Ireland and that she is imprisoned by a brutal tyrant and will remain so until her true love comes from overseas and liberates her. The poet pledges himself to her and promises to do all in his power to expedite her liberation. (108)

According to Kearney, Davin fails to recognize the Ballyhoura peasant woman as Ireland herself because he has been too rigidly trained in a rude nationalism that romanticizes Ireland. His particular politics places a strong restriction on the sexual adventure this woman offers. In other words, it is precisely Davin's nationalist training that prevents him from taking the romantic role of the poet in the aisling, who recognizes and liberates the Irish nation.[8] In rendering the incident, Joyce highlights the connection between sexual liberation and national independence.

The figure of this woman as a representation of Ireland subverts common assumptions about the role of gender in the politics of colonization. She is not recognizable as the beautiful woman to whose side the nationalist poet rushes, nor does she fit the type of the temptress in historical legends. She is a distorted combination of these two, equal parts dark and light. (Joyce presents this mingling of oppositional categories metaphorically by the woman's placement in the vestibule between the lighted cottage and the darkened landscape.) And Stephen, in remembering Davin's confidence, processes the memory in a peculiar way that continues to subvert the hackneyed view of Mother Ireland as the woman who welcomes the colonist into her homeland only to find she needs the poet to rescue her from her plight. Davin's encounter recalls these myths at the same time that it undermines the assumptions arising from them:

> The last words of Davin's story sang in his memory and the figure of the woman in the story stood forth, reflected in other figures of the peasant women whom he had seen standing in doorways at Clane as the college cars drove by, as a type of her race and his own, a batlike soul waking to the consciousness of itself in darkness and secrecy and loneliness and, through the eyes and voice and gesture of a woman without guile, calling the stranger to her bed. (*Portrait* 183)

The description of the peasant woman as a "batlike soul waking to the consciousness of itself in darkness and secrecy and loneliness" anticipates precisely the words Stephen later uses in thinking about E.C.: "she was a figure of the womanhood of her country, a batlike soul waking to the consciousness of itself in darkness and secrecy and loneliness" (*Portrait* 221).[9] Given Stephen's puerile comparison of women with marsupials in the draft form of this novel, this observation can be read as purely misogynist.[10] But I think his comment is complicated by his realization at this moment that he has wronged E.C., who has the right both to her innocence and to her desires. The comment is also complicated by the identification with the batlike woman as a "type of her race and his own." Stephen is not necessarily thinking that sexually experienced women are either mothers (marsupials) or whores (bats), nor is his metaphor solely an attempt to imply an animal lack of consciousness. Rather, her mind, like his and like that of their common "race," is waking into consciousness of itself.

It is precisely this trajectory from the unconscious into consciousness that Stephen associates with the act of artistic creativity later in the fifth chapter, when he culls from Percy Shelley's "Defense of Poetry" the idea of the fading coal that is for both Shelley and Stephen the image of the mind in the act of creation. In the "Defense," Shelley writes:

> Poetry is not like reasoning, a power to be exerted according
> to the determination of the will. A man cannot say, "I will
> compose poetry." The poet cannot even say it; for the mind
> in creation is as a fading coal, which some invisible influence,
> like an inconstant wind, awakens to transitory brightness; . . .
> and the conscious portions of our natures are unprophetic
> either of its approach or its departure. (503–4)

Shelley proposes that the impulse for poetic expression has its
origins in the unconscious. When an inconstant and unpredictable wind lights on the coal, it glows. He draws this image, in his
brilliantly literal-minded way, from the word *inspire*, which means
"to blow into." Creativity, then, is a record of the invisible movement of unconscious thought into conscious expression (just as
pregnancy is the sign, partly visible and partly invisible, of the
movement of potential creativity into actual creation in the biological context). As Stephen explains it in his conversation with
Lynch, "This supreme quality" (by which Stephen means "radiance," the last in his four phases of apprehension) "is felt by the
artist when the esthetic image is first conceived in his imagination.
The mind in that mysterious instant Shelley likened beautifully
to a fading coal" (*Portrait* 213).

Stephen might not consciously associate the radiant moment
of apprehension with E.C. and the pregnant woman as types for
the Irish race coming into awareness of itself. And some have
made the argument that his point is precisely to delimit the creativity of women as a purely physical phenomenon. Judith A.
Spector notes:

> The message is clear; since women have physical wombs, they
> must be relegated to the realm of the physical. The female
> characters in *Dubliners, A Portrait,* and *Ulysses* are limited to their
> physicality and preoccupied with their sexuality; they are as-
> suredly not intellectuals or artists. (83)

Spector argues that Joyce opposes women's physical creativity to
men's intellectual creativity. But while Stephen may be guilty of

such a simplified opposition, Joyce's objective is to reconcile physical and intellectual creation. Joyce draws an analogy between the
woman's process of coming into consciousness and the artistic
endeavor through the metaphor provided by pregnancy. And
while pregnancy, labor, and delivery have long provided male
writers with an image for their act of poetic creation, Joyce's
version of this comparison is quite different. The pregnant
woman, casting light into the shadows through her open door
and moving between consciousness and its lack, replicates the
movement of wind on Shelly's partially lit coal. The metaphor
that balances light with dark in the woman's placement in the
doorway and in the fading coal's brightened response to wind
presents the woman's physical creativity as analogous to the poet's
creativity, a waking into consciousness. The woman's role in creativity is not wholly subsumed by the author nor is she made a
passive object in this representation. It is important to note also
that Joyce does not imagine the pregnant woman as a muse. Nor
is this woman a receptacle, merely, for the seed of masculine
creativity. For it is not on her pregnancy that the representation
of this memory lays its emphasis. Rather, our attention is drawn
to her initiating erotic impulse as an act of creativity; the desiring
impulse itself is coupled with the darkness and secrecy of her soul
in the moment that it begins to waken to consciousness of itself.

It is curious that the text places the peasant woman in this
liminal space between consciousness and its lack. Intuitively, I
would be inclined to associate the political oppression of a colo-
nized Irish woman with the structures of repression in the unconscious itself. We need look no further than May Dedalus to
understand the oppression suffered by Catholic women in colonial Ireland. And Joyce's texts abound with examples of such
women, visibly suffering the ill effects of a repressive culture that
confines them to a few, preferably invisible and certainly restraining, roles. But in following that intuitive judgment, I would be
guilty of precisely the error that Stephen makes more flamboy-
antly in calling women marsupials. I would assume that social
oppression relegated Irish women clearly and irretrievably to the

territory of darkness and mute physicality. Joyce draws our attention to the peasant woman to indicate that there is always excess that erupts beyond the borders of any oppression. While the conditions in which the woman lives demand monogamy and fertility, her sexuality moves against and distorts these cultural boundaries. She uses her pregnancy to mark her husband's absence with an expression of desire that transgresses community sanctions.

Joyce marks the porous borders of repression with the sign of creativity in the same gesture that marks the woman's body with the sign of biological creation. The transition between the pregnant woman's reproductive function and her erotic impulse, as differing signs of creativity, marks a portal of escape from repression, an opportunity to "fly by those nets." From that portal of escape, Joyce traces the barely perceptible movement of creativity along subversive pathways away from the reservoirs of cultural oppression, whether it is imperialist or nationalist. Stephen's remembrance of the woman subverts the clichéd stories that frame her choices. Joyce's image equates the coming into consciousness of a nation with the coming into consciousness of desire. Davin's withdrawal from desire reminds readers that for Joyce, Irish nationalism, like the literary movements that support it, is hampered by an investment in sexual repression and that aesthetic creativity requires creative receptivity.

Notes

1. Vincent Cheng makes this argument compelling in *Joyce, Race, and Empire*.

2. Joyce's pun on *The Celtic Twilight* as "cultic toilette" resonates on a number of levels. With this phrase, he signals the cult influence of Irish nationalism, a label that would indicate both the unexamined adherence of its members and the movement's transience. The French *toilette* gestures toward the hypocritical purism of the movement. *Les toilettes* are water closets and indicate Joyce's role as the sewer into which the movement deposits the more undesirable and unacknowledged aspects of

experience. *La toilette* refers to a woman's clothing or outfit and indicates the extent to which this cult dresses up, clothes, and disguises the actual corpus of Irish experience.

3. One prominent example of Roman Catholic church involvement in Irish liberation politics is the local parish aid for Daniel O'Connell's mass meetings, which reformed penal laws and allowed Catholics more rights under British rule in the nineteenth century.

4. In *Ulysses*, Stephen, quoting Jesus, describes himself as a servant to two masters and refers explicitly to the Roman Catholic church and the imperial British state.

5. This classroom is the location in the draft version where Stephen delivers his essay on aesthetics. Retaining this location in the revision, Joyce introduces the figure of the dean, who asks Stephen about his aesthetics and unwittingly introduces the problem of language in the same context. The dean's conversation and the location are one indication of the connection between the loss of a national language and identity and the artist's aesthetic responsibility.

6. For a more complete account of this event, see Foster.

7. The pregnant woman's autonomy is echoed by an "Ithaca" narrator in *Ulysses* during Bloom's sleepy reverie about his wife's sexual history: "To reflect that each one who enters imagines himself to be the first to enter whereas he is always the last term of a preceding series even if the first term of a succeeding one, each imagining himself to be first, last, only and alone whereas he is neither first nor last nor only nor alone in a series originating in and repeated to infinity" (17.2127–31).

8. Mary Reynolds offers a different explanation for Davin's refusal. She points out that his reaction is partly defined by years of English terrorism among Irish peasants. For although the Irish countryside at *Portrait's* narrative time, 1902, was prosperous (as indicated by Davin's well-made boots), the people who resided there still reacted to centuries of English oppression. "Stephen realizes that what repels him in his peasant friend . . . is Davin's slow reluctance of speech and deed—these qualities are actually a survival of the peasant response to English terror, a dehumanizing effect" (231).

9. Vincent Cheng in "The Bawk of Bats" explores this bat metaphor by drawing on its implication of prostitution. Certainly the element of prostitution in national and sexual politics is a strong part of the material with which Stephen struggles in assessing Davin's story. Stephen's

metaphor questions whether Ireland prostitutes herself or expresses desire.

10. Suzette Henke eloquently presents this point of view.

Works Cited

Cheng, Vincent J. " 'The Bawk of Bats' in Joyce's Belfry: The Flitter in the Feminine." In *Joycean Occasions: Essays from the Milwaukee James Joyce Conference*, edited by Janet E. Dunleavy, Melvin J. Friedman, and Michael Patrick Gillespie, 125–37. Newark: University of Delaware Press 1991.

———. *Joyce, Race, and Empire*. New York: Cambridge University Press, 1995.

Foster, R. F. *Modern Ireland, 1600–1972*. London: Penguin, 1988.

Henke, Suzette. "Stephen Dedalus and Women: A Portrait of the Artist as a Young Misogynist." In *Women in Joyce*, edited by Suzette Henke, Elaine Unkeless, and Carolyn G. Heilburn, 82–107 Urbana: University of Illinois Press 1982.

Joyce, James. *The Critical Writings of James Joyce*, edited by Ellsworth Mason and Richard Ellmann. Ithaca, N.Y.: Cornell University Press, 1989.

———. *Finnegans Wake*. New York: Viking, 1939.

———. *A Portrait of the Artist as a Young Man: Text, Criticism, and Notes*, edited by Chester G. Anderson. New York: Viking, 1968.

———. *Stephen Hero*, edited by John J. Slocum and Herbert Cahoon. New York: New Directions, 1963.

———. *Ulysses: The Corrected Text*. New York: Vintage, 1986.

Kearney, Colber. "The Image of Ireland in Joyce's *Portrait*." In *The Artist and the Labyrinth*, edited by Augustine Martin, 101–20. London: Ryan, 1990.

Reynolds, Mary. "Davin's Boots: Joyce, Yeats, and Irish History." In *Joycean Occasions: Essays from the Milwaukee James Joyce Conference*, edited by Janet E. Dunleavy, Melvin J. Friedman, and Michael Patrick Gillespie, 218–34. Newark: University of Delaware Press, 1991.

Shelley, Percy Bysshe. "A Defense of Poetry." In *Shelley's Poetry and Prose*, edited by Donald H. Reiman and Sharon B. Powers, 478–508. New York: Norton, 1977.

Spector, Judith A. "On Defining a Sexual Aesthetic: A Portrait of the Artist as Sexual Antagonist." *Midwest Quarterly* 26 (1984): 81–94.

"Goodbye Ireland I'm Going to Gort"

Geography, Scale, and Narrating the Nation

MARJORIE HOWES

◆ ◆ ◆

> This locality is more *around* temporality than
> *about* historicity: a form of living that is more
> complex than "community"; more symbolic than
> "society"; more connotative than "country"; less
> patriotic than *patrie*; more rhetorical than the rea-
> son of state; more mythological than ideology;
> less homogeneous than hegemony; less centred
> than the citizen; more collective than "the sub-
> ject"; more psychic than civility; more hybrid in
> the articulation of cultural differences and iden-
> tifications—gender, race or class—than can be
> represented in any hierarchical or binary struc-
> turing of social antagonism.
> —Homi Bhabha, "DissemiNation"

> A nation is the same people living in the same
> place . . . Or also living in different places.
> —James Joyce, *Ulysses*

I

GEOGRAPHY HAS ALWAYS HAD an important place in
Irish political thinking, whether in British arguments for the
inevitability of colonization, republican patriotism, unionism,
moderate or militant nationalism. As Oliver MacDonagh has observed, "In one sense, the Irish problem has persisted because of
the power of geographical images over men's minds" (*States of*

Mind, 15). Irish studies shares with postcolonial studies an interest in the multifarious transactions between material and symbolic geographies that enable this wide range of discourses. My epigraphs organize the problematic of defining or narrating the nation around the confusions and complexities of place that arise from such transactions. Homi Bhabha claims that the nation is "a ubiquitous and obscure form of living the *locality* of culture" ("DissemiNation," 292) that can only be defined through a potentially endless recitation of what it is distinct from, yet related to. Leopold Bloom appeals to an apparent tautology whose central comparative term is missing—the "same people"—and whose spatial elements appear to cancel each other out: "the same place" or "different places." There is a long tradition in Joyce scholarship of delineating Joycean geographies (see, for example, Seidel, *Epic Geography*), and more recent critics have offered various fruitful approaches to the issues surrounding the nation in Joyce's works (Cheng, *Joyce, Race, and Empire*; Duffy, *The Subaltern "Ulysses"*; Kiberd, *inventing Ireland*; Nolan, *James Joyce and Nationalism*). Here I will argue that Joyce takes up the issue of narrating the Irish nation in a kind of geographical representation that has received scant attention from either critical tradition. These representations foreground spatial scales—local, regional, international—which are sometimes thought to represent alternatives to the category or ideology of the nation.[1] In contrast, I will argue that it is precisely through these alternative scales, and the opportunities and obstacles they pose for imagining the scale of the national, that Joyce's engagement with the problematic of the nation appears most vividly.

Although I will focus on "The Dead" and *A Portrait of the Artist as a Young Man*, this particular geographical approach to narrating the nation appears in *Ulysses* and *Finnegans Wake* as well. In "Cyclops," just after Bloom utters his definition and the Citizen challenges his right to be included in any conception of the Irish nation, Joe's handkerchief swells into an "intricately embroidered ancient Irish facecloth" (*Ulysses*, 12.1438–39). The cloth parodies (among other things) a nationalist geography of Ireland. It is inscribed with a diverse collection of places, some of which would be natural fodder for nationalist sentimentalizing, like the lakes of Killarney and Croagh Patrick. Others remind us of how colonialism shaped Ireland, like the three birthplaces of the first Duke of Wellington and Tullamore jail. The absurdity of still other places undercuts any dream of an Irish nation that claims to encompass them, like Fingal's Cave, which is actually in Scotland, and Kilballymachshonakill, which is not a place at all. One could read the cloth as an illustration of Joyce's much-quoted claim in "Ireland, Island of Saints and Sages" that "our civilization is a vast fabric, in which the most diverse elements are mingled" (*Critical Writing* 165). But if the cloth represents the hybridity of the Irish nation, it also indicates how persistently and thoroughly Joyce thought through national issues in spatial and geographical terms.

If we focus on the geographical imagination at work here, its critique of naive nationalist equations of the nation with its physical territory points in two related directions. On the one hand, the imagined community of the nation is far too complex and dispersed to be metaphorized as a space, with its suggestions of contiguity, wholeness, and fixed boundaries. On the other, the actual physical spaces over which nation-states exercise sovereignty are far too complicated to be analyzed solely through reference to that sovereignty, as integrated and natural national territories. One thing that is lacking in both cases is an appreciation of the importance of, and the relations among, different spatial scales. The nameless narrator of "Cyclops," who displays equal scorn for the conceptions of the nation offered by Bloom and the Citizen, brings up this issue when he announces his intention to step outside to urinate: "Goodbye Ireland I'm going to Gort" (*Ulysses*, 12.1561). The usual form of this colloquial phrase is "Goodbye Dublin I'm going to Gort" (Gifford, *Ulysses Annotated*, 366). The narrator's humorous revision of it, which suggests that Gort somehow is not "in" Ireland, is in keeping with the parody of nationalist geography on Joe's handkerchief. Gort lies in County Galway, near Augusta Gregory's Coole, and the phrase represents one of Joyce's many assertions that the idealized West offered by the cultural nationalism in which she was a central figure is not to be found anywhere in the real Ireland. It also crosses geographical movement westward, between two comparable material locations, with two other kinds of movement, from the scale of the national to a more local scale and from the material to the metaphorical. Joyce's rendition of the problems of narrating the nation repeatedly organizes itself around this combination.

While my epigraph from Bhabha's influential essay appears to insist on the specificity of locality, the essay displays the tendency common to much postcolonial and poststructuralist work to employ a myriad of spatial metaphors but to treat the materiality of space as fairly transparent and unproblematic. Bhabha approaches the complexity of the nation, metaphorized consistently, though not exclusively, as the "space of the nation" ("DissemiNation," 303), through time, most notably in his widely cited articulation of the contradictory "double-time" of the nation (297). Bhabha wants to show that "the space of the modern nation-people is never simply horizontal" (293), to investigate its "irredeemably plural modern space" (300), and his theoretical vocabulary of terms like "enunciatory position" (298), "space of cultural signification" (299), and the "site of writing" (297) relies heavily on spatial metaphors. At the same time, the essay often characterizes the conceptions of the nation it critiques as forms of spatial thinking that naively equate people, territory, and nation. The crude, and crudely spatial, conception of the nation is disarticulated through an analysis of the complexities of temporality. Thus while narrating the nation is rendered wonderfully, helpfully problematic, the materiality of national space and the category of space itself remain fairly inert, naturalized, and abstract.

Neil Smith's *Uneven Development* offers a useful counterexample which approaches the complex materiality of space through scale. For Smith, space is "deep space," which is "the space of everyday life in all its scales from the global to the local . . . quintessentially social space" (160–61). He argues that geographical space, including nature itself, is produced in a particular way under capitalism; uneven development is the "geographical expression of the contradictions of capital" (152). Uneven development is organized through the "continual determination and internal differentiation of spatial scale" (136). Each scale—the urban, the nation-state, and the global—is determined as "an integrated space-economy" (135–36), a geographical unit which represents an identifiable and separate scale of social activity. At the same time, it is also subject to internal differentiation and shaped by its relation to larger scales, factors which both enable and threaten each scale's drive toward realizing itself as "absolute space." This contradictory structure in which the drive toward equalization and the drive toward differentiation confront each other at various scales is the central feature of the production of space under capitalism, and the contradictions of capitalism appear in the problematic doubleness assigned to scale.

Bhabha's and Smith's approaches are complementary. Together they suggest ways of examining relationships that are at the center of the problematic of the nation: relationships between material and metaphorical space and between capitalist modernity and the modernity of the nation. A number of scholars have argued that Ireland's entry into a specifically colonial modernity was especially traumatic and uneven (Hechter, *Internal Colonialism*; Gibbons, *Transformations*; Eagleton, *Heathcliff and the Great Hunger*, 273–319). However "belated" Joyce might find the Irish (*CW* 70), colonial Ireland was not simply backward or underdeveloped in relation to Britain, whatever one might mean by that. Instead, through colonial intervention, it became a disorienting mixture of the archaic and the modern. The beginnings of the economic and social transformations of the nineteenth century—the extermination of the cottier class, the rise of the strong farmer, the establishment of high rates of celibacy and late marriage age, the hemorrhage of emigration—preceded the Great Famine of the 1840s. But they were greatly accelerated by it, and the Famine constituted, among other things, a sudden, disastrous, and incomplete transition to modernity, especially in agricultural production and the social organization of rural life. If the relative indifference and ineptness with which the British handled the catastrophe of the Famine provided one source of the juxtaposition between the archaic and the modern, a highly modernized state apparatus and a willingness to intervene in Irish society provided another. Historians have often argued that Britain treated

Ireland as a "social laboratory in which Englishmen were prepared to conduct experiments in government which contemporary opinion at home was not prepared to tolerate" (Lyons, *Ireland since the Famine*, 74). Ireland had a national school system before England did, and, as Terry Eagleton observes, "[by] 1850, Ireland had one of the most commercially advanced agricultures in the world, and was fast developing one of the world's densest railway systems" (*Heathcliff and the Great Hunger*, 274).

Thus the uneven development that expresses the contradictions of European capitalist modernity was especially acute in Ireland. Some of Benedict Anderson's work since *Imagined Communities* offers a way of tying the material geography of uneven development to the rise of specifically national forms of consciousness and culture. Anderson metaphorizes the displacements of modernity—geographical and otherwise—as forms of exile. He argues that in the nineteenth century the migration of populations, the standardization of printed languages, and the establishment of national school systems represented forms of exile from local origins and affiliations and that nationalism constituted a compensatory "project for coming home from exile" (Anderson, "Exodus," 319). It was "the essential nexus of long-distance transportation and print capitalist communications" (316), a nexus that was well developed in largely preindustrial Ireland, rather than industrialization per se, that first prepared the ground for the rise of nationalism. For Anderson's exile, geographical movement (and the other displacements for which it stands) provokes a nostalgia for a local scale which is eased when individuals transfers some of their energies and affections upward to the scale of the national: "It was beginning to become possible to see 'English fields' in England—from the window of a railway carriage" (318). Anderson's theory fits well with the long-standing observation of historians that modern Irish nationalism took hold first in the modernizing, relatively prosperous agricultural regions and small towns that experienced these changes earlier than the poor and underdeveloped Gaeltacht (Boyce, *Nationalism in Ireland*). However, because Ireland's modernization was inextricably bound up with the uneven development of colonialism, highly modernized com-

munications and transportation systems and the forms of exile
they generated occurred in conjunction with archaic or residual
social, economic, and cultural formations. In addition, emigration, the decline of the Irish language, and the imperial origin of
national schools were traumatic, much-discussed, and specifically
colonial issues. And the nationalisms that emerged were revolutionary rather than state nationalisms. Both materially and symbolically, the specifically colonial nature of Ireland's capitalist modernity helped produce a national imaginary related to but
distinct from European statist nationalism.

In nineteenth-century Ireland, the transfer of loyalties to a
national scale was an uncertain and incomplete process, and other
supposedly regressive responses to the exilic dislocations of modernity were available. For example, part of Daniel O'Connell's
unprecedented success in mobilizing and nationalizing the Irish
masses was due to his genius for tapping into specifically local
grievances and loyalties and tying them to a nationalist project.
At the same time, however, he worked hard to discourage the
agrarian disturbances and secret societies whose motives and tar-
gets were regional rather than national, and which were an attempt to enforce the traditional social and economic structures
and values that were being destroyed by agricultural modernization (MacDonagh, *The Hereditary Bondsman, The Emancipist*). The notion of a "transfer" is itself somewhat misleading; local issues and
affiliations operated simultaneously within a wider national
framework without necessarily ceasing to be (problematically)
local (Gibbons, *Transformations*, 134–48). With this caveat, Smith's
attention to the complex materiality of geographical space and
Anderson's metaphorical use of geographical movement demonstrate, in very different ways, that the national is to be grasped
most fully in its relation to other scales, rather than in opposition
to them. Both differ from the standard observations that some
nationalisms are more cosmopolitan or more respectful of regional and local difference than others because they insist that
these other scales are structurally, simultaneously, both necessary
and inimical to the national.

Seamus Deane has acutely observed that Joyce's civilization was "the civilization of Catholic Dublin, related to but distinct from that of Catholic Ireland" ("Joyce the Irishman," 40), and much Joyce scholarship understandably focuses on Joyce's Dublin as exemplary of Ireland's uneven development or the relationship between the national and more local scales (Jameson, *"Ulysses* in History"; Duffy, *The Subaltern "Ulysses,"* 53–92; Leerssen, *Remembrance and Imagination*, 224–31; Fairhall, *James Joyce and the Question of History*, 64–79). Certainly, during the nineteenth century, Dublin underwent various forms of industrial decline that made equating progress, modernity, and urban life impossible, and well into the twentieth century, the city experienced massive backwardness in terms of housing and public health in comparison to other cities in the United Kingdom (O'Brien, *Dear, Dirty Dublin*). But Dublin's incomplete and uneven colonial modernity had a counterpart in what we might call the perverse modernity of the Irish countryside. Rural villages in postfamine Ireland were not modern anonymous collectivities. But they were also not the kind of totalizable, knowable, face-to-face community that some scholars associate with precapitalist forms of social life. The main reasons for this were Ireland's uniquely high rate of emigration, driven in part by agricultural modernization, mostly (during this period) to the United States, and the specific cultural meanings attached to emigration in Irish culture. Every village, virtually every family, had sons, daughters, or other relatives over the water. They remained absent yet active members of the community—they wrote letters, sent money home, financed the emigration of siblings or other relatives, and followed events in Ireland through the Irish-American press. The anthropologists Arensberg and Kimball observe that often many members of the same family or village emigrated to the same place, even over several generations, a practice that forged lasting international connections with specific foreign localities. These diasporic relations between emigrants and those at home were quite continuous with local affiliations; they were "part of the general 'friendliness' by which the Irish countryman sums up the family obligations" (*Family and Community*, 144) and were expressed in the same terms. There were also various uniquely Irish cultural traditions organized around the departures of emigrants, many of whom viewed themselves as unwilling exiles, such as American wakes, the all-night parties resembling wakes that were often held before a boat sailed (Miller, *Emigrants and Exiles*, 556–68). The sheer size of the international Irish diaspora and its intimate incorporation into everyday social and cultural life in Ireland meant that rural communities did not coincide with the local territories they occupied. We might call them communities of mourning or melancholy, or see in them something resembling an Irish Atlantic.[2]

The ambiguous modernity of rural Ireland and the concomitant porousness of local and regional geographical scales posed a problem for the cultural nationalism that appropriated the Irish countryside, and especially the West of Ireland, symbolically, as an ahistorical and antimodern repository of Irishness. In many ways a bourgeois, modernizing movement, cultural nationalism sought less to return to or recreate this version of the West than to unify the Irish people around the idea of its (safely distanced and enclosed, both temporally and geographically) worth. In Joyce's works, the geographical mode of inscribing the problematic of the nation that I am tracing centers on characters like Gabriel Conroy and Stephen Dedalus, who reject the conventional forms of national belonging offered to them by cultural nationalism only to find themselves drawn in some manner into alternative narratives of the nation. The narrator of "Cyclops" is, in a minor way, another such figure. This paradigm is well established in Joyce studies and represents a dominant view of Joyce himself. Here I will try to show that Joyce organizes his alternative narratives of the nation around a series of distinctions enabled by the recognition of rural Ireland's perverse partial modernity: material versus metaphorical geographical movement, the complex materialities of spatial scales versus their symbolic appropriation or metaphorization, and movement over space versus movement from one scale to another.

II

The much-debated engagement of "The Dead" with questions of national ideology and community is organized around two re-

lated regions—the West of Ireland and "that region where dwell
the vast hosts of the dead" (*Dubliners*, 224)—and their crucial,
ambiguous role in the versions of the national to which various
Dubliners subscribe. Much of the story does what the imagination
of the cultural nationalism Joyce overtly scorned also did: it
merges the two regions into one, a conflation that Joep Leerssen
has described as "one of the dominant modes of nineteenth-
century Celticism" (*Remembrance and Imagination*, 188). Each region
represents something that Gabriel feels able to reject or master
early in the story but that threatens to overwhelm him at its
close. Gabriel's resolution not to "linger on the past" (*Dubliners*,
205) in his speech gives way to his helpless subordination to the
dead, and he resists the critical but flirtatious Molly Ivors's invitation to "come for an excursion to the Aran Isles" (189), only
to "swoon" (225) before the ominous seductions of another "journey westward" (225), this one associated with Gretta and Michael
Furey. Gabriel's self-conscious cosmopolitanism is, in Bernard
Benstock's words, "mere window-dressing" (*Undiscover'd Country*, 5);
in his worship of things foreign, Gabriel is simply the last and
most sympathetic in a series of provincial Dubliners. Molly looks
west, Gabriel looks east, and they are linked through their competing versions of Irish provincialism, as well as through their
commensurate educations, professions, and superior intellectual
status (in Gabriel's mind, at any rate).[3]

Molly's nationalism and Gabriel's cosmopolitanism represent
equally undesirable relations to the national. Much critical debate
has revolved around what Emer Nolan calls "a revivalist sub-text"
in the story (*James Joyce and Nationalism*, 29), which raises the question of what, if any, alternative relation to the national Gabriel
establishes or is forced into by his "journey westward." Nolan's
provocative reading of "The Dead" incorporates a number of
competing interpretations by appealing to formulations of the
nation's doubleness suggested by Anderson and Bhabha. She argues, following Anderson, that Gabriel's final epiphany represents
both death and immersion in the community because it is the
job of nationalism to transform mortality into continuity (36).
Nolan also asserts that readings which claim that Gabriel capit-

ulates to the communal or Irish lures of the West and those that claim he achieves a self-realization that isolates him from any larger community are in fact complementary because "national belonging is an enabling illusion for individuals who, in spite of it, live in real social isolation" (34). Gabriel's "intensely solitary but yet shared experience" (36) is his incorporation into the community-in-anonymity of the nation, symbolized by the reference to the unifying snow in the newspapers, one of the cultural forms that Anderson uses to exemplify the homogeneous, empty, clock time of the modern nation.

Nolan's reading synthesizes elements in the ending that had often appeared as alternatives to critics: death and continuity, isolation and national belonging, the West as social or literal death and the West as Ireland. She focuses on Gabriel, while other analyses emphasize that the West signifies a diverse and even conflicting constellation of entities and concepts for different characters. Luke Gibbons suggests that "The Dead" presents a struggle, which Joyce outlined in his 1907 essay on Fenianism (*Critical Writings*, 188), between two competing forms of nationalism: constitutional nationalism and a "dissident, insurrectionary tradition" (Gibbons, *Transformations*, 146). This struggle is "articulated through the competing strategies of the newspaper, and the popular ballad" (146); the former is allied with Gabriel's symbolic appropriation of the West, the latter with "The Lass of Aughrim" and the meanings the song and the West have for Gretta. In a similar vein, Cóilín Owens claims, "To Gretta [the West] is that which she can never recover; to Gabriel, it is that which he can never know; to the reader it is a radically ambiguous symbol of the differences between Gretta's and Gabriel's temperaments, and of the differences between Gaelic Ireland as a cultural ideal and the impossibility of a reconciliation between it and the 'thought-tormented age' into which modern, urban, bourgeois Ireland is being assimilated" (Owens, "Mystique of the West," 84–85).

Nolan, Gibbons, and Owens all read the West as embodying the national, whether as a vehicle of reconciliation or of division. But there is another, related set of ambiguities surrounding the West in "The Dead," one that is organized through competing geographical scales and the perverse modernity of rural Ireland. This set of ambiguities resists the conflation of the West with the dead. To the aporias about what the West *means*, the text adds a related series of uncertainties about what it *is* as a physical region. Joyce crosses the complexities of the movement over space—the journey westward—with the problem of scale in defining the region that represents the destination. The West is a shifting, semi-modern, marginal set of regions that both enables and defies the fantasies that Gabriel, Molly, and Gretta construct, and the text carefully renders it ambiguous in geographical and scalar terms.

Molly combines her invitation to the Aran Isles with an observation about Gretta's origins: "She's from Connacht, isn't she?" (*Dubliners*, 189). Voicing her enthusiasm for the trip, Gretta says, "I'd love to see Galway again" (191). Terence Brown's note to Gretta's remark comments, "Presumably she means Galway city, the principal city of County Galway and of the province of Connacht" (311). The slippage in these exchanges between the particular places and geographical scales that stand in for the West—a set of islands, a city, a county, a province—gives the West a physical ambiguity which is related but not reducible to its symbolic richness. Other elements of the story give the region a further geographical complexity. Michael Furey's people live in Oughterard, a small village seventeen miles north of Galway city, and he works in the gasworks of Galway city, a typical rural-urban migrant in a semideveloped region. Gretta lived in a district of Galway city called Nuns' Island, which suggests both the inner differentiation of the city scale and a Catholic alternative to supposedly pagan, primitive Aran. And, as Vincent J. Cheng has argued, the town of Aughrim in County Galway evokes two catastrophic Irish military defeats in the face of British imperialism: the battle of the Boyne and the battle of Aughrim (*Joyce, Race, and Empire*, 143–44). Various private and public histories—imperial, industrial, romantic, nationalist—are embedded in competing scales and geographies.

Five years later, Joyce again combines a consideration of the West's relation to the past and the dead with an analysis of its ambiguous and uneven modernity. In his 1912 essay on Galway, he begins by invoking the ideas, which he describes as both right and wrong, of "the lazy Dubliner, who travels little and knows his country only by hearsay" (*Critical Writings*, 229) and who thinks of Galway as the exotic "Spanish city." Joyce goes on to offer his own blend of fantasy and reality, lamenting the city's decline from a vibrant international trading center and cultural contact zone to its current isolated, decaying modernity: "Outside the city walls rise the suburbs—new, gay, and heedless of the past, but you have only to close your eyes to this bothersome modernity for a moment to see in the twilight of history the 'Spanish city' " (*Critical Writings*, 229). What we might call the true modernity of Galway, with its surprising and energizing contradictions and juxtapositions of the archaic and the modern, regional particularity and international connection, in contrast to its current backward modernity, Joyce finds in a sixteenth-century travel narrative, "in which the writer says that, although he had travelled throughout the world, he had never seen in a single glance what he saw in Galway—a priest elevating the Host, a pack chasing a deer, a ship entering the harbour under full sail, and a salmon being killed with a spear" (230).

One might be tempted to read the inclusion of so many actual western locations in "The Dead" as an instance of the kind of Joycean referential mapping that means, for example, that contemporary readers who visit Dublin can retrace Lenehan's walk in "Two Gallants" and that the route and landmarks of this walk assemble a fairly coherent set of references to English domination, or that Leopold Bloom and Stephen Dedalus can be read as versions of the flaneur (Duffy, *The Subaltern "Ulysses,"* 53–92; Wills, "Joyce, Prostitution, and the Colonial City"). In contrast, the point in "The Dead," with its emphasis on different scales rather than on streets, buildings, and monuments, is to portray the region as rich, problematic, deep space, rather than to define it as something readily mappable or easily traversable. The West as Molly's Aran may be that clichéd embodiment of Irishness worshiped by cultural nationalism. But Gretta's reference to Galway, which introduces a tension between the city and the county, is ambiguous; it signifies cultural nationalism's idea of the primitive rural heartland, the perverse modernity of its material space, an idealized, cosmopolitan past for the "Spanish city," and the backwardness of Ireland's industrial centers.

Taken together, these references to different material features of the region's uneven modernity, embodied in different geographical scales, both multiply the possible nationalist appropriations of the West and highlight the obstacles that the area in question presents for them. Similarly, the last paragraph of "The Dead" accomplishes the unifying, symbolic journey westward, but at the same time it suggests a material journey by including the "dark central plain," "the treeless hills," and the "Bog of Allen" (*Dubliners*, 225), all of which belong to the supposedly uninspiring midlands that travelers from Dublin to the West must cross. Joseph Valente has suggested that Gabriel's failure of vision at the end of "The Dead" springs from "his inability to identify with the *otherness* of the other" ("Cosmopolitan Sublime," 73) and his penchant for revivalist myth making, arguing that the primitive and self-immolating Michael Furey is not an alternative to such myth making but a symptom of it (69–73). Furthermore, Gabriel is "humiliated" (*Dubliners*, 220), not simply by Furey's romantic, archaic death, but by the contrast between that death and Furey's mundane, modern working life.[4] The conflict Joyce stages between the symbolically freighted journey westward and the material, geographical ambiguities of its destination indicates that the real Otherness of the Other is symbolized not by the fiery depths of Furey's passionate heart but by the flames of the gasworks where he earned his living.

III

In *A Portrait of the Artist as a Young Man*, Stephen, like Gabriel, rejects conventional Irish nationalism and finds himself engaging with an ambiguous and sometimes threatening alternative mode of the nation. Rather than emphasizing the scalar ambi- the West or the local as material regions, *A Portrait* highlights the role different conceptions of scale play in different versions of the nation. And instead of focusing primarily on a largely symbolic journey to the West, *A Portrait's* analysis of the impulses and obstacles to the formation of Stephen's national consciousness foregrounds the importance of his mundane travels between home and school. Stephen is a complex version of Anderson's exile, struggling with competing ways of transforming the local affiliations he has lost into membership in a national community. This process depends upon two major factors: first, Stephen's geographical movement, other displacements, and the homesickness they produce, and, second, fantasized but threatening constructions of rural Ireland.

Early in the novel, Stephen, unable to learn the geography lesson that maps the spatial divisions of the New World in straightforward topographical terms—through "the names of places in America" (*Portrait*, 12)—thinks about a different conception of space. In the flyleaf of his geography book he has written:

Stephen Dedalus
Class of Elements
Clangowes Wood College
Sallins
County Kildare
Ireland
Europe
The World
The Universe   (12)

Stephen's alternative geography involves an extensive but incomplete list of different scales; he wonders, "What was after the universe?" (13). It also signifies one potential avenue for Stephen's incorporation into a conventional nationalist community. Stephen's list of scales does not include Great Britain; instead he places Ireland in Europe. His formulation offers a model of the relations among scales as orderly and commensurate, with each scale neatly enfolding the smaller ones, something it has in common with the explicitly nationalist verse that Fleming has written on the opposite page:

> Stephen Dedalus is my name,
> Ireland is my nation.
> Clongowes is my dwellingplace
> And heaven my expectation. (13)

Fleming's verse harmonizes the individual and national scales through a narrative of salvation that links the individual's affiliation with the national—his recognition of Ireland as his nation—with a projected movement from home—his dwelling place—to heaven. Both inscriptions figure the individual climbing the geographical scales from himself to the Irish nation (and beyond), according to the dictates of conventional nationalism.

This process takes place at school and is catalyzed by the kinds of exile school represents. Torn from his home, which is associated with the maternal and the local, Stephen is encouraged to transfer his loyalties to the protonationalist male community, which expresses its resentment of authority through a parody of insurrection: "Let us get up a rebellion, Fleming said. Will we?" (44). As critics have often noted, this change involves his incorporation into a related set of discourses succinctly described by Vicki Mahaffey as "the necessity of homosocial bonding, homophobia, and misogyny" ("Père-version and Im-mère-sion," 124). The fact that there is no right answer to the question "Do you kiss your mother before you go to bed?"[5] indicates that local affiliations are both mandated and forbidden by nationalism; they acquire a problematic doubleness or ambivalence, the experience of which binds the members of the national community together. Stephen is interpellated into the community, not by answering correctly, which is impossible, but by "try[ing] to laugh with them" (11) at his own newly created discomfort with his maternal origins.

The forms of transportation that brought Stephen to school—

trains and hired cars—figure heavily in the first chapter of *Portrait* and are associated with his feelings of exile. When Stephen feels that he is "sick in his heart if you could be sick in that place," he consoles himself by alternately covering and uncovering his ears, comparing the resulting auditory changes to those that occur when a train enters and leaves a tunnel (10). They are also connected with the vehicle that enables Stephen simultaneously to reject and reconstitute his local, maternal loyalties as part of his membership in a nationalist community: a fantasized construction of rural Ireland. This fantasy revolves around a vision of the women another boy has seen in the village of Clane "as the cars had come past from Sallins" on the way to Clongowes: "he had seen a woman standing at the halfdoor of a cottage with a child in her arms" (15). Stephen finds the rural Ireland they represent both appealing and frightening. While he thinks, "It would be lovely to sleep for one night in that cottage before the fire of smoking turf," he also feels afraid, and his fear focuses on the road that enables his transportation from home to school, from the local to the national, by way of such rural areas: "But, O, the road there between the trees was dark!" (15). The roads, signs of rural Ireland's perverse modernity, of Stephen's exile from home, and of his partial return home via national identification, are dark and threatening because they do not resolve the conflicts of scale—between the local/maternal and the national—that they initiate.

Such resolution is only possible at a further remove of fantasy, in the context of imagined rather than actual geographical movement homeward. Anticipating the holidays, Stephen imagines the cars carrying him past the same emblematic women at Clane, and the journey creates an image of community through geographical movement:

The cars drove past the chapel and all caps were raised. They drove merrily along the country roads. The drivers pointed with their whips to Bodenstown. The fellows cheered. They passed the farmhouse of the Jolly Farmer. Cheer after cheer after cheer. Through Clane they drove, cheering and cheered. The peasant women stood at the halfdoors, the men stood here and there. (17)

Bodenstown is where Wolfe Tone is buried, and in his note to this passage Deane speculates that the drivers are pointing their whips toward his grave ("Joyce the Irishman," 282). This vision includes the peasant women of Clane, but their threat has been neutralized, the drive is merry, and the nationalist community is based more on the reciprocal (masculine) cheering and the unifying memory of a nationalist hero than on the attractive but disturbing female figures.

The topographical geography that the exiled Stephen rejects in favor of an ambiguous journey from the local to the national scale is allied with the stridently anti-Parnellite Dante: "A little boy had been taught geography by an old woman who kept two brushes in her wardrobe. Then he had been sent away from home to a college" (*Portrait*, 98). It also displays imperialism's preoccupation with the mapping and territorial conquest of exotic places: "She had taught him where the Mozambique Channel was and what was the longest river in America and what was the name of the highest mountain in the moon" (*Portrait*, 7). Of course, a major lesson of Stephen's actual visit home (and of chapter I generally) is that nationalist politics are more about division and ambivalence than they are about the kind of cheery, unproblematic unity figured in Stephen's imagined journey. In addition, Stephen later rejects the nationalism fostered at schools and other institutions while groping his way toward some alternative exilic relation to the Irish nation.

When an older Stephen contemplates his ambivalent relation to the category and ideology of the nation—his rejection of nationalism, his separation from the national community, his desire to learn "the hidden ways of Irish life" (196) and to "hit their conscience" (259) to help revive his nation—his imagination returns to the women of Clane, now remembered in the context of his own geographical movement and associated with the woman who tried to seduce Davin:

The last words of Davin's story sang in his memory and the figure of the woman in the story stood forth, reflected in other figures of the peasant women whom he had seen standing in the doorways at Clane as the college cars drove by, as a type of her race and his own, a batlike soul waking to the consciousness of itself in darkness and secrecy and loneliness and, through the eyes and voice and gesture of a woman without guile, calling the stranger to her bed. (198)

It has become possible for Stephen to see the "peasant women" of villages like Clane as representatively Irish figures and himself as part (however problematically) of the national community they embody—from the window of a car or train. His conflation of these women and Ireland consistently involves versions of a contrast between a stationary rural woman and a traveling man: "A woman had waited in the doorway as Davin had passed by at night" (259). Stephen's actual travel through the space of rural Ireland has helped him produce an imaginary and specifically national geography, in which a national male subject performs the integration of the local into the national by his movement through space and his symbolic appropriation of the peasant women as national types.

But the country roads that link rural and urban areas, carry the displaced into exile, and create the modern, traveling national subject continue to frighten Stephen: "I fear many things: dogs, horses, firearms, the sea, thunderstorms, machinery, the country roads at night" (264). The processes they represent are ambiguous and incomplete; Stephen cannot complete a "project for coming home from exile" (Anderson, "Exodus," 319) by embracing a national scale and narrative. The other regions and scales such a narrative seeks to integrate are not as commensurate as Stephen once believed. As in "The Dead," the West emerges as both necessary and recalcitrant to a national narrative, a problem embodied in a different representatively Irish figure: the Irish-speaking old man with red eyes. Critics usually assume that the old man represents the cultural nationalist ideal of primitive Irishness that Joyce rejected. But he also signifies an alternative, and problem-

atic, conception of scale to match Stephen's ambivalent alternative to conventional nationalism: "Mulrennan spoke to him about
universe and stars. Old man sat, listened, smoked, spat. Then said:
—Ah, there must be terrible queer creatures at the latter end of
the world" (274). Mulrennan's remarks, so to speak, give the old
man a chance to repeat Stephen's earlier trip upscale from his
own individual being, through the nation to the universe. But
the old man refuses, and his reply figures space in terms of im-
mense, mythic geographical distance and utter alienation, rather
than in terms of linkage and commensurability. What the young
Stephen, along with conventional nationalism, imagined as a progression of ever-widening frameworks, each one neatly enclosing
the smaller ones, has become the radical incommensurability of
scales. Like the country roads, the old man represents something
that is both enabling and crippling for a national narrative, and,
like them, he is ambiguous and threatening. Stephen's initial
claim, "I fear him" (274), and his conclusion that he means the
old man "no harm" (274), indicate that his famous resolution to
narrate the Irish nation, to forge in the smithy of his soul the
uncreated conscience of his race, must incorporate or acknowledge these contradictory elements.

Both Gabriel and Stephen fail to arrive at coherent visions of
the Irish nation or, more precisely, arrive at visions of the nation
notable for their ambiguity, in part because the real rural landscape both supports and resists the imagined national geography
they attempt to project onto it. The material geographies of Ireland's uneven development and their various possible relationships with imaginative appropriations of space form a basis for
Joyce's critique of cultural nationalism as well as for his alternative narratives of the nation. Both "The Dead" and *A Portrait*
combine a focus on the materiality of space and physical journeys
with an investigation of the metaphorical uses of geographical
movements, regions, and scales. They figure versions of the
"double-time" of the nation, not by simply metaphorizing the
nation as a space, but by teasing out the complex relations between metaphorical and material space, between the Gorts that
are in Ireland, and the Gorts that not.

Notes

1. For a recent collection of essays in geography in which investigations of regional particularity or international connection in Ireland often present themselves as critiques of the national, see Graham, ed., *In Search of Ireland*.

2. Paul Gilroy's *The Black Atlantic* offers a model that is suggestive for the Irish experience, though of course it is by no means strictly analogous to it.

3. The text emphasizes the parallels between Gabriel and Molly in this passage: "He wanted to say that literature was above politics. But they were friends of many years' standing and their careers had been parallel, first at the University, and then as teachers: he could not risk a grandiose phrase with her" (*Dubliners*, 188), which marks an obvious contrast to the superiority Gabriel feels in relation to all the other guests.

4. His exchange with Gretta makes this clear:

—He is dead, she said at length. He died when he was only seventeen. Isn't it a terrible thing to die so young as that?

—What was he? asked Gabriel, still ironically.

—He was in the gasworks, she said.

Gabriel felt humiliated by the failure of his irony and by the evocation of this figure from the dead, a boy, in the gasworks. (*Dubliners*, 221)

5. I do not agree with those critics (for example, Williams, *Reading Joyce Politically*, 106–7) who claim that "I do not" would have been a correct initial answer; when Stephen does give that answer, it is wrong.

Works Cited

Anderson, Benedict. "Exodus." *Critical Inquiry* 20 (1994): 314–27.

———. *Imagined Communities: Reflections on the Origin and Spread of Nationalism.* London: Verso, 1991.

Arensberg, Conrad M., and Solon T. Kimball. *Family and Community in Ireland.* 1940. Cambridge, Mass.: Harvard University Press, 1968.

Benstock, Bernard. *James Joyce: The Undiscover'd Country.* New York: Barnes & Noble, 1977.

Bhabha, Homi. "DissemiNation." In *Nation and Narration*, edited by Homi Bhabha, 291–322. London: Routledge, 1990.

Boyce, D. George. *Nationalism in Ireland*. London: Routledge, 1991 (1982).

Cheng, Vincent J. *Joyce, Race, and Empire*. Cambridge: Cambridge University Press, 1995.

Deane, Seamus "Joyce the Irishman." In *The Cambridge Companion to James Joyce*, edited by Derek Attridge, 31–54. Cambridge: Cambridge University Press, 1990.

Duffy, Enda. *The Subaltern "Ulysses."* Minneapolis: University of Minnesota Press, 1994.

Eagleton, Terry. *Heathcliff and the Great Hunger: Studies in Irish Culture*. London: Verso, 1995.

Fairhall, James. *James Joyce and the Question of History*. Cambridge: Cambridge University Press, 1993.

Gibbons, Luke. *Transformations in Irish Culture*. Cork, Ireland: Cork University Press, 1996.

Gifford, Don. *Ulysses Annotated*. Berkeley: University of California Press, 1988.

Gilroy, Paul. *The Black Atlantic: Modernity and Double Consciousness*. Cambridge, Mass.: Harvard University Press, 1993.

Graham, Brian, ed. *In Search of Ireland: A Cultural Geography*. London: Routledge, 1997.

Hechter, Michael. *Internal Colonialism: The Celtic Fringe in British National Development*. Berkeley: University of California Press, 1975.

Jameson, Fredric. "*Ulysses* in History." In *James Joyce and Modern Literature*, edited by W. J. McCormack and Alistair Stead, 126–41. London: Routledge & Kegan Paul, 1982.

Joyce, James. *The Critical Writings of James Joyce*, edited by Ellsworth Mason and Richard Ellmann. Ithaca, N.Y.: Cornell University Press, 1989.

———. *Dubliners*. New York: Penguin, 1993.

———*A Portrait of the Artist as a Young Man*. New York: Penguin, 1976.

———*Ulysses*, edited by Hans Walter Gabler with Wolfhard Steppe and Claus Melchior. New York: Random House, 1986.

Kiberd, Delcan. *Inventing Ireland*. Cambridge, Mass.: Harvard University Press, 1996.

Leerssen, Joep. *Remembrance and Imagination: Patterns in the Historical and Literary Representation of Ireland in the Nineteenth Century*. Cork, Ireland: Cork University Press, 1996.

Lyons, F. S. L. *Ireland since the Famine*. London: Fontana, 1982.

MacDonagh, Oliver. *The Emancipist: Daniel O'Connell, 1830–47.* New York: St. Martin's, 1989.

————. *The Hereditary Bondsman: Daniel O'Connell, 1775–1829.* London: Weidenfeld & Nicolson, 1988.

————. *States of Mind: A Study of Anglo-Irish Conflict, 1780–1980.* London: Allen & Unwin, 1983.

Mahaffey, Vicki. "Père-version and Im-mère-sion: Idealized Corruption in *A Portrait of the Artist as a Young Man* and *The Picture of Dorian Gray.*" In *Quare Joyce,* edited by Joseph Valente, 121–38. Ann Arbor: University of Michigan Press, 1998.

Miller, Kerby. *Emigrants and Exiles: Ireland and the Irish Exodus to North America.* Oxford: Oxford University Press, 1985.

Nolan, Emer. *James Joyce and Nationalism.* London: Routledge, 1995.

O'Brien, Joseph V. *Dear, Dirty Dublin: A City in Distress, 1899–1916.* Berkeley: University of California Press, 1982.

Owens, Cóilín. "The Mystique of the West in Joyce's 'The Dead.' " *Irish University Review* 22, no. 1 (Spring 1992): 80–91.

Seidel, Michael. *Epic Geography: James Joyce's "Ulysses."* Princeton, N.J.: Princeton University Press, 1976.

Smith, Neil. *Uneven Development: Nature, Capital and the Production of Space.* Oxford: Basil Blackwell, 1984.

Valente, Joseph. "James Joyce and the Cosmopolitan Sublime." In *Joyce and the Subject of History,* edited by Mark A. Wollaeger, Victor Luftig, and Robert Spoo, 59–82. Ann Arbor: University of Michigan Press, 1996.

Williams, Trevor. *Reading Joyce Politically.* Gainesville: University of Florida Press, 1997.

Wills, Clair. "Joyce, Prostitution and the Colonial City." In *Ireland and Irish Cultural Studies,* edited by John Paul Waters. Special issue of *South Atlantic Quarterly* 95, no. 1 (Winter 1996): 79–96.

Between Stephen and Jim

Portraits of Joyce as a Young Man

MARK A. WOLLAEGER

◆ ◆ ◆

S TANISLAUS JOYCE, James Joyce's younger brother and "whetstone" (*Ulysses* 9.977), recalls in his published remembrance of James that his older brother's personality descended from their paternal grandfather, whose

> serenity of temper, skipping a generation as often happens, descended to his grandson, who was named after him and who in boyhood and youth was of such a cheerful and amiable disposition that in the family circle he was given the nickname (borrowed from an advertisement for some patent food) of "Sunny Jim." (*My Brother's Keeper* 23)

Always fascinated by popular culture, Joyce must have been amused by a nickname borrowed from advertising copy, but the sunny side of the street is not where most readers of *A Portrait of the Artist as a Young Man* are inclined to imagine that novel's gloomy adolescent, Stephen Dedalus, who feels that his childhood is "dead or lost and with it his soul capable of simple joys" (*Portrait* 96).

Nor are readers likely to confuse the yet more world-weary Stephen of *Ulysses* with the exuberant figure in Zurich who would "suddenly interrupt a Saturday afternoon walk in the fashionable Bahnhofstrasse by flinging his loose limbs about in a kind of spider dance" (Ellmann 430).

These discrepancies alone ought to raise doubts about the occasional critical practice of referring to a composite figure "Stephen/Joyce," as if *Portrait* and *Ulysses* were autobiographies instead of autobiographical fictions. Influential early theorists of modernism, such as Joseph Frank in "Spatial Form in Modern Literature" (1945) or Harry Levin in "What Was Modernism?" (1960), made Stephen the poster child for modernism as a form of aesthetic self-enclosure by citing Stephen's words as if they were Joyce's, thereby producing an apolitical version of modernism that recent criticism has tried to dismantle (Wollaeger 692–93). Despite more recent efforts by critics such as Robert Bell, who points out that "Stephen's morbidly egocentric humor [in *Ulysses*] is the opposite of Joyce's antic energy" (33), or Roy Gottfried, whose treatment of *Portrait* as a comic novel aims to recover forms of humor to which Stephen himself is usually deaf, some *Portrait* critics still analyze the two-headed creature Stephen/Joyce. To be sure, the naiveté of early criticism has been replaced by more self-conscious usage, but the practice still tends to remove Stephen from the complex mechanics of meaning in which Joyce situates him. The persistence of the composite figure derives in part from the influence of psychoanalytic theory, which often uses characters as windows onto the author's hidden desires, but also from the undeniable fact that much of *Portrait* retraces the contours of Joyce's biography.[1]

While it is true that most of the characters and events recounted in *Portrait* are lifted from Joyce's life, Stanislaus, who provides the most reliable skeleton key to the book's biographical provenance (apart from Richard Ellmann's monumental biography), also provides the key qualification: "Jim is thought to be very frank about himself but his style is such that it may be contended that he confesses in a foreign language" (*Complete Dublin Diary* 103). Joyce's openly symbolic name for his fictional surrogate provides an index to his self-mythologizing: St. Stephen was the first Christian martyr, Daedalus the pagan prototype of the artist-inventor. What's more, many of the scenes in *Portrait* that Joyce modeled on his own experience are radically changed in the fiction. To cite just one example, Stephen's momentary gust of boyish excitement before stepping onstage as the schoolmaster in the Whitsuntide play gives no hint that Joyce himself took the same opportunity to indulge in an extended parody of the school rector, who was seated in the first row (Ellmann 56); in *Portrait*, Stephen ignores his classmate's suggestion that he undertake precisely this prank. If the slash dividing Stephen/Joyce is to acknowledge difference as well as identity, we need to look carefully at portraits of the writer's youth.

Critics like stories about Joyce's fear of dogs and thunder because they mirror Stephen's. But what of Joyce the deadpan comedian?

> Playing "Adamant," in a variation of a charade, he listened expressionless to the reports of catastrophes: his house was on fire, his goods destroyed, his wife and children burned to death. Then a look of concern came over his face as he said, "What happened to my dog?" (Ellmann 53)

As a kindergartner, when he wasn't putting salt in the other children's drinks, Joyce enjoyed fabricating horror stories about his family life, telling one girl that his mother would punish her offspring by pushing their heads down into the toilet and flushing (Ellmann 26–27). John Francis Byrne, the model for *Portrait*'s Cranly, remembers Joyce at age twelve sitting in class at Belvedere College "in an elfin crouch waiting and hoping for a blunder," in response to which he would shout with what sounded "like a howl of agony, as if his little frame were being torn apart" (Mikhail 3). Stanislaus's earliest memory of his older brother is of a playful though telling dramatization of Christian mythology:

> I was Adam and a sister, my elder by less than a year, was Eve. My brother was the devil. What I remember indistinctly is my

brother wriggling across the floor with a long tail probably made up of a rolled-up sheet or towel. (*My Brother's Keeper* 3)

The Eileen of *Portrait*, Eileen Vance, recalled a related scenario:

> When James wished to punish one of his brothers or sisters for misconduct, he forced the offending child to the ground, placed a red wheelbarrow over him, donned a red stockingcap, and made grisly sounds to indicate that he was burning the malefactor in hellfire. (Ellmann 26)

So much depends upon the stories one tells. Joyce's adventures at Clongowes Wood College, beginning at age six and a half, may have included the famous scenes of pandying and vindication, but he was not "the weak, shrinking infant who figures in *A Portrait of the Artist*" (*My Brother's Keeper* 17). He in fact won prizes for his skill in hurdling and was avidly interested in cricket.

Joyce's playfulness grew more prankish in later years. His classmate at University College Eugene Sheehy recalls Joyce's fun during French class with George Clancy, the model for *Portrait*'s Davin:

> Joyce would snigger whilst Clancy was translating into English a passage from a French text-book. Clancy pretended to take offence, demanded an instant apology, which was refused, and thereupon challenged Joyce to a duel in the Phoenix Park. The Professor intervened to prevent bloodshed; the performance ended with handshakes all round; and the guileless Frenchman never appreciated what a farce it all was. (Sheehy 15)

Byrne remembers another farcical scene that got Joyce thrown out of the National Library. Byrne was reading a book entitled *Diseases of the Ox* to help out a farming friend when Joyce came in and sat down beside him:

> At that period Joyce was cramming himself with the Norwegian language, and he had brought with him to our table a

pile of books on Ibsen including some of his plays, a Norwegian dictionary and a Norwegian grammar. For a moment he was silent, but then he leaned over to look at the large book I had open before me. "Good Lord, Byrne," he ejaculated, "what *are* you reading?" I didn't say anything but I turned the pages to the title of the chapter where printed in large type was "DIS-EASES OF THE OX." The instantaneous effect on James Joyce was the detonating expulsion of a howl that reverberated through the reading room; and no Assyrian ever came down more swiftly on a fold than did Lyster on Joyce, who was in a con-vulsion of laughter. (Scholes 185–86)

Perhaps if the librarian Lyster had known that he would become a character in *Ulysses* he would have thought twice before throw-ing Joyce out. Most of us have collapsed into giggles in inappro-priate places, but what makes this moment characteristically Joy-cean is that he and Byrne proceeded to take a walk in order to analyze what precisely had made the title so funny.

Thomas Kettle remembered Joyce from University College days as "wilful, fastidious, a lover of elfish paradoxes . . . the very voice and embodiment of the literary spirit" (Scholes 164). But the elf could also be a bit of a troll, and it is this side of himself that Joyce tends to develop in Stephen. Not yet twenty-one and the author of only a few essays, Joyce arrived uninvited just before midnight at the house of the famous poet and mystic AE (George Russell). Once admitted, Joyce proceeded to shower contempt on contemporary men of letters, including the most famous poet in Ireland, William Butler Yeats. AE, evidently a patient man, at a later date permitted the arrogant young writer to read some of his poems aloud to Yeats and himself, and when Yeats offered encouragement, Joyce responded: "Your opinion isn't worth more than another's. It doesn't matter whether you or he (A.E.) likes them. Your work will all be forgotten in time" (Scholes 166). Joyce's arrogance was justified to the extent that today AE is familiar to many people not as a historical figure, certainly not as a writer, but as a character in *Ulysses*. But Yeats was equally justified at the time for saying of Joyce, "never . . . have I encountered so much pretension with so little to show for it" (Scholes 201). Yeats must have been thinking of Joyce's table-turning response to his commentary on Joyce's poetry: "You're past developing—it is a pity we didn't meet early enough for me to be of help to you" (Scholes 166).

Sometimes Joyce seemed unwilling to offer much more than a song to others, let alone help. Joseph Holloway described in his diary his first encounter with Joyce in June of 1904, a pivotal period in Joyce's life. At the Cousins's home,

> Mr. J. Joyce, a strangely aloof, silent youth, with weird, pene-trating, large eyes, which he frequently shaded with his hand and with a half-bashful, far-away expression on his face, sang some dainty old world ballads most artistically and pleasingly. . . . Later he sat in a corner and gazed at us all in turn in an uncomfortable way from under his brows and said little or nothing all the evening. He is a strange boy. I cannot forget him. (Scholes 163–64)

Joyce's mother had died the previous August, which may account for some of his moody brooding. At this time he had begun to write the early version of *Portrait* entitled *Stephen Hero* but was still contemplating a career as a singer. A month earlier, he had entered a singing contest only to forfeit the first prize when he refused to sight-read a song after performing those he had prepared. A few days after his performance at the Cousins's, Joyce would meet and fall in love with his future wife, Nora Barnacle; he later memorialized the event by setting the action of *Ulysses* on the day they first walked out together, June 16, 1904, a date now known around the world as Bloomsday. The following month, he wrote and published the first of his *Dubliners* stories, "The Sisters," and within three months would begin his nearly lifelong exile from Ireland.

Holloway's memory of Joyce's eyes are echoed in many portraits. W. K. Magee (who wrote as John Eglinton) recalls young Joyce in Dublin:

A pair of burning dark-blue eyes, serious and questioning, is fixed on me from under the peak of a nautical cap; the face is long, with a slight flush suggestive of dissipation, and an incipient beard is permitted to straggle over a very pronounced chin. (Scholes 197)

Sheehy's portrait of Joyce around this time is equally vivid and also begins to bring out another side of his character:

He was a tall slight stripling, with flashing teeth—white as a hound's—pale blue eyes that sometimes had an icy look, and a mobile sensitive mouth. He was fond of throwing back his head as he walked, and his mood alternated between cold, slightly haughty, aloofness and sudden boisterous merriment. (Sheehy 21)

Sheehy was not the only one to detect a certain coldness in Joyce's character. In 1922, Djuna Barnes sat down with Joyce in Paris at the cafe Deux Magots and reported in *Vanity Fair* that she saw in Joyce's eyes "a little jeer that goes with a lift and rounding of the upper lip" (Barnes 293). Long-suffering Stanislaus often notes how his older brother rarely spared his feelings, whether by reminding Stanislaus of the inferiority of his mind in comparison to his own or by reading Stanislaus's diary without permission and appropriating what he found for his fiction. Stanislaus's portrait finds more than haughtiness in his brother's face:

Though he dislikes greatly to be rude, I think there is little courtesy in his nature. As he sits on the hearth-rug, his arms embracing his knees, his head thrown a little back, his hair brushed up straight off his forehead, his long face red as an Indian's in the reflexion of the fire, there is a look of cruelty in his face. (*Complete Dublin Diary* 4)

Stanislaus also observes that his brother had "a proud, wilful, vicious selfishness, out of which by times now he writes a poem or an epiphany, now commits . . . meannesses of whim and appetite" (*Complete Dublin Diary* 3). There was a clinical quality to Joyce's selfishness. In later years, he seemed genuinely unable to understand why he should be grateful to Stanislaus for having tended to his many needs for so long in Trieste and came to feel that he had discharged all duties to his family while a teenager by sharing, as Stephen does in *Portrait*, his academic exhibition prize winnings.

Stanislaus often waxes eloquent on his brother's aloof arrogance: "To judge by his unaffected imperturbability, he might have been assisting at a badly rehearsed comedy that did not concern him" (*My Brother's Keeper* 71). Alessandro Francini Bruni provides a glimpse of such theater in his account of Joyce's arrival in Pola to teach English at a Berlitz school. Expecting a well-dressed Cambridge don, those who greeted Joyce on his arrival found instead an impoverished "bunch of rags":

> Joyce didn't think for even a minute about the state of his clothing. The problem of sartorial harmony never crossed his mind. On the contrary, Joyce in his greatness was so aloof, so aware of his role, that he waited motionlessly for the others to approach and welcome him on behalf of the city. When they were face to face they began to measure one another, each trying to spy into the other's eyes what he was thinking. The clear-eyed, poised Joyce stared into the puffy eyes [of the Berlitz assistant], as if he really were Charles V surveying his realm. (Potts 11)

In Pola and later Trieste, Joyce was given to unorthodox teaching ploys in the classroom, but he also seems to have undertaken his duties with great seriousness and commitment. In Trieste, where he finished *Portrait*, Joyce was seen "hastening from house to house to give their hour of English to all the Triestines. Energetic and punctual in his work, devoted to his wife, his children, his house, he was remarkable for his sobriety" (Potts 52). Or so remembered Silvio Benco. Francini and Stanislaus suggest that Joyce's sobriety often ended with the daylight. Still, Benco's portrait of a Joyce whose "paradoxical *diablerie*" increasingly found expression in his writing rather than in shocking people with his conversational candor rings true. In his university days, Joyce sometimes enjoyed crude sexual banter with his close friends and Stanislaus, but in later life the author whose *Ulysses* was banned for obscenity and whose fetishistic sexual fantasies in letters to Nora provide rich material for psychoanalytic criticism was notably prudish in conversation. Cohabitation with Nora and the birth of their son Giorgio may not have been cures for public drunkenness, but family life does seem to have elicited from Joyce a new discipline and restraint.

Nevertheless, the "cold lucid indifference" Stephen feels in *Portrait* after his debauches with prostitutes clearly corresponds to a need for sensual gratification and a capacity for detachment that were fundamental to Joyce's character. The same qualities were evident much earlier in what otherwise might seem an unexceptional anecdote about the casual sadism of older brothers:

> On Pancake Night one pancake was left on the platter, and all four boys—James, Stanislaus, Charles, and George—dove for it. James made off with the prize and ran up and down stairs, protesting to his pursuers that he had already eaten it. At last they were convinced, and he then imperturbably removed the pancake from the pocket where it lay hidden, and ate it up with the air of little Jack Horner. (Ellmann 45)

But if Joyce's pleasure in flaunting his power over his siblings testifies to the selfishness of his appetites and an early capacity for emotional distance, Ellmann offers a plausible explanation for the hypertrophy of Joyce's calculated detachment from others over the years:

> The fact that he was turning his life to fiction at the same time that he was living it encouraged him to feel a certain detachment from what happened to him, for he knew he could reconsider and re-order it for the purposes of his book. At the same time, since he felt dependent for material upon

actual events, he had an interest in bringing simmering pots to a strong boil, in making the events through which he lived take on as extreme a form as possible. The sense that they were characters in his drama annoyed some of his friends. (Ellmann 149)

The more hungry Joyce became for experience, the more detached his attitude. This character trait does much to justify David Hayman's coinage for the extradiegetic narrator in *Ulysses* who is thought to be responsible for manipulating the text into its final form: the Arranger.

For friends, the sense that behind his detachment Joyce was living in a parallel universe in which even the most insignificant moment was radiant with private significance could be acute. After eye surgery in 1924, Joyce was forced to recuperate in a dark room with his eyes bandaged. Myron Nutting visited the clinic in Paris and experienced a moment of peculiarly Joycean surrealism. The now-famous writer was

lying on his back in the dark, his eyes under dressings as big as small pillows. "Hello, Joyce," he said cheerily. Joyce remained silent and motionless for a few seconds, then reached under his pillow and drew out a composition book and a pencil. Slowly and carefully, by touch, he made an entry, put his book and pencil back under the pillow, then held out his hand to say, "Hello, Nutting." Aware of his friend's bafflement, he took up the notebook again and showed him the words, "Carriage sponge," which left Nutting no wiser. (Ellmann 566)

The moment recalls two episodes in *Portrait*. Joyce's self-contained linguistic world is suggestive of Stephen's often-quoted description of the artist's Olympian detachment: "The artist, like the God of the creation, remains within or behind or beyond or above his handiwork, invisible, refined out of existence, indifferent, paring his fingernails" (215)—and thinking about carriage sponges. The enigmatic impenetrability of the words also recalls the oddly charged, elusive materiality of language when Stephen flees from his humiliation after the school play and stops to gaze up "at the sombre porch of the morgue and from that to the dark cobbled laneway at its side. He saw the word *Lotts* on the wall of the lane and breathed slowly the rank heavy air" (86). In a novel bound tightly together with chains of symbolic images—birds, water, flowers, falling, rising—the word "Lotts" remains stubbornly unassimilable, as if only in the mute standoff between contemplative mind and stark literality could Stephen find something like a secular version of the peace that passes all understanding.

Stephen is often in a state of detached reverie in *Portrait*, and we view his surroundings through the increasingly complex mediation of his mind. Stanislaus, present as Maurice in *Stephen Hero*, is gone,[2] and his sisters only heard offstage at the beginning of chapter 5. The attenuation of Stephen's siblings may reflect Joyce's egotism and relative neglect, yet he could also be a model of the loving older brother. When their mother died and the youngest sister, Mabel, seemed unable to cope with her grief, Stanislaus remembers Joyce "sitting on the top step of the first flight of stairs with his arm around her, talking to her in a very matter-of-fact voice":

—You must not cry like that, he said, because there is no reason to cry. Mother is in heaven. She is far happier now than she has ever been on earth, but if she sees you crying it will spoil her happiness. You must remember that when you feel like crying. You can pray for her, if you wish. Mother would like that. But you mustn't cry anymore. (*My Brother's Keeper* 236–37)

Here, Joyce is far from the Stephen who in *Portrait* cites Pascal, Aloysius Gonzaga, and Jesus as precedents for discounting a mother's love. The genuine warmth of Joyce's poem on the birth of his grandson, "Ecce Puer," bears little relation to the affectation of Stephen's villanelle in *Portrait* or to the Stephen who later bumps into E. C., the young woman who inspired his poem, and turns on "the spiritual-heroic refrigerating apparatus" (252). Rarely glimpsed in *Portrait*, Joyce's sentimentality, joy in life, and pleasure in domesticity register frequently in accounts of those who knew him in Trieste. Francini for one, remembers the care Joyce devoted to tracking down all the ingredients for a plum pudding—nine days in the making!—in celebration of St. Patrick's Day.

It would take a larger gallery than this to do justice to the complexity of Joyce's character. Magee claimed not to remember any of Joyce's "strange sententious talk" from his Dublin years but believed he could hear his voice again clearly in Stephen's esoteric discourse on aesthetics in *Portrait*. That surely was one of Joyce's voices. Francini records the more demotic voice in which Joyce held forth in Trieste, a voice largely refined out of existence in *Portrait*, save for the occasional outburst from Stephen's father, Simon Dedalus:

> The tax collector is an idiot who is always annoying me [Joyce declaimed]. He has filled my desk with little sheets marked "Warning," "Warning," "Warning." I told him that if he didn't stop it, I would send him to be f . . . ound out by that swindler, his master. Today, the swindler is the government in Vienna. Tomorrow it could be the one in Rome. But whether in Vienna or Rome or London, to me governments are all the same, pirates. (Potts 27)

A similar contrast may be found between the lyrical, soft-focus treatment of prostitution in *Portrait* and the diary entries in which Stanislaus recalls Joyce's vulgar remarks about women and the exuberant profanity of the prostitutes his brother frequented. Francini tries to capture Joyce in paradoxical metaphors: "His head is a hive of discordant and disconnected ideas. All the same there is perfect order in it"; "He is an alloy composed of elements which, according to the laws of physics, should repel one another but which instead hold together through a miracle of molecular aggregation" (Potts 34).

Stanislaus, who deserves the last word, says more with less. Stanislaus claims to have disliked his brother but acknowledges that everyone else took to him easily. This was so, he surmises, "because he is so much alive. He seemed to me the person in Ireland who was most alive" (*Complete Dublin Diary* 146).

Notes

1. For additional commentary and bibliography, see McBride 33–37.

2. A trace remains, however, in Simon Dedalus's seeming meta-comment: "—O, Holy Paul, I forgot about Maurice" (71).

Works Cited

Barnes, Djuna. *Interviews.* Edited by Alyce Barry. Washington, D.C.: Sun & Moon Press, 1985.

Bell, Robert H. *Jocoserious Joyce.* Ithaca, N.Y.: Cornell University Press, 1991.

Ellmann, Richard. *James Joyce.* New York: Oxford University Press, 1982.

Frank, Joseph. "Spatial Form in Modern Literature." *Sewanee Review* 53 (1945): 221–40, 433–56; 643–53. This influential three-part essay was published in revised and expanded form in Frank's *The Widening Gyre* (Bloomington: Indiana University Press, 1963).

Gottfried, Roy. *Joyce's Comic Portrait.* Gainesville: University of Florida Press, 2000.

Hayman, David. *"Ulysses" and the Mechanics of Meaning.* Madison: University of Wisconsin Press, 1982.

Joyce, James. *A Portrait of the Artist as a Young Man.* Edited by Chester G. Anderson. New York: Penguin, 1977.

———. *Ulysses: The Gabler Edition.* New York: Vintage, 1986.

Joyce, Stanislaus. *The Complete Dublin Diary of Stanislaus Joyce.* Edited by George H. Healey. Ithaca, N.Y.: Cornell University Press, 1971.

———. *My Brother's Keeper.* Edited by Richard Ellmann. New York: Viking, 1958.

Levin, Harry. "What Was Modernism?" *Massachusetts Review* 1, no. 4 (1960): 609–30.

McBride, Margaret. *"Ulysses" and the Metamorphosis of Stephen Dedalus.* Lewisburg, Pa.: Bucknell University Press, 2001.

Mikhail, E. H. *James Joyce: Interviews and Recollections.* New York: St. Martin's, 1990.

Potts, Willard, ed. *Portraits of the Artist in Exile.* Seattle: University of Washington Press, 1979.

Scholes, Robert. *The Workshop of Daedalus*. Evanston, Ill.: Northwestern University Press, 1965.

Sheehy, Eugene. *May It Please the Court*. Dublin: Fallon, 1951.

Wollaeger, Mark. "Stephen/Joyce, Joyce/Haacke: Modernism and the Social Function of Art." *English Literary History* 62 (1995): 691–707.

Suggested Reading

Brady, Philip, and James F. Carens, eds. *Critical Essays on James Joyce's "A Portrait of the Artist as a Young Man."* New York: Hall, 1998.

Buttigieg, Joseph A. *A Portrait of the Artist in Different Perspective.* Athens: Ohio University Press, 1987.

Carens, James F. "*A Portrait of the Artist as a Young Man.*" In *A Companion to Joyce Studies,* edited by Zack Bowen and James F. Carens, 255–359. Westport, Conn.: Greenwood, 1984.

Cixous, Hélène. "Joyce: the (r)use of writing." In *Post-Structuralist Joyce,* edited by Derek Attridge and Daniel Ferrer, 15–30. Cambridge: Cambridge University Press, 1984.

―――. "Reaching the Point of Wheat; or, A Portrait of the Artist as a Maturing Woman." *New Literary History* 19, no. 1 (1987): 1–21.

Deming, Robert H. *James Joyce: The Critical Heritage.* vol. 1. London: Routledge & Kegan Paul, 1970.

Eco, Umberto. *The Aesthetics of Chaosmos.* Translated by Ellen Esrock. Cambridge, Mass.: Harvard University Press, 1989.

Ellmann, Richard. *James Joyce.* 2d ed. New York: Oxford University Press, 1982.

Farrell, James T. "Joyce's *A Portrait of the Artist.*" In *James Joyce: Two Decades of Criticism*, edited by Seon Givens, 175–97. New York: Vanguard, 1948.

Friedman, Susan Stanford. "(Self) Censorship and the Making of Joyce's Modernism." In *Joyce and the Return of the Repressed*, edited by Susan Stanford Friedman, 21–57. Ithaca, N.Y.: Cornell University Press, 1993.

Froula, Christine. *Modernism's Body: Sex, Culture, and Joyce*. New York: Columbia University Press, 1996. 33–83.

Gabler, Hans Walter. "The Genesis of *A Portrait of the Artist as a Young Man*." In *Critical Essays on James Joyce's "A Portrait of the Artist as a Young Man,"* edited by Philip Brady and James F. Carens, 83–112. New York: Hall, 1998.

Gifford, Don. *Joyce Annotated: Notes for "Dubliners" and "A Portrait of the Artist as a Young Man."* 2d ed. Berkeley: University of California Press, 1982.

Givens, Seon, ed. *James Joyce: Two Decades of Criticism*. New York: Vanguard, 1963.

Goldman, Arnold. *The Joyce Paradox*. Evanston, Ill.: Northwestern University Press, 1966.

Hawkins, Hunt. "Joyce as a Colonial Writer." *College Language Association Journal* 35, no. 4 (June 1992): 400–410.

Henke, Suzette. "Stephen Dedalus and Women: A Portrait of the Artist as a Young Misogynist." In *Women in Joyce*, edited by Suzette Henke and Elaine Unkeless, 82–107. Urbana: University of Illinois Press, 1982.

Joyce, James. "A Portrait of the Artist." In *A Portrait of the Artist as a Young Man*, edited by Chester G. Anderson, 257–72. New York: Penguin, 1977.

———. *A Portrait of the Artist as a Young Man*. Edited by Chester G. Anderson. New York: Penguin, 1977. Includes useful annotations of the text, excerpts from related texts by Joyce, and a selection of criticism.

———. *A Portrait of the Artist as a Young Man*. Edited by R. B. Kershner. Boston and New York: Bedford, 1993. Includes a valuable editor's introduction and a selection of essays using representative critical approaches.

———. *Stephen Hero*. Edited by Theodore Spencer. New York: New Directions, 1944.

Kenner, Hugh. "The Cubist *Portrait*." In *Approaches to Joyce's "Portrait,"* edited by Thomas F. Staley, 171–84. Pittsburgh, Pa.: University of Pittsburgh Press, 1976.

———. *Dublin's Joyce*. New York: Columbia University Press, 1987.

————. *Joyce's Voices*. Berkeley: University of California Press, 1978.

Kershner, R. B. "The Artist as Text: Dialogism and Incremental Repetition in *Portrait*." *English Literary History* 53, no. 4 (Winter 1986): 881–94.

————. "History as Nightmare: Joyce's *Portrait* to Christy Brown." In *Joyce and the Subject of History*, edited by Mark A. Wollaeger, Victor Luftig, and Robert Spoo, 27–45. Ann Arbor: University of Michigan Press, 1996.

Leonard, Garry. "When a Fly Gets in Your I: The City, Modernism, and Aesthetic Theory in *A Portrait of the Artist as a Young Man*." In Leonard, *Advertising and Commodity Culture in Joyce*, 175–208. Gainesville: University of Florida Press, 1998.

Levin, Harry. *James Joyce*. New York: New Directions, 1960.

Mahaffey, Vicki. "Père-version and Im-mère-sion: Idealized Corruption in *A Portrait of the Artist as a Young Man* and *The Picture of Dorian Gray*." *James Joyce Quarterly* 31, no. 3 (Spring 1994): 189–206.

————. *Reauthorizing Joyce*. 1988; reprint, Gainesville: University Press of Florida, 1995.

MacCabe, Colin. *James Joyce and the Revolution of the Word*. London: Macmillan, 1979.

Norris, Margot. "Stephen Dedalus, Oscar Wilde, and the Art of Lying." In Norris, *Joyce's Web: The Social Unraveling of Modernism*, 52–67. Austin: University of Texas Press, 1992.

Riquelme, John Paul. *Teller and Tale in Joyce's Fiction*. Baltimore, Md.: Johns Hopkins University Press, 1983.

Scholes, Robert. "Stephen Dedalus: Poet or Aesthete?" *Publication of the Modern Language Association* 79 (September 1964): 484–89.

————. *The Workshop of Daedalus*. Evanston, Ill.: Northwestern University Press, 1965.

Scott, Bonnie Kime. "Emma Clery in *Stephen Hero*: A Young Woman Walking Proudly through the Decayed City." In *Women in Joyce*, edited by Suzette Henke and Elaine Unkeless, 57–81. Urbana: University of Illinois Press, 1982.

Spoo, Robert. *James Joyce and the Language of History*. New York: Oxford University Press, 1994.

Staley, Thomas F., ed. *Approaches to Joyce's "Portrait."* Pittsburgh, Pa.: University of Pittsburgh Press, 1976.

————. "Strings in the Labyrinth: Sixty Years with Joyce's *Portrait*." In *Approaches to Joyce's "Portrait,"* edited by Thomas F. Staley, 3–24. Pittsburgh, Pa.: University of Pittsburgh Press, 1976.

Valente, Joseph, ed. *Quare Joyce*. Ann Arbor: University of Michigan Press, 1998.

Wills, Clair. "Joyce, Prostitution, and the Colonial City." *South Atlantic Quarterly* 95 (Winter 1996): 79–85.

Wilson, Edmund. *Axel's Castle*. 1931; reprint, New York: Modern Library, 1996.

Wollaeger, Mark, Victor Luftig, and Robert Spoo, eds. *Joyce and the Subject of History*. Ann Arbor: University of Michigan Press, 1996.